OFF THE RECORD

OFF THE RECORD

The Trials and Tribulations of a Travelin' Troubadour

LIGHTNIN' CHARLIE

Copyright 2008 by Lightnin' Charlie. Second edition copyright 2012 by Lightnin' Charlie. All rights reserved. No portion of this book may be reproduced, stored in a retrieval system, used in the housebreaking of young animals, or transmitted in any form or by any means – electronic, spitball, mechanical, photocopy, recording, message in a bottle, paper airplane, or any other – except for brief quotation in printed reviews, as long as they're positive, without the prior permission of the author. Please dispose of this book properly, in appropriately designated receptacles, or in adequately ventilated rest rooms.

This book is a work containing parody and satire. Any resemblance to actual events or locales or persons, living or dead, is entirely intentional. Names, characters, places, and incidents are products of the author's imagination, and are limited by the author's diminished recollection. Or they are actual people, places, and things, purposely portrayed by the author facetiously, thus eliminating the opportunity for any and all litigation against the author by any and all attorneys, living or dead. The author does admit liability for his obsessive overuse of puns, parentheticals, and alliterations, and hereby throws himself upon the mercy of the reader.

Edited by Beth Dolinger.

Cover Art & Layout by Excello Designs, Chicago, Illinois.

Printed in the United States of America.

ISBN: 978-1-58275-320-1.

To my darling wife, Beth

CONTENTS

Introduction: Dangers, Toils, And Snares   i

1. A New Leaf, A New Blog, And Old Sour Grapes   1
2. Rock Rock Rhythm And Blues   7
3. My Record: One's At The CD Store, And One's At The Police Station   11
4. Why I Don't Come Down Off The Mountain Anymore   19
5. Leopard Skin, Lookalikes, And Law Enforcement   27
6. Fire In The Hole   37
7. Luck Lightnin' Charlie Style or If I Said You Had A Beautiful Moustache, Would You Hold It Against Me?   45
8. Lightnin' And The Snake Lady   53
9. Brown Gravy And White Lies - A Satire   59
10. Photographs And Memories   69
11. What's The Word?   73
12. Daddy's Home   79
13. Death And Taxes   85
14. Writer's Block or The Psychiatrist Is Out   89
15. An American Trilogy   91
16. Buckets, Broomsticks, And Bullhorns   117
17. A Horror Story   121
18. The Re-Invention Of Me   131

19. Don't Worry, Be Happy   145

20. It Was A Very Good Year   161

21. Stranger Than Fiction, The Story Of Me   169

22. The Squeaky Wheel   189

23. Al Roker And The Miracle Cure   203

24. Taking The Fifth . . . Commandment, That Is   211

25. Kissin' Cousins, I'm My Own Grandpaw,
    or It's All Relative   237

26. Rednecks, Spandex, And Car Wrecks
    or Get Off My Alley, Pally   253

27. Lightnin's Log Cabin On The Hill   261

28. Lightnin's Quotations For A Happy Life   273

29. Famous Last Words   301

30. The Curtain Falls   363

31. The Indian Rope Trick,
    And Like A Good Neighbor – Sanskrit Is There,
    or How Much Is That Doggie In The Rickshaw?   365

32. The World's Fair   399

33. Proverbs   431

    Afterword   437

    About The Author   445

INTRODUCTION

DANGERS, TOILS, AND SNARES

This book you are reading was never intended to be a book. The *Lightnin' Lowdown* began in April 2005 as a monthly anecdotal journal, or "blog" on my website, LightninCharlie.com. I soon started receiving emails from Lightnin' Bugs all over the world, from folks who were just lovin' the Lowdowns, and these diatribes quickly became my site's most popular feature. Naturally I felt good about the Lowdown's popularity (and the traffic it was causing on my website), but I felt a greater obligation to use this newfound forum I had to glorify God, and all He's done for me. *Off The Record* is a compilation of these *Lightnin' Lowdowns,* presented here, in their entirety.

Folks are naturally curious about the lifestyle of a professional, touring musician, and have often asked me what it has been like. Of course, after three decades of living it, I've accumulated a wealth of stories and anecdotes, and I always believed I could someday write a book with all this stuff. My belief that the book would be enjoyable to read was reinforced every time I'd tell one of these tales, and people would howl with laughter, or react with disbelief, or with tears. I've even had folks request a story, rather than a song, at my gigs! And I'm not sure if that's a compliment to my storytelling, or a criticism of my singing, or both!

I soon found out that the more outrageous my offering, the more folks seemed to enjoy them. As Will Rogers said, *"Everything is funny, as long as it's happening to somebody else!"* But I am not simply telling these tales for shock value. I feel convicted to tell people of exactly where I came from, and that an Almighty God has brought me from a mighty, mighty long way indeed. These stories, my story, are part of the body of Christ, and the Greatest Story Ever Told.

I've been blessed with this life and its many gifts. But it has not been easy, and it has not always been fun. Much of it has been depraved, treacherous, and brutal. But I felt that it was my duty, to my Lord, to tell of the horrible and hellish situations I've been in, that He's delivered me from, and show others that He'll deliver them too, no matter what their circumstances, if they'll let go and let God. Through many dangers, toils, and snares, I have already come. And it's Grace that's brought me through.

My hope is that you enjoy reading these wild and crazy rants, and that this book will please Abba God, the Father. My wish is that the Spirit of these sagas will bless and be a witness to many. These stories, rough as they are, are my testimony. My fervent prayer is that they illustrate to every reader, that Jesus Christ is the way, the truth, and the life. He has led me from the desert, and to the Promised Land.

Lightnin' Charlie
April 2008

APRIL 2005

1

A NEW LEAF, A NEW BLOG, AND OLD SOUR GRAPES

Dear Lightnin' Bugs,

Thanks for visiting my brand new website. The Lightnin' Lowdown will let you know what's happening in my world, in my heart, and in my head. Sometimes it'll be funny, sometimes sad; sometimes it'll be outrageous. But I promise... it'll never be boring.

And I solemnly swear to tell the truth, the whole truth, and nothing but the truth, except in cases of my stretching the truth a little to get a laugh. In the words of Dean Martin,

"If you want to hear me bein' serious – you buy an album!"

I'll post a brand new Lowdown each month, so surf in when you can, and see what's happenin' in Lightnin' Land...it's like reality TV, without the commercials.

Speaking of no commercials, I am appearing 'live-to-tape' on ARC-TV four times per week, so you local Lightnin' Bugs check out your cable TV listings to see when I can be seen. We are working on putting a DVD together of live Lightnin' Charlie stuff, so watch my online shop and ARC-TV for more details.

And speaking of work, I just finished up a cantankerous three-year run at a high-rise Hotel and Convention Center in Bristol, Virginia. Let's call it the Squaliday Inn. Or the Squall-A-Day Inn. You pick...they're pronounced the same (and as you will see from my story, both are accurate). And 'squalid' is a very suitable pseudonym – not for the hotel itself, which was very upscale and nice – but for the management at the hotel, as it means 'filthy', 'foul', and 'fetid'. How apt is that? And all 'F's', just like the general manager's personal hygiene rating. The owners of the hotel, a real colorful and eccentric married couple, were always fair and kind to me. They loved me. And the majority of the audiences who were filling the place were in love with me too. (How else could I gig there 5 nights a week for 3 years?) So what's the trouble? Well friend, anytime there's anything constructive and mutually pleasurable going on, and everybody's happy...look out...because someone will be looking to tear it apart. Can I get a witness? Watch any daytime soap opera and you'll see what I'm talking about. Night after night, I was subjected to some of the most bizarre, devilish, and sickening situations that I've ever seen (or heard of). All thanks to management. Standing on her hairy knuckles, between me and my loving audience, and between me and my loving boss (the owners), was this vile beast of a woman, gumming up the works, and taking ugly to a whole new level. Boy did she have it in for me. Maybe it was because I made more dough than she did, or maybe it was because I didn't have to sneak up on the glass to get a drink of water. She was Godzilla going through menopause. From day one, she (and believe me, I use the term 'she' loosely) simply hated me, and plotted hard and long to get me out of there. She finally succeeded. But she had help – the devil never acts alone. Scheming and squealing, this whopper (let's just call her 'The Whopper') soon attracted and surrounded herself with others of her ilk. Pigs of a feather. The swine flew together. And there's no shortage of swine on the Bristol state line.

But the funny thing (for me) is that this battleground of a gig changed my life forever, and for the *better*. In spite of the hateful people and evil spirits there, in spite of their unclean ambitions and constant ill will, and in spite of the pure, seething malice they had for me (and my family), I now regard them – certainly not as friends – but as huge benefactors to me. I'll try to explain how I was helped, personally and professionally, by my eternal enemy. I've got to give the devil her due. I wish I could say thanks to The Whopper in person, but I'll put it in print, and maybe someday, someone will read this to her. So here goes...

Performing for The Whopper in the hotel lounge for four hours a night, five nights a week, for thirty-six grueling months in a row was brutal. It was like a blood bank for the soul. Difficulties in life abound, and those that don't kill you, only serve to make you stronger. But today, I am grateful for the many, many good things that came from my association with the Squaliday Inn, its malevolent manager, and its onsite drunk tank, Flop's Lounge. Let me explain...

A very lucrative and long contract such as I had there (unheard of among my musical peers, by the way), allowed me the financial freedom to conquer three very large and imposing monsters: debt relief, *A New Leaf*, and one nasty old beef. Let's explore these one at a time.

First things first. Of paramount importance to me are my wife, my family, and the future of my kids. I would like to thank the Squaliday Inn Hotel and Redemption Center, for allowing us to do something which will have considerable impact on the rest of our kids' lives, and our own. We were able (praise God!) to get completely out of credit card debt, forever. That's forever and ever, amen.

We had, like too many Americans, accumulated a large debt on several credit cards. Unlike a lot of Americans though, ours wasn't due to frivolous spending. It was just one of those things that happened while trying to get through some tough times.

My wife (who graduated at the top of her class, Magna Cum Laude) was not able to find a job in her field (physical therapy) for over a year after graduation, due to the physical therapy market being saturated at that time. She was wonderfully qualified, and had applications everywhere, but to no avail. So we were living on only one income – mine. And my gigs, at that time, were very poor, and therefore, so were we.

We would use a credit card to pay for an occasional car repair, or a dental bill, or something of that nature. But we would also, from time to time, use a credit card to pay for groceries, or a dinner. Because of the card's exorbitant interest rates, compounding over time, a gallon of milk would end up costing us $95. As many of you know (unfortunately), from your own personal experience with credit cards, that despite years and years of payments, our debt kept getting bigger and bigger. But thanks to my gig at the Squall-A-Day Inn (and my large weekly paycheck, which came, regular as rain, for 150 weeks in a row) – we paid off our debt, completely and for good. You can probably imagine what a great time my wife and I had at our own, private, emancipation party, cutting up all those cancelled cards. Free at last! The Whopper and her Squalid Squad of Knuckle-Walkers made that possible.

Being the musical houseboy for Rosemary's Baby and her uncircumcised society (performing approximately 780 shows!), allowed me to conquer a second monster. And that was financing my soon-to-be-released, career-changing, tour-de-force CD *A New Leaf*.

I was able to record and produce this CD without compromise, due to the fact that I didn't have to cut corners, creatively, due to cost and expense issues. I was able to make artistic decisions that were not based upon monetary concerns for the first time in my recording career. That is huge.

My previous two CDs were made on a very tight budget, for record companies, and are not nearly the powerhouse record that *A New Leaf* is. I worked on *A New Leaf* for the same three years that I worked at the hotel, making time for recording and arranging as I could (a high-wire balancing act, to say the least, with a five-night-a-week job that included a 500-mile per week commute, plus a house, a wife, and two babies – I was Mr. Mom during the daytime while my wife worked).

I was personally responsible for every facet of the CD-making process (writing, arranging, scheduling, recording, photography, layout and design, mixing, mastering, pressing, etc.). And these are all projects that are very time (and money) consuming. But I had the brotherly love and tireless commitment of my dearest friend and partner, Harmonica Todd Levine, without whom, it would not have been possible. He and I, day by day, built this record from the bottom up, and was no small feat, but we did it. And to quote Marvin Gaye, it's some kind of wonderful.

Early on in the creation process of this new CD, I made the conscious decision not to compromise, not one bit, on this record. I would take my time, taking as much time as I needed to get the results I wanted. I brought in musicians from as far away as Chicago, redoing songs over and over and over again. I was determined to do this, for as long as it would take, to produce the record I had always wanted to make.

Since I was producing it, and paying for all of it myself, this was a mighty big commitment. The recording studio cost $60 per hour, for example, and, in case you're wondering, I didn't charge one minute of it. I paid in cash, in full, at the end of each session, for three years, before leaving the studio. In for a penny – in for a pound. I needed a CD at a new, higher level, to take me, and my career, up to the next level. And I've finally got it. And ironically, it's all come from my God and my torturous tenure at the Squaliday Inn.

I am forever indebted to the intellectually-challenged and humorless enemies of American music (and American musicians) at the Ball-A-Day Inn Hotel and Depression Center, in Bristol, Virginia. You fleas know who you are, but do you know what you did, for my family and me? While constantly striving to make my 3120 hours there most miserable, you (in spite of yourselves) helped me make the record of my life. A million thanks.

And last but least, that nasty old beast. Hail to Ms. Chief, that big side of beef. My very special thanks goes out (and down) to the third and final monster: that messy-haired, cud-chewing, bean bag of a gal; yes friends, that she-devil curmudgeon of a manager of Bristol's Heartburn Hotel and Contemption Center; that refrigerator with a head; ladies and gentlemen, let's give it up for that simian in a suit, who ruled with an iron hoof, that pantyhosed pug-dog in power, who seethingly signed all of those pretty, plump, pink paychecks personally... *The Whopper!*

How can I begin to repay her for all she's done for me? Well, how 'bout with a song? I just wrote this little ditty, just for her, even though she's not exactly a connoisseur of music. It's called *She's The One*. It only has one verse, but that's okay, her family tree only has one branch. So here goes...

She's the one.
She's the one with the cloven hoof and high heel shoes.
She's the one singin',
"In the Shallow End of the Gene Pool Blues".
She's the one who's made all this come true.
She's the one.

Yes friends, she's the one, at the Call-It-A-Day Inn Hotel and Confusion Center, she is. She put the "Miss" in "Mismanagement". But I wonder who put the "Bomp" in the "Bomp, sh-bomp, sh-bomp?" And who put the "Dip" in the "Dip, da-dip, da-dip?" But I digress. Anyway, for her information, and with the faint hope that one of her drunken associates is reading this to her... Mike Ditka called, and he wants his

SUITS BACK!

I would also like to thank local health department officials, in advance, for faithfully looking into the sickening situation at the Squaliday Inn Hotel and Salmonella Center in Bristol, Virginia (just a rat's run off Interstate 81). Thanks to the gag order now being lifted (nice pun!), I can freely and frankly discuss my felonious food poisoning from Flop's. But I won't.

Although opposite of her ruinous intentions, The Whopper and her crop of Philistines really did me a world of good and I feel compelled to say thanks. Whopper (if you're listening), you gave me the opportunity to play lots of great music for lots of great people. You introduced me to some fine folks who have become dear, precious, and lifelong friends. Plus, you unintentionally provided me with some fantastic music industry contacts, which will be a huge help to me in the future. All this is due to my appearing tirelessly and faithfully – night after night – in spite of you. And year after year – with an ogre in my ear, at the smarmy smut-hut you mismanaged, Flop's Lounge. Whopper, you have my gratitude!

In closing, I leave you with two verses of scripture, which perfectly describe and define my experience with this bad-tempered troglodyte. The first scripture, from Jesus' Sermon on the Mount, describes what I did, during my thorny, three-year tenure with her, and the second describes what God will do, with *all* situations, if we'll let Him.

"Do not give dogs what is sacred; do not throw your pearls to pigs. If you do, they will trample them under their feet, and then turn and tear you to pieces."

– Matthew 7:6 NIV

"And we know that God causes all things to work together for good to those who love God, to those who are called according to His purpose."
– Romans 8:28 NASB

My wife and I are going on a much-needed vacation cruise to the Bahamas this month – just the two of us. We are leaving our boys (ages 2 and 4) at home. In case any potential burglars are reading this, I must warn you...they are both 6th-degree black belts in Tae Kwon Do, and along with our Chinese manservant, Kato, are very capable of defending the fort against intruders. Speaking of intruders...a definition:

Pokemon (*n.*) a Jamaican proctologist.

Sorry folks! I guess you realize (after reading this diatribe), that old Lightnin's in desperate need of a vacation. I promise and vow, right here and now, that the jokes will be better in a few weeks. And so will I.

So stay tuned y'all...more trash in a flash, more dancin' on the ceilin' and wallpaper peelin'. I love you and hope to see you again next month, right here in the Lightnin' Lowdown, where the sky's the limit, the air is rare, and everything is everything. Come back soon and often, and tell your friends. I'll tell a good story, and give God the glory.

An old-fashioned hug,
Charlie

MAY 2005

2

ROCK, ROCK, RHYTHM AND BLUES

Well, old man winter has finally given up the ghost and, here in the South, it is spring at last.

When my wife and I got back from our trip to the Bahamas in March, we both had a terrific tan. I was darker than Bryant Gumbel. But it's been so cold and rainy here that we now look like plain old white people again. I be *"Lightening!"*

My name gets misspelled that way quite a bit, but right now it's quite fitting. I'm dropping a shade a day, at least. (Michael Jackson and me) I've got the connections, but I sure ain't got the complexion. And I'm afraid I'm starting to sing like Pat Boone or The Association (God forbid). I noticed just yesterday as I was holding a cup of coffee that my pinky finger was sticking out. This has got to stop. I need a tan, man!

So now that Mister Sun is shining, I've been able to spend a lot of time with my kids working and playing in our backyard, listening to music, and hanging out. To facilitate this (Facilitate? See? It's even affecting my vocabulary!)...Anyway, to take my tunes outside, I bought some of those wireless speakers for the yard that look like a rock. A Rock Speaker (appalling pun).

I thought it might be interesting to give you Lightnin' Bugs an idea of what kind of music Lightnin' Charlie is listening to while he cuts down trees and eats his lunch.

I'll list a top ten, in no particular order, of artists and albums that are in my CD changer at the moment. Please feel free to e-mail me and tell me that you dig it, and find it interesting, and to please do it again next month. And I will.

Or, if the Spirit moves you to tell me that I am being a self-indulgent bore, that nobody cares what I'm listening to while mulching flower beds, and to cease and desist immediately, then by all means, do. And I will.

I've always found it real insightful to know what the musicians I listen to are listening to. But what do I know? Maybe you would prefer something a bit more risqué: stories of police brutality and street violence, for example (I've got plenty of those, if that's more your style). Let me know. This is your forum, and your world too. I'm just writing in it.

So here goes. And by the way, I do take requests from my neighbors.

1) Otis Redding – Stax Box Set
2) Lefty Frizzell – Essentials
3) The Isaacs – Pieces Of Our Past
4) Sam Cooke – Live At The Harlem Square Club
5) King Cole Trio – Best Of Nat "King" Cole Trio
6) LaVern Baker – Blues and Ballads
7) Frank Sinatra – Come Dance With Me
8) Gaither Homecoming – Israel and Jerusalem
9) Elvis Presley – Fun In Acapulco FTD
10) Lonnie Johnson – Unsung Blues Legend

You might happen to hear me doing some of these songs at my shows this month, and you'll see that I am truly the luckiest guy in the world because I get to play the music that I love and get paid for it. Thanks to you.

By the way, my CD *A New Leaf* is now being pressed (like a suit) and will be available at my online store and at my shows by the end of the month. Please buy one – the babies need shoes and I need a new weed-eater.

And I'm so sure you're gonna love it that I'm offering a money-back guarantee to my Lowdown readers (this means you). If you buy *A New Leaf* and are not completely satisfied, simply return it to Obie Joyful (my albino tambourine player who is also in charge of complaints and refunds), and he will give you a Lightnin' Charlie Online Shop gift card for your purchase price (minus a 15% restocking fee). But be sure to speak slowly, because Obie Joyful is deaf, but he reads lips very well. In most situations, deafness would be considered a handicap, but for complaint department managers and tambourine players, it's actually a benefit!

If *A New Leaf* is not (by far) the best record that I've ever done, then James Brown ain't funky and King Kong ain't a monkey! I'm very excited and thankful to God that after three years of hard work, *A New Leaf* is finally finished and coming to fruition. It is a CD that represents me, my music, and my sound far better than anything I've ever recorded. *A New Leaf* represents more than the fulfillment of three years of hard work, it's the culmination of forty-three years of life, and it's the record I've always wanted to make. God willing, by next month's Lowdown, it'll be here.

Until we meet again, stay well, my friends. Take good care of each other. See you in the funny papers.

Love,
Light-brown Charlie
the artist formerly known as "The Mighty Whitey"

JUNE 2005

3

MY RECORD: ONE'S AT THE CD STORE, AND ONE'S AT THE POLICE STATION

Hallelujah!!! My CD, *A New Leaf,* is enjoying long-awaited release parties and is now walking on its own. After very long and difficult (understatement) labor pains, I am the proud papa of a brand new CD baby child. It is getting very favorable (another understatement) reviews and is now available in stores regionally, in Tennessee and Virginia, and at my online shop. Thanks for being so patient and for continuing to ask me when the new CD would be available.

I've been performing songs from *A New Leaf* for over a year now and introducing them by saying,

"This is a tune from my new record which is due out any day..." (blatant overstatement).

The gestation period for a Lightnin' Charlie CD must be longer than any other mammal on earth. However, it is finally here, and free...free at last. But understand, in this case, 'free' means 'turn loose' or 'liberated' or, in other words, you can set one 'free' for fifteen US dollars. That is to say, if you 'turn loose' of fifteen bucks from your wallet, you can own my masterpiece. This is for the benefit of so-called 'friends' that seem to feel that they're entitled to own your life's work without paying for it because of 'friendship'. Uh-uh. Bona fide friends have money, fifteen bucks anyway. And don't mind paying for things they want. If you want to own a copy of *A New Leaf,* but don't think it's worth fifteen bucks, I've got bad news for you partner; you're out of luck! Do I need more friends like that? I've got so many friends now that I can't get all of their phone numbers into my cell phone. Enough already – I'm only going to need six pallbearers. And furthermore, if I want a good, loyal, and true friend till the end, I'll buy a dog.

Now let's move on to other business. A lot of you have heard me tell stories of my days on the road, breaking the law, dealing with life's curveballs, etc. and have asked me to include some of these anecdotes in the Lowdown.

So, due to popular demand and the fact that folks always seem to enjoy hearing of my personal misfortunes, here is one of those stories, offered for your enjoyment, from my sordid, but not too distant past. And remember as you read these tales of my old days, old friends, and wild oats, that Lightnin' Charlie is just an old sinner – saved by grace. And away we go…

One day while driving my bandbox, which at that time was a gaudy, green Ford van (the color of money), I was pulled over for having an expired tag. The policeman routinely wrote me a ticket, which, he explained, would be thrown out when I appeared in court with a valid registration on the court date. Okay, no problem.

Later that same day, I was pulled over again on my way to work (I was tending bar at a local cut-and-stab), and when I got out and showed the policeman the ticket for the expired registration (that's what he had pulled me over for), he just waved "OK" and let me go on my merry way. I had the ticket, and had until the court date to get my tag. Ba-da-bing, end of story.

Later that same night (I knew I should have stayed in bed), this time on my way home from work, I was pulled over a third time. And guess what, Lightnin' Bugs? Third time's a charm. Knowing the drill, I stepped out of the car with my ticket in hand, politely telling the officer, this time a policewoman (uh-oh), that, if I was being stopped for my expired registration, that I had already been given a citation that morning. This is where the fun begins, folks (yours, not mine).

The policewoman instantly dropped her hand to her pistol and yelled for me to,

"*Git yore hands where I can see 'em!*"

Obviously, she had misunderstood me. I reiterated that if she had pulled me over for the tag, I had already been given a ticket that day, and was only trying to show her the ticket. Then she *drew* her pistol, pointed it at me (with military grip and stance!), and shouted again for me to stop and put my hands up, which I surely did; immediately this time. No misunderstanding here, boss! I've got my mind *right!*

Now, those of you who know me know that I am not the type to argue with law enforcement officials, let alone act aggressively or even rudely towards them. My plan-of-attack (or defense) is to be as nice and cooperative as possible so that both of us can go our separate ways as quickly as possible. We both have our jobs to do. That being said, I was as surprised then, as you are now, at having a police officer's .40-caliber Glock pointed at me for driving home from work with an expired tag.

She approached me slowly and cautiously and, holstering her gun (whew!), started her interrogation with the $64,000 question,

"Have you been drinking?"
"No ma'am", I replied weakly, *"I'm on my way home from work."*

Trained to disregard this honest answer, she barked back at me, loudly, her fat paw still on her pistol grip – my hands still in the air,

"Well, you smell like beer", she growled,
"Well ma'am", said I, in my most diplomatic tone, *"I'm sure I do. I'm a bartender, and I'm covered with beer. But I can't drink alcohol while I'm working – I've been drinking cokes and coffee all night."*

She obviously didn't want to hear the truth, she couldn't handle the truth, and she was becoming enraged at the prospect of having pulled over an innocent and ordinary citizen, who really was simply on his way home from work, and she snarled at me, trying desperately to create an offence, where there was none,

"Oh Yeah? Why are yore eyes all red, then?"

Well friends, I was quickly becoming a bit agitated myself. I still had my hands up in the air like a gangbanger, and since my innocence didn't seem to make any impression on her, I thought I might try sarcasm. Bad idea. Honesty is always the best policy, even when it gets you nowhere, but my truthful responses seemed to only be making her madder. I could've told her the truth – that I was allergic to cigarette smoke, and that my eyes were red because I had been working in a smoke-filled bar for the last ten hours, earning minimum wage, and was tired and sleepy. I was also tired of having my hands in the air, having a loaded pistol aimed at my chest, and being questioned like a terrorist. So instead of giving her a straight answer (she wouldn't have bought it anyway), I gave her my sly, sweet look (as sweet as I could muster under the circumstances), and with a large dose of syrupy cynicism, cooed,

"Honey, I'm a musician. My eyes are always this color!"

Well, that did it. I had said the 'M' word (musician) to an angry cop, and there was no turning back now.

"GIT YORE HANDS ON THE CAR!!!"

she squealed triumphantly, her tail finally becoming untwisted in triumph.

She was in a bit of a quandary: she couldn't ticket me (again) for the expired registration, she couldn't arrest me for DUI, she definitely couldn't let me go, but she finally had something to bust me for that would surely stick...my admission of guilt (although coerced), of being a musician. And a wise guy. Maybe addressing her as "Honey" was a contributing factor to my arrest, too. Judging by her extreme butchy appearance and manner, she probably had not been called "Honey" for quite a long time; at least not by a man.

At this point, I'd like to address the naysayers, who are positive that this type of thing does not occur, and I am either making all or most of it up, or I am leaving a lot out. I am guilty of omitting a few parts, but not to affect the veracity of the story, but to allow kids to safely read it. I've told this story to some folks, who immediately dismiss my version of the facts with,

"They can't do that!"

Listen babe, they can do whatever they want to do, until they get caught doing it, same as any other criminal. A badge doesn't automatically make them pure of heart. But don't get me wrong. I respect policemen (and women!) for their courage and for their underpaid protection of me and my family. It's a thankless and terrific job they do. But that's the good cops, the true law enforcement officers. Some people believe all cops are good, just because they're cops; and that all politicians are good, and all priests are good, etc. Some people believe professional wrestling is real. Some simple people simply believe what the people in power tell them as truth. Let a bad person gain power, and they're very bad; they're dangerous. Power corrupts, and absolute power corrupts absolutely.

I respect the law, and its officers, but there are some out there, boys and girls, who are not in it for the right reasons. Maybe they were bullied as kids, and seek revenge on the world via their badge, or maybe they have been bullies their whole life, and seek employment that affords them the opportunity to keep on bullying. Whether you believe it or not, there are many goons in law enforcement, who relish the opportunity to bully innocent people. That's why they became cops in the first place – for the badge and the gun, and the freedom to act irresponsibly and without culpability for their actions. I know these bad cops exist, and so do the good cops. But I believe that bad cops are still the vast minority, thank God.

Police brutality isn't necessarily a bad thing, depending on whom it's directed towards. I don't object to cops bullying criminals. Bully for you! That's what you're paid to do. Public safety requires the police to apprehend and throw the bad guys into jail. But does having bloodshot eyes, an expired registration, and a guitar make me Public Enemy Number One? It did that night. So before you give me too much credit for an over-active imagination, let me assure you that this story is true, and that I ran into one bad, she-bully, of a sow-cop that night. And she had some kin at the station too, as you shall soon see.

I was handcuffed and taken into custody by the policewoman, whose name, I found out, was "Baron". That has a nice Nazi ring to it, eh? I knew I had to get her name because I had seen people on TV that are wrongfully arrested, and after they ask the arresting officer for their name and badge number, the cop then repents, relents, and lets them go. Handcuffed, under arrest, in the back of her squad car, and on my way to jail, I boldly asked for her name.

"Baron", she said, glaring at me in her rear view mirror.
"Barren?" I said, making sure, *"Like infertile?"*
"No!" she yapped, *"Baron. Like the Red Baron!"*
"The Bloody Red Baron of Germany?" I asked.
"Yeah! You got it!" she growled.

Yeah, I got it, all right. She was proudly referring to her namesake (and soul mate), Baron von Richthofen, the Red Baron. A sworn and declared enemy of the American people, the German top gun and flying ace of World War I garnered fame and made his living by shooting down more British and American airmen than any other WWI flyer. His job was taking down the good guys. Well, that's quite apt in our story, is it not? Declaring herself the enemy, the gauntlet had been thrown down. Any sworn enemy of America is certainly an enemy of mine; likewise, any friend of America's enemy is also my enemy. I rode to the police station, seething, and contemplating the enemy, the Kaiser, and World War I (not to mention the long combat history between the Red Baron and my beloved Snoopy and his Sopwith Camel).

The bloody Ms. Red Baron of Germany, still unrepentant, took me to the police station (amid a lot of very un-ladylike speech), where I was "processed" and placed in a cell. And on the many occasions, at the scene, in her car, and at the jail, when I demanded to be told what I was being arrested for, I was cursed and told to shut up, Gestapo-style. They wouldn't treat O. J. that way. But then O. J. was quite different; he was guilty.

I was glad to be put into my jail cell, grateful even. Because part of the grisly process of being "processed", included (are you ready for this?) being

STRIP-SEARCHED!!!

Yes, our naked hero and author, Lightnin' Charlie, guilty of being a musician and having an expired vehicle registration, was forced to bend over and grab his ankles for the benefit of a very cheerful, and very cross-eyed cop. This ghastly duty didn't seem to cause Cross-Eyed Cop any alarm. Much to the contrary (and much to my horror), it seemed to provide him with great delight, and the only reason I'm not writing this from prison today, is that he only looked, and didn't touch. Over time, though, this repeated tedious inspection had most likely been the cause of his becoming cross-eyed. Although feeling very wretched and most hopeless by then, I performed this ankle-grab with relative ease, as I am very flexible from years of Tae Kwon Do injuries. But I wasn't at all used to the naked part. If I had access to a firearm, and thought I could possibly escape, I would probably be known today as "Cop Killer". You see, I wasn't living the life of a committed Christian back then. I didn't forgive my enemies. And neither did I turn the other cheek (jolly good pun!). Let's move on.

I was never told what I was being arrested for, never given my Miranda rights *(Hey, Johnnie Cochran!)*, never given a Breathalyzer or any field sobriety tests, never given a phone call, and never charged with anything. And here I am, naked, bent over, and grabbing my ankles, in what anyone would call a completely compromising position, with Cross-Eyed Cop looking for a valid vehicle registration in a place where I didn't know people hid them!

I was humiliated and released, wondering if photos of this event would someday hit the tabloids. Hit the hemorrhoids is more like it. I was released after two or three hours in jail (long enough for my car to be towed), and was never told why I was arrested. Not that it mattered; they could just make something up. The attorney I went to see afterwards told me the same thing.

Allow me to tell you what I think. Me thinks Ms. Red Baron's comrade and co-conspirator, Cross-Eyed Cop, must've been the type who, besides enjoying his work, had a soft spot (no pun intended) for musicians with bloodshot eyes; or anyone else, for that matter, as long as they were male, and handcuffed. The butch and bloody Red Baron would troll around (no pun intended!), looking for victims to wrongfully incarcerate, violate, humiliate, infuriate, and desecrate. She makes her arrest, and takes her innocent victim downtown, to be "processed" and jailed by her friend and fellow lowlife, Cross-Eyed Cop. Then, for dessert, she calls her cousin, or her girlfriend's cousin, to tow the victim's vehicle away and impound it. "Cousin Tow-Job" commands a handsome fee for this service (I had to pay him $150 to get my car back). Ms. Red Baron gets her jollies by bullying and violating helpless innocents. And Cross-Eyed Cop gets his jollies by...well, "processing".

What a sick and twisted trio – East Tennessee's thin blue line. And what a successful little enterprise...everybody wins: the Nazi sow-bully Red Baron, the homo-hillbilly Cross-Eyed Cop, and their grimy, tattooed accomplice, Cousin Tow-Job. The attorney I consulted told me it would be a case of my word against theirs, and to forget about it. Nice world, huh?

But this sick miscarriage of justice did teach me one valuable lesson. This horrible experience has established in me a lifelong habit to never, *EVER,* let my vehicle registrations expire again. Never. And I own four vehicles. I've got my mind *right,* boss! All that bending over must've brought all the blood to my head and fixed me for life! All my plates are up to date, boss!

Well, that's it for this installment of "So You Want To Be In Show Business?" See you next month, right here in the true blue tales of the Lightnin' Lowdown. Y'all mosey along and stay out of trouble now, ya' hear?

God loves you and God knows I love you too,
Lightnin' Charlie

P.S. I forgot to mention my top ten CDs for this month. Here 'tis, in no particular order.

1) The Isaacs - Heroes
2) Sister Rosetta Tharpe - The Gospel Of The Blues
3) Gordon Lightfoot - United Artists Collection
4) The Rat Pack - Live At The Sand's
5) Big Jack Johnson and Kim Wilson - The Memphis Barbecue Sessions
6) Ivory Joe Hunter - 16 Greatest Hits
7) Barrelhouse Chuck - Salute To Sunnyland Slim
8) Louvin Brothers - Tribute To The Delmore Brothers
9) Bob Margolin And Nappy Brown - Down In The Alley
10) Sam Cooke - The SAR Records Story

JULY 2005

4

WHY I DON'T COME DOWN OFF THE MOUNTAIN ANYMORE

My darling Lightnin' Bugs, hope this finds you all well and enjoying the dog days of summer. Thanks for surfing in and thanks for buying my new record, *A New Leaf.* Thanks also for coming out to see the shows - I'd look pretty silly up there without you.

Here is my backyard CD top ten list, in no particular order:

1) Johnny Cash - American IV The Man Comes Around
2) Percy Mayfield - The Poet Of The Blues
3) Little Willie John - Fever
4) Various - There's A Riot Going On (The Songs Of Leiber And Stoller)
5) Jimmy Rogers - The Complete Chess Recordings
6) The Isaacs - Carry Me
7) Various - Ultra Rare Rockabilly
8) Mahalia Jackson - Gospels, Spirituals, & Hymns, Vol. 1 & 2
9) Hank Williams - Alone With His Guitar
10) Elvis Presley - The Complete Sun Sessions

Okay boys and girls, for this month's installment of "So You Want To Be In Show Business?" we are going to be traveling back to a place some of you East Tennesseans/Southwest Virginians will definitely remember - the historic downtown train station in Bristol, Virginia. The Bristol Train Station, situated directly (and conveniently) across the street from the Bristol Police Station, was home to many a shady nightclub through the years, and the opening scene for this sentimental saga of musical misery takes place here. So let's start with a song...sing children sing, to the tune of *House Of The Rising Sun:*

There is a club in Bristol
Right across the street's "the man"
With fightin' freaks and migraine geeks
In the back of Lightnin's van

This is a tale of a typical night's employment for yours truly (before I saw the Light).

Once upon a time, after playing a non-eventful three-set gig in a nightclub in the aforementioned train station, the band had finished the load-out and retired to a table to sit, talk, and have a nightcap (Sprite for me) with four or five patrons who were still hanging around.

It was after closing time, but they were apparently friends of the bartender and were enjoying the tranquility (and the smell of stale beer) that permeates a bar after closing. I knew one of the guys at the table – I had bought my wife's engagement ring from his local jewelry store. So we were just hanging out, making friendly small talk, when I got up to go to the front desk and telephone my wife to tell her I was running late and I'd be home soon. When I hung up the phone and turned to go back to the table, I saw my bass player, Jack (his real name), and one of the guys from the table engaged in fisticuffs (that is, they were rolling around on the floor, punching each other in the head and face). I ran over and got between them, pulling them apart, to break it up.

My drummer was standing there, a chair raised over his head, shrieking and screaming as only he could do. Let's call him "Mork" (not his real name, but just a vowel away). Mork was wearing a powder blue tuxedo, the latest of his borrowings from me, and was quite a sight...and a sound...and a mind.

> *"You're traveling through another dimension, a dimension not only of sight and sound but of mind; a journey into a wondrous land whose boundaries are that of imagination. That's the signpost up ahead – your next stop, the Twilight Zone!"*

Mr. Mork was not only dependent upon me for clothing, but for housing, driving, and food as well. Mork had been kicked out of his previous abode (and several others before that), and I took him in, dumbly thinking that I could keep him under control, and at least I wouldn't have to go looking for him when it was time to go to the gig (Mork didn't have a car either).

Mork might not have had a home, a car, clothes, or social graces, but I'll tell you about one thing Mork did have. Mork had this extraordinary shrill tone (the understatement of the century) when he would scream or yell loudly that was like no other. It would loosen the fillings in your teeth. I have never heard anything else like it, before or since. He was a big fan of the rock band, K.I.S.S., and idolized the deviate drummer Tommy Lee. Mork looked up to sociopaths as his sole role models, and he was always screaming, loud and long, about something.

I can't overstate the mind-blowing ferocity of Mork's cry. We put him out of the van onto the street several times for taking these fits. We'd literally throw him, bodily, out of the van, after begging him to stop. One would go blind from a sustained exposure to Mork's screaming in a small, confined space like a van; it was unbelievable. You've heard of people whose voices could break glass? Well, his could break plaster. It was deafeningly loud, but it wasn't the volume that got you. It was the tone. Mork's howlings had the tonal quality of fingernails on a chalkboard. It made you feel like you were chewing aluminum foil. It was maddening and quite unbearable; torture in the truest sense of the word.

Another benefit of having Mork in the band (a Mork perk!) was that occasionally, when the spirit (spirits is more like it) moved him, he would strip off all of his clothes (my clothes) while playing drums at a gig (my gig), and then shriek/recite some terribly vulgar lines from the movie *Full Metal Jacket* (at his trademark head-splitting volume). This was always a Tennessee showstopper and real deal-breaker of the highest order (for me). My drummer Mork: what an asset. Well, that's almost the right word.

Anyway, let's get back to our Bristol brawl, y'all. I had left Mork, our asset, holding a chair over his head, and yowling like a thousand hyenas with their tails stuck in an old clothes-wringer, and Jack, our bassist, rolling on the floor, in a no-holds barred wrestling match. I just noticed, while typing, that our asset (Mork) and our bassist (Jack) have something in common. If you'll look again at the words *asset* and *bassist*, I'm sure you'll see it too. It's a personality trait that the two of them shared. And it's also another name for a mule.

I managed to separate the two fighters and was demanding to know what in the wide world of sports had happened. Jack said that this guy just sucker-punched him in the eye (which was already swelling shut) for no reason. The guy denied it, to which Jack, pointing to his quickly closing left eye, replied logically that,

"Yeah, I guess I just punched myself in the eye."

This other fellow, the Sucker-Puncher, was no spring chicken, but he was big, and he was tough. He had the kind of face that looked like you could strike a match on it. He was at least twenty years older than Jack, and a lot bigger, but he was obviously one rough-dried old dude, and was not the type of guy to mess with. His looks reminded me of some of the crusty pirate mutineers in *Mutiny On The Bounty* (not the glossy remake with Marlon Brando, but the killer original with Clark Gable). Why this codger cracked Jack remains a mystery, but the reasons for the fight don't matter, as they don't affect the rest of our story.

It was at this point that the two of them decided that there was nothing left to do but "take it outside and settle it" and they started towards the door. And we all followed; to make sure that the Marquis of Queensbury rules of bar fighting were strictly adhered to. After all, we were not barbarians. There would be no guns, no knives, no standing eight-count, no saving by the bell (no bell), and no calling of police.

And so Jack and the Sucker-Puncher, Mork and I, along with another guy and girl from our table left the club and entered the long corridor of the train station, which led outside where the dispute was to be settled. All of a sudden, this other guy begins belligerently shoving his chest and beer-belly into Jack's back as they're walking out. I should mention that Jack was only about five and a half feet tall, weighing somewhere in the neighborhood of 130 pounds, and this guy bumping and bullying Jack was another big 'un, standing six foot two or so, and tipping the scales at around 225 pounds. This guy wasn't involved in the fracas at the table, and was simply taking the opportunity to be what his mother raised him to be, a redneck. Bullying someone 100 pounds smaller than themselves is typical of rednecks. About the only time they'll pick on someone their own size, is when they outnumber the guy five to one (or when their victim is handcuffed – see last month's Lowdown). Perhaps this redneck was puffing up and bumping his chest into Jack for the want of some personal attention from him. If so, he was about to get it.

Jack spun around and, quick as a cat, had this big lummox down and was applying a Royce Gracie Ju-Jitsu stranglehold to his throat. Jack was so fast; he looked like a spider monkey climbing that guy. Jack's superb chokehold completely shut off the carotid artery from delivering much-needed blood to the brain, causing the redneck to turn gray immediately (grayneck?), and pass out. This procedure took all of two or three seconds. His girlfriend or wife was now in a state of panic, hitting my one-eyed bassist in the face with her purse and screaming. I was panicking as well, trying to get Jack's spider monkey hands unlocked from the guy's throat (he wasn't letting go), and I was doing my fair share of screaming, too, pleading,

"Let him go, Jack! You're gonna kill him!"

Jack did let go of him and it was then that we noticed the foul odor coming from the fallen redneck.

Yes friends, I'm sorry to say his bowels let go about the same time Jack did. Quickly regaining color and consciousness (such as it was), he was led into the men's room of the club by his faithful girl Friday, never to be seen or heard from again. Good riddance to bad rubbish. The Sucker-Puncher, who thought he might be on his way to meet a similar fate, now reconsidered, and smartly decided that he wanted to be friends.

So the two of them, the Sucker-Puncher and the One-Eyed Jack, shook hands and became fast friends. Bosom buddies, even. So much so, that the jewelry store owner even told Jack that if he'd come by his store the next day, that he'd give him a diamond ring for his girlfriend, which he did.

There was much "slapping fives" and "man hugs", and I was quickly sickening and tiring of the entire affair. I had had a bellyful of the slugging and the screaming, the judo-ing and the choking, the defecating and now the lovemaking between these yahoos, and suggested strongly to the boys in the band that it was high time we made tracks. Let's get while the gettin's good.

Remember, the Bristol police station (and jail) was located directly across the street from the train station, and I really didn't want to deal with the police (as readers of last month's Lowdown will certainly agree) or any more redneck shenanigans. So we tiptoed to my van to start the 30-minute journey home. I was oh, so very grateful to be getting out of there in one piece (with the exception of 'one-eye') and without the intervention of law enforcement.

But as fate would have it, about halfway home, our drummer Mork started into a screaming fit, telling me at the tip-top of his lungs to...

"PULL OVER CHARLIE, I'M NOT GOING HOME SOBERRRR!!!"

I pulled my diesel van ("plub-plub-plub-plub") and 12-foot trailer into an all-night gas station/convenience store along the side of the highway, thinking that a quart of beer might well appease my Turret's Syndrome-afflicted drummer. My intent in pulling over was solely to shut him up. I realize the road to Hell is paved with good intentions, and this, as you will see, was no exception.

Mork leaped out of the van, violently slammed my van door, and now full of fight (back at the real fight he didn't do anything except hold a chair over his head and scream like Tina Turner on helium), promptly proceeded to kick a metal newspaper bin through the gigantic plate glass window of the convenience store, smashing it, and leaving a hole the size of a Volkswagen Beetle.

I'm parallel-parked right in front of the store, in full view of the open-mouthed clerk who was (up till now) enjoying a quiet night and playing a quick game of Ms. Pac-Man in front of the window. Mork-Maniac jumps right back into the van and screams,

"LET'S GOOOOOOO, CHARLIE!!!"

To which I replied,

"Go? Go where? You stupid [many expletives deleted] moron!"

Funny, I just couldn't see myself outrunning every cop car and helicopter in Bristol in my GMC diesel van with loaded 12-foot trailer. *Plup-plup-plup-plup...*

I got out and tried to explain to the freaked-out clerk that we were Lightnin' Charlie and the Upsetters, and that my drummer was a hopeless psychotic who had just been involved in a bar fight where he witnessed his buddy (and fellow asset) get his eye blacked and he's just upset (pun intended), and if he would just allow me to clean up the mess and give him my driver's license with my home phone number, that there surely would be no need to involve the police in this matter, etc. etc. He didn't answer me or say a single word.

Well, the next thing I see is about fifteen police cars, lights spinning, sirens wailing, pulling into the scene of the crime. This battalion of cops all jump out of their cars and, whom do you think they throw against the wall of the building??? How'd you guess? Me, the sober babysitter who's been busy singing songs, loading and unloading equipment, breaking up fist fights and strangulation murders, dealing with spoiled, suburban, shrieking banshee-brats and big, bowel-moving rednecks. Me, who had been apologetically picking up pieces of broken glass the size of card tables and offering up my name, address, phone number, driver's license, and lots of cash to the clerk (in exchange for some silence), while One-Eyed Jack is sitting in my backseat thinking about what kind of free diamond ring he'll get tomorrow and my screeching asset of a drummer is sitting in MY van wearing MY powder-blue tuxedo and griping about how long this is taking ME to straighten out, because he's in a hurry to get his quart of beer and go home to MY house!!! Do I sound bitter, friends? I still get migraine headaches occasionally, but not nearly as often as I used to.

So after being roughly handcuffed and searched (not stripped this time, thankfully) by the police, I was allowed to explain what had happened – that my drummer, who is a hopeless mental case, had kicked the newspaper bin in anger, but had in no way intended for it to bust out the window of the store, and that I'm sure that the clerk would vouch for my sober cooperation and for taking complete responsibility for this mishap and that I would gladly pay for the damages. I was told to sit down and shut up and wait while they phoned the storeowner. They called him, woke him up (it must've been 2:30 AM by then), and told me he was "on his way to the scene". It would then be up to him whether or not charges were placed and arrests were made.

By the way, Mork (the other white meat), who has a history of law-breaking and outrageous public misbehavior a mile long, has never, to this day, ever been handcuffed, let alone arrested, by law enforcement. I was extremely confident that if any arrests were made that night for the window Mork kicked in, that the guilty party's clean record would not be tarnished, and I would surely be the one to go downtown and face the music. Why? That's easy: because I was the only one present who hadn't done anything wrong. Call me crazy.

While we waited, the police did remove the cuffs from me, as I must not have appeared to be a threat, and I was even allowed to videotape my drummer (in my powder blue tux) and my bass player (with one eye swollen shut) sitting on the curb in front of the massive hole in the plate glass window. It's a wonderful moment that sums up the 1980s for me in a five-second video clip.

At this point, as if things couldn't get any weirder, an old, jalopy pick-up truck, that looked like something Fred G. Sanford would abandon, pulls up to the gas pumps and two long-haired, bearded, dirty dudes get out. The driver yells at his passenger (in front of twenty cops),

"Yew pump the gas and I'll git the beer!"

I'm standing at the counter inside the store, still trying to schmooze and sweet-talk the clerk into putting in a good word with his boss for us, to allow ME to pay for the damage, in cash, but the clerk was having none of it, when this new kid on the block lurches in. This nouveaux idiot (in a lot full of idiots) wobbles up to the counter with his 12-pack. He slowly looks me up and down (I'm in my funky stage clothes), and then, looking at the gigantic hole in the glass, says sneeringly to the clerk,

"That's the reason I don't come down off the mountain anymore."

I was not in a position to argue that point, although I'm still not sure if he was referring to the assets, to the hole, or to me.

Bearded Beer Breath, the Tennessee Mountain Man, pays for his half-case, gives me one last dirty look, and swaggers back out towards his truck, where every cop in Bristol is waiting for him. One smiling policeman goes up to him and says,

*"Put the beer down on the ground
and put your hands on top of your head."*

While having nothing else to do while waiting for my arrest order, the cops got some ID from the passenger, and ran the truck's license plate, and it comes back with fugitive warrants on both of them. Not to mention a sure DUI for the driver and probably possession of any number of other types of illegal mountain contraband and paraphernalia. Now my question is this: if you are drunk and driving, and wanting to buy *more* beer, and you have a fugitive warrant out for your arrest, and one on your passenger also, why pull into a gas station where every cop in town is present, and not hiding behind some trees, but with all their lights and sirens on? I'm looking at these two rednecks in disbelief (as I know the cops are), knowing that we three will surely be cellmates soon, and fearing that they'll be blaming all this, and all these cops, on me. I remember thinking then how I wished I knew a little Ju-Jitsu.

The storeowner finally arrived an hour or so later (in his pajamas and robe – bless his heart), and after I handed him $500 in cash, I was allowed to drive to the ATM where I withdrew $500 more for him. He took my contact information and profuse apologies, and said that if I called him in the morning, he would let me know how much more the glass was going to cost (it ended up costing $1200), and that he didn't see any need to press charges. Mork was still sitting unmolested (as usual) on the curb and smoking cigarettes that he was bumming off the cops. He gets free cigarettes and I get frisked, handcuffed, and touched for $1000.

Today, Mr. Mork the Psychopath is living comfortably in Nashville, Tennessee, righteously rent-free. By night, Mork is still wearing **K.I.S.S.** makeup and still stripping off borrowed clothes in public. By day, he drives a delivery truck for a liquor store. That's perfect, like putting the fox in charge of the henhouse.

Jack recovered nicely from his shiner and got a free diamond chip ring from his sucker-punching new best friend (I had to drive him to the store to get it – he didn't own a car either). Jack is now out of the music business and working as a river raft guide, taking tourists rafting on the rapids. Funny, I've spent a lifetime getting taken up and down the river by musicians and malcontents (very redundant), so it's very comforting for me to have this forum, to share these stories, to vent my many frustrations, and to avoid shock treatment. You Lightnin' Bugs are saving me a bundle in therapy.

I'd like to close this installment of *American Midol* with a quote from the novelist, Tom Clancy, who said,

> *"The difference between writing fact and fiction is that fiction has to make sense."*

Said a mouthful there, Tom.

See you next time, for more lore, in store!
Charlie

AUGUST 2005

5

LEOPARD SKIN, LOOKALIKES, AND LAW ENFORCEMENT

Well, well, my little chickadees...hope all is well with you and yours. As for yours truly, I've been busier than a long-tailed cat in a room full of rocking chairs. And hotter than Michael Jackson at Boys Town (sorry). But it's good to be busy. And healthy and happy...and hot. It sure beats the alternative. Summertime, and the livin' is easy...

My new CD, *A New Leaf* is doing very well and getting rave reviews regionally. Lightnin' Charlie will be in 30,000 local mailboxes on Saturday, August 6th in the News And Neighbor newspaper. I am anxious to hear the national and international reviews on *A New Leaf*, which will be coming soon, and I will pass those on to you as they happen.

This month, before I tell y'all a true blues band bedtime story filled with sugarplums, fairies, and the joys of being a traveling rock star, I thought I'd list some books and movies that I'm enjoying at home right now instead of the usual CD top ten, so here's a nickel's worth of each, in no particular order...

LC's Book Of The Month Club

1) The Great Divorce - C.S. Lewis
2) Band Of Brothers - Stephen E. Ambrose
3) First On The Moon - Neil Armstrong, Michael Collins, Buzz Aldrin
4) Shiloh - Shelby Foote
5) The Everlasting Man - G.K. Chesterton

LC's Movie Picks Of The Month

1) It's A Gift - W.C. Fields
2) Rear Window - Jimmy Stewart, Grace Kelly
3) Pride Of The Yankees - Gary Cooper
4) The Harder They Come - Jimmy Cliff
5) The Great Escape - Steve McQueen, James Garner, James Coburn

Okay, for this month's edition of

COPS - LOCATION: LIGHTNIN' CHARLIE...

let's go back to a gig I played several years ago in a downtown nightclub in North Carolina. I had some difficulties that night with my bass player, not the spider monkey from last month's Lowdown, but another unhappy camper with a bit of a drinking problem. He was the nicest guy in the world until he finished his third Budweiser. And he was *way* past number three by the time we finished the show. He and I had been having mild-to-heavy disagreements all that afternoon during the drive, and the night wasn't bringing us any closer together.

Let me give you a little background on this guy. His first name was "Danny" (almost), but as soon as he got into a blues band, he dropped his first name and started using his middle name, "Leroy". This was a much more "dangerous" and "bluesy-sounding" moniker. But for the purposes of our story, let's call him "Mini-Me", which he was occasionally called, but never to his face. Leroy had an eccentric penchant for emulating me and my style of dress. Here are some items that, taken together, made the use the term "Mini-Me" appropriate for Leroy. Firstly, and through no fault of his own, Leroy was white like me (we all look alike, right?), he played a Fender sunburst guitar like mine (his was a Precision bass, mine was a Stratocaster), and after he joined the band, he took to wearing sport coats and black berets (hats) which is what I usually wore on stage back then. I always encouraged my band members (through the effective use of monetary fines), to dress the part when onstage. But I never intended for two-thirds of the band to look like twins. This must have appeared strange to the audience because here's two white guys (one just a shade away) in a three-piece band wearing sport coats, black berets and playing almost identical guitars onstage. The only differentiating factor between us was that he was about a foot shorter than I (hence the "Mini-Me"), and he always wore sneakers instead of dress shoes like I did. He wore those cheap, canvas, Chuck Taylor Converse Hi-Tops (he had two in every color).

The third character in this odd trifecta was my rockin', redheaded drummer Chuck (his real name), who sported a big Duran Duran hairdo and earrings, wore leopard-skin vests and leather pants tucked into cowboy boots. With real silver spurs. Yeah, I know. Chuck, Charlie, and Mini-Me. Chuckles (his nickname) must have appeared to the audience to be the 'redheaded stepchild' along with these two weird twins – one short, one tall.

Looking back, I realize that maybe the constant problems we were having with rednecks, drunks, etc. was at least partly due to our looking like freaks from a musical circus act. Plus there was the fact that I would take very little crap from people (except on-duty police officers and bandmates). This zero tolerance of mine has created many a colorful incident, and has provided me with a wealth of ribald stories and a lifetime of Lowdown episodes.

Anyway, before this particular road trip, much to my horror, Leroy asked to borrow a pair of my dress shoes to wear at that night's show. We both wore the same size – Mini-Me had big feet (remember, we were a circus act). For this show, Mini-Me would forego his usual Converses (which he comfortably wore on the four-hour van trip down to North Carolina). Mini-Me went shopping in my shoe closet, picking out a pair of wild, black patent-leather loafers, with cheetah fur on the tops (I rarely wore these because of my drummer's affection for animal fur and my present discontent at dressing like the other guys in the band).

By the way, let's explore the reason that I always wear hats onstage. It, too, is a matter of style. The reason I wore hats onstage was that I am *BALD*. The fact that bandmates with perfect heads of hair were taking my cue and wearing the same hats as I was wore, always seemed strange to me and was also quite insensitive to my particular handicap. Imagine if Ray Charles' band, all with 20/20 vision, wore dark glasses and had assistants lead them to their spots onstage, and then rocked back and forth while leaning on white canes at their side. Would that be a tad bit insensitive to their bandleader's handicap? Today it would be considered a hate crime. How dare they do that to Brother Ray? But the double standard that is still alive and well, as it applies to my career, my gender, my demography, and my ethnicity, made it perfectly acceptable to be insensitive to old baldy. And it really gave me the creeps.

Now back to our story. After we finished playing the gig, I was talking to a very nice, middle-aged couple that was sitting up front for the show and really digging us – clapping, dancing, laughing, and having a good time. They came up after our show to say hello to me and tell me that they had really enjoyed the band, etc. The man's wife then asked me if we had any Lightnin' Charlie t-shirts for sale. I said I was sorry, but we were out of them. As Mini-Me came out of the men's room and was staggering our way, this lady motioned toward him with her hand and said that she had noticed his Lightnin' Charlie and the Upsetters t-shirt he was wearing under his jacket and would have bought one. Mini-Me, you'll recall, was way past Budweiser number three, and by this point, had a chip on his shoulder the size of a beanbag chair. Seeing (but not hearing) our conversation, and seeing this woman point toward him, walked up to us and said slurringly,

"I shee y'all talkin' 'bout me...[BLEEP] YOU!!!"

Without hesitation, after years of training, I immediately launched into my "Let-Me-Apologize-For-The-Drunkard-In-My-Band" speech, which I had down pat, due to much practice. Then these two very nice folks left the building very upset (after all, they had just met one of the Upsetters up-close and personal). Naturally they were never seen at any of my gigs ever again.

I then tried to explain to my evil twin, the drunken "Mini-Me", what we were talking about and why the lady had pointed at him – that she liked his Lightnin' Charlie and the Upsetters t-shirt and had asked to *buy* one. Of course he just drunkenly sneered at me and walked out to my van, in my shoes, to chain-smoke and reflect on what a terrible jackass Charlie was.

I had made arrangements for us to spend the night with a friend of mine, a guy everyone called "Bobo". I didn't know where his house was, so Bobo was going to pull his car around to the front of the club for us to follow him home. After loading out (just my drummer and I, with no help from Leroy), I went out to the van to wait for Bobo.

When I got there, Mini-Me was sitting on the floor of my van, carelessly huffing his Marlboro reds. His legs were stretched out the open side door, his feet against the curb. He was cussing and carrying on, calling me various and sundry names under his beer-breath, while waiting to get paid. Reaching my limit, I told him,

*"If that's how you feel, Leroy,
then why are you still wearing my $100 fur shoes?"*

So Leroy loathingly removed my cheetah loafers by kicking at the heels, one foot after the other, and leering at me through bloodshot eyes, he knocked them off into the gutter. Then he started to put on his $10 hi-tops. Observing this, becoming enraged, and wondering why I hadn't stayed in college, I furiously yanked his hi-tops away from him. He had tied the sneakers together by the shoelaces. I got out of the van and stood triumphantly in the middle of the downtown street and, taking a running-go, hurled them down the street just as far as I could throw them. They must have gone two full city blocks – spinning through the air like some medieval weapon of war...

Whooop-whooop-whooop-whooop

Maturity obviously not being my strong suit, I turned and screamed at Leroy,

"That'll teach you to kick my shoes into the gutter!!!"

Well, Mini-Me knew he'd been whipped. Now silent, sheepish, and shoeless, Leroy started walking down the street to get his Chuck Taylors, and I got into the driver's seat to wait for Bobo.

While Leroy was fetching his sneakers, a guy comes staggering out of the club, climbs into the back seat of my van (through the open side door), and starts yelling at me to,

"GO TO THIS FIRST RED LIGHT AND HANG A LEFT!!!"

Not recognizing him, but assuming he must be here to direct us to Bobo's house, I asked him politely,

> "You a friend of Bobo's?"

He smartly responds with,

> "[BLEEP] BOBO!!! GO TO THE FIRST LIGHT
> AND HANG A LEFT!!!"

Well, if this guy thought my van was his taxi, he was surely mistaken. And if this sweet-talker thought that charm would persuade me to drive him someplace, he was also very much mistaken. I already had my hands full with one drunken malcontent. So, realizing that this guy was no friend of ours, but was just another malevolent barfly with no ride home, I graciously said,

> "Sorry man, I can't take you anywhere. We're from out-of-town
> and we're waiting to follow our friend home."

Sitting comfortably in my back seat, he glared at me and bellowed,

> "WHY DON'T YOU GO [BLEEP] YOURSELF??!!!
> I SAID TO GO TO THE RED LIGHT AND TURN LEFT!!!"

I had already heard a similar hyperbole from my own drunken employee, my bassist wearing my shoes. Now I'm being told to perform this unnatural (and quite impossible) act on myself by a drunken stranger sitting cozily in the back seat of my van. I said to him, much louder, and much less graciously this time,

> "I'M NOT TAKING YOU ANYWHERE –
> GET OUT OF MY VAN, NOW!!!"

To which he wittingly countered with,

> "[BLEEP] YOU!!!"

and again demanded,

> "GO TO THAT [BLEEP-BLEEP-BLEEP] LIGHT
> AND TURN LEFT!!!"

Yes friends, just another in a long line of very satisfied customers with very limited vocabularies.

Well, that being the proverbial last straw, I jumped out of the driver's seat and was quickly making my way around the front of the van to, by God, *pull him out*. This psychopath had gotten into a stranger's vehicle with three full-grown strangers in it (well, two were in it, and one's on the way). After cursing them and ordering them to drive him someplace, he had enraged the owner of the vehicle to the point of violence. The vehicle's owner was now righteously infuriated and on his way to physically eject him from the vehicle. Surely even this pub-crawling boozer would have the mental capacity to back off and leave in the face of such holy fury, right? Wrong again, Charlie.

Regular readers of the Lowdown will already know that, based on my selection of bandmates alone, judging character isn't one of my strong suits either. As our hero was quickly making his way around the front of the van, this guy was running towards me, hooping and hollering and, more importantly, reaching his right hand into his front pants pocket. For what, I didn't know. And I wasn't waiting around to find out. My spontaneous strategy was to 'divide-and-conquer': I intended to separate his head from his body before he could separate whatever was in his hand from his pocket. Well, my right fist started traveling up like a supersonic, spiral ham, starting way down below my hip (somewhere around Tupelo, Mississippi), and it met the oncoming point of this idiot's nose with a terrific 'bang' that sounded like the noise made when you blow up a paper bag and bust it with your other hand...

POW!!!

I'll bet he had to use a shoehorn to get his hat on for a week after that smash. It was a thing of beauty, really. He went down, falling flat on his back like a sack of bologna, and was knocked out. Cold. Another first round KO for our winner and still champion, Lightnin' Charlie! The extraordinary thing was, and I swear this is true, that as he lay there, his eyes were wide open and his eyeballs were spinning wildly around in their sockets like a cuckoo clock in some Looney Tunes cartoon.

Yes, fight fans, just another loud-mouthed redneck, now residing on "Queer Street", compliments of our hero, and still undefeated champion, Lightnin' Charlie, Skinny Street Fighter! Be sure and tune in next week for an exciting welterweight bout between Felix "Boom Boom" Bastogne and Carl "The Cat" Carter. That's all for tonight. Thanks for joining us on Friday Night At The Fights...

But wait... As I turn to get back into the van and make tracks for anyplace, the sock-footed Leroy, disgruntled employee, is finally returning from his sneaker-fetching exercise. Having seen the altercation that was taking place outside the van, Mini-Me, is coming hard, in a dead run, in his socks. Then Leroy (remember, he has large feet for a little guy), without breaking stride, on a two-block run, attempts to place-kick this unconscious guy's head like a football.

If he had succeeded, I'd be writing this from prison, but instead of connecting with the side of the sot's skull, the Good Lord made him barely miss his mark – directing the path of my shoeless evil twin's right foot into the top edge of the curb. Life truly is a game of inches.

Apparently, Mini-Me had heard the yelling, and sprinted, sock-footed, all the way back to the van and kicked the top of the concrete curb with all his momentum and might, soundly breaking his big toe and sobering him up immediately. This was kind of a ghetto version of Charlie Brown and Lucy Van Pelt's football fiasco. Leroy made a wretched, garbled hissing sound through his teeth that was not unlike the sound of air escaping from a tire, and fell into the open door of the van. I put her in gear to pull out.

That's when the cops arrived. Lots of 'em. They were on foot (pun intended) and had heard the commotion from the police station conveniently located directly across the street (again). One might think (if one has never been a touring blues musician), that having a police station right across the street from where you are being victimized in a violent crime might be a good thing. Why is a police station always right across the street from us? And why is that never a good thing?

Some of the cops were helping old slot machine-eyes up off the sidewalk and others were getting me out of the van ordering me to explain what had happened. I told them excitedly, but honestly, and in one breath,

"We're the band, playing inside the club. I'm waiting for my friend to drive around so we can follow him home to spend the night. Then this drunk gets into my van and starts cussing me, ordering me to drive him somewhere. After telling him nicely that I couldn't, he continues to cuss at me and yells at me to drive him up the street. I tell him to get out of my van. He refused. I got out to make him get out and here he comes running at me and screaming and trying to pull something out of his front pocket. That's when I hit him and he went down and I got into the van to leave. Then you all showed up and that's what happened!!!"

I am wide-eyed, huffing, puffing and praying that I am not going to jail. There's a lady cop standing closest to me [see the June Lowdown for more on lady cops and me]. She looks right at me and says,

"Well that's all fine and good, but why did you then try to kick him in the head like that? You could've killed him!"

Friends, *now* do you see why I wanted to be the only one in the band with a black beret and tiger-striped sport coat? Do you think identity theft only occurs with credit cards and social security numbers? Do you think my evil twin jumped to my aid, and confessed to the police that it was *he* who ran fifty yards and tried to punt that dead head like a pigskin? I hope you've answered, yes, no, and no. I started stammering (like Ralph Kramden – *"Hammenna-Hammenna-Hammenna")*, and trying to quickly come up with a better explanation than the truth,

"No Ma'am. It wasn't me who tried to kill the guy... it was someone else dressed up like me."

Thank God that before I had to come out with that one, the deranged knockout victim had regained consciousness and, once on his feet, started fighting with the cops. So they figured rightly that he was their man. The lady cop then told me I could go and they commenced to roughly routing the wacko across the street to bed. He had gotten a lift home after all.

I slowly idled out from the curb and just to make sure, asked another cop through my open window if it was all right for me to go. He said "Yeah", and I pulled out, turned the corner at the end of the block where Bobo was waiting for me when – you guessed it, friends...

BLUE LIGHTS!!!

The police apparently wanted to get me for DUI (although I wasn't the one drinking – again a case of mistaken identity). So they told me to drive away and then pulled me over, intending to arrest me for driving drunk. Actually, I was driving drunks. They would arrest me though, and probably put me into the same cell with the guy I wouldn't drive home. Why they didn't arrest me at the scene for attempted murder, I don't know. Must have been the paperwork.

"*License and registration,*" growled the cop.

Defensively I said, "*But the lady officer told me I could leave...*"

"*License and registration,*" the cop repeated.

I shakily dug my license and registration out of my wallet and handed to him. Meanwhile, the alcoholic, shoe-borrowing Mini-Me is in the back seat sucking air through his clenched teeth, doing a pretty good Kirk Douglas imitation, when the cop, looking at my driver's license says,

"*You guys from Johnson City, Tennessee?*"

"*Yes sir*", says I, not knowing where this line of questioning was headed. "*Well,*" he grins, handing me back my license, "*if y'all are from Johnson City, you can't be all bad. I went to college there. Used to go see a killer blues band called Lightnin' Charlie and the Upsetters. Ever heard of 'em?*"

I grinned real big at that sweet cop and pointed toward my bass player in the back seat (you know, the one with the black toe and the grimace). Ah yes, my evil twin who had just attempted murder in full view of an entire police station while dressed up like me. Yes sirree. Intuitively (and soberly), Mini-Me knew his cue, and opened up the front of his jacket, showing the policeman his Lightnin' Charlie and the Upsetters t-shirt, *proudly* this time.

Funny, the last time someone pointed at his t-shirt, he let go with some real raunchy expletives. This time, however, Mini-Me was all smiles. It's a wonder what a little exercise and a blackened, smashed great toe can do for one's attitude.

As for me, I was extremely grateful for two things: One, to be on my way to a bed that didn't have steel bars around it, and two, that the cops didn't see the silver spurs on the boots of my redheaded drummer, Chuckles. Yep, I'd rather be lucky than good.

The End???
Not by a long shot, hot shot...

See you in next month's episode, tentatively titled,

"Too Lazy To Work And Too Nervous To Steal"
or
"Mamas, Don't Let Your Babies Grow Up To Be Bluesboys"

Till then,
Stayin' alive and keepin' it real,
Lightnin' "the Cop-Magnet" Charlie

SEPTEMBER 2005

6

FIRE IN THE HOLE

Greetings and salutations, my dear Lightnin' Bugs. If you are having half as much fun as I am this summer, then I am twice as happy as you.

Thanks for surfin' in and hope to see you soon at Lightnin' Charlie Dillpickle's Traveling Circus and Merchandise Mart featuring the Moondogger Magic Show and Charlie's own trained mice! Trained mice? Check my calendar for event dates. I don't really have a circus, and a magic show, and trained mice, I'm just trying to make my worn-out little rock 'n' roll road show sound more interesting. It is what it is.

Here is a nickel's worth of my CDs and movies-of-the-month club for September, in no particular order:

<u>CDs now playing in Lightnin' Land</u>

1) Guitar Slim - Sufferin' Mind
2) Barrelhouse Chuck - Slowdown Sundown
   (featuring my brother-in-the-blues, Harmonica Todd Levine)
3) Honi Deaton & Dream - Promise To A Soldier
   (featuring my brother-in-law, Joe Clark)
4) Tarheel Slim & Little Ann - The Robin & Fire Years
5) Stevie Ray Vaughan - Raisin' A Little Sand (bootleg)

<u>DVDs now playing in Lightnin' Land</u>

1) The Beatles Anthology
2) Kojak - The First Season
3) The Akira Kurosawa Collection (Rashomon, Seven Samurai, Throne Of Blood, Yojimbo, etc.)
4) The Bridge On The River Kwai - Alec Guiness, William Holden
5) Public Enemy - James Cagney

   P.S. I'm still working on last month's books...I'm a slow reader.

For this month's story, I wanted to share a personal event with you. As I'm writing this, I am watching television coverage of the Katrina hurricane disaster in Louisiana and Mississippi. My heart goes out to those poor people who are in the midst of terrible suffering at the loss of their homes and all of their material possessions. Greater sympathy, have I, for those who are grieving the loss of a whole lot more than merely material things. I would like to relate to you a story of how I lost my home and most everything I owned at Christmastime 1983.

At that time, I was in college and living in a run-down old rental house-trailer in the sticks with a roommate. Although the digs were shabby, we had a lot of real nice things in the house. We were the only guys around that had a videotape player (Betamax!) complete with some of the obligatory videos of the day – Scarface, Pink Floyd's The Wall, Richard Pryor Live In Concert, Easy Money, etc. We were superbad. Then there was my collection of vinyl (LPs, EPs & 45s) that numbered about 1000 that I had been collecting my whole life. I also had some really cool things framed like: Stevie Ray Vaughan's autograph on a club poster along with some guitar picks he had given me, photos of my aunt Jeannette with Elvis and his family at Graceland, as well as a lifetime's worth of irreplaceable family photographs. And there was also my wardrobe. I once asked Jerry Portnoy, the harmonica player in Muddy Waters' band for his advice on leading a blues band. He looked at me and said, *"Dress like a pimp."* And I did.

Early one morning, a few days before Christmas, it was cold, gray, and, as we say around here, spitting snow. My roommate Derek was leaving for work. I was asleep on the couch in the living room, wearing a groovy set of custom pajamas – long-john bottoms and a sleeveless, American Flag t-shirt. I need to point out, for the benefit of our story, that there was nobody alive that was a heavier sleeper than I. Not one. I used to buy the loudest alarm clocks and clock radios I could find, and then to wake me, I'd set several of them around my room to go off like a symphony. Friends spending the night, trying to wake me in the morning/afternoon would become fearful that I was comatose or dead. Honestly. When I was a kid growing up in Miami, we lived in a duplex apartment. Our apartment was upstairs and another family's apartment was downstairs. My parents were good friends with the couple downstairs and I was pals with their son who was my age, about 6 or 7 years old. Late one night, a regiment of plainclothes cops drove vans and pickup trucks across the sidewalk onto the lawn around our house and, using axes on the front door and rifle stocks on the windows, busted their way into the downstairs apartment and opened fire on the dad who was standing in his bedroom, in his pajamas, with his wife in bed beside him, and his son a few feet away. He died from multiple gunshot wounds. Supposedly, he had ties to drug-traffickers from South America, but my folks never knew of it (he was a solid family man, vice-president of a bank, etc.). The undercover police (who most likely were the ones high on cocaine) said in their report that they told him to "freeze" and he "moved toward his wife" who was lying in bed. They opened up on him. But all the screeching tires, the breaking-and-entering with axes, the massive amounts of shotgun and small arms fire, and the screaming and chaos which followed, didn't rouse me from my slumber upstairs. I slept right on through it all and doubt that I even turned over. This was a blessing to my parents who didn't figure these pony-tailed, blue-jeaned, van-hippies with shotguns for policemen; they thought these thugs were crazed killers who were coming upstairs for us next. Sorry to digress, but you needed an understanding of just how deeply I slept once I was asleep – you could not wake me up.

This particular snowy December morning, at about 6 AM, as my roommate Derek went out the front door to drive to work, for some reason, I woke up. Me waking up at six o'clock in the morning was more than very unusual; it was next to impossible. Then, instead of just turning over and going back to sleep, I got up to go to my bedroom. This was not only abnormal, but also totally unprecedented for me. If I fell asleep at the top of a ladder, that's where I would stay until I was ready to get up. And it wouldn't be at six o'clock in the morning, either. But on this morning, I woke up, got up, and went down the hall to my bedroom. If I had made it back to my bedroom at the end of the hall, I would not be writing this today.

Halfway down the hall, I stopped at the bathroom to get a drink of water out of the sink. This also was a very peculiar thing for me to do. And when I stopped in the hallway bathroom, I smelled smoke. It was coming from Derek's room, which was adjacent to the bathroom. I rushed into his room and saw his small clock radio was on fire (firemen later ruled ours an electrical fire and the cause of the blaze faulty wiring). When Derek left his room and turned off the light at the switch, it apparently had shorted and caught fire.

Now wide-awake, I ran into the bathroom, three feet away (this is a two-bedroom, single-wide house-trailer, not a sprawling southern plantation). At this point, I was fully aware that I had a problem, but I wasn't yet thinking that my house was burning down. The flames were only about a foot square and I would simply put the fire out. I grabbed the big bath towels off the shower rack in the bathroom and returned to smother out the fire. But when I hit that fire with those towels (we stupidly didn't have a fire extinguisher – but I've got one in every room of my house today), the flames shot out onto the wall and flew up the wall and across the ceiling faster than you can imagine. I remember the sound it made,

"FLOOOF!!!"

The best way I can describe it is that the flames didn't look small and separate from one another like a fire in a fireplace; these were one, single flame, the height and width of the entire room, that spread up the wall and across the ceiling toward me like an ocean wave rolling in to the shore – only faster. *Much* faster. Then, realizing that this wasn't a just a little fire, but that, in fact, the house was burning down, I slammed the bedroom door closed and ran into the living room (at the front door) to throw as many of our earthly belongings out to safety as I could. For your information, the time elapsed between my first smelling the smoke from a tiny little fire to running for my life from a room engulfed in flames was about eight or ten seconds, tops.

But I was not panicked and was bound and determined to get as much stuff out as possible. On my first run through the living room to the front door, I grabbed my Fender guitar and amp, and in one sweeping motion, *threw* them out the front door. Then I turned to go back down the hall to my bedroom and get the jewelry box that contained my most prized possessions – the rings, watches, and cufflinks I had inherited from my father. But already, the hallway and living room was full of thick, gray smoke. I was still going to my bedroom to get my dad's jewelry box – I would simply hold my breath. There weren't any flames outside of Derek's room yet, as I had closed his door – just smoke. I would hold my breath, run to my room, grab the jewelry box from my dresser, and run back into the living room to continue throwing other things of value and importance out the front door into my driveway. But I immediately learned that, in a smoke-filled, burning building, you couldn't hold your breath, no matter how you tried. You choke and gag regardless of whether you're holding your breath or not. I don't know if this is true of all building materials when burning, but I know it's true of burning trailers. You know, when hearing this story, some people (cowards mostly) will tell me how *they* would've reacted and how *they* would've got this and that out, and how *they* wouldn't have been overcome by the heat and smoke. I say that's what a bull leaves a big pile of in a field after he's eaten a bunch of wet grass. Remember Richard Pryor talking about the never-been-there brothers who say,

"Man, if I was a slave back then, I wouldn't have taken that, I would've..."

But no one with any real experience in making personal life-or-death decisions (firefighters, combat veterans, etc.) has ever said to me that they would've (or could've) done anything differently than I did. They know in those situations, it becomes a matter, simply, of survival. They realize that the result of what I did, and didn't do, is that I survived. And based on that fact alone, that I am here to tell the story, is good enough for them. And me.

We never know what we'll do in a vital situation like that until we're in it. A life-or-death situation, that is. I'm not so stupid as to tell soldiers, who have been in battle, live rounds whizzing by their heads, artillery exploding all around them, their buddies getting blown apart right next to them,

"If I were there, I would've grabbed a grenade, and ran out there, flanking the enemy, and I would've..."

I don't know what I'd do in a situation like that, and neither do you, unless you've been there. I only know of two things I would definitely do, in that situation, and that is, one: be terrified, and two: try to live through it.

When I tried to run down the hall to my room, the smoke got into my eyes and lungs and it felt like they were on fire, too. I couldn't see or breathe and couldn't hold my breath, either. Within seconds, the living room was full of smoke and hot as an oven. It was time to go. I turned; taking the last of my things and the one that means the most to me now. So that's how, approximately two minutes after waking up (or being woke up), I left, coughing and gagging, through my front door carrying my first guitar – the classical guitar that my dad had given me as a kid, never to see any of my other worldly possessions again. I wonder at what a sight I must've been – long-john bottoms, USA flag shirt (sleeveless), emerging like a lunatic phoenix from the thick gray smoke, the roof of the trailer already in flames, clutching a guitar, choking and gasping for air...Nowadays it sounds like just another scene from a Garth Brooks concert, but man, I'd love to have a photo of *that!!!*

I now turned my attention to my car, which was parallel-parked on the hill right in front of the trailer. I needed to move it in a hurry. The problem was, its doors were locked and the keys were inside the house. By now, the entire living room was in flames and the heat coming out of the front door towards my car was extraordinary (understatement) and would literally knock you down. Only firemen and hotdogs at a weenie-roast understand the kind of heat I am talking about. Luckily though, the driver's side of the car was away from the house. Crouching under the top of the driver's side of the car (if I stood up, the heat would've taken my head off), I was able, with the help of the Almighty, to kick out the side window, leap in with my legs hanging out the window, and rip the automatic transmission down into neutral, rolling the car down the hill to safety. Now there was nothing left to do but to sit down in the snow, in the only clothes I owned (long-john underwear bottoms and a sleeveless American flag t-shirt), and cry.

Neighbors arrived and said they had called the fire department and that a fire truck was on the way. The boiler/gas tank for the heater in the trailer was located between the bathroom and my bedroom at the end of the trailer, and if only the firemen could stop the fire before it reached that tank (it was obviously very combustible), some of the belongings in my bedroom might be saved (my bedroom was at the far end of the trailer and my door was also closed). Water damage from the fire hoses would still have ruined all of my clothes, furniture, etc. but I was praying that my father's rings and things would somehow be saved. Because I was in the county, however, a volunteer fire department had to be awakened in their homes and dispatched to the scene. Ironically, there was a city fire station with firemen ready and on call only five minutes away from me, but because I was outside city limits, I had to wait for the volunteer fire department to arrive. That took 45 minutes. Five or ten minutes before they arrived, the flames reached the middle of the trailer. Desperate for the sound of a fire truck, I painfully watched the gas tank explode, sending flames throughout the house and killing, absolutely and finally, any hope I had of saving anything else I owned. So on Christmas 1983, all I had to my name and my 21 years was: two guitars, an amp, a 1978 Pontiac Grand Prix with a stripped transmission and no driver's side window, a pair of long-john bottoms, and an American flag t-shirt. That's it. Sound like a starter kit for a blues singer? It was.

Later that afternoon, two friends who Derek and I had a date to play basketball with showed up at our place. There was nothing left of the trailer except for the concrete foundation and smoldering rubble. They were positive that I was dead, having seen the way I slept, and knowing that I was home. They were hopeful that Derek might have been at work when the fire happened. They found me at a Red Cross shelter downtown trying to figure out a way to get some clothes (I had no wallet, no checkbook, no money, no ID). They had a real surprised look on their faces when they saw me (alive). And that's the happy ending to this story – that *I was alive*.

You cannot persuade me that there are not supernatural "beings", (angelic, I believe) which intercede on our behalf, unseen by us. My waking up and getting up (when I didn't have to) at 6 o'clock in the morning and then stopping to drink water out of a sink with my hands is so completely out-of-character for me as to be nearly impossible. It was so unlike me, that it would be less incredible if I stood up right now and started dancing like Gene Kelly and reciting Tolstoy. In Swahili. With trained mice. Trained mice?

If I had not awoke at all, or if I had awoke and gone back to sleep, or if I had awoke, gotten up, and gone straight to my bedroom, I am positive that I would not be here today. That's a fact. I was lucky to get out alive anyway, being fully aware of the danger and still trying, foolishly, to go back in and get things out. But it was not my time yet. The Good Lord knew I had songs to sing and records to make and a girl to marry and two sons to raise. And many lives to touch with music. And if you think that what we say and do in our everyday lives doesn't affect other people, brother *you're* asleep and need to wake up.

Maybe reading this will cause you to take a fire extinguisher home tonight instead of a pizza; or to simply go and hug your kids real tight; or to say a little prayer before you go to bed. As I am watching Katrina's devastation on the gulf coast on TV, and the helpless thousands suddenly without a home or clothing, I can sympathize with them as someone who has been there.

And as I see the bodies of people killed by the disaster, I realize that there, but for the grace of God, go I. We easily forget how precious and fragile the gift of life really is. Maybe this little story will help to remind you how very lucky you are to be alive and well enough to read this in a home that has a roof on it. It has also reminded me.

May God bless you and keep you all in His care, until we meet again, either here in hyperspace or at the shows. I am and will remain,

Your friend,
Lightnin' Charlie

OCTOBER 2005

7

LUCK, LIGHTNIN' CHARLIE STYLE
- OR -
IF I SAID YOU HAD A BEAUTIFUL MOUSTACHE, WOULD YOU HOLD IT AGAINST ME?

Hello out there in TV Land! This is the Lightnin' Man coming to you live from his bomb shelter in East Tennessee. Hope all is well with you – my dear Lightnin' Bugs. But *all* is never well with anyone. You know, life is a lot like baseball. The greatest hitter of all time, Ted Williams, in his best season, only hit safely in 4 out of 10 at bats. And that's a feat that hasn't been equaled in 60 years. And so goes life – if we find a *few minutes* of peace and painless content in a 24-hour day, *we're cookin'*.

As for me, I've spent the last few days dealing with a septic tank problem in my house. These kinds of emergencies always seem to occur on Friday evening so we can suffer until Monday morning when the commode cavalry comes. Pray for me. I'll spare you the gory details, for the benefit of those who might wish to enjoy food in the days following the reading of this. I did take some photos for a new diet book I'll be writing. Talk about a way to lose weight fast! One look at these photos, and you'll fast for days. But suffice it to say that I am now in the market for new sneakers, new gloves, a new shovel and wheelbarrow, and a new shop vac. And while we're at it, throw in a new garage. But I don't expect FEMA is going to buy them for me. This emergency and expense (and the disaster flowing down the wall inside my garage) is mine, all mine, and mine alone. Where are George W. Bush and the Reverend Jesse Jackson? Where, oh where, are Geraldo and Bill Clinton? Where is the Easter Bunny? I don't suppose the Septic Tank Fairy is going to appear and build me a new garage (at taxpayer's expense). Despite the fact that I've been injured through "no fault of my own", I don't anticipate Congress taxing everyone in the United States for years to come to compensate me for it. I don't think someone having compassion and sympathy for me and my misfortune requires them to build me a new house. So as I'm getting to know slop as never before, I won't be looking for the Fat Man to come sleigh-riding in from the North Pole with a team of raw sewage-eating reindeer.

Nor will I be waiting for the Man Of Steel to make the trek with a big blank check from the planet Krypton. One of the big troubles with this generation of Americans is too much entitlement and too many "victims". *Everyone* has to blame *someone* for *everything*. Sometimes bad things happen to good people. Where's the personal responsibility? When's the last time you heard someone put the blame on *themselves* for something? Or realize the natural fact that some adversities are random and blameless, that sometimes things just happen, and it's nobody's fault. So if I'm still up to my knees in feces tomorrow, I won't sue the federal government, I'll get a bucket. And if I don't have the money to pay for it, I'll get a job. I know I could probably sue the restaurant where I bought the tacos that ultimately led to my septic tank explosion and be awarded a few million dollars, but I guess I'm just too old-fashioned. Sue me if you don't like it.

By the way, do you know what my attorney friend named his new baby daughter?

"Sue"

I phoned my attorney the other day and said,

"Frank, how much will you charge me to answer three questions?"
He quickly replied, "A thousand bucks."
I said, "A thousand bucks! Frank, don't you think that's a little steep?"
Frank answered, "Yep, what's your third question?"

Times like these require levity. And since I'm doing an unusual amount of radio and TV spots lately for my upcoming American Heart Association gig, this month's story has to do with TV. Live TV. Here 'tis, complete with its very own theme song.

[Sung to the tune of "Gilligan's Island"]

Just sit right back and you'll hear a tale
a tale of a fateful ad
On live TV in Tennessee
and a guitar amp gone bad...a guitar amp gone bad

LC was a mighty singin' man
the Upsetters short of cash
With soundman in hand, this blues band ran
into a thick moustache...a mighty thick moustache

The TV spot was getting rough
the tiny band was tossed
if not for the courage of the Lightnin' Man
the Upsetters would be lost...the Upsetters would be lost

*The band still lives on the shore of this
world's fastest half-a-mile
With Lightnin' – his guitar too
two baby boys and his wife
A sideburned cat in a cowboy hat
are here Lightnin' Charlie style*

Once upon a time, Lightnin' Charlie and the Upsetters was booked to play live on a local TV news program to promote an upcoming music festival. Being young, fresh, and "chomping-at-the-bit", we were plenty excited about performing on television and showing the whole world (or at least our little hometown) what we already knew – that we were *great.*

We had long thought ourselves to be superstars, yet we weren't getting our due respect locally. When Jesus said, "You can't be a prophet in your own hometown", He was talking about us. Musicians as terrific as we were naturally deserved all kinds of preferential treatment. After all, we were icons of the blues. We knew it. It was just that our hometown didn't know it – not yet. This five-minute TV appearance was going to change all that. It would make us instant sex symbols with the ladies. It would forever cement our status as hometown heroes – never again to pay a speeding or parking ticket. And maybe best of all, we would – *for the rest of our lives* – be automatically upgraded to "BIGGIE SIZE" at no extra cost.

We showed up at the TV studio bright and early and eager to set up our equipment. We brought our own soundman to insure that we would sound good. TV people are notorious for being, well...TV people. They're not concerned with audio at all. They just concentrate on the video aspect of the production, and that's why we thought it important to bring our soundman. We were leaving nothing to chance – this was just too big.

The song we chose to play was a tune called *TV Crazy*, made popular by Little Charlie and the Nightcats. It was a tongue-in-cheek story about a guy whose wife paid no attention to him or to her wifely duties. All she cared about were the TV shows she was addicted to – *Dallas, Dynasty, Love Boat,* etc.

"She's TV crazy and it's about to drive me insane..."

My choice of material for the TV spot would surely showcase my wit and my overall clever nature to all who watched – after all, we were *playing on TV.*

After we set up, we did a thorough sound-check, which our soundman recorded and, listening to the playback on headphones, were thrilled at the result. We sounded killer-diller. I remember slapping my soundman five and telling him that this one was "in the bag". Famous last words.

One unusual thing for us though was that they made us set up real far apart from each other so that the cameras could maneuver around between us. These cameras were great big jobs on wheels that looked like golf carts on steroids and they had huge floodlights on top (klieg lights – the brightest in the world). These things were a wee bit intimidating, and I didn't particularly like my vocal mic being a country mile (twenty feet or so) away from my guitar amp. We didn't feel comfortable playing so far apart from each other, and our amps, but after hearing the sound-check, we were confident of what we had, so everything was cool.

The director introduced himself and told us that we should be in place and "at-the-ready" by 12:00. He would give us a hand cue at 12:06, and then the news anchor (a real attractive young blonde woman whom I shall call "D.D.") would introduce us from her desk. I always preferred to watch D.D. at home in lieu of the other two local anchors that were not-so-attractive older bald men – this was pre-cable days and there were only three channels. This was also pre-Charlie becoming a not-so-attractive older bald man himself! So at 12:06, when D.D. says, "Heeere's Lightnin'...", we would hit it. After we had murdered 'em with our song, they would go to a two-minute commercial break and then D.D. would come over and do a quick interview with me. I was looking forward to this portion of the show too, because D.D. would surely be all flustered and flushed after witnessing my sexy performance and this would show everyone in town the dynamic effect I have on women. This would take place at 12:12. There wasn't any room for error or fooling around – this was live television. It was also our big break. And we had it all planned out *perfectly*.

Having about thirty minutes until showtime, my drummer, bassist, and I sat down to relax and go over the song's arrangement, which was fairly simple. In a three-piece blues band, the rhythm section (bass and drums) basically churns out the chord changes and backbeat while the front man (me) provides all the flash and fireworks on guitar. And man, were we gonna let 'em have it with both barrels!!!

At 11:55, we took up arms and stood loosely at attention in our places. At 12:00, the lights came on in the newsroom part of the studio (it was all one big room) and D.D. started reading the top stories. At 12:06, the director gave us the "high sign" and D.D. said that now, everyone was "in for a treat" (my sentiments exactly)

> *"...because local blues band Lightnin' Charlie and the Upsetters are in the studio and all set to perform a song for us. So without any further ado, here's Lightnin' Charlie and the Upsetters!!!"*

Here we go. The director gave us the finger (not that one, you fool – the index finger) to "hit it!" and lights, as bright as the sun, shone from the tops of those moving cameras. Magic time! I shouted to the band, in my best John Lennon, *"1, 2, 3, 4!!!"* and the rock started *rollin'*. For about two seconds. That's when my guitar amp quit. Just stopped. I was standing at the vocal mic, you remember – the one a country mile away from the amp. I turned back toward the amp (20 feet behind me) to try and see what the problem was. Then, immediately, it came back on. So I swiveled back around toward the vocal mic. The amp stopped again. I turned back around – it came on. I swung back around to the mic. You get the picture – I looked like some whacked-out, 6' 2" tall, sideburned ballerina doing pirouettes. For what seemed to me to be an eternity. The camera-dollies were circling around me like the Sioux around Custer and those klieg lights now seemed brighter than ever. How long a minute is depends on what side of the bathroom door you're on.

I was familiar with the expression "sweating bullets" beforehand, but was now getting a newfound, personal understanding of the term. Torpedoes of sweat that felt like they were the size of pool balls *flew* out of my forehead and face. Just like projectiles from a gun. Sweating bullets – what an apt expression! Cameras rolled in on each side of me for close-ups of my face and guitar-playing (not) hands. I decided that my best (and only) bet was to cut my losses and just start singing.

> *"Well people I usta have a happy li-ife,*
> *till this chaaaange come over my wife..."*

And there's nothing the rhythm section could do but go,

> *"Bomp, bomp-bomp, bomp-bomp, bomp-bomp..."*

The next three minutes passed like a kidney stone – slow and painful. My pony-tailed soundman tried valiantly to resurrect my dead amp, but to no avail. He was shown, on-camera, on all fours, pounding futilely on the top of the Fender amp, behind me, looking to all like a deranged hippie giving CPR. The amp would buzz a little when he would strike it on the sconce, so I turned my head around a couple more times during the song, exhorting him to "JUST HIT IT, MAN!!!"

My poor bass player ("Mini-Me"), who had figured that television stardom would, among other things, allow him to quit his day job (ironically as an electrician!), had the classic "deer-in-the-headlights" look on his face. My drummer (to his credit – or discredit) had a "couldn't-care-less" grin on his face. This is typical of drummers. I still don't know if he was just game-faced, if he truly didn't care, or if he didn't realize that anything was wrong (that would be typical of drummers, too).

The song finally gave up the ghost, amid the swooping around of those bloody cameras and a smattering of sympathetic applause from D.D., the two or three technicians, and the jovial co-anchor and weatherman, "J.W." (J.W. later experienced some technical troubles of his own with his weather maps, and declared on-air, *"Lightnin' has struck the studio today – nothing is working!"*). And check this out... "J.W." recently told me that he was STRUCK by lightning while fishing a few days after this doomed appearance. I don't know if I am infected with a contagious curse, or if I am just a carrier, or both.

As they broke for commercial, my bass player and I collapsed into a nearby sofa and mutually swore our suicides. It was the end of the world for us. Instead of showing everyone how great we were, everyone in town would see us in musical death-throes. And I would be shown in close-up, from three angles, sweating bombs out of my face, spinning round and round, and yelling over my shoulder, *"JUST HIT IT, MAN!!!"*

This was the end of all our dreams, but as the commercial break ended, my day of cruel surprises was just beginning. For here comes D.D. for the interview segment and as I take my place beside her, I see that her upper lip is sporting a moustache that would make Albert Einstein's moustache appear pencil-thin in comparison. It was unbelievable. And it was covered with that pancake makeup that television people wear. Richard Nixon refused to wear it on television in 1960, putting JFK into the White House, who then put us into Vietnam. Nixon finally got into the White House in 1968, got us out of Vietnam, then went on television wearing that aforementioned pancake makeup and resigned the presidency. It's a weird world.

So there I was, fresh from the greatest public disgrace of my life, standing next to D.D. (the ex-real attractive young blonde) trying desperately not to look at her lip. Look, I've seen lots of women with peach-fuzzy, little feminine hair problems on their lip, *but this was an obscenity.* I've never seen anything like it – in or out of the circus. The pile of flesh-colored makeup on top of it wasn't helping matters either – this made it even bigger and more hideous.

After this moustache revelation, I would tune in to watch D.D. on the news to closely inspect her upper lip on my TV screen. I would get my face right up in front of the TV set to try and see what I saw. But somehow that bush was *invisible* on screen. Her upper lip just looked *blurry* – I guess from the depth of that thing. The klieg lights would light up the skin-colored makeup on the top of it and the camera would just make it look *blurry* – not *furry!!! Ha! That's a good one! Blurry not furry!* I crack myself up sometimes. Oh, excuse me...back to our story.

It was ten seconds to go. There was a horrible car crash on her upper lip and I was hopelessly trying not to look...*" Don't look at her lip. Don't look at her lip. Don't look at her lip.* Five seconds...standby...lights, camera, action!!!"

DD: "I'm back with Lightnin' Charlie. Hey, *great job* on that song! Thanks for joining us today."

LC [looking at his shoes]: "Thank you D for having us."

DD: "So tell us about the Blah-Blah Music Festival. What night are you and the Upsetters going to be there?"

LC [still looking at his shoes]: "Well, God and Fender amps willing, we'll be there on..."

I have a videotape copy of the debacle, and I just took a break from writing to watch it. Needless to say, it's not something I watch very often. I've not seen it in ten years or more. Although I find myself to be a very handsome devil, I do not enjoy watching myself on video. If I have a video copy of an appearance, I'll usually watch it once to see how it came out, and how I can improve upon what I was doing, etc. Generally speaking, it's not something that is a very big deal to me, either way, for good or bad. But watching this catastrophe is like watching close-ups of one's own slow, agonizing death – it's excruciating. Unbearable. But I saw something bizarre in the video that I had forgotten about. During our performance of *TV Crazy*, the television video feed suddenly breaks to a family of Orientals. The horrible audio of us (of course) continues to play though. They're on-screen for a long time too, ten or fifteen seconds. They're just sitting there – a man, a woman, and five little toddlers; they're not doing or saying anything. You know the look on a newsperson's face when they finish a story and say, "Back to you Fred", but the camera mistakenly stays on them, not cutting away to Fred, and there's that pregnant pause, when they are stuck, staring stiffly into the camera, not saying a word? That's what these people looked like. Like they were awaiting sentencing, or the reading of the will. Then a caption comes on underneath them that explains everything:

Korean Newlyweds Strike Oil – Adopt Quintuplets.

Behind this I'm crooning away, with bass and drums,

"She's watching Whe-ee-el Of Fortune and uh, Twilight Zone. She's diggin' Johnny while she's tapin' Joan. Star Search and Jeopardy, reruns of Fame – she even wants me to go on the Newlywed Game..."

Newlywed Game? Korean Newlyweds Strike Oil? Quintuplets? Why are guitar amps and anchorwoman's upper lips not working? Is it hormonal? What planet am I on? Twilight Zone? Yeah, Twilight Zone indeed.

"The best-laid plans of Mice and Men often go awry, and bring nothing but grief and pain where joy had been promised." – Robert Burns

Every success I've ever had has been in private while every failure has been in full public view. For years afterward, people would come up to me and *unanimously* say,

"I saw you on TV, y'all were pretty good."

Pretty good? I kid you not. Those are the exact words of everyone who saw it (not just friends) – that we were "pretty good". Well, thank you *pretty much* (I was pretty, anyway). Were they just being polite? I think not. Strangers don't go out of their way to compliment you on something, which is obviously a fiasco. Either they were just *completely* clueless and didn't know the difference between an electric guitar that's on or off (drummer) – or perhaps I have considerable acting abilities to go along with my musical prowess, dashing good looks, wit, humility, etc. Is that it? If I could pull that off, on live TV, without a guitar, and without the audience knowing that anything was wrong, well…to use the name of another 1980s television show, *that's incredible!* And most likely impossible. Nobody's that good an actor; Marlon Brando, James Dean, Sir Laurence Olivier, *nobody.* Not even me. It had to be that they were, sadly, just clueless.

"Father, forgive them, for they know not what they do." – Luke 23:34

So how could I expect to awaken these friends and neighbors to the fact that I was a musical genius when they couldn't tell the difference between off and on? Ah, there's the rub. Even if I had been at my *supreme best*, I still would only have been "pretty good" in their eyes. To discern genius, one must be able to recognize a disaster. They just didn't get it. They didn't see it. Ah, will they ever? I'm out here, *still* trying to show 'em…

Your friend,
Still alive and kickin',
Lightnin' Man

November 2005

8

LIGHTNIN' AND THE SNAKE LADY

Greetings sweethearts and Lightnin' Bugs. Welcome to the Lowdown where we explore the darker side of superstardom. Here we go again with another tale, tall and true.

A few years ago, a promoter phoned me and asked me if my band would be interested in playing a show for him. He explained that he had booked a large outdoor arena for a music festival showcasing various retired musicians from the 1920s and '30s. They had been active in vaudeville and burlesque shows of that era. Now, however, they were mostly confined to nursing homes and assisted living facilities. They hadn't performed in many, many years and obviously didn't have a backup band. That's where we came in.

This promoter/guitar player, whom I'll call "Guido", knew that we were a band that could play many different styles of blues as well as the rags and popular tunes from their day. And he knew that we could work well without any rehearsal. Due to the age and health conditions of the performers, we would have to meet them on the day of the show and just "wing it". Naturally, Guido didn't have a lot of money to pay for our services. However, he told me that there would be a ton of great publicity and exposure for Lightnin' Charlie and the Upsetters. The festival would be broadcast live on the radio and filmed for a documentary-style television broadcast. *Rolling Stone* magazine had promised (and eventually delivered) a big feature article on the event. So I agreed, being young and dumb and under the false impression that "publicity" and "exposure" would somehow buy gas and groceries. It was the best of times...it was the worst of times.

When we arrived at the club after a four-hour drive in my van (with no air-conditioning), it was mid-afternoon and miserably hot. We met Guido and a few of the performers in the side stage dressing room. The festival was to take place in an outdoor arena, which was adjacent to a big rock club. The floor was concrete and there weren't any walls – just open air. There was a metal roof over all of it, which kept out the rain but intensified the murderous summer heat. This was the Deep South, y'all...in July.

One of the roadies took us backstage and introduced us to a couple of the performers who looked pretty good for their age – keep in mind that these guys were in their 80s and 90s. They seemed to be real happy to be getting the opportunity to get out there again. I particularly liked one tall, dapper cat, dressed in a pinstriped zoot suit, complete with the obligatory overlong pocket-watch chain, named "Mister Q" (I didn't know what the "Q" stood for and I didn't ask). I was then shown side stage to a sofa where Guido was rehearsing his acoustic guitar part with the only female in the show – a tiny, little woman whose years probably outnumbered her weight. She must've been in her 90s and probably weighed 80 pounds soaking wet. Guido planned to play guitar and accompany her on her only tune in the show, a sweet little ditty about her long-lost puppy named "Prince".

"I had a little dog, Prince was his name. I had a little dog, and Prince was his name. Since I lost my little doggie, my life ain't been the same."

Guido was slowly strumming along and she was lightly clapping her hands together and singing softly – the stereotypical sweet little old lady. When they finished, Guido introduced us to "Willa Mae" who starred in burlesque shows throughout the chitlin circuit in the 1920s and '30s as "The Snake Lady". She earned this title due to the fact that she performed her striptease and sang the blues with a huge live python wrapped around her naked (or darn-near next to naked) body. In their subsequent article, *Rolling Stone* ran some really wild pictures of the Snake Lady in her heyday. She must have been something. I said,

"Hello Miss Willa Mae, nice to meet you."

She reached up from the sofa, took my hand and said,

"Lord, bless your heart, honey. God love you."

She was just the sweetest thing!!! It being unbearably hot in there, I asked her if I could get her a drink of water. The rock club Samaritans had left a little thermos jug of warm water out there for us.

"Oh, that would be so nice, honey. Thank you. Bless yore heart", she cooed.

I gladly went to the jug to fetch that sweet little old lady a pail of water. I was gone for maybe two minutes.

When I returned, Willa Mae was up, off the couch, and, shuffling slowly behind her walker, coming toward me. I reached out with the cup of water and said,

"How you doin', sweetie?"

She looked up at me and slurred,

"NONE OF YOUR [BLEEP]-ING BUSINESS! NOW GET THE [BLEEP] OUT OF MY WAY!!!"

Well, you could've knocked me over with a soda straw. I stood there for a moment, transfixed, with my mouth hanging wide open and my arm outstretched with the cup of water. Sometimes the brain just refuses to accept what the senses submit to it. This was one of those times.

She buffaloed her way past me and was angrily jerking her arms away from Guido and the stagehands who were desperately trying to help her/hold her.

What had happened was, just after I left for the water, one of the other performers pulled out a little pint of brown whiskey and was happily passing it around. When it got around to Willa Mae, who was eagerly grabbing for it, Guido told her that she "better not", but she insisted, and so they poured a sip into the screw cap from the bottle for her. How much could a bottle cap hold – off a pint bottle? A tablespoon? She had grabbed that cap, drank it down, and was immediately transformed from Sweet Grandma Jekyll to the Evil Ms. Hyde. I have never seen anything like it. It was like her blood had turned into alcohol. She apparently had been (still was) an alcoholic who, upon having one sip of booze, was instantly drunk. And I mean rip-roarin', cross-eyed, out-of-the-box, choke-your-momma-till-she's-dead drunk. I left the sweetest little old granny *("God love your heart, honey")* and came back two minutes later to this werewolf with a walker *("GET THE [BLEEP] OUT OF MY WAY!")*. Liquor IS quicker.

For the next couple of hours, while we were setting up and sound checking, Guido and Company tried their best to keep the Snake Lady under control. But she was having none of it. She kept shuffling out onto the stage from the adjacent dressing room, harassing everyone, and bumming smokes. During our sound check, she came out onstage, grabbed me by my neck, and pulling me down, tried to kiss me full-on-the-mouth while I was singing. It was a nightmare. And then, Snake Lady, having pushed aside the two 200-pound roadies now assigned to hold her, wiggled her way, with walker, to the front of the stage. This is the stage of our story (pun intended) that nobody believes, myself included. Snake Lady was standing, facing us (her back to the room), at the front of the stage. Listen, this stage was at least five feet high off the concrete floor below. Snake Lady stumbled backwards into one of the big monitor speakers setting on the floor at stage front, and, losing her balance,

FLIPS OVER BACKWARDS AND FALLS OFF THE STAGE!!!

Snake Lady landed flat on her back on the concrete floor below. *Five or six feet down – onto concrete!* Roadies and stagehands rushed down there to see if she was still alive. But Snake Lady, still alive, was not even *fazed*. Helped to her feet (with some assistance) and grabbing her walker (which landed right beside her), Snake Lady then begins (continues) cursing and pushing away the guys trying to help her, and away she goes. *Like nothing happened!*

Everyone was completely dumbfounded. I hardly believe it myself today, and I saw it with my own eyes, along with plenty of witnesses. That plunge would've killed me. Snake Lady did a one-and-a-half gainer, back-flipping off of a six-foot stage, onto a concrete floor, landing on her spine, and, God as my witness, got right back up and didn't even *FLINCH!* It's no wonder Snake Lady had lived to be ninety – what could possibly kill her...a silver bullet?

Needless to say, her performance that night was less than perfect. She somehow had stayed drunk throughout the day and the rest of the night, although she didn't see another (get ready for the pun) *drop* of booze. She wasn't left alone for a minute by the stagehands, for fear of her getting another sip of whiskey, and killing someone. A female stagehand even accompanied her to the bathroom.

Once onstage, Snake Lady's sweet, gentle, little tune about her long-lost pup became a drunken diatribe. Her adorable, tender, ballad of Prince was twisted into a blood-curdling curse-fest. She cursed Guido (who was hopelessly trying to accompany her on guitar), she cursed the dumbstruck audience (who were clueless as to what was going on), and she even cursed her poor little doggie Prince. Doggone-it, that's going too far – poor Prince didn't have a dog in this race!

What this must've sounded like to a live radio audience is beyond me. I'll bet drivers had to pull off the road to keep from wrecking. Although I've never seen the television documentary (and wonder if it was ever finished), I am sure her "song" was cut. I do have film footage of our set (a friend of ours was videotaping) and Snake Lady can be seen sitting on the piano bench, smoking heavily, under heavy guard.

Snake Lady did provide one bit of unexpected help to me. Her good deed of the night occurred when a young keyboard player came onstage, uninvited, during our set. He sat down at the piano, and started loudly banging away. This local longhair had asked me, backstage, if he could sit in with us, and I politely declined. Then, during our performance, in spite of being told "no", he comes out anyway (there being a total breach of stage security, due to the number of stagehands assigned to Snake Lady). I don't know what made me madder – the fact that he didn't care about ruining our set, or that he didn't seem to fear me, or my wrath. But he didn't know the kind of day I'd had. Before the song ended, and I had the chance to throw him off the stage, and onto the concrete floor to his death, Snake Lady came to the rescue. She sat down next to him, and, likewise uninvited, began obnoxiously kissing him, all about the face and neck! That did the trick. One obnoxious, uninvited keyboard player – *exit stage left!* You gotta fight fire with fire! That dude *ran* off the stage. And Snake Lady sat there, smoking, for the rest of the night. There was a roadie assigned to each of her elbows, with instructions to keep giving her cigarettes and maybe she'd stay put, which she did.

Rolling Stone didn't include any of this in their feature story about the Snake Lady and the Old-Timer's Festival. They focused instead on the young Willa Mae, and also on the other cool old-timers (who were all terrific), who appeared with us that night. Nor did *Rolling Stone* write a single word about us. Not even our name was mentioned. So much for publicity and exposure. What Lightnin' Charlie and the Upsetters were publicly exposed to that night was upsetting enough on its own. But it certainly makes for a good story.

Hope all your stories have happy endings. Have a joyful Thanksgiving, Lightnin' Bugs and *Lord bless yore heart too*, Snake Lady, wherever you are.

                          Happy Landings,
                                Charlie

DECEMBER 2005

9

BROWN GRAVY AND WHITE LIES – A SATIRE

Well friends, here we are at the end of another year. And the most important question we should ask ourselves, at the end of 2005 is...

Is our planet any closer to realizing the enormous, superstar talent I possess? And will my hometown finally give me the key to the city that I've deserved for years? The fact that I can't park my car any closer to Wal-Mart than you can is, by all accounts, a travesty of justice. I've petitioned the local DMV to issue me an honorary license plate, allowing me to park my Cadillacs wherever I please, but to no avail. Fact is, I am no closer to "making it" than I was last year, or the year before that. That's because the system that creates superstars refuses to acknowledge my musical genius. They're all vicious; they're all jealous; they're all bitter. And they're all stupid. And they're all out to get me; keeping me from what's rightfully mine. But before I tell y'all about the way poor Lightnin' was molested in our hometown press, I do have some good things on my horizon to tell you about.

This month, on the 12th of December, I am performing at the world-famous Barter Theatre in Abingdon, Virginia – on the same stage that was once graced by some of my contemporaries like Gregory Peck, George C. Scott, and Patricia Neal. It's a shame that none of them lived to see this glorious occasion.

Next month, on the 7th of January, I will be performing at the famed Lincoln Theatre in Marion, Virginia, for the *Song Of The Mountains* Concert Series - filmed for national television by Blue Ridge Public Television and PBS.

On the 13th of January (my Dad's birthday), I will be at our regional entertainment mecca, the Paramount Center For The Arts in historic downtown Bristol (the Birthplace of Country Music) for an album release party with my band The Upsetters.

I will be featured in the December/January issue of the stunningly beautiful (even when I'm not in it) *Marquee Magazine.*

I'm selling CDs and playing great gigs. It seems that I should be happy and content with the way my career is going. And I was beginning to feel good about myself again. But then the other night, without the benefit of Prozac, I sat through the CMA (Country Music Association) awards show on television, and I was so disgusted with this sick and filthy music business that I snuck out of my house (without my bodyguards) and went to the Cracker Barrel to drown my sorrows in brown gravy and sweet tea.

It was there that I met an old "friend" of mine named Moe Lester, who writes for a local muck-rag called the *Tri-City Enquirer*. He sat down with me and we talked "off-the-record" for a while. Then this weekend, I see this article on the cover of the magazine. I've reprinted it here in the Lowdown allowing you Lightnin' Bugs to share in my grief. But realize that I was being taped without my knowledge or consent. And Lord knows I probably had too much sweet tea to drink. Let's all pray for Lester that he'll come to his senses and print a retraction. Otherwise it'll be his funeral and my trial.

Tri-City Enquirer
Dec. 1, 2005

LIGHTNIN' CHARLIE – HERO OR MONSTER?
Fantasies Of "Making It" Haunt Local Music Legend

Lightnin' Charlie in happier days   Lightnin' Charlie in Cracker Barrel

By: Moe Lester
molester@tricityenquirer.com

Lightnin' Charlie Dolinger, if that really is his name, has been part of the local music scene for twenty-five years, and has developed into one of the area's finest singers and premier entertainers. But he is considered an enigma to most folks – even those who know him well.

Lightnin' Charlie possesses all the gifts a performer could want – charismatic stage presence, hot guitar licks, lots of flashy clothes, and corny jokes. But Dolinger may also suffer from long-term brain damage, as evidenced by his seven ex-wives, his sudden hair loss, and his off-the-wall tirades.

Those who visit Stratland, his comfortable, guitar-filled, ranch-style gated compound on the outskirts of Johnson City, Tennessee will immediately sense that something is terribly wrong here. Three gas-guzzling 1960s Cadillacs (one of them a limousine with tail-fins, for God's sake), a guitar-shaped jacuzzi, a shag-carpeted basement severely damaged by recurring sewer drain problems, all demonstrate the hopelessness of a man consumed with excess.

There is a constant stream of traffic at the gates of Stratland – fans and bill collectors wanting to catch a glimpse of Charlie. If Lightnin' is in town and is out of bed (he sleeps until 4 PM every day), he will gladly come down to the gates, sign autographs for fans, and tell vague, half-true stories of the "good old days". Often, he will invite some of these folks (as long as they're female), up to the house to eat pork chops and cheese fries and watch Japanese samurai films or Dracula movies on his big-screen, rent-to-own, plasma TV. Dolinger can be completely unaffected and charming in one-on-one situations like these. He is the type of man, who, during our recent phone interview, said matter-of-factly,

"Lester, hold that thought. Ol' Lightnin's gotta pee in the pottie to get rid of some of this sweet tea." [sound of flowing urine]

Dolinger is, if nothing else, a down-to-earth Southern gentleman and a huge natural talent. But beware of his dark side. Just mention one of the subjects that are forbidden by his inner circle of lackeys and watch the miserable metamorphosis that instantly occurs in Charlie. Some of these taboo subjects are: Hollywood, the Internet, FEMA, tort reform, unsweetened tea, Michael Jackson, Olympic sporting events, 21st century blues music, septic systems, Al Gore, non-fat foods, and many, many others. I am routinely given a list of these keywords-to-avoid upon entering Stratland for interviews. Lightnin's handlers are specially trained to steer him clear of discussions about contemporary music (especially rap) and the music business in general. These are topics that turn Lightnin' Charlie into a sour, cynical suffragette – sending him into uncontrollable fits of ranting and raving. It's times like these that he appears to be a sad, bitter, balding old man. And he's probably the most politically incorrect person I've ever encountered.

I recently caught Lightnin' alone at the Cracker Barrel, without his bodyguards, where he was pouring brown turkey gravy on his salad, drinking sweet tea, and alternating between abusing and flirting with the waitresses. Thanks to the fact that Charlie didn't know he was being recorded (my recorder was in my pocket), I was able to garner some of his unguarded and candid opinions on these nerve-touching subjects that sent his blood pressure soaring! But I must warn you, dear reader, that what follows is the most offensive tirade I've ever had the good fortune to record as a reporter. So brace yourself...

On hippie "jam bands":

"They deliver pizza all week to have marijuana money, they live with their parents, they whine their anti-establishment, commie crap, their mommy is folding their underwear, their daddy is giving them money to go to Starbuck's, then on the weekend...SHAZAM!!! They're Bob Dylan. You know, Dylan couldn't sing, but at least he did his own laundry."

On why Lightnin' Charlie isn't headlining local music festivals:

"I'm invisible to the local yokels. I'm probably better known in Mongolia than I am in Johnson City. I was belting out Jimmy Reed songs for a living when these other guys were pooping yellow. Do they think I'm too old? I do 10 pushups almost every day. I eat two fishes and five loaves of bread every day. I'm 43 years old and I still get pimples! I've played these cut-and-stab bars for 25 years and there isn't a mark on my face. I'm still pretty. I SHOOK UP THE WORLD!!! I MUST BE THE GREATEST!!! CAN I GET SOME MORE SWEET TEA???"

On the media:

"Freaks with laptops. Near-sighted geeks who were never spanked as children. Don't misquote me. Don't misspell my name. The media can't get my name right. They always mess Lightnin' up. It's a third grade word. I don't care what they say about me anymore, just spell my name right."

On recalling his first band, the Southside Sheiks, and the brutally awful onstage banter between himself and bandleader Brian Bar-Sinister, an aged ex-vaudevillian midget:

"It was excruciating shtick. Brian saw us as the next Amos and Andy...of East Tennessee. We played real tough, gutbucket, Chicago blues. But then, in between songs, there's this cornball shuck-and-jive. It was like Hee Haw and Harlem all mixed up together. And he was only about three-and-a-half feet tall – we looked like some demonic ventriloquist act. Here's a small bit of what I (and our poor audience), went through on a typical night at the office...

Bar-Sinister: "Last month my wife and I flew to the islands for a second honeymoon."

Charlie: "Jamaica?"
Bar-Sinister: "No, she claimed she had a headache."
Charlie: "Oh, that's too bad. My last vacation was with my uncle. We took a cruise to Alaska."
Bar-Sinister: "Nome?"
Charlie: "Of course, he's my uncle."
Bar-Sinister: "You've traveled a lot – what do you think of South America? I'm going there soon.
Charlie: "South America? What part?"
Bar-Sinister: "Uruguay."
Charlie: "Well, you go Uruguay, and I'll go mine!"
Bar-Sinister: "Why, I oughta...!!! And now, here's one by Howlin' Wolf..."

On his memories of twenty years of live performances:

"It's the same with my ex-wives; I can only remember the weird ones."

On the state of the blues:

"The blues is a fetid, stinking corpse. No blues clubs, no blues singers, no blues fans, and no blues records. They oughta give the blues a funeral already...book me to do the eulogy, and Harmonica Todd to blow harp. At least we'd give it a proper send-off."

On blues bands:

"As a living art form, real blues has been hijacked and murdered by a pack of poor, no-talent wannabes who will play for peanuts and close clubs down because of how awful they are. And because people, for the most part, don't know any better, that will be the legacy of the blues – four or five scrubby guys playing rocked-out, ten-minute versions of "Stormy Monday". And after these blue-jeaned bums are finished hacking away at the classics, and are back at their trailer park doing bong hits, the club owner won't book any more blues bands, and audiences won't go near the blues, because of the schlock they just heard masquerading as blues. They're terrorists; Osama Bin Ladens with Les Pauls."

On white blues players:

"A guy that used to get beat up daily in high school gets a harmonica, a fedora hat, and a pair of Raybans, and it's instant cool, tough, ramblin' blues man. It makes me sick. I'd like to choke the ugly out of Dan Ackroyd."

On black blues players:

"Disco on crack."

On female blues singers:

"Ex-prostitutes and porno stars releasing so-called blues records. And they're all called "Divas", every one. Just because your pituitary gland produces estrogen doesn't automatically entitle you to the title, "Diva". Isn't there more to it than that? What about the music? It used to be about the music. Every press photo and album review I see lately has some fat skank bending over in a thong and a bikini top. Or a big-footed, anorexic Olive Oyl with furry underarms. Divas. That's beautiful...while Bessie Smith and Ella Fitzgerald and other TRUE DIVAS are spinning in their graves. Can I do the same thing? Hey, Lightnin' Charlie's got a new CD out...look at me... I'm bending over my motorcycle in a thong...I'm a Diva...my tattooed butt is hanging out...look at my moppers...I'd probably get the Grammy Awards I've always deserved, and headline all the major blues festivals, too...[his two straws slurping at the bottom of his glass and yelling loudly] Can I PLEASE get some MORE SWEET TEA???"

It is obvious that the world has beaten Lightnin' Charlie down into an emotionally distressed, jealous old man who has lost touch with reality and would gladly sell his soul (but not his Cadillacs), for stardom (or a chance at a hot music video). Dolinger feels the music industry has, to quote him from the Cracker Barrel interview, "turned its scaly back" on him but still anticipates the commercial success that has cruelly passed him by. I asked the Lightnin' Man to reflect on fate, fame, and hard work:

"Never squat with your spurs on."

Well, who can argue with that? Even a broken clock is right twice a day.

In the wee hours of the morning, Lightnin' can often be found in his damp basement, breaking boards with karate kicks and playing gospel songs on his gigantic pipe organ. He loves for friends and fans to drop in and sing along and help him stretch out his hamstrings.

"Y'all come on out (anytime after 4 PM) and I'll cook us up some chicken and dumplins, break out the sweet tea, and we can start doin' some really high kicks!"

Much to the chagrin of his stressed-out handlers and his pompadoured sports therapist, Dr. Nick Nack, who says,

"Lightnin' Charlie has pulled his hamstring so many times that if he continues to put on these impromptu displays without proper warm-up, I can't be responsible for the long-term damage he's creating for himself. He's liable to be in a Rascal scooter before he's 50. He needs to make up his mind whether he wants to be a gospel singer or a martial artist."

Dolinger is currently appearing at nursing homes, Pentecostal churches, posh charity fund-raisers and lakeside boat docks, pathetically expecting his big break to come any day.

"I taught Kenny Chesney how to plug in a microphone. But does he return any of my emails? NOOOOO, he's much too big a star for me now. Garth Brooks opened for me at the National Guard Armory on Hwy 11-E back in '84. But does ol' Garth remember me? Does he let me backstage at his shows? NOOOOO, he sends his big bodyguards out to put me in a headlock and throw me out of the building! They tossed me onto a parked bicycle at Freedom Hall last year and CRACKED THREE OF MY RIBS! And then there's Hootie and the Blowfish, another bunch of super-rich superstars. They used to panhandle quarters off me to play Donkey Kong in the sports bar I was playing in Myrtle Beach, South Carolina. Now look at them – they're richer than Imelda Marcos. And I'm stuck playing boat docks and bar mitzvahs and watching vampire movies with grandmothers with braces on their teeth! Not that I'm bitter though...And here I am, sitting in a Cracker Barrel with an empty glass while every single waitress walks right by me taking care of EVERY FAT NOBODY IN THE PLACE...HEY STUPID!!! WHY CAN'T LIGHTNIN' CHARLIE GET SOME MORE SWEET TEA??? DON'T YOU PEOPLE KNOW WHO I AM????" [Ed. note: Charlie's voice rises steadily here to a hair-raising shriek]

Lightnin' Charlie's latest double-album, *The Bass Player Is Not My Twin,* is available online, at Flop's Lounge in Bristol, Virginia (where Charlie himself is not allowed, due to a restraining order against him, and a pending defamation and slander lawsuit), and at all Tower Records stores in Croatia ("My home away from home – those Serbs are my homeboys!"). You can visit his website at www.lightnincharlie.com and purchase CDs and merchandise. Lightnin' also has his own line of designer shirts, tae kwon do uniforms, bumper stickers, and assorted aromatherapy goods. You can also sign various wacko, right-wing petitions. But the highlight of his website is Dolinger's grossly embellished tales of woe in his *Lightnin' Lowdown* – soon to be released as a major motion picture starring Samuel L. Jackson, Billy Crystal, and Morgan Fairchild. Unfortunately for Charlie though, the film, tentatively titled *Thunderboy and Lightmeat*, won't put one dime in his pocket. Nor will Lightnin' be given any screen credit.

Dolinger's attorneys, *Dewey, Cheatham, and Howe*, have recently issued a statement. They say that, while watching "Seven Samurai" late one night at Stratland (a film Charlie swears is about his ex-wives), he unknowingly signed over his rights to *Thunderboy and Lightmeat* to a precocious and pimply teenager who apparently was working undercover for the movie studio. She asked Lightnin' for his autograph – at the bottom of twenty separate sheets of blank paper. Charlie says he didn't realize he was signing away his life story, he just thought she was a really big fan. Litigation is pending.

It's sad to see such a gifted man fall so far from grace. Due to poor sales of his new tour-de-force CD, *A New Beef*, a reluctant Lightnin' Charlie seems to be slowly but surely adjusting to the fact that fame and fortune have truly passed him by. He has good days and bad days like anyone else, but thanks to large doses of anti-depressants like Prozac and Lithium, along with his intake of sweet tea being closely monitored, I've noticed that his moods are a lot more "even" lately. But his blood pressure is still a source of constant concern to his handlers.

He has recently told me of his plans to write a book – his own memoirs of course, horribly titled *Lightnin' Lowdown – The Trials and Tribulations of a Travelin' Troubadour*.

Of his upcoming book, Lightnin' Charlie says,

"Outside of a dog, a book is man's best friend.
Inside of a dog, it's too dark to read!"

Until next time, this is your mild-mannered, and muck-raking reporter, Moe Lester, signing off, and wishing Lightnin' Charlie, and you, the best of luck.

THE END

And all God's people said...*AMEN!* And by the way, my attorneys advised me to use the word SATIRE more than once in this fractured fairy tale (My wife suggested I add it to the title, as well), and to put it in all caps, for the benefit of folks without a sense of humor (other attorneys).

But seriously folks, here's wishing you all a very Merry Christmas and a blessed and bountiful New Year. I'll see you at the shows...

Don't meet me there – beat me there
And I'll see you back here – in the Lowdown next year.

Thanks, Lightnin' Bugs, for a great 2005!!!

God bless you all,
Charlie

JANUARY 2006

10

PHOTOGRAPHS AND MEMORIES

Happy New Leaf, everybody! Glad to be alive and with you this New Year. Those of you who know me will bear witness that I should be glad to be alive and anywhere. And believe me, I am. 2006 marks my twenty-third year of traveling and performing as a full-time musician. The truly amazing thing to me (and to those who have firsthand knowledge of some of these fracas) is simply that I've survived this tempestuous and crazy life, touring the world for so many years and getting through so many close and ugly calls, usually without a scratch.

We have dealt with drunks and derelicts of every sort. We have wrestled with slimy, ex-con, club owners (redundant) for our money. We have had to defend ourselves against guns, knives, glassware, pool balls, baseball bats, and most anything else that can render a singer silent. Sticks and stones may break my bones but, oh brother, some of the words...

We have driven almost a million miles, have broken every part that can possibly break on a motor vehicle at least once, and always seemed to be a dollar short or a day late and a long way from home.

We have had innumerable scrapes with the law, gotten police escorts to gigs and gotten ordered out of town after them. But by the mystery of God's Grace, Lightnin' Charlie's still here. There are several of my bandmates that are not, and I know that I don't deserve to be. All I can say is that God spreads grace like a 4-year old spreads peanut butter: He gets it all over the place; places it doesn't seem to belong and places it doesn't deserve to be. And He has gotten it all over me, patiently and lovingly carrying me to the place I am today – where I can play good music for good people. Thank You.

I thought I would do a top ten list this month – a list that would give my readers a glimpse into what life on the road has been like for me and my band of brothers, The Upsetters. They say a photograph is worth a thousand words, and I am lucky to have tons of memorable photographs through the years, but there are lots of photographs that were never taken, that I wish I had today; of moments in time that would speak volumes of what a road musician's life is really like. No 8X10 glossy publicity pics here. Talk about a reality show with teeth, this is it! So with no further ado, here is my . . .

TOP TEN PHOTOGRAPHS I WISH I HAD FROM A LIFE ON THE ROAD

10) The face of my harmonica player Brian Bar-Sinister who, while vomiting violently in a parking lot, was told nonchalantly by our too-cool drummer King Edwards, *"No wonder you're sick, Brian...Look at all that puke that was in yo' stomach!"* An all-time classic.

9) The horrified faces of our sweet hosts (a kindly, retired couple that had invited us to stay with them in their ultra-fancy beachfront condo during a weekend gig in Myrtle Beach, South Carolina), when one morning while we were having coffee, Chuck, our drummer and red-headed stepchild, galloped downstairs and announced excitedly, *"I need a plunger and a mop!"* Priceless.

8) The dumbstruck expression of the lowbrow motorcycle gang member who took offense at the way I was dressed onstage, and had yelled at me that I was *"a white nigger"*. I immediately turned on him and said, in one of my quickest, sharpest retorts to a heckler ever, *"Who are you callin' white?!?"* He looked like something out of a Tex Avery cartoon, only dumber. And yes, they were waiting for us outside.

7) The scene at my favorite private concert I've ever done. I serenaded a young couple at their table in a restaurant's private room while he popped the question. He had hired me to sing to his girlfriend as he proposed. Of course, she said, *"Yes!"* It's not been all bad.

6) The eyes of my hairdo-crazy drummer Chuck [see #9] after a gig, when we were told by the bartender that, instead of getting the money owed the band (the crooked club-owner had took off and disappeared with our cash), that he would, instead, let us into the crooked club-owner's hair salon next door and we could *"Take whatever you want."* Chuckles the Coiffured Cowboy went ape. He was like a kid in a candy store, and I was just a broke bald guy in a beauty shop.

5) The face of a Virginia hotel/nightclub manager when the band van arrived an hour late for our gig, but with a full police escort – complete with sirens and lights. We were having an electrical problem with our van and had driven the last 50 miles to the gig without any headlights and therefore, very slowly. When we were finally pulled over by the police, just a mile shy of the gig, they courteously (and surprisingly) offered to escort us the last mile of the way to the hotel where the manager was furiously pacing, waiting

and watching for us, at the front door. Funny, he didn't say a word to us about being late. What could he say? We were late, but we were there, and we had a *police escort!* First time for everything.

4) The face of my loud-mouthed drummer Mork [see July 2005 *Why I Don't Come Down Off The Mountain Anymore*] upon seeing his first month's cell phone bill – for $2003. He was rendered completely speechless. Sweet justice, that.

3) The flabbergasted faces of my band and road manager (all male) upon being asked for a tampon by a flustered female patron in a Florida nightclub. *Whuuutttt????* And no, wiseguy – it wasn't in Tampa.

2) The incredulous faces of our road manager Nat and myself when, after finally landing a long sought-after winter tour of Florida, we were informed by our whiny, malcontented bassist Kevin that, *"I can't go to Florida, Charlie...I'll have to buy food!"* This one would make a great poster for welfare reform.

<u>And The Number One Photograph
I Wish I Had From A Life On The Road</u>
is...

The crazed, pony-tailed redneck who (after a long, and protracted heckle session with me) pulled a huge hunting knife out, and demanded that I

"PLAY A BOB SEGER SONG...NOW!"

I coolly replied, *"Okay man, but this Seger song's probably a little before your time...it's off Seger's Live Silver Bullet record..."* and we tore into *Got My Mojo Working* by Muddy Waters. This is the polar opposite of a Bob Seger song. But the mangy mutt instantly holstered his Bowie knife, ran cheering out onto the dance floor, whoopin' and a-whompin', delighted and proud to have (once again) gotten his way.

This is the number one photograph because it typifies the barroom brawler I've encountered so often through the years – someone who was willing to kill (or be killed) and go to prison (or the cemetery) over something he knew so little (nothing) about. Sad but true.

A Laurel and Hardy handshake,
LC

February 2006

11

WHAT'S THE WORD?

Greetings Lightnin' Bugs! This month's Lowdown deals with honesty, and the lack of it. This true tale, and the deceit that's contained in it, addresses the real reason that most guys (myself included) started playing music, especially guitarists. And that is...basically, to have the opportunity to meet lots of girls. If you were to ask a hundred guitar players why they picked up their instrument in the first place, around fifty would say, *"to get chicks"*. And the other fifty would be lying. Take it from the Lightnin' Man himself. It's all about dem girls. It is for me. Or it was. And ladies, take it from me, there is no end to what we'll do, or say, to getcha. Listen up y'all...

Once upon a time, way back when I was single, the band and I were playing one of my favorite gigs, a club in a nearby college town that was absolutely loaded with the most gorgeous young female patrons you could shake a stick at (or a guitar). It was fabulous. Since we had always packed the place, we were given a posh hotel suite as part of our pay. It had a large living room, complete with kitchen and bedrooms, and we decided on this trip to make the best of an already splendid situation by planning an after-hours affair with some female fans. We intended to invite every woman at our gig (and there were no dogs in this bunch, boys) to come over to our sweet little suite and hang out with us after the show. And since we had to have something to serve them once they got there, we stopped at a local liquor store for some party favors. But naturally, we were broke. Well, not broke, but badly bent.

After browsing around the wines and fancy liqueurs for a while, all of which we found to be way too pricey, we saw the answer to our budget problem – a not-so-fine domestic wine that's known on the street as "the Bird". Needing to get the most bang for our buck, and cognizant of the fact that quantity - not quality, was the way to go, we finally and frugally opted for two gallon jugs of Thunderbird white wine, chilled. I think it cost us around eight bucks, total. We all pitched in. I remember my part being around two dollars. We, Lightnin' Charlie and the Big Spenders, took "the Bird" to our suite and put it in the fridge.

There were two small obstacles to our party plan, though – quality and quantity. First, the quality issue – how we were going to get any of these sweet, young college girls to come to a blues band's hotel room at three o'clock in the morning to drink Thunderbird? I remember our bassist, Kevin, suggesting that we tell them,

"Yeah, it's Thunderbird...but it's *chilled.*"

God love him. Secondly, the quantity issue – was two gallons going to be enough brew for the amount of people that we would invite? One thing we were sure of, and that was the fact that we four guys were going to be the only men at this here party. We wanted an all-girl cast. We swore an oath not to mention the party even within earshot of any male at the club. And we figured, judging by our past performances at this nightclub, that we could probably extend personal invitations to two hundred girls or more. And if only *half of them* showed up...well Houston, we'd have a problem – we only had two gallons of wine. It was our crafty little New York democrat harmonica player, who was by far the best liar in the band, who suggested an ingenious method of solving both problems. He proposed that we should tell the girls, nonchalantly, that we had somehow procured a case of "imported Japanese saki", and that they would be more than welcome to stop by on their way home and try some. Real casual. Then, once they were there, we would never allow the bottles to be seen. We would pour the "saki" ("Bird") in the kitchen, which had swinging saloon-style doors making it private from the living room. This would prevent our guests (victims) from ever seeing the jugs of Thunderbird.

Furthermore, as fate would have it, this kitchen was stocked with hundreds of little bowls. Restaurant people would call them "monkey dishes" – small, almost flat bowls that, for example, a side order of applesauce or extra salad dressing would be served in. I am not going to elaborate any further on the term "monkey dish"; you all know how I do adore the pun, but a little restraint goes a long way, and discretion truly is the greater part of valor. Shall we be pressing on?

We would further our psychological assault; Bar-Sinister said, by serving the "saki" in these dainty, little dishes. Since our guests would never see the bottles of "Bird", and would be sipping it from diminutive, petite, little "Japanese-style" mini-bowls, we thought the illusion just might work. In fact, we were *sure* it would work. We didn't completely understand the power of suggestion, but we were big fans.

All hats were off to our harmonica player, Brian Bar-Sinister for the cruelly brilliant plan. Brian, the New York liberal and the architect of this devious machination, later went to work for the Clinton Administration. Although I am not at liberty to divulge what his job title was, I can tell you that it rhymes with "limp", and he answered directly to the President.

My bass player (One-Eyed Jack), who had never heard of "saki", had one complaint. He was afraid that if he told a girl in the club to come over to our suite for some "saki", she'd slap him in the face. Bless his heart. We told him to say "Japanese plum wine...imported."

So the stage was set – we rinsed the hundred or so monkey dishes in the sink (we were pigs but we weren't filthy), got dressed for the show, and went to the club for our twelve-bar blues ambush upon the innocence and naivety of the daughters of Eve.

The club was jam-packed as usual with the beautiful bevy of birds that we were accustomed to seeing there. After three sets and two lengthy breaks spreading the word about our "little get together" – Brian Bar-Sinister thought it best to refrain from using the word "party", reasoning, that "little get together" takes all the pressure off the girls. He felt that chicks might show up at a hotel at 3 AM for a "little get together" that would never have showed up for a "party". Man, Bill Clinton must've loved Brian! So the news of our imported libation (accent on "Lie") was buzzing about the club's females. We hustled back to the hotel to see what we saw.

When we arrived, the parking lot was already full and we were tickled pink (pardon the pun) to see 30 or 40 babes anxiously waiting for us in the lobby. We retired to our suite, girls in tow, and proceeded to make introductions and small talk, trying to make everyone comfortable, and downplaying the fact that there appeared to be only ladies present. The ones who were slightly ill at ease were comforted by the strength of their numbers. It looked like the Playboy Mansion at feeding time. There obviously wasn't sofa space for that many people, so our diabolical little harmonica player seized the opportunity to turn a negative into a positive again – he had all the girls sit next to each other, on the floor, cross-legged, Japanese-style. I've got to give the devil his due – that guy was a genius. He then politely excused himself and went into the kitchen to prepare the "saki".

He was accompanied by our drummer, whom we called "King Edwards", who wasn't nearly as interested in these delicate, young college girls as we were. He was much more interested in the Thunderbird wine. King Edwards was a real sweet guy who unfortunately had a bit of a drinking problem. He would drink Miller High Life at the gig until he was literally speaking in tongues. We *lived* with him and still couldn't understand a word. But his drumming was never (almost never) affected. He could play the blues in his sleep. In spite of drumming in a touring, hardcore Chicago-style blues band, King Edwards desperately wanted to play funk; Parliament Funkadelic-style stuff, and he took terrible fits from time to time pleading with us to change our style to his. This was, of course, inherently impossible. On the road, King didn't go in for a lot of the fandanny that we would cook up, as far as the women were concerned. He was older (40) and wiser than we were, and had a girlfriend back home who would've cut his throat if she caught him messin' around. I need to point out here that King Edwards happened to be black. I am reluctant to mention this, because it otherwise makes no difference, except that it ultimately has a huge effect upon our story. Let me also point out that the 30 or 40 young ladies in our living room were all white. Lily-white.

We had decided upon our arrival, appropriately I thought, to keep what we had as far as party guests were concerned, and to not answer the phone after we got inside for fear that letting more folks in might spoil our "perfect party". That is to say, "perfect" in the sense that 100% of our guests were female. What's a perfect party? Us and forty beautiful girls. And not even one ugly one. We figured we had more than we could handle now, and that the more people we let in, the more chance that there would be other guys ruining the mix. This is the natural law of diminishing returns. If it ain't broke, don't fix it. Or, as I said that night with fiendish laughter,

> "A bird in the hand is worth two in the bush."

Sorry...I warned you about me and the puns.

Well, as you must be dying to know by now, and probably have already guessed, the girls were served our "imported saki" in the little dishes, and they *loved* it. They *"oooh-ed"* and *"aaah-ed" and "mmmmm-ed"* and went on and on about how smooth and delicious it was.

> *"This saki is so yummy! Where can I buy more of this?"* one child asked.
> *"You can't get this stuff in the States. This here's the real deal – imported all the way from Japan",* came our reply (emphasis on "Lie").

Seconds and thirds were poured all around and I was glad we had splurged for the second gallon. It was going so well, that even we couldn't believe it. There was a killer vibe – we were playing some Marvin Gaye and Curtis Mayfield & The Impressions on our little stereo (we didn't have any Japanese music in our collection, but we vowed to get some as soon as we got home), everybody's relaxed and in-the-groove, laughing and giggling and cutting up. The perfect party – for under ten bucks! This was just too good to be true. And that's when the bomb dropped.

King Edwards, who had been spending most of his time in the kitchen (we hadn't noticed), apparently had drank/drunk most of the second gallon of Thunderbird himself, and now, being happy with his world, had decided to pull the rug out from under ours. King Edwards exploded through the swinging western-style saloon doors of the kitchen, wearing his turquoise slacks from the show, but no shirt or shoes, waving the empty gallon jug of Thunderbird over his head, and looking like some ghetto Gary Cooper, screamed...

"It's Thunderbiiiiiiirrrdd!!! Hey girls...it's Thunderbiiiiiirrrdd!!!
YYYAAAAAAAHHH!!!!
THHHUUUNNNDDDERRRBBIIIRRRDDDD!!!!!!!!!!

The result was instant and immediate buzz-kill, followed by panic, and a mad dash for the door. Yelling *"FIRE!"* in a crowded theatre wouldn't have incited the stampede that followed King Edwards' charge. Forty girls who were *"oooh-ing"* and *"aaah-ing"* the "saki" a minute ago were *"ugggh-ing"* and *"yecchh-ing"* the "Bird" now. More accurately, it was the *idea* that they had drunk the Thunderbird. It was *"Oh so yummy"* a minute ago when they thought it was imported plum wine, but now that they realized that they were drinking four-dollar-a-gallon street wine, well, they ran like a foul and disgusted wind for the door. *Come back...Shane!!!*

Alas, all good things must come to an end, but we were not big fans of King Edwards for weeks following his terrorist testimony at the party. We all had our own ways of getting back at him – though we could never get even. I personally took pleasure in opening all of his unopened packs of Newport menthol cigarettes at the foil on top (where you're supposed to open them), rather than his preferred soul-brother method of opening them at the bottom. Actually, this benefited King as he smoked much less over the next few weeks. Yet it was all soon forgiven, but not forgotten, as we all developed our own peculiar impersonations of King Edwards busting shirtless through the saloon doors, Thunderbird in hand, crowing,

"It's Thunderbiii-iii-rd!!! It's Thunderbiii-iii-rd!!!"

As a footnote to our story, I should tell you that we subsequently played that club once or twice, but due to a lack of attendance, we were forced to move on. Let go, laid off, our phone calls not returned, you get the picture. We were now persona-non-grata in this well-to-do little college town. We had gone from big shot celebrity status to musical pariahs in no time. We were suddenly and disastrously (for us) the untouchables.

Apparently, word had gotten around at this liberal arts college that we were not to be trusted and that Lightnin' Charlie and His Upsetters were nothing but despicable cads and lecherous scoundrels. And that proved to be our demise. They wouldn't go near us after that. We were the guys their mothers had warned them about. Funny, those same traits would put us on Leno today. But hey, Lightnin' Charlie, King Edwards and the gang had provided these young students with a valuable bit of education in human nature (accent on "man") that probably proved more practical to them in the long run than all the college courses on Keats and Shelley and Henry David Thoreau combined (that their parents were spending a fortune on). Oh well. I don't require any thanks. Just the doing of a good deed is its own reward. It's the kind of guy I am...or was.

And that's how we blew one of the best gigs we ever had. The kind of gig that we had dreamed of playing from the time we were teenagers. The kind of gig that was the reason for our learning to play music in the first place. The kind of gig that was always a mess of delightful, dancing, hot, blooming young babes that all seemed to be "tens". And they loved us. And we blew it. It's the kind of gig that every garage band in the world fantasizes about while practicing hour after hour. Believe me. And it's the one gig I think of each and every time I hear the phrase,

"What's the word? It's Thunderbird!!!"

Until we meet again, I bid you all a fond farewell.

Your friend and teacher,
Lightnin' Charlie
(accent on the "Lie")

MARCH 2006

12

DADDY'S HOME

Good Evening Buggies,

Before we launch into our ignoble narrative, I want to bring back (by popular demand) my top-ten list of books, movies, and CDs. These are, in no particular order, some stuff the Lightnin' Man is into lately.

First, a few books...

1) That Hideous Strength – C.S. Lewis
2) Escaping The Delta – Robert Johnson And The Invention Of The Blues – Elijah Wald
3) Miss Rhythm – The Autobiography Of Ruth Brown, Rhythm & Blues Legend

A trio of favorite films...

4) A Face In The Crowd
5) Say Amen Somebody
6) Red River

And, last but not least, a mess of music...

7) The Bobby Darin Collection (Box Set)
8) Little Walter – Southern Feeling
9) Smokie Norful – I Need You Now
10) Sam Cooke – The Man And His Music

This month's little frolic is a sweet, happy tale of fatherhood. Proud papas can be a little crazy. Case in point: in 2000, when my wife & I found out that there was going to be a "blessed event" in our lives, I took crazy to a new level. I was (and still am) completely cracked and madly in love with my wife and our two boys. But people in love do crazy things. Maybe that's why the word *"love"* is synonymous and completely interchangeable with words *like "crazy"* and *"nuts"*.

"I'm nuts over her, and she's crazy about me!"

I'll never forget all the joy and fervor of that mysterious, soul-stirring season when my wife was carrying our firstborn son. Expectant Papa Charlie did a lot of cuckoo things during that time, but the craziest thing, or more accurately, the craziest-*looking* thing I did must be the following.

From around the fourth month or so, I would sing into my wife Beth's grand belly every night, hoping to reach the developing eardrums of our little unborn baby. We had read about the way that unborn fetuses could respond while in the womb to music that is playing in the outside world. I remember being particularly interested in the way that newborn babies were said to be able to recognize their mother's (and father's) voices. So every night, and I do mean *every* night – I don't think I missed a single night – I would kneel down beside my wife and, using the weird-looking thing that used to be her belly button, croon loudly into her tummy. My sweetheart's cute little belly-button, that through the course of her pregnancy grew to look more and more like the flowery top of a piece of cauliflower – kind of like a mini mushroom cloud – was now being utilized as a vocal mic by her batty husband. She often complained about the sensitivity of her navel and the irritating stubble of my not-so-clean-shaven face and chin, but I pressed on.

Lightnin' Charlie, being a professional vocalist and amateur dad, speculated that bass tones would probably resound and "carry" more (pun intended) inside her, getting through all of that amniotic jazz, so I sang a lot of doo-wop bass lines, hoping to connect with my boy. *Blue Moon* by The Marcels, *Get A Job* by The Silhouettes, *Duke Of Earl* by Gene Chandler, and *Why Do Fools Fall In Love* by Frankie Lymon and The Teenagers were some of my favorites. I also sung a lot of Sinatra and Dean Martin into the tum-tum because that's the stuff I remember my dad singing to me when I was a kid.

"Flyyyy me to the moo-oo-oon...Let me sw-ingggg among the stars..."

In the '60s though, dads probably waited until the baby was out-and-about before they started singing to them.

The January 2006 Lowdown *[Photographs And Memories]* lists the top ten pictures I wish I had from my life as a road musician. Well, picture *this* – me kneeling beside my wife, who would pull her shirt up over her big, bare belly to allow me access to the belly-button microphone, or the "womb-mic" as I called it, singing "Bowser-style"...

"Dip-Di-dip-Di-dip, Bomp-bomp-Ba-bomp, Ba-bomp-ba-bomp-bomp, Bomp-ba-bomp-ba-bomp-bomp, Ba-dang-a-dong-ding, A-ding-a-dong-ding, Blue Moooooon!!!"

You know America...if our neighbors could see the unglued lives we actually lead, within the confines and privacy of our own homes, there wouldn't be a one of us that wouldn't be committed permanently to a mental institution. People in glass houses... And who would be left to guard the patients at the nut house? No one – we would all be inmates. I know I would. I'd be on top of the cuckoo's nest, crowing,

"Sha-na-na-na, Sha-na-na-na-na, Ba-ooo, Sha-na-na-na, Sha-na-na-na-na, Bow-yip-yip-yip-yip-yip-yip-yip-yip-boom-boom-boom...Get a job!"

Added to this disturbing image was the fact that, at that time, I had huge, bushy, black, "Aloha From Hawaii" Elvis sideburns. I am just telling you this to complete your mental picture (emphasis on *'mental'*). In retrospect, I am glad that I used an old Elvis/Dracula trick in our bedroom – taping black shower curtain liners over the bedroom windows (and under the thick velvet drapes) to keep out the unwanted sunlight. This was much more efficient and more permanent than the aluminum foil used in Elvis' hotel rooms. It would allow me to get my beauty sleep after rockin' and rollin' into the wee wee hours. It also, thank God, kept out the nosy neighbors, the peeping toms, and the *nice young men in their-clean-white-coats-and they're-coming-to-take-me-AWAAAYYYY!!! HA-HA!!!*

Close your eyes and imagine me and my sideburns warbling into my wife's navel, which used to be an 'innie', but was now very much an 'outie'...

"Duke-Duke-Duke-Duke Of Earl-Duke-Duke-Duke Of Earl-Duke-Duke-Duke Of Earl-Duke-Duke..."

You get the picture...I was gone...Real gone. And head over heels, crazy in love with my wife and our baby boy.

"To us a child is born, to us a Son is given." – Isaiah 9:6

Our son was born in December and was the greatest Christmas gift I have ever gotten. On the third day, Proud Papa Charlie took his wife and bouncing baby boy home from the hospital – no rest for the weary. Nowadays, hospitals quickly kick you to the curb getting you out of their bed and out of their rooms, making valuable space available to new sick people (with insurance). They're very caring. Not about the patient – about making money. In Japan, new mothers are treated to a month of pampering and "R & R" in the hospital before they are turned out to the brutally hectic life called parenthood. Kudos to the Japanese on this one. But here in America it's *"BONSAI!!!! GET OUT!!!"* It's all about turnover, baby.

On our first day home, my mom, who came to take some of the load off the new parents, joined my wife and me, and our three-day-old king-of-the-castle. We hadn't slept well in days (and were not going to get much sleep for months to come, but we didn't know that yet...) and my dear considerate mother wanted to help us by doing the laundry, cooking the meals, etc. I say that *"we"* hadn't slept well, but in fact, it was *"I"* who hadn't slept at all. You see, in the hospital, my wife had an IV (intravenous) in her arm, which was connected to a big jug of self-serve morphine. It had a nifty little trigger button that, when pushed, would dispense a single dose of morphine for the pain (my wife had a C-section and was going through the usual post-op distress). But unfortunately for my wife, only a certain amount of painkiller could be dispensed per hour, and if the patient pushed the button for more dope, before it was time for more dope, the gizmo would go...

"BEEP-BEEP-BEEP-BEEP!!!"

So, as I tried to get some sleep in a disagreeable recliner-chair in our hospital room for two nights (and days) after the birth, all I heard every couple of minutes was...

"BEEP-BEEP-BEEP-BEEP!!!"

My wife slept pretty well though. I wonder why. But I guess that morphine stuff makes one awfully thirsty, because she ran my legs off bringing her fountain cokes with crushed ice (don't forget the "bendy-straw") from the nurse's break room on our floor. The nursing staff slyly told me that I could just "help myself to drinks", as we wanted them. I initially thought that this was pretty cool and quite generous of them to allow me access to the "coke-fountain", but they apparently knew what I didn't, and that was, that my wife was going to guzzle drinks by the gallon for the next couple days. It was unbelievable. The second night I counted fifty-six Pepsi's in a nine-hour period. And I was using large, Styrofoam cups that must've held ten or twelve ounces. And the minute I would sink back into that awfully dolorous [dol-or-ous (do'-ler-as) adj. to cause grief or discomfort] recliner for a bit of shut-eye, I would hear the sound of her straw sucking air and backwash off the bottom of the cup...

"Sccchhh-lllll-uuuu-rrr-pppp....Sccchhh-lllll-uuuu-rrr-pppp"

This nerve-wracking sound was followed at once by...

"BEEP-BEEP-BEEP-BEEP!!!"

This was then followed promptly (and routinely) by this request...

"Honnnney, could yew git me shome more Pepshi, pleashe?"

I am sorry to digress here, but doggone it America, we men just don't get the credit we deserve for all the pain and suffering *we* go through dealing with this labor and childbirth business. Seriously, that recliner was unbearable! But it's all about you women, ain't it? It's your world and we're just living in it. I didn't have a joystick filled with morphine. And you women don't have the market cornered when it comes to the postpartum blues either. I was exhausted, America. And I just need to pat myself on the back right here and now for being such a good, dutiful (if not beautiful) husband and never complaining (until now) about the Pepsi and recliner torture. My wife just read this over my shoulder and informed me of two things...one, that she has no recollection of any of this

[Ed. note: That's a big surprise...BEEP-BEEP-BEEP-BEEP!!!]

and two, that *nobody* could drink that much Pepsi. Well, I'll let *you* decide who is telling the truth, America – me or the new mom with the black tongue. And now that I've gotten *that* off my chest, I need to apologize to Brother Bernie Mac and get back to our story...

On this, our first day home, my wife and my mother were sitting on our sofa with the baby lying between them. I was going to the fridge to get a drink (as had become my custom) and when I asked them if they needed anything from the kitchen, my son, hearing my voice, turned his head toward me and got real "wide-eyed" with recognition. This thrilled me because it was obvious that he had recognized the *sound of my voice!* And not only did he *recognize* my voice, it was quite apparent by his expression that he *enjoyed* and *appreciated* it as well. This was, of course, very meaningful to an old singer and a new daddy. So Lightnin' Charlie, being not only a chip-off-the-old-block but also a major ham-off-the-old-hock, took this opportunity to gloat a little. I spread my arms out in a gesture of immodest modesty and proclaimed proudly...

"Ah yes, his master's voice..."

My son's anticipatory grin now told me that he knew something great was coming and he was ready for it. He had grown to love my songs and especially my singing and was now clearly in love with the *sound* of my voice and was anxious to hear more. He had that look of glad expectation in his eyes. You know, the *"look of love"*. Haughtily I knelt, full of myself, on one knee in front of my son and began to swing and swagger, singing Sinatra's *Fly Me To The Moon...*

"Fill my heart with song..."

Eager to see the magical effect and psychic connection I had conjured with my child, I sang this one line, and stared deeply into his brand new eyes.

My son's instantaneous reaction was a nonchalant but blistering bowel movement. He responded to my singing with the loudest, soggiest, most explosive and booming butt-turbulence I believe I have ever heard. His timing was impeccable. As soon as I sung *"Fill my heart with song"*, before I could even deliver the next line, he went to work – thunderously filling his diaper (not his heart), with something very different from song.

It knocked all of us onto the floor laughing. It was just too hilarious – too perfectly set up to be true.

After all of my

"Bomp-bomp-Ba-bomps"

After months of

"Bow-yip-yip-yip-yips" and *"Boom-boom-booms"*

When the strains (poop-pun intended) of

"Duke-Duke-Duke" and *"Dip-Di-dip-Di-dip"*

were just a memory, my beautiful baby boy was finally here with me, grinning up at me and *showing* me how much he loved me. His master's voice, all right.

Maybe that was just his way of telling me,

"Daddy, I love you."

Or maybe he was begging,

"Dad, for God's sake, stop it!"

Or maybe, just maybe,

"Yeah Daddy, sing another one! And this time, really swing it!"

Maybe this was his way of applauding. Or booing. I guess I'll never know. But had he been responding that way to my nightly concerts all along? My *poor wife!* The things women go through...

Well America, I'm off to fetch my wife a nice cold Pepsi. She didn't ask me to, but I need to get busy and try to spoil her just a little bit. Like I used to. I don't have any crushed ice, but I can make some right quick with some ice cubes, a baggie and a hammer. She deserves it. She's my hero. And she puts up with me.

"BEEP-BEEP-BEEP-BEEP!!!"

That's right America,
Yours truly,
Lightnin' Charlie (what I do)
AKA Daddy (who I am)

APRIL 2006

13

DEATH AND TAXES

If you are reading this, as you obviously are, I assume that you are finished filing your 2005 income tax return. Some of you poor souls might be paying still more taxes and penalties after working and paying all year (as I did last year). Some of you might even be reading this from a federal prison (although I am glad to be ignorant of whether or not federal prisoners are allowed access to computers in federal penitentiaries). And some of you lucky ones are already enjoying a refund. God bless you. "Refund" is an Internal Revenue Service term meaning the portion of your money that they are generously giving back to you. But at least you are finished filing and done with the yearly nightmare of being threatened with imprisonment and financial ruin for not turning over all your hard-earned pay to the government weasels. And if you're not finished, what are you doing reading this? As for yours truly – I'm still working on mine – hence the delay in putting up this installment of the Lowdown. My apologies to you, my loyal readers, for my tardiness, and foul and bloody curses on the IRS, my annual nemesis, for putting me through this every year.

If you are reading this, as you obviously are, and did not work or pay taxes last year, my compliments to you – you are the bright one. You're probably perusing this on a nice big LCD flat-screen monitor with a speedy new computer and a high-speed Internet connection. I'm the chump who, along with my wife, worked all year to buy it for you. I'm the chump who's typing this on an antique, slower-than-you-know-what-through-a-goose desktop PC with a dial-up modem. Call me "Chump Charlie", with my rapidly receding hairline (along with my rapidly receding refund), and blurred vision from staring at TurboTax for weeks and weeks after working all year. I'm the chump. Maybe someday I'll wise up and quit working so I can have something. I can see it now...I'll be a stay-at-home hippie, smoking dope and churning out offspring like tadpoles and getting rewarded for my efforts with a big fat check from the government. Of course, it isn't the government's money – they've just hijacked it and wrote the check. It's working chumps like me who earned the money. It wouldn't be a very pretty picture...me lying around on a sectional sofa all day, chain-smoking, eating Doritos, and watching Jerry Springer on my big-screen plasma TV, complaining about this rotten country that feeds me and all my kids, wherever (and whosoever) they are. I wouldn't be expected to pay rent or utilities. I'd get tattoos and liposuction (all for free) and yak with my bum-friends on my cell phone (also free) about how much better things are in countries like France or Canada. But I won't go live there. Not while I've got chumps like Charlie getting up every day and going to work for me.

I'm reminded of a story of a young Sir Arthur Conan Doyle, author of the Sherlock Holmes detective stories, who was an ophthalmologist before he turned his talents to creating the most popular fictional character of all time. In his first year of independent medical practice, his earnings were 154 British pounds (the equivalent of $270). He filled out his income tax forms for the year showing that, based upon his income, he was not liable to pay any income tax, and sent it in. The authorities returned the form with the words

"Most Unsatisfactory"

scrawled across it. Doyle returned it again, this time with his own subscription,

"I entirely agree".

This reminds me of another story of a brash youngster named Lightnin' Charlie, who once got a speeding ticket from one of those automated gizmos that takes a picture of your speeding car, and then sends you the photo with the ticket in the mail. Fearlessly, Lightnin' Charlie took a photograph of a check, made out to the police department for the proper amount, and sent the police department the photo of the check. The police department (who must always have the last word) sent Charlie back a photo of a pair of handcuffs. End of story.

Historically, Tennesseans like myself were never big fans of the federal government. There's the story of a ragged, young Tennessean, a soldier of the Confederacy, who was caught alone outside Murfreesboro and surrounded by a company of Federals. The Federal army, seeing the hopeless condition of this shoeless and tattered lad, began to mock him. This barefoot soldier couldn't possibly grasp any of the intricate issues that had incited the war. He obviously didn't own any slaves and, by the looks of him, didn't know much about the complexities of the U. S. Constitution, or much else for that matter.

"Why are you here, fightin' this war, Reb?" the Federals taunted him.

"I'm fightin'", the Rebel replied, *"cause y'all are down here."*

It's no small wonder to me that our Great Republic was born as a direct result of the labor pains from excessive taxation without representation. Some things never change. My state representative is subsidizing (with my hard-earned pay) a Nashville "performance artist", who spreads peanut butter and ketchup all over her naked body and crawls around onstage, howling on all fours while urinating on crucifixes and American flags and screaming,

"Katrina!!! Katrina!!!"

I agree that she has the right as a free American citizen to defecate and desecrate like the heathen freak she is and sell tickets to consenting adults (superfreaks). Also guaranteed in our Constitution is the free enterprise system – the right of "folks" to buy tickets to watch this "artist". But where in our Constitution does it say that I have to pay for all of it? Is this what Jefferson, Washington, Monroe and the others had in mind? Press "1" for English. Godfrey Daniel, mother-of-pearl, I'm a man without a country...

I am going to cut my rant-therapy short this month as I am probably "preaching to the choir" about the debacle of our tax laws, and I still have a lot more work to do on my return before the April 15th deadline. For one thing, I need to figure out the difference between amortization and depreciation. And I'm not sure about the difference between directly allocable deductions and indirectly allocable deductions.

However, I do know the difference between the 2005 unit sales of Lightnin' Charlie's *A New Leaf* and the 2005 Oscar-winning piece of work by Memphis thug-rappers (redundant to the extreme) called *It's Hard Out Here For A Pimp*. I don't know the exact figure, but I know it's got a lot of zeros. But at least they're finally out of government housing, and can now pay me my money back. I'm entitled to reparations, right?

Yep, death and taxes...but not in that order.

Your loyal friend and colleague,
Charlie

14

WRITER'S BLOCK
- OR -
THE PSYCHIATRIST IS OUT

Sorry Lightnin' Bugs. I'm suffering from writer's block. Check back next month.

Actually I am suffering from writer's *cramp* from endorsing so many checks due to my superhuman schedule this month (24 shows in 19 days) and I just haven't had the time to write. All this lovely income will kill me on next year's tax return though [see the April Lowdown *Death and Taxes*], but is good news for America's drug dealers on federal assistance. Welfare? How about farewell?

So I apologize for the delay (I realize that a lot of you depend on the Lowdown as an alternative to therapy), but I promise you an extra good 'un in June...God willing and the creek don't rise.

Till then, I am and will remain,
your humble and lovable servant,
Sir Charles

JUNE / JULY / AUGUST 2006

15

AN AMERICAN TRILOGY

This long-awaited Lowdown, late as it may be, will hopefully bring a bit of pleasure to my readers, as well as bring to an end my apathy about writing these diatribes.

I've received a ton of emails inquiring about the reason for the delay (it's the first lapse in Lowdowns since I started writing these monthly sagas sixteen months ago). Some well-meaning folks asked if I was ill or suffering from writer's block, while others, less well-meaning, seemed to revel in the misconception that I had finally run out of things to say.

As delightful a prospect as that must seem for some, it is nonetheless wholly untrue. The fact is, I've been so busy and deluged with work, all good, that I just haven't had the time nor the inclination to hammer out a tale worthy of inclusion in Lightnin's Lowdown.

Here are a few selected e-mails from you, my friends and fans:

Travis T. of Dew Process writes:
What's up? Three months and no Lowdown? It ain't fair. Since my divorce, the Lowdown is the only thing I have to look forward to that makes me smile. If there's not a new one online by June 1st, and a darn funny one, too, I'll kill myself.
Yours Truly,
Travis (deceased)
P.S. Could you please send me your summer concert itinerary and three cases of Dasani water?

A. Lapse in Judgment Falls writes:
I knew a bigmouth fancy pants like you was bound to come up short sooner or later. People like you make me sick. Thank God you've finally shut your festering gob.
Love your music,
Reverend & Mrs. Arthur Lapse

Miss Carriage of Justus writes:
Dear Charlie Blowhard,
I just want to know what the problem is. Three months and no Lowdown from Mr. Big Shot? Has the long arm of the law finally caught up with you? Have the snide comments you make about our local men and women of Law Enforcement finally come back on you? I guess them chickens have come home to roost now, haven't they, you self-righteous prig. Couldn't happen to a nicer guy. Put your show times and dates up on the web, as I am sure you'll soon be strumming your way out of latrine duty while in county lockup, you prancing piece of prima donna. You deserve every bit of bad luck that comes your way, Mr. Lightnin' Charlie. Expect to see me when you least expect it, punk. When you hear someone sneaking up behind you, it'll be me. I am 6 feet, 2 inches tall; I weigh 250 pounds, and have wavy brown hair with auburn highlights. I enjoy lifting weights, Southern Rock, and taking long walks around the yard with special friends. My measurements are 46-54-46, and I am a Libra. Please play some Skynyrd for me.
C-Ya,
Miss Carriage (Jim)
Cell Block C,
Justus County Penal Institution
Bristol, Virginia

Miss Take of Sumagnitude writes:
Yo Charlie,
Where ya' been? I've been worried sick over here. I haven't seen a Lowdown in months. Are you okay? Sal and me, we're scared something bad has happened to you. Is there someone or something keeping you from writing your little soap opera stories? If so, Sal and me – we're here to help you. All you gotta do is ask, *capice?*

Look, I don't wanna know about your past association with the Lumbago family out of Miami Beach. I'm not talkin' about that mess down there with the Cuban cigars and the olive oil. That's ancient history. Things have changed inside the Lumbago family since you were a boss, and any problems you had with Carlo (formerly of the Winnebagos of Detroit) is all in the past. You know they found Carlo sleeping with the fishes in Biscayne Bay wearing cement skis. But that's none of my business. I might've heard a few things, you know, about how business got ugly in Jersey after you sold your screenplay to HBO. But hey, I always say, let

sleeping dogs lie. If the government wants to set you up in Elvis Country in Tennessee somewhere with a new name bangin' away on a guitar like some moulingnon, who am I to question it, God bless you. You need anything, you call us. Forget about it.
Your paisan,
Big Miss Take
c/o Victoria's Secret
104 East River Street
Sumagnitude, NY 10015

Yes, my beloved readers, you have come to expect these raucous and ribald rants at a certain literary level, and you have become spoiled with their welfare check regularity. But you know it don't come easy. Once I've come up with an idea for the story, I usually spend 2 or 3 nights typing a rough draft, then 2 or 3 nights tweaking it and putting it up on the web. This I do on my earthworm-speed desktop PC, down in my basement/office, which is famous for flooding and has flooded twice since the last Lowdown (I still have not heard from the Racist-Reverend Messy-Jesse, the Clinton-Bushes, or FEMA in response to my sad and soggy plight). But that tirade is included in a previous Lowdown. As for the present, I simply haven't had the desire to snorkel into the basement of my house nor the energy to delve into the dark recesses of my mind from which the Lowdown lackadaisically flows.

This lack of energy is due to a wonderful explosion of bookings – the most in my 23-year career. And thanks to my letting go and letting God, it's gigs of quality as well as quantity. I don't have to cast my pearls before swine any more. So ends this "note from home", hopefully excusing my absence. I would like to make up for my three-month lapse with a gratuitous trilogy, all three episodes starring former bass players of mine. But first, a lucky list of 13 killer CDs spinning at my house, in no particular order:

1) Amos Milburn – The Motown Sessions
2) The Five Blind Boys Of Mississippi – Millennium Collection
3) Magic Sam – Rockin' Wild In Chicago
4) Sister Wynona Carr – Dragnet For Jesus
5) Carl Perkins – Original Sun Greatest Hits
6) Paul Rishell & Annie Raines – Goin' Home
7) Smokie Norful – Nothing Without You

8) The Fabulous Thunderbirds - Painted On
9) Charlie Rich - Complete Smash Records
10) Sam Cooke - Live At The Harlem Square Club (Remastered)
11) Nick Curran - Player!
12) Bobby Blue Bland - The Duke Recordings
13) Johnny Guitar Watson - 3 Hours Past Midnight

And now, on with the show...

Episode One

"Cheap On The Sunny Side"
or
"As The Worm Turns"

The first episode of our trilogy centers on a wild cat whom I'll call "Marvin". Marvin played bass for me from 1985 to 1988 and was quite a character. Marvin is the only Upsetter to have died twice and was, among other things, the absolute cheapest human being I have ever known. Or, for that matter, I've ever heard of.

Any story about Marvin begs a detailed physical and biographical description of him. Marvin had been a pretty hardcore drug addict when he was in his twenties, and his party came to an end with a severe heart attack at the ripe old age of twenty-nine. While in the hospital, Marvin's heart stopped for several minutes and he was clinically dead before being resuscitated. After recovering, Marvin never touched any drugs or drink again and was clean and sober during his stint in the Upsetters. Marvin's troubles started long before his twenties, though. Born with a cleft palette and severe asthma, a young Marvin was at home when a fire broke out in his family's house and he received terrible burns to his face and body before being rescued by firemen. As an adult, Marvin had considerable facial scars from the burns and the many surgeries and skin grafts that followed. We used to kid him about his expression of "constant surprise" because of the way his skin was stretched so tightly around his eyes and I never saw Marvin with his mouth closed - I don't think he was physically able to close it - which accounted for his being unable to drink through a straw. These days, Hollywood is full of aging stars with this same look of "surgical surprise". But Marvin came by his honest.

So picture a man in his early thirties, having come back from drug and alcohol addiction (and back from the dead), diminutive in stature at five foot six inches tall, maybe 125 pounds, with a cleft palette and facial burn scars, with two black

"Bozo" shocks of afro-kinky hair (despite being hopelessly Caucasian) thrusting out horizontally like wings from the sides of his head. I used to call him "the Phantom Of The Opera's stunt double". One positive albeit necessary trait Marvin possessed was a good self-deprecating sense of humor.

If all this wasn't enough, poor Marvin constantly had to use prescription CO_2 inhalers for his asthma ("pocket rockets", we called them; "Vaso-dilators", according to Marvin). And the more nervous or upset Marvin got, the more he would huff on that pocket rocket. And believe me, being recently back from the dead and living in the Upsetters in 1985 was a mighty nerve-wracking and plenty upsetting undertaking for Marvin. Both puns (Upsetter, undertaker) intended.

And now that you have an idea of Marvin's background and appearance, a word or two about Marvin's personality. Okay, I'll splurge – three words – that completely describe Marvin's personality: *cheap, cheap, and cheap.* I cannot overstate the case for Marvin being the world's cheapest mortal. When we would be setting up at a gig, Marvin would thirstily saunter up to the bar, and when the bartender asked what he would like, Marvin would reply, "How much for a coke?" If the bartender replied, "Oh, you're in the band – I won't charge you for cokes", Marvin would grin ear-to-ear like the proverbial Cheshire cat and say, "I'll have a coke" (you've heard of a big [bleep]-eating grin? This expression of Marvin's was a "free soda-drinking grin") and times like these were the happiest I ever saw Marvin. But if the bartender replied to his query, "A coke? 50 cents", Marvin would say dejectedly, "I'll have ice-water". Marvin refused to pay 50 cents for a fountain coke (even with free refills) and would drink foul tap water all night long to keep from spending two quarters.

Needless to say, the word "tip" was considered by Marvin to be profanity and he never spoke the word nor engaged in the practice in all the years I knew him. Not a nickel. Not once. This served to endear him to waitresses and bartenders everywhere we played. But to see Marvin's mug with a fistful of free bellywash was to see the ultimate expression of joy and satisfaction on a person who knew that all was right with the world.

Let me illustrate another example of the excruciating extent of Marvin's cheapness. Marvin once told me that he had every penny he had ever made playing with the Upsetters in the bank. The *same* penny. In other words, let's say Marvin's pay for a certain night's gig was $52.47, he would deposit *that very same* $52.47 into the bank the next morning. He would not, for example, stop and buy a 25-cent pack of gum on his way home, spending 25 cents of his pay. Even though he could *replace* the 25 cents the next day with another quarter to make his full $52.47 bank deposit. It had to be the complete amount of his pay, and even sicker still, it had to be the *same coin and paper* that he was paid. Neither would he consider for a moment depositing $52.22 and having fresh breath, for five sticks of gum anyway. Forget about it. I could not possibly believe this to be true if Marvin hadn't told me this himself. Proudly. I often told Marvin that he was so tight, he squeaked. He would say, "Charlie, I'm not tight, I'm parsimonious." Look it up for yourself – I did.

It should also be stated that Marvin was not a pauper who, out of necessity, had to scrimp and save. He came from a fairly well-to-do family, and he still lived at home. You don't think Marvin would pay rent, do you? Marvin never had, nor ever would have, his own house or apartment in his life.

There was only one thing that Marvin would occasionally spend his money on. And this one indulgence was unfortunately, like his indulgences in his drug days, very self-destructive to his bass playing and a detriment and disaster to the Upsetters. I am referring to Marvin purchasing records by his favorite musician, Thelonius Monk. Lightnin' Charlie and the Upsetters were then, and are now, a gutbucket mix of blues, soul, and rock 'n' roll. The Upsetters' bassist plays a key role, especially in a small 3-piece band, in creating that sound. We could always tell when Marvin had been listening to that Monk junk, because we would sound like a train wreck. In the toilet. Thanks to Thelonius Monk. On those nights, I would introduce Marvin onstage as "the loneliest monk". He would look over at me, open-mouthed and looking surprised. To this day, I can't stand Thelonius Monk or Marvin's other fave and destroyer of Upsetter grooves, the bi-polar bassist Jaco Pastorius. Thelonius and Pastorius (sounds like a 1st century Roman governor and his bath-buddy) were not musicians that I wanted the Upsetters to sound like. This was the only thing Marvin ever did that made me angry. His parsimony only hurt him – his taste for junkie jazz hurt the band.

Now that you have an idea of what made Marvin tick, let's get on with our fable...

Once upon a weekend, in a little hamlet in Virginia, the Upsetters and Lightnin' Charlie were holding court in a local Ramada Inn lounge. Our drummer had to drive back home to work his day job on Saturday, and would return Saturday night for the gig. This left Marvin and I alone to contemplate the meaning of life (between Ramada Inn shows). We hung around the hotel Saturday afternoon until our barren bellies couldn't wait any longer and we took our grub-lust to a local steakhouse. Life on the road usually only provided one decent square meal per day, if you were lucky. A typical day's victuals would be lots of black coffee, greasy fast food and sodas, followed by more coffee and maybe some potato chips or a candy bar (I once tried, unsuccessfully, to get a corporate endorsement from Milky Way and Kit Kat bars). Then, after the show, when most everything was closed for the night, we were forced to forage like bears through gas stations, convenience stores and hotel vending machines for sustenance. If someone would open a 24-hour Cracker Barrel, they'd get rich from just feeding the bands.

On this day, Marvin and I ended up at one of those low-priced steakhouses where you order, cafeteria-style, and carry your tray to your table. Going through the line, I sensed the tension I had grown accustomed to feeling when Marvin was about to be forced to spend money. But Marvin was about to be sporting one of those grins I spoke of earlier, because his muscles relaxed and his eyes lit up at the sight of a small sign behind the counter that read:

TODAY'S SPECIAL
ALL-YOU-CAN-EAT
SOUP & SALAD BAR WITH DRINK
$3.95

Marvin looked at the cashier and, with a satisfied mind said, "I'll have the special." She handed him a soup bowl, a large salad plate, and a coke, then turned to take my order. "Separate checks, please", I declared, "Rib eye, medium-rare, baked potato, butter and sour cream. Ice water with lemon. Coffee, black." I had found that separate checks were required when dining out with Marvin (or anyone else in the Upsetters' entourage), because the courtesy of picking up a check was never, ever reciprocated by the sponges in my band. I invariably inherited most of the tipping duties as well. Traveling with these guys was just one joy after another.

Marvin and I easily found a table in the empty dining room. It was around 3 or 4 PM and we were the only patrons in the place. A nervous young waitress brought me my coffee. "Do you want cream?" she asked. "No thanks, black", I answered. She looked at me blankly and set the creamers in her hand down onto the table anyway. I noticed, from her nametag that her name was Susan and, feeling sorry for her, said, "Thanks a lot, Susan". This seemed to make her even more uneasy and, without another word, Susan turned and scurried off. Marvin, having deposited his coke (with free refills) on the table, had bolted to the salad bar to get his four dollars worth.

I happen to despise "buffets" and consider them to be nothing but horse troughs, the food fodder for animals. By the way, you know what the term "BUFFET" stands for, don't you? "Big Ugly Fat Fellers Eating Together". I, personally, rank buffet-style dining on a par with the culinary experience found in prisons, elementary schools, hospitals and military mess halls. I find the whole idea ghastly – sharing my food, crockery, and utensils with a society of gluttons.

Every time I'm forced into one of these cattle drives, I always go to the men's room to wash my hands prior to going to the food bar. And every time, just as sure as baby bunnies, a big, ugly, fat feller will come into the men's room, pee in (and around) the urinal, and then exit without washing his hands. I then have the pitiful pleasure of meeting him again, in the food line, directly in front of me. He hands the serving spoon to me. It's my destiny. He's handling everything that I am expected to put my hands on and put into my mouth? Uh-uh, not me – I know where his hands have been.

Marvin returned to the table with a cup of soup and a tremendous salad, covered with ranch dressing. He dove, wholeheartedly, into that mess, rushing to get it down so he could go back for seconds. Remember, with Marvin, it isn't about the food; it's about the money. My steak and baked arrived and I was able to leisurely finish my meal about the same time that Marvin had finished flying through his – that's how big his salad was. Marvin was greedily tidying up the last bits off the bottom of his plate when he stopped, sat back, and said, "Oh God, *look!*"

There on the bottom of Marvin's salad plate, in the flat pool of chalk-white ranch dressing, was a jet-black, live worm, swollen to about the size of my index finger. I recognized it (from having worked in lots of bad restaurants and filthy kitchens) as one of those worms that gets into old, rotten heads of lettuce. They're a big, freaky-looking bit of vermin, and have lots of legs on each side like a centipede. And this guy was just a-gittin' it, swimming vigorously through the remnants of Marvin's lunch.

I remember making some jive comment about the rain forest, which Marvin didn't even hear. He was wide-eyed, frantically squeezing off a double-dose from his pocket rocket and, wheeling his head round-and-round like Linda Blair in The Exorcist, was desperately seeking Susan, our waitress. Could I make this up?

But Susan, not exactly a "people person", was hiding, literally, behind a floor-to-ceiling column at the edge of the dining room. Peering around the edge, she could see Marvin and I looking around for her (it wasn't that she was too busy – we were still the only customers in the joint) but just as eye contact was made between our server and our selves, Susan would pull her face back behind the pole. The poor girl had apparently been victimized by some type of terrible trauma, such as sexual abuse or a violent shaking, which had led her to this point, where she's hiding behind a post from Marvin and me.

But trauma, at our table at least, was a condition, which belonged wholly to Marvin. He got up, and calmly and quietly, carried his plate (with the fat, black Flipper rollicking in the deep end of the salad sauce) over to the pole behind which our waitress was lurking. The conversation that ensued (pun intended) between Susan and Marvin was so surreal as to be beyond belief. I would not believe it, if I had not heard it with my own ears.

> Marvin: *"I need to show you something."*
> Susan: [blank stare]
> Marvin: [holding out his plate, showing, as clear and obvious as ugly on a pig, the great black wiggling worm – impossible to miss in the shallow bleach-white dressing]
> Susan: [still blank and blinking, looking down at the plate and up at Marvin with absolutely no reaction] *"Do you want another plate?"*
> Marvin: [blinking harder than Susan] *"No, I don't want another plate!"*
> Susan: [vacantly oblivious to what was the matter with Marvin] *"Do you want me to take this plate?"*
> Marvin: [louder now] *"Yes! Yes, I want you to take this plate!"*
> Susan: [taking plate and wordlessly turning and walking away]

Marvin returned to our table, stunned and surprised-looking (even more so than usual) like a punch-drunk fighter who has to be led back to his corner. I told him I couldn't believe what I had just heard. *Another plate?* Did she think he wanted to go back for seconds and fish for Son Of Flipper? *Take this plate?* Did she think he was a vegetarian who was acting silly to be appalled at the sight of a little undercooked (ALIVE) meat on his salad plate? Did she see nothing *wrong* with what was on Marvin's plate? Marvin sat silently, hitting his inhaler, and thinking hard (I'm sure), about three hundred and ninety-five little craven images of Abraham Lincoln.

Needless to say, Susan remained cleverly camouflaged behind the column, never returning to our table. Nor did she tell management about the problem. The problem with Susan was that she didn't see a problem. Susan apparently saw nothing out of the ordinary in a dinner plate crawling with insects (reptiles?).

Now anxious to get out of there and hopefully to forget this grisly grub (though I've yet to forget it and it's been twenty years ago), Marvin and I got up to leave. Since Susan never brought us our checks, we should have, in hindsight, just cut our losses and split. But that was also impossible, because, if the cops came before we could get away, we'd, at some point, have to admit to them that we were a band from out-of-town, and then we'd go directly to jail for not paying our check, regardless of worms. So, being eager to tell a manager what had happened, and indignantly bracing for an apology, we dumbly went to the cashier and stood, waiting for justice.

A manager (actually an assistant manager who was pimpled and probably not quite twenty years old) arrived shortly with our checks. While adding them up, he asked nonchalantly if "everything was alright?" Marvin said that everything was "most definitely *not alright*" and proceeded to tell him the story of Flipper the grub worm and Susan the grubby waitress. Mr. Manager responded in kind, saying he was "very sorry that happened" and he would "gladly remove the salad from our bill".

Well, Marvin was a new man. Now *exhilarated* at the prospect of *saving* some money, Marvin couldn't care less that he had just eaten roughage in which a giant worm had been running amok. Remember folks; it was all about the money to Marvin. So young Mr. Manager proceeds to ring up Marvin's bill and says,

"That'll be $5.78 please."

Marvin looks at him and says,

"But I had the Special - salad, soup and drink for $3.95."

Get ready...Boy Wonder says,

"I know, but I took the salad off your check and so now I'll have to charge you the ala carte price for the soup and drink."

I was dumbfounded. Marvin started hyperventilating. I remember this as one of the most outrageous moments in my life, when the impossible was happening right before my eyes.

"Wait a minute!" I yelled, *"Are you telling me that he's getting charged two dollars extra for having a live worm in his food?"*

I know I said earlier that I never picked up a check, but honestly, Marvin was about to go into cardiac arrest, and desperate times call for desperate measures. Telling Boy Wonder to forget it - he and the waitress were obviously in this together and both descendants, mentally at least, of the grub worm - I told him to add the two checks together and give me the total. This unexpected turn of events put Marvin's already badly rattled psyche into further confusion. How should he react to this - yes, he had eaten that squalid salad, but now his entire meal was going to be *free*? Praise God Almighty, free at last...

Life on the road meant dealing with all kinds of abuses, injustices, and transgressions. We always seemed to be at the mercy of the seamiest of sewer rats and the dirtiest of dunghill dictators. Whether in hotels, in bars, in our cars, or in roadside restaurants, we were routinely subjected to wanton insult and injury. And by definition - being traveling musicians, often hundreds of miles from home, knowing no one, but knowing better than to ever get the police involved in our disputes, we generally had little or no recourse other than to simply grin and bear it.

But I had, for only the most extreme cases of personal persecution, always carried what I referred to as "the equalizer". Not the equalizer you're thinking of though. I've never carried a gun for fear (and certainty) that I'd use it, and if I were traveling around the country, packing heat, it would add the problem of body disposal to my already overwhelming list of duties.

No, the equalizer I am referring to was truly an inspired feat of immorality and a real thing of beauty. It evened out the score and hit 'em where it really hurt 'em – in their pocketbooks. The offending swine wouldn't know, until it was too late, what hit 'em. Or who. And the best part was, by the time they realized they had been had, we would be history – out of town – gone like a cool breeze. Long gone daddies that had gotten even. And I got even with that Western Wormhouse.

Unfortunately I am not able at this time, under the advice of my attorney, to elaborate further on the specifics of my great equalizer. But rest assured that ol' Lightnin' came out on top in the "Great Virginia Steakhouse Massacre" and perhaps in a future Lowdown, when the statute of limitations for counterfeiting has run out, I'll tell you all about it.

More about Marvin in Episode Three, but now let's move on to...

<u>Episode Two</u>
a sophomoric little offering called:

"You're Just Steakin' And No Givin'"
or
"If It Feels Good, Blue It"

Once upon a time and twice within this trilogy, our story revolves around a restaurant. A bad restaurant. As in Episode One, the plot involves a bad Virginia restaurant and an Upsetter unable or unwilling to make the proper choices in life. Also as in Episode One, our story costars a slightly flighty-headed waitress. Well, more than slightly. Thoroughly. Intensely. And maybe flighty is too kind. How about cuckoo? Or cracked? Wacked? Bone-headed. Thoughtless. Asinine. Madcap. Goofy. Half-baked. Dixie-fried. In the dark. Elevator doesn't go all the way to the top floor. Screwed-up. Loony. Bats in the belfry. Bent. Gone. Real gone. Way out there. Sorry folks, I got a little carried away there with Microsoft Word's synonym feature.

And that just begins to describe the acumen (or lack thereof) of my poor bass player, Kevin, who ordered the Steak Special at Waffle House early one morning. By the way, Kevin, if you're reading this, 'acumen' is not the white of an egg.

Kevin (not his real name, but darn close) was a real trip. He was the bass player in the January 2006 Lowdown *Photographs and Memories* [see #2 (no pun intended) on the Top Ten list] who nagged me for years to book some gigs in Florida. Then when I booked us some real sweet gigs in – you guessed it, friends – in *Florida*, Kevin immediately snapped at me,

"I can't go to Florida, *Charlie*...I'll have to buy *food!*"

This has become one of my all-time favorite lines and I repeat it often, especially when someone asks me what it's like to make a living as a bandleader. Sorry for repeating it here.

Kevin breezed through life, constantly depending on (and usually demanding) the kindness and blind benevolence of others for his survival. Kevin didn't have a place of his own – he was living on the "sofa circuit" (a term musicians use for being homeless) – crashing wherever he could – with friends, family, freshly-picked females, etc. And Kevin's biggest fault was his belief that nothing about his circumstances was ever Kevin's fault. My pet peeve with Kevin was the way that he would always put the proper noun, *"Charlie"* at the end of any sentence that was a complaint.

"I can't go to Florida, *Charlie!*"

or

"How am I gonna get home from the gig, *Charlie?*"

or how about

"My stage clothes look like I've slept in them because I *slept in them*...I don't have a house with a washing machine, *Charlie!*"

The first couple of years Kevin was with me, I thought he was ending all of these whiny decrees, not with the proper noun, *"Charlie"*, but with the noun, "Charity". You know, generosity toward the poor (pronounced in Kevin-ese as *"Char - tee"*, as in *"char*-broiled"). Kevin's constant moans like,

"You've *got* to drive me home – I don't have a car, *Char-ity!*"

or the plaintive plea,

"Introduce me to that chick, *Char-ity!*"

or his worn-out wail for a lift,

"Come on, it's just thirteen miles to my Grandma's house, *Char-ity!*"

These weepings all sounded (at first) like he was begging for charity, not demanding his due. But I soon learned better, that I personally owed these things to Kevin.

Whether Kevin was asking for a 3 AM ride over the mountain to Grandma's house or a large monetary loan, he always was tactless, and completely devoid of charm. He made his requests for favors sound like edicts from on high. He *demanded* things of you because you *owed* it to him.

"I can't pay you the money I owe you - I don't have a job, *Charlie!*"

Kevin has the distinction of being the most pompous pauper that I have ever known. But it must be said here that we were *all* very young and very dumb in those days, myself included. And, thank God, Kevin and the rest of the slobs mentioned in the Lowdown, myself especially, have matured (to some extent) and become semi-responsible adults today. Most of us, anyway. And the fact that I now possess this wealth of memories and a lifetime's worth of great anecdotes is due to the fact that I wasn't traveling with Rhodes Scholars - I was traveling with musicians.

STUPID IS AS STUPID DOES

You all know Forrest Gump's famous line, "stupid is as stupid does". Well, here's a practical example. One night, driving back from some gigs in Virginia, we were traveling southbound on Interstate 81, when everyone agreed that it was time to stop and get some chow. If you have ever motored south on I-81 through Virginia, you're aware of the many Waffle Houses scattered (and smothered) across the Commonwealth. You are probably also aware of their specialty-of-the-house (if you can read their sign) - it's waffles. Plain old waffles. Not Braised Portobello Mushrooms in a Caper Mayonnaise Roulade. That's the point of this episode - live within your means. Watch what Kevin orders at Waffle House, and watch what it gets him. Stupid is as stupid does. And if Kevin is reading this, I sure hope he's forgotten that Ju-Jitsu stranglehold!

The minimum-wage crew working at these late night, little snack shacks usually consists of longhaired fugitives with multiple outstanding arrest warrants and recent parolees on work release. I've seen lots of Waffle House workers wearing ankle bracelets. That doesn't mean that the food isn't good or the service is bad or that the cooks can't cook. I'm simply saying: don't order something that's over their head. Or yours. Waffles, scrambled eggs, BLT's. As in life, shoot for things within range, and things won't get too messed up. Stupid is as stupid does.

FREE ADVICE ON LIFE, THE ROAD,
AND EATING AT WAFFLE HOUSES

Generally speaking, if you're driving long distances and putting on the feedbag at a Waffle House or any other "greasy spoon", breakfast items are the best bets. Take it easy - make the safe bet. You don't want to drive back onto the Interstate and suffer violent amoebic dysentery at 70 mph from eating the Kung Pao Pork.

If, while ordering at Waffle House, the spirit hits you, and you get the *urge to splurge*, you know…you're feelin' a little froggy and in the mood for some culinary exotica, try a slice of American cheese whipped up in your scrambled eggs or hash browns.

But for God's sake, stick to the program, Sam. I don't recommend ordering the Shrimp Cocktail or the Raw Oysters with Goat Cheese or the Sardinian Lamb Kabobs over Couscous from any restaurant that has a jukebox or has chili on the menu. All over it. I realize this lifestyle I'm espousing – playing it cool and close-to-the-vest is a very conservative ideal, but most liberals, just like Kevin, are shooting the works with other people's money.

ENTER THE AWFUL HOUSE AND ENTER THE DRAGON

The Upsetters entered Waffle House and, after Charlie had gone to the men's room to wash his hands [see Episode One], the waitress was poised and ready to take their order.

Now, I'm not an elitist or a germophobe, but I feel that anyone working with food, and with the public, (even at a Waffle House) should at least give the *impression* of cleanliness. That being said, let me describe the dragon, our Waffle House waitress. The first thing that struck me was the smell. She reeked of smoke (cigarettes of both the legal and illegal variety). Then I looked up to see her filthy fingers, putting our silverware down on the table holding the wrong end of the cutlery (the tines of the fork, the bowl of the spoon, the blade of the knife). Perfect, a stoned, greasy hag with long, filthy fingernails handling the business end of my spoon. And I mean really filthy fingers. I'm talkin' black muck at a Jiffy Lube level, corrupted to the quick, with the obligatory jailhouse tattoos all over her hands, wrists, and arms (and God knows where else).

As my eyes, wounded but unable to turn away, moved on up a little higher, I noticed something else – the name her cruel parents had cursed her with. I realized that this wasn't her fault though, as I read the name printed on her soiled nametag: "Froda". *Froda?* What was that, a female hobbit? I dare you to try to make this up.

Then, mine eyes would see the glory of the coming of the coup-de-grace: yes friends… no teeth. Froda was toothless – top and bottom. A gummy bear. I won't comment on her face because Froda's face, like Froda's name, was not Froda's fault. She was born with it. And her face didn't affect my health or my healthy appetite the way Froda's many other sins did.

As Froda went around the table, taking our order, my drummer was first. "I'll have three scrambled eggs with hash browns, smothered and covered. And orange juice." Okay fine. Our roadie was next. "I'll have two BLT's on white.

And a coke." Beautiful. Now my turn, "Just black coffee, thanks" (I didn't want cream or sugar, because I couldn't use my spoon). Although I was famished, I figured that someone had to be physically able to drive us home – or to the hospital, if things suddenly got ugly (uglier). Anyway, I reckoned coffee to be relatively safe because of its temperature – Waffle House coffee is always piping-hot. Nothing could live in boiling coffee, *could it?* Surely not. And the name's not Shirley, it's Froda.

Now it was up to Kevin. Kevin had apparently slept at someone's house recently where they watched a lot of Food Network and cooking shows on TV. Completely alive in his arrogance, he sermonized to the waitress/felon:

> "I see tenderloin steak on the menu. As I am very strict about eating only Angus beef from grain-fed Angus beef cows, and I only eat bone-in steaks that come from the short loin section of the animal, I need to know if your tenderloin comes from the strip loin section, which is more flavorful, or from the tenderloin section, which is more tender. Go ask the Chef *(the Chef?)* if the cut is a Porterhouse or a T-bone? Porterhouse steaks have more tenderloin and T-bones have a larger strip loin section, and I'll need to know which cut you serve before I make my decision."

This was Kevin's all-time longest string of consecutive sentences that didn't have a "Charlie" before the period.

Froda's retort was priceless and to the point:

"Whuuuutttt?"

Well, we fell out laughing. Everyone thought it to be a hilarious exchange except for the two principals, namely Kevin and Froda. Kevin tried again, sullenly summing it up this time,

"Just find out what kind of tenderloin it is."

Froda turned and sauntered across the room to the pony-tailed cook, whose full attention we now had as a result of our loud guffawing. Froda spoke to him briefly, and he answered her even more briefly, by gruffly shaking his head and muttering something at her. Froda then shuffled back to our table. With her hand on her hip and looking at the wall, she said,

"It's tenderloin steak."

Froda seemed to be well-schooled in the ancient art of circular argument.

"Okay, I'll try it," his homeless majesty replied, dejectedly, "but just make sure it's cooked rare."

When Froda returned with our food, *their* food that is, we were all naturally curious about the state of Kevin's steak. He immediately cut into it to see if it was cooked properly, and what we saw took our breath away. For out of Kevin's tenderloin, and onto his plate, came gushing forth a dark blue liquid. A gush that slowed to a gurgle and then stopped. Like opening a vein.

Being rendered momentarily speechless, we stared dumbly into his plate, with the strip loin or the short loin or whatever it was lying there like an ancient pagan sacrifice gone very wrong. It was then, as I was mesmerized and transfixed by this horror, that I first became aware of the Waffle House logo that runs around the inside edge of their plates and coffee cups. I had eaten off of those plates more times than I can (or want to) remember, yet I had never really *seen* what their logo looked like. I realized in bewilderment (now that time was standing still), that the letters that spell out "WAFFLE HOUSE" are of the type, or font style, that are supposed to look creepy or scary. It's the same style calligraphy used on old monster movie posters. Every time I see Bela Lugosi's name in print, it's in those letters. All caps and all squiggly. Do you remember the kid's toy, "Creepy Crawlers"? It had a little heat chamber or mini-microwave that you put these little clods of colored plastic into. Then you'd pretend to be Dr. Frankenstein Jr. and when you took the plastic out, *PRESTO!* They had been transformed into spiders and snakes. Remember that toy? Well, the letters "CREEPY CRAWLERS" were exactly the same as the letters "WAFFLE HOUSE".

The words "WAFFLE HOUSE" on Kevin's plate were plenty creepy-looking to us now. It was 4:30 AM, we're in the middle of nowhere, we're all alone in a diner, our only company a probable serial-killer cook and a witch-hag waitress named Froda (who made Margaret Hamilton, the actress who played the Wicked Witch of the West in The Wizard Of Oz, look like Grace Kelly), watching some mysterious, viscous, dark-blue fluid ooze and swirl around Kevin's unclean meat.

I don't know how long that moment lasted in real-time. It seemed to me that time just hung there, suspended, until the spooky spell was broken by Kevin, who let out a loud yelp, and, pushing himself away from the table in abject horror, cried out,

"Hey! What is this?"

Froda was in no rush coming over to see what the fuss was all about, and when Kevin showed her his blue steak, she simply dismissed it, drawling,

"*Aw, honey*, that's just blue food coloring they use to stamp the grade on the side of the steaks. You know, USDA or *whutever.*"

Whatever indeed. Now comes the most unbelievable part of the story for me – that Froda's weak explanation seemed to satisfy Kevin completely. Apparently the episode Kevin had seen on the Food Network didn't mention anything about blue steak, so having nothing to base an opinion on, he just took Froda at her word. And dug in.

We watched Kevin's every bite go from his fork into his mouth. It wouldn't have done any good trying to talk him out of eating a blue steak from Waffle House, either ("It's just ink from the USDA stamp, *Charlie*"). Nor would it have done any good to reveal to Kevin the main fallacy with Froda's conclusion: that a blue stamp on the edge of the steak would not flow from the *inside*.

Kevin finished, leaving only some fat, gristle, and blue drippings as evidence, and leaned back in the booth with a sated, proud, glassy look in his eyes. Remember that Kevin was proud of everything that Kevin did. So it was that Kevin had a supercilious look (look it up, baby!) about him even after eating a blue steak.

Let's pause here long enough for me to let you know where we are in the story. Kevin has just eaten a blue steak and is even more glassy-eyed than usual. Now let me tell you where we are, geographically speaking. Pay close attention, because I assure you, this is not a digression.

Founded in 1790, Wytheville, Virginia is nestled quietly in the southeastern edge of the Blue Ridge Mountains, 80 miles southwest of Roanoke, Virginia, and 120 miles south of Charleston, West Virginia. Wytheville, along with having beautiful landscapes and mountain vistas, happens to be a long way from nowhere and pretty much "in the sticks". There wouldn't be, say, a *doctor of forensic medicine* for example, for hundreds of miles. This wayward Waffle House, in Wytheville, where my bassist has just eaten (and enjoyed) unnatural meat, is so far out in the country that air has to be shipped in.

It behooves me, at this point, not to digress further, but to give you a quick (and very relevant to our story) history lesson on Wytheville, Virginia. Wytheville was named after a true Renaissance man, George Wythe, who was Thomas Jefferson's lifelong friend and childhood mentor until Wythe met with a tragic and violent death.

"No man ever left behind him a character more venerated than George Wythe," Thomas Jefferson wrote. "His virtue was of the purest tint."

Tint? As in *blue tint?* See how this applies to our story? Just you wait...

George Wythe's signature is first among the Virginia signatures on the Declaration of Independence. He was so highly respected by his fellow Virginians that the other delegates left a space so that his signature would appear first, as he was absent from the meeting the day they signed the document.

Jefferson learned the law from Wythe, and, in a manner of speaking, Wythe's signature on the Declaration was the teacher's endorsement of his pupil's finest brief.

If Wythe had accomplished nothing more than signing the Declaration of Independence and teaching Thomas Jefferson, he would have earned a place in history, but his life was crowded with achievement. Wythe was Virginia's foremost classical scholar, dean of its lawyers, a Williamsburg alderman and mayor, a member of the House of Burgesses, and House Clerk. He was the colony's attorney general, a delegate to the Continental Congress, speaker of the state assembly, the nation's first college law professor, founder and president of the Waffle House restaurant chain *(not really – just checking to see if you're still there!)*, Virginia's chancellor, and a framer of the federal Constitution.

Thanks for staying with me; here's where it gets good. Near the end of his life, Wythe wrote his will in favor of a grandnephew, George Wythe Sweeney, but also gave generous bequests to his former slaves Matthew Brown and Lydia Broadnax. A ne'er-do-well, nephew Sweeney forged checks against Wythe's accounts to cover unpaid debts ("I can't pay the people I owe, I'm a ne'er-do-well, *Charlie!*").

Hoping to avoid detection and inherit his great uncle's entire estate, Sweeney then resorted to murder. He conspired to murder his great uncle by poisoning him. And, are you ready for this? Strawberries or coffee *(COFFEE?!?)* were the vehicle by which Sweeney poisoned both his great uncle, George Wythe, and the former slave, Matthew Brown. Brown died quickly, but Wythe endured two weeks of agony. But as he lay dying, Sweeney's forgeries were discovered, and Wythe quickly revised his will – removing his murderer.

A grand jury indicted Sweeney for murder. But all the evidence against him was circumstantial. No witness was able to testify in court that he saw Sweeney poison the food. There was a witness, but she was the wrong color. Even though Lydia Broadnax said she was in Wythe's kitchen and saw Sweeney with the poison, she was not allowed, as a black woman, to testify against a white man. So Sweeney the murderer was released, albeit without the fortune that he murdered for.

Okay, let's cut back to a bright orange booth in 20th century Wytheville, where ne'er-do-well Kevin is sitting with a bellyful of blue meat. I am sitting across from him, my stomach nervously boiling with black coffee, and considering irony itself. I wonder if George Wythe thought he was being "safe" when he had ordered his strawberries and coffee? I wonder if Sweeney had any progeny, like any toothless great granddaughters with filthy paws? I wonder what the odds were on us getting poisoned in a town named after a guy who was poisoned? And why was I the only guy that ordered coffee? Oh poor me, poor me (just don't pour me any more coffee!)

Froda finally made her way back to our table and, while clearing the plates, had a very unusual thing to say. Typically, a waiter or waitress might say, as they clear the table of plates, "Was everything alright?" or "May I get you anything else?" But that weird morning in Wytheville was anything but typical. Froda appeared shocked at seeing an empty plate where there once was a blue steak, and staring straight at Kevin, with her voice full of concern, said...

"Honey, are you *feelin' alright???*"

One word, and one word only, immediately ran through my mind: *"Whuuuutttt???"* Kevin sat bolt upright, eyed fully dilated, and wailed,

"What do you mean, am I *feelin' alright?*"
"Well," replied Froda, "you *ate that steak!*"
Kevin howled, *"But you said it was just food coloring!"*

Froda here had no rebuttal. What could she say? Her bluff had been called. Kevin, now taking the lead and doing what he does best, became the crass commander:

"I *DEMAND* to know the designation of this Waffle House, so if I take sick and die, my lawyers will know who to *SUE!*"

Froda's slurred and gummed, three-word response, mumbled from a toothless craw in a greasy spoon in Wytheville, Virginia, will forever be burned in my memory.

"The Wiffle Waffle"

was all she said. And that really says it all.

Episode Three

"S Is More Than I Can Stand"
or
"Happy Entrails To You, Until We Meet Again"

This third and final episode of this trilogy is a story about sound check. After a band sets up all of their equipment, and before they begin their show, there is a crucial portion of the process called the "sound check". I think most of you already know what that is, but I'm not sure if most of you realize just how very important it is – in more ways than the obvious one.

The primary purpose of the sound check is to make sure all the amplifiers and the sound system are working properly, then to get the instruments and vocals mixed together well, and then to "dial in" or tweak the EQ to the particular room so that everything *sounds* good. The real difficulty in dialing in a PA system is due to the fact that every room is different – your settings from the night before are liable to squeal like a pig the next night.

There is always, in my experience, a moment of holding-of-one's-breath while turning on the PA system (public address system) for the sound check, because if the PA doesn't come on when you turn it on, you're in trouble. Typically, guitars and basses use their own amps, and the vocals and any instrument mics are run through the PA. So, if the band is all set up and their amps for their instruments are working, then it's time to check the PA. A band without a working PA would be forced to play instrumentals all night, because there would be nothing to sing through. This would not be good for business, and when you're far from home (and any spare pieces or parts), the whole gig rides on the PA coming on and working when you flip the switch. That's why I wait with baited breath every time I turn that baby on.

Regular readers of the Lowdown will realize also, that it was routine for the Upsetters, and more specifically, Lightnin' Charlie, to have to jump through a host of hoops just to get everyone together and to the gig. Some examples of the happy hoops I would habitually encounter, *prior to arriving* at work, would be:

Upsetter – sick
Upsetter – lost
Upsetter – drunk (is this redundant?)
Upsetter – jailed
Upsetter – refusing to go to work ("I can't go to Florida, *Charlie*...I'll have to buy *food!*")
Upsetter – upset and quitting (redundant, yes, but nonetheless, the norm)
Upsetter – vehicle breakdown, police roadblocks [see Upsetter – drunk, jailed, etc.]

The list of obstacles, personal and circumstantial, to any road band simply *making it to a gig* is staggering. Factor in the sleep deprivation, the fights, the drunks; the lack of a decent wage, the terrible food [see Episodes One and Two], and it's likewise no small wonder that the shows played are ever *any good*.

In my twenty-three year career, I've played approximately 3600 shows, and I'm proud of the fact that I've only had to cancel five or six. This is an amazing tribute to my health, my commitment, my perseverance, my diplomacy ("I can't go to

Florida, *Charlie*...I'll have to buy *food!"),* and, most of all, the amazing grace of almighty God. It is also a reflection of why my head is so bald.

The nature of the public, being so fickle and so quick to embrace the dark side, can be evidenced by the example of "No-Show Jones". Country music legend George Jones, over a span of fifty years, has probably performed 10,000 concerts. But as soon as he cancels four or five, he's "No-Show Jones". Nobody remembers the other 9,995. If you think nobody is paying attention to you, make a mistake. And if you think nobody cares if you're alive or dead, try missing a couple of car payments.

Once the band is all present and accounted for, all set up on stage and ready to go, that's when the sound check begins. And due to the aforementioned list of troubles, sound check is often late. Ideally, sound check should be finished before the audience arrives. But, like the well-laid plans of mice and men, it doesn't always work out that way. One of the ramifications of sound checking in front of the audience is obvious - it's annoying (at best) and a nuisance, and it can sound from bad to painfully bad. An audience doesn't want to hear, "Check. Check. Check one, check two", etc. upon arriving at a nightclub. And they definitely don't want to hear a sound system sharply and agonizingly feeding back - that's torture. The other effect of sound checking in front of the audience, *your* audience - the same folks that you are about to perform the show for, is a little less obvious but much more detrimental. And that has to do with the natural law of first impression. Let an audience in to see Sinatra setting up a PA system, sweating like a hog on Sunday (pick any two items from the aforementioned list of obstacles), crawling around onstage on all fours, running speaker and mic cables, then squealing *"check, check"* into a microphone that's roaring and screeching. That impression is going to remain with them for the rest of the night, and even more disastrous to the artist, for the rest of their lives [see George Jones above]. No matter how good you sound a half-hour later, the audience is going to remember that first, awful-sounding, ugly impression for as long as they live. And if they should happen to temporarily forget it, the latent memory of it will immediately be conjured up at any mention of the artist's name *("Lightnin' Charlie?* Man, I saw him in concert years ago, and he was *terrible...").*

In situations where I am forced to sound check in front of my audience, I never say the word "check". I'll say *"shoop-shoop"* or *"chantilly"* or *"sufferin' succotash"* - anything to distract them from the irritating nature of what I'm doing. When checking a vocal mic, it's important to use words with "S's" (that's the plural of "S") to check the treble or high end. If the treble is too hot, you'll know it when you say sibilant things like *"send me some"* or *"superfly".* Likewise, to check the low end and midrange on a PA, you should use words with hard consonants that pop, like "P's" and "B's" *("Ping-pong"* and *"Papa"* work well). If the PA pops or rings on these words, the lows and/or mids are too hot.

Once the mic is on and sounding halfway decent (not feeding back, not "underwater-sounding", etc.), then, rather than continuing to yelp monosyllabically like an imbecile, I'll sing a little something. I always try to sing something silly, in the hope that a little levity will offset the poor fidelity of the sound. A little devil-may-care attitude goes a long way in these situations. I'll never sing more than a verse or two of a song either. It's imperative that the audience realizes that this is not *the show*. The only benefit to robotically saying, *"check one, check one"* over and over is that, at least the audience will realize that it's a *sound check*.

One thing I've learned over the course of 3600 shows is to never underestimate the intelligence of an audience. Another (much more important) thing I've learned is to never, ever *overestimate* the intelligence of an audience. Take nothing for granted. You might announce,

> *"Sorry we're running a little late, folks, our bass player was in the hospital getting his stomach pumped, so I apologize for having to check this microphone..."*

But someone might come in after your explanation and during your fingernails-down-a-blackboard sound check, and just hate you. Don't assume they understand English. You've got to cover all the bases all the time when you're in the spotlight. You have to be all things to all people. And if you're not, they'll remember forever.

Let's drop in on a typical sound check (late) with the Upsetters and Lightnin' Charlie. This particular sound check was significant because of how our bass player Marvin [see Episode One] decided to check his microphone in a biker bar.

Brother Marvin was an intellectual (an intellectual is a person who can hear the William Tell Overture and not think of the Lone Ranger). Aside from dumbly denying himself nearly all of the smallest comforts and simplest joys in life, Marvin was a very smart guy. The problem with Marvin and his intelligence, as with so many educated fools, was twofold. For one thing, Marvin didn't possess one ounce of "street smarts" and for another thing, Marvin always made sure that everyone around him was aware of his infinite depth and perspicacity (look it up!). Of these two issues, the former affected the band more adversely than the latter – Marvin would often get himself into situations that he couldn't get himself out of, without more than a little help from us. The latter of these two issues was irritating, and could also lead to trouble, when Marvin was left in a one-on-one situation (which I tried hard to avoid). This occasion turned out to be a very dangerous (but very funny) combination of the two.

We were set up and sound checking in what was a fairly rough joint. One night, a guy was stabbed to death right in front of the stage, on the dance floor. The police made a chalk outline of the body where it fell. The powers-that-be at this club apparently thought the incident funny or good advertising or both, because when we arrived to play a show the weekend after the murder, they had made a masking tape outline over the temporary chalk outline. They wanted to preserve the memory of the corpse for their own enjoyment. It's probably still there. That's the type of place it was. Frequented by a lot of rowdy bikers, ex-cons, trouble-making females, and once and future murderers, (redundant-a-plenty), it was far from my favorite place to play. And the feeling was definitely mutual. Lightnin' Charlie and the Upsetters was not their favorite band. After all, we didn't play Seger OR Skynyrd.

Since Marvin sang some background vocals on a couple tunes, we usually set up a vocal mic for him. Marvin wasn't a singer, but he helped out a little on tunes like *Got My Mojo Workin'* and *Bo Diddley* for example. These songs were call-and-response things where the band just repeats back what the singer says – no big deal – you don't have to be a great singer to just repeat after me: *"Got my mojo workin'!"* or *"Hey Bo Diddley!"*. Even audiences (after enough booze) can do it. Anyway, I had enough trouble already without trying to make Marvin a singer.

[Ed note: Remember folks, as you read the following, it's imperative for you to keep in mind the physical description I gave of Marvin in Episode One. Try to picture the Phantom Of The Opera's stunt double playing a Jazz bass in a biker bar.]

On this particular night, we were running late and just needed to make sure everything was up and working and we'd dial it in on-the-fly – it was already past showtime, and it wasn't a good time (or place) to fool around. All eyes were upon us. And in this audience, "all eyes" was an odd number.

We had checked everything but Marvin's vocal mic (it being almost a non-entity with Marvin only having to say a couple words on a couple songs), so just before we started the show, I called across the stage to Marvin, almost as an afterthought, with the directive to "Check your mic".

Marvin stepped up to the mic and said, loud and proud,

"Sibilance, si-bi-lance. Yeah...sibilance, SSSSSIBILANCCCCE. YEAH!"

I was on the other side of the stage nervously crouched over the mixing board. When I heard this, my head jerked around toward Marvin, and then at the audience. It was then that I knew – we were going to die here. Everybody in the place was staring a hole, figuratively, in Marvin and was making plans to put a hole, literally, in him, too. I hissed across the stage at Marvin through clenched teeth,

"*What are you DOING?*"

Marvin looked back at me, unalarmed and unaware that he had probably just signed all of our death warrants, and said, not on-mic, "I'm checking my mic..." and turning back on-mic bellowed again,

"*Ssssiii-bi-lanccccceeee!*"

A low humming was now coming from the audience, which sounded like a bunch of tattooed and angry hornets. I glared at him and seethed,

"*What???*"

Marvin turned again toward me and, in his most professorial manner, exulted,

"Sibilance, it's a word that means a hissing sound or..."

"I KNOW what it means", I raged, "Why are you saying it?"

"To check the high end", spoke Professor Marvin to his pupil, "if you want to check the treble, you should always use words with a lot of S's."

"If you wanna check treble", I shot back, "*say chitlins!*"

Marvin obediently turned back on-mic and slowly enunciated (in his Marvin-esque way that made everything he said sound like the ding-dong of a doorbell) the four syllables that probably saved our life that night,

"*Chit-lins...Chit-lins.*"

The audience, now thinking that this was a joke and all part of the show, let out an instantaneous and uproarious peal of laughter – the kind of laughter that Martin and Lewis used to get in the clubs in the '50s – people turning tables over kind of laughter. It was like the scene in *The Producers*, when the angry audience realizes, incorrectly, that *Springtime For Hitler* is a comedy.

Deciding not to kill us, and even coming around to digging our music (a little), they really were plumb crazy about Marvin from that moment on. He'd gone from chump to champ in just four syllables.

A few weeks later, when we returned to do another show, we realized the extent of their newfound love for us and especially Marvin, when we saw our name up in lights on their marquee...

TONIGHT
LIGHTNIN' CHARLIE AND THE CHITLINS

From then on, whenever Marvin checked his mic, he would confidently coo,

"Chit-lins!...Chit-lins!...YEAH! Chit-lins!!!"

It became a kind of catch phrase for Marvin. I saw the "double dose of chitlins" (as I called it) really give Marvin a boost socially. Pretty women would come up to him at shows and ask him to say it for them. I kid you not. And Marvin ate it up. Since Marvin was a guy who hadn't gotten very many breaks in life, it was great to see him catch a small one.

THE END

Hope you Lightnin' Bugs enjoyed this tremendous trilogy of terror. Come see us.

Lovingly,
Charlie

Postscript

Marvin passed away in July 1998.

Marvin had left the Upsetters in 1988 to take a job with a large software firm as a computer programmer. Marvin had been on an exercise kick for a couple years and, every day after work, rain or shine, Marvin rode his bicycle.

One brutally hot July afternoon, while bike riding, Marvin suffered a massive coronary. He died in the hospital early the next morning. He was 47 years old.

We shared much good music, good times and had a lot of laughs together. I only wish that I had bought him an ice-cold coke every single time he wanted one.

SEPTEMBER 2006

16

BUCKETS, BROOMSTICKS, AND BULLHORNS

Hello, my dear Storm Chasers and Lightnin' Bugs! Welcome to this September installment of the Lightnin' Lowdown – a monthly narrative so silly that only you would be wasting time reading it. For newcomers, the Lowdown is a kind of comic book – set in rock 'n' roll hyperspace – that documents the extraordinary exploits of our hero, Lightnin' Man. Although Lightnin' Man possesses no super-powers (other than attracting fiasco and mayhem everywhere he goes), he does have the ability to somehow survive these scrapes, and the audacity to proudly retell them here in the Lowdown. Mild-mannered Charlie by day, when night falls (or trouble calls), that's when Charlie dons his trusty hat and guitar – he never uses a cape – and becomes the psycho-magnet, semi-super hero we know and love as Lightnin' Charlie.

For this month's escapade, let's travel down memory lane to Destin, Florida, where our hero and his beautiful bride are honeymooning in the golden sunshine and white sands of the Gulf Coast. Charlie and Beth are typical newlyweds – taking hedonistic pleasure in loving, laughing, lying in the sun, and most of all, rejoicing in the eternal mystery of being newlyweds and SO IN LOVE.

The honeymooners were out for a late lunch one rainy afternoon, celebrating another special occasion – Charlie's thirty-fifth birthday. Always one to try and combine opportunities for gifts, compliments, and personal accolades, Charlie's birthday falls five days after his wedding anniversary (Beth's birthday is the week after his). Our hero is a bit of a glutton when it comes to adulation and attention. On this gray day in March, Beth and Charlie were dining at a famous local eatery known for its stone crabs. Everything about this restaurant was large-scale. Its dining room was humongous, as large as an airport. Its portions ridiculous – they served their crab legs in a large metal bucket. Most of their patrons were biggie-sized too, being regular customers and obviously accustomed to slurping down buckets full of crab and bowls full of melted butter. After a wonderfully delicious, but perversely massive, meal of crab legs, Charlie excused himself and went to the men's room to, well...to bathe, basically. After a meal of this magnitude, one is covered, lip to lap, with melted butter, bits of crab (meat and shell), and is in dire need of a washroom. Newlywed Charlie, still full of all the aforementioned joys (and as anyone who knows him personally or professionally will surely attest – full of other things as well), was now fully gorged and thick as a tick. Lightnin' lumbered off to use the facilities, partially expecting to see a sign on the restroom door saying *"Vomitorium"* – not *"Men's"* – and find it complete with fresh togas and a trough. It was while Charlie was freshening up that Beth went to work setting him up.

While her clueless hubby was in the men's room, Bethlehem was alerting their waiter that the buttery, bald man with her was not only a celebrity, but that they were celebrating his thirty-fifth birthday. Beth asked if they "did anything for birthdays", apparently hoping for some free ice cream to follow the buckets of crab and butter. Many of you are now thinking along one of two lines, both logical but incorrect. Firstly, that Lightnin' must've married some kind of fat pig to want free dessert after that kind of gross gluttony. For your information, Beth weighed 105 pounds then and 120 pounds now, nine years and two kids later, and could hardly be classified as a fat pig. Secondly, that Beth must've been a world-class gold-digger and black widow – trying to murder her older husband with food, thereby inheriting his rock star estate and collecting on his huge life insurance policies. If one wasn't aware of the abject poverty that was Lightnin' Charlie circa 1997, with no life insurance and no estate, one might be misled into thinking one of these or the other was her motive. The fact was that Beth was just being Beth, innocently trying to do something to surprise the old man on his birthday. And free ice cream was about all they could afford. The waiter asked Beth for the birthday boy's first name (ignoring the fact of his celebrity status), and casually walked away.

When Charlie returned to the table, his chin and chest considerably cleaner, but still so full of his heavy lunch that he could hardly breathe, *"Check",* was all he could manage to grunt to the waiter, who was standing by their table. What Charlie would have noticed, had he been able to see straight, was the bullhorn and broom the waiter held by his sides. As Charlie, his britches tighter than the nuts on the Brooklyn Bridge, tried to get his eyes to focus on what was happening, the waiter raised the electric bullhorn to his lips and announced to the dining room (airplane hangar),

"LADIEEEES AND GENTLEMEN, YOUR ATTENTION PLEASE! WE HAVE A BIRTHDAY BOY OVER HERE!!!"

The bullhorn was the type the police use in hostage situations, and his voice had that big, metallic quality of a SWAT team sergeant. Charlie, still trying to focus, stood halfway up and gave the "little wave" to the crowd of uninterested eaters and sat back down, happy as always to be recognized, but unable at the moment to stand up straight.

"OH NO, CHARLIE...WE'RE NOT THROUGH WITH YOU YET!"

The cruel waiter continued,

"AS ALL BIRTHDAY BOYS MUST DO HERE AT MOE'S CRAB SHACK...

(not the restaurant's real name, but very close)

...YOU'VE GOT TO STRADDLE THIS HERE BROOM...AND RIDE IT LIKE A HORSE...ALL AROUND THE ROOM...AND DON'T FORGET TO WAVE TO ALL YOUR FRIENDS HERE CELEBRATING WITH YOU!"

Charlie (and Beth) looked up at him in horror.

"WHAT DO SAY, FOLKS? ARE YOU READY TO SEE CHARLIE-THE-BIRTHDAY-BOY RIDE AROUND OUR RANGE ON THIS HERE 'HORSEY'?"

So our hero, bristling a bit at the humiliation (which was the intention, no doubt), but rising spectacularly to the occasion, took the bull by the horns, so to speak. After all, I *am* in show business. Unable to disappoint the four or five people (out of 200) who lamely applauded, Lightnin' Man (incognito without his hat and guitar, now sporting a white shirt, flecked with bits of pink crab shell and spattered with yellow butter spots) bravely took the 'horsey' (broomstick) from the evil waiter, and with a hearty

"Hi-Yo Silver...AWAY!" off he rode.

So as Lightnin' trotted around this prodigious Ponderosa, huffing and puffing, waving idiotically at guests, and loudly neighing *"whinny"* for the 'horsey' and gamely adding *"giddy-ups"* and *"hy-aaas"* for effect, patrons seemed to be moved by the sheer spectacle of it all. What a sight this must've been to behold – a bald, bloated cowboy on a broom, in broad daylight, obviously on the verge of a massive butter-induced coronary (and/or in the midst of a severe mental breakdown), yee-haw-ing, yippee-yi-yay-ing, and galloping around the vast perimeter of a two-acre dining room where the strongest drink served is sweet tea.

Like so many marathon runners who dream of simply finishing the race, who reach and cross that mystical 'point-of-no-return' – the point of physical and spiritual exhaustion after which they claim to be in a sort of trance or out-of-body state, and are driven forward only by the dream of finishing, Charlie recalls that the only thing that kept him going after he had reached his 'point-of-no-return' (somewhere around the salad bar) was his new-found dream of becoming a newlywed widower. That is, if he didn't drop dead and make his newlywed wife a widow first. Charlie remembers swearing an oath (somewhere around the salad bar) that, if God would only spare his life, that just as soon as he got out of that restaurant/torture chamber and regained sufficient sight, strength, and stamina, he was surely going to kill Beth.

Lightnin' Charlie the Newlywed, by the grace of God, finished the entire, embarrassing run, and pulled his 'horsey' up to a halt at his table/stable with a grandiose gesture that was pure Lightnin' Charlie. An appropriate, albeit over-the-top *"WHOA BOY!"* signaled the end of Charlie's performance. The sadistic waiter was there, waiting for him. Taking the broom from the Lightnin' Man with a look of surprised awe mixed with utter and complete respect for the buttered birthday boy, he looked deeply into Charlie's glazed and bloodshot eyes and said worshipfully,

"Wow man, you're REALLY cool!
We've NEVER had anybody actually DO IT before!"

I am loathe to admit it, and may God forbid that one of Lightnin' Man's many enemies gets hold of this information, but to this day, our hero's bane is buckets, brooms, and bullhorns. This Man of Rock, Lightnin' Charlie, who's faster than a flying beer bottle and able to leap tall rednecks with a single bound, recoils from these harmless (?) household items like Superman from Kryptonite, and although Charlie is known to occasionally use a dust buster, you'll NEVER see him with a broom. Nor will you ever spot him around sandcastles or hostage negotiations.

Yes friends, even our heroes have their Achilles heels. Please don't think any less of Lightnin' Man for having his. He's only human. And he's out-of-here.

HI-YO and *AWAY!!!*
The Lone Lightnin' Man
(AKA Beth's loving husband Charlie)

OCTOBER 2006

17

A HORROR STORY

Look out, Lowdown fans of the musical macabre! This month, I'm commemorating a sick and twisted holiday (obviously invented by pediatric dentists and fake cobweb manufacturers), by telling a real-life Lightnin' Charlie horror story...

MEET! . . . a deranged eight-foot tall green monster
     with bolts in his neck!
WATCH! . . . his sickening self-destruction and
     heinous criminal larceny!

WHAT'S GOT LIGHTNIN' PRAYING TO DIE???

  READ ON . . . IF YOU DARE!!!

HEAR! . . . a ghastly tale with an
 UNBELIEVABLE CLIMAX OF TRUE HORROR . . .
  SO SHOCKING . . .
   YOU'LL BE GLAD . . .
   YOU'RE NOT LIGHTNIN' CHARLIE!!!

Lightnin' Charlie-O-Lantern

This month's Creature Feature enjoys lots of wailing and weeping, gnashing of teeth, and, of course, plenty of the usual Lightnin' Charlie rants, digressions, diatribes, and silly exaggerations. And the best thing is... it's all free for you. But the worst thing is... it's all true for me. Bon appetit!

Halloween used to be a great night for a bar band, especially if it fell on a weekend. Clubs would raise their cover charges, have costume contests with big cash prizes, book hot bands, and be packed with partiers. All this translated into a big payday for the band; generally, Halloween was the second-biggest paying one-nighter of the year, second only to New Year's Eve. But times have changed. At least they have for Lightnin' Charlie. I don't do Halloween no more (triple negative). Halloween will never be the same again. Halloween is forever soiled (future pun) for me. I can't watch Boris Karloff movies anymore, either. I can't have anything. You'll see. Here's a gruesome tale, offered for your approval, another rough trip down my memory lane.

Ten years ago, on a cold dark night... the Upsetters and Yours Truly were booked (for big bucks) at a local club for a Halloween show. I'll call the joint "Skipper's" (not it's real name, but kind of close – from the same goofy '60s "Island" TV show). Halloween happened to fall on a Saturday that year making the fat night even fatter. Our manager, Nat, an ex-funeral director, had even held out for more money when booking the gig because we knew that Skipper's wanted us to play their big Halloween shindig and we knew we would get it. Yeah, we got it all right...

The night started out badly. The first thing that I noticed as being way out of the ordinary was the club DJ was spinning records at *eyeball-busting* volume. When playing at this club previously, we were always told to keep our stage volume down because of a noise ordinance that was being enforced due to the club's close proximity to a residential neighborhood. The DJ's volume was likewise always monitored very closely. This Halloween night must've been an exception. The DJ was *so incredibly loud,* that I swear you could hear him from a mile away. We had to take our breaks in the parking lot because we just couldn't stand it – it was physically unbearable. Even from outside, it was making the fillings in my teeth hurt. Literally. I wondered why the boss (all of a sudden) didn't seem to care at all. And he was not only careless, but also participating. He was hanging out in the booth with the DJ, carryin' on and playing records. Bad ones. *Really* loud.

And now a word about the boss. The owner and manager of Skipper's was in his forties and a big, big man – six foot six, two hundred and seventy-five pounds, probably played pulling guard on his college football team. We'll call him "Will" (not his real name, but dreadfully close). As we were about to start our first set, Will was making his way up onstage to "introduce us". The problem with this was twofold. One, Will was in costume; an elaborate Frankenstein (that's *his* real name) monster costume. He had green makeup on his face and hands. He was wearing a big Frankenstein half-head that sat on top of his own head, attaching invisibly with makeup across the top of Will's brow, his head must've measured a grotesque two and a half feet from the bottom of Will's natural chin up to the flat, green, plastic top. This seemed to make Will dangerously top-heavy, too. He was sporting the obligatory bolts in the neck, and his pants and shirt – both way too small, were righteously torn and ratty. Then there was the gigantic, black Frankenstein shoes that had big, heavy lifts in the bottoms adding another eight or ten inches to the monster's height and making it very difficult for Will to walk.

That leads us to the other problem that was making walking (and introducing the band) very difficult for Will that night – Will the Frankenstein monster was stupid drunk. We found out later that he was an alcoholic who hadn't touched a drop for fifteen years and had fallen, fabulously, off the wagon that Halloween night. So here comes the drunken Willenstein monster, measuring a good eight-feet tall with the shoes and head, lumbering onstage to slurringly introduce the band.

"Laaadieeeessshh an gennlemen, guys and ghouls,
lemme have yer attenshun, pleassh (believe me – he had everyone's attention)
I would like to introdoushh my favrit ban,
Linin Sharlie an the Upshettersh!

Then Will raised his big, green fists over his head (friends, please try and visualize the huge, imposing figure the eight-foot tall Will-monster made on a five-foot high stage), closed his eyes, threw his head back, and screamed,

"NOW LET'S [BLEEP]-ING PAAAAARRRRTTTTYYYY!!!!"

The rest of the night was downhill from there – an absolute nightmare. Immediately upon finishing each of our three forty-five minute sets, we would bolt (there's a bad pun) for the backdoor as the DJ (also rip-roaring drunk) would start his brutal assault on the senses. I think my migraine started during his "Play That Funky Music, White Boy" sin, which was undoubtedly mistaken for ordinary turbulence by passenger jets flying over Bristol that night. Between the gross gig and the usual bickering with the guys in the band (I don't recall what specifics we were fighting about that night), I was getting a frontal lobe headache that would soon develop into a real humdinger.

I used to suffer routinely from these merciless migraine headaches, and they were *always* caused by stress. And always band or gig related. Since I don't allow bums in my band anymore and I refuse to play gigs that I know, going in, are going to be horrible...guess what? *PRESTO!!!* No more migraines. The guys in the Upsetters at that time were responsible for lots of migraines. Lots of nights and early mornings with Lightnin' lying in a dark room with ice-cold towels over his eyes. They were the group that I used to call "Lightnin' Charlie and the Hemorrhoids" because of the severe rear pains they were. But the agony was always reserved for my top, not my bottom. Every three or four gigs with those guys (the Hemorrhoids), I would get a migraine that felt like King Kong was pulling a barbed-wire slip-knot around my head at the temples and there was some little guy (probably my bass player) inside my skull, right behind my eyeballs, trying to knock them out of their sockets with a hammer and chisel. I always imagined it to be some kind of gremlin like the one destroying the engines on the wing of the plane in that Twilight Zone episode with William Shatner. You know the type – killing you and enjoying it. Anyone who suffers with these bad boys has my complete sympathy and is all too hip to the intense pain I'm talking about. Hip to the tip. When having one of these Hemorrhoid-induced migraines, this is what I would do when I got home:

1) Eat six maximum-strength Advils
2) Lie flat and completely still in a pitch-dark room
3) Place ice-cold towels over my eyes
4) Have total silence
5) Beg God for relief or death

Notice #2, 3, & 4 are very much like death's sweet repose. The whole scene was very death-like, except for the pain. Usually after three hours or so, I would finally throw up, take a cold shower, and go to bed feeling like I'd been run over by a long, slow-moving train. All the while, the Hemorrhoids were happily spending the cash I had paid them for doing this to me. Ah yes...those were the days.

Once back in bed, usually daylight by then, I would have a moment to reflect on the stress and the sources of stress that had put me in this place.

> *"Hey Charlie"*, my gremlin would whisper to me, *"You better get some sleep – you've got to be fresh for the next gig tomorrow!"*

Some musicians have monkeys on their backs. I had a gremlin in my skull. And Hemorrhoids for bandmates.

And the bed and the cold towels and the shower and the Advil – those were only available if I was lucky enough to be at home. The migraines I suffered out on the road are another story altogether. I've blocked most of them from my memory. Those terrible headaches are the closest (along with seasickness and food poisoning) that I ever came to slow death – dying a miserable, violent, painful death – in which I was so helpless and so sick, I'd be praying fervently for death to come. But here's some free advice for those who suffer, like I did, from crippling co-dependency and migraine headaches: Lose the losers and lose the migraines.

Let's digress further, shall we? As long time fans of the Upsetters and Lightnin' Charlie realize, the only band member that has remained constant through the years is Lightnin' Charlie himself. The many members of the Upsetters, spanning three decades, are too numerous to name. Often people (well-meaning fans) will ask me,

"What ever happened to so-and-so?"

I'll reply that they quit or got fired, went to prison or died, went back to being a plumber or an electrician, or a funeral director, or whatever. Some folks (lovely people) then get the mistaken impression that since the Upsetter-in-question is no longer with *me,* that *I* must be the problem; that *I* must be a hard case and impossible to work with. Still others (the most charming) will even say this to my face. When this happens, I'll ask them (the charmers) if they are married. They (being so lovely and charming) will invariably answer "no", that they are divorced (these delightful types are always divorced – if they treat people on the street this rudely, how did they treat their spouses?). Then I will ask if they were in love with their ex's when they got married. Even the dumbest of the dumb will answer, "yes" to this. I'll tell them how sorry (and surprised) I am that it didn't work out. Then I'll explain to them how I have lived with two or three other men (that I'm *not* in love with), eating, drinking, and sleeping with them, working and traveling with them, for better or worse (usually the latter), for richer or poorer (always the latter), in sickness and in health (my sickness – their health), for more years than they could stay married to someone that they were once madly in love with. This burst of logic always leaves the boorish barflies charmed and completely convinced (not about my irrefutable point of view, but that they were right to begin with – that I *was* impossible to be around!).

Though I've never been *in love* with any of my bandmates, there's some I've loved dearly. And still do. And over my twenty-three year career, I've had several guys who were with me for five, six, or seven-year stretches. And some who are no longer in my band are still my good friends. My 21st Century Upsetters, Joe Dean and Chris Carroll, have been with me for five years now, outlasting lots of marriages and millions of relationships. So there. Please tell Dr. Phil to quit calling. I'm all right. Clean up your own backyard. That is all. As you were. And now that I've gotten that off my chest, on with our story...

The costume contest was a big success, featuring some real lulus. A guy and girl dressed up as John and Jackie Kennedy with the back of JFK's head blown off from the gunshot wound and Jackie's dress covered with blood. Good taste, that.

There was a crew of four or five pregnant nuns. What does one call a bunch of nuns...a pack? A bevy? A throng, perhaps? I don't know, but they were cute. There were several Elvises, two Marilyns, a Richard Nixon, way too many demons, a matador and an Indian chief, and four guys dressed up like the rock band, K.I.S.S. Plenty of people turned out, dressed in outlandish and very extravagant costumes, due to the first prize of $2000 cash. I'll give you a minute to ponder that: two thousand dollars. That's not a typo. Two grand. Our Halloween "big bucks" turned out to be "chump change" compared to that. Once again, I'm in the wrong business.

All the contestants came onstage between our second and third sets to be judged by audience applause, and since the DJ wasn't killing us softly with his song, we stood side-stage to watch. The DJ (stands for "Drunk Jerk") introduced the contestants on microphone one by one. My personal fave was a beautiful Carmen Miranda look-alike, complete with giant fruit salad headdress and brightly colorful sundress, but when she came onstage to the microphone, Drunk Jerk was clueless as to who she was or why she had all that fruit on top of her head. He sneered at her like *she* was the idiot, and asked,

"What are *you* supposed to be?"

"Carmen Miranda", she said sweetly.

"What?" the waste of good organs replied, *"Miranda? You have the right to remain silent? Whatever!"*

This, and the dull throbbing behind my right eyeball, only served to make me love the DJ even more. He was a drunk, a sadist, *and* a moron. Terrific. See? Listening to the Village People on ten *does* rot your brain. If you have one to begin with, that is. You can't spend what you ain't got and you can't lose something you ain't never had.

Anyway, first prize went to a real class act called "The Insane Gynecologist". Dressed in scrubs splattered with fake blood, carrying a mangled plastic baby doll, a hunk of raw liver, and a bloody butcher knife, this young entrepreneur took home two large. In cash.

The Insane Gynecologist smartly took his money and ran, leaving Skipper's immediately. He probably split to avoid getting mugged and/or having to buy people drinks. More than likely, he was also hurrying off to another club's costume contest to win another couple grand. Who needs a college education? I'm *still* bitter about *that* guy, for reasons you'll soon see. I just don't like people smarter than me (I). Two thousand bucks for ten minutes work – no loading and unloading, no setting up equipment, no decades spent practicing and paying dues to play the blues, no fighting with stoned Hemorrhoids, and no migraines. The Insane Gynecologist? On the contrary. He was insane like a fox.

We finished our last set and I staggered offstage. I was going into labor now, in the full dilation of headache giving birth to migraine. The gremlin was pounding away at the back of my right eye and I knew I had to get out of there quick. I went straight to our manager, who was dressed like Elwood Blues from the Blues Brothers, but it was not a costume, and told him,

"Nat, get my stuff, get our money – I've *got* to go home."

And home I went. Thankfully, Beth (my wife's real name) was with me and she drove us home in her car. We were only a ten minute drive from the club, and had just gotten home, having dry-swallowed six Advil on the way, and was getting situated in the bed. Beth was getting the cold compresses for my eyes when the phone rang.

It was our manager, Nat (not his real name, but...ah, forget it). Beth answered the phone and came into our bedroom handing the phone to me.

"I can't talk", I mumbled to her, "find out what the problem is, and don't tell me."

"You'd better talk to him" was all she said, and gave me the phone.

I thought Nat must've had a question about loading out – how to break down my amps, where to pack microphones, or something of that nature. Perturbed, I took the phone. Before I could say anything, I heard sounds from the other end of the line that made me think I was getting a phone call from Hell itself. There was wailing. And yelling. Screaming and crying. Cursing. Lots of moaning and groaning. It sounded like the Wailing Wall and the waiting line in every "early bird" dinner restaurant in South Florida combined.

"What's going *on down there?*" I said into the phone, which was an appropriate question for either Skipper's or Hell.

"Charlie, you're not going to believe this", Nat began, "and I know you have a migraine and can't talk, so just listen. First of all, we're not getting paid for tonight."

"WHAT?" I barked.

"We're not getting paid", Nat repeated over the sounds of people sobbing and wailing in the background like the lowest rung in Dante's Inferno, "nobody's getting paid. There's no money."

"NO MONEY?" I shouted. I was sitting up in bed now, *"What do you mean – no money? Where's Will?"*

"He's in his office", said Nat matter-of-factly, "but someone has left with all the money from the drawers and the safe and nobody knows where it is."

"Put Will on the phone", I ordered.

"I can't – he's passed out", Nat answered.

"Well, *WAKE HIM UP!!!*" I demanded.

Nat had to talk louder now over the din of misery. This was before cell phones – he was using a phone at the bar and it was all hell and hysterics around him,

"Charlie, we've *tried*. The *bartenders* have tried. Kevin (our bassist) has been hitting him in the face and jabbing him in the ribs with a *mop handle* and he's not moving. They've called 911. The waitresses are crying, everybody's real upset – they think he might be dead."

I was dumbfounded. "Does he have a pulse?" I asked, wondering if I had passed out and was dreaming this.

"That's the thing, Charlie", Nat the ex-funeral director replied, "No one can get close enough to him to tell."

"*Get close enough to tell?*" I echoed, shaking my heavy head, "What are you *talking about?*"

I heard Nat let out a big exhalation in preparation of what he was about to tell me, and you the reader, might want to do the same.

"Charlie, listen, because I can only say this once...Will is unconscious in his office chair", Nat began. "His pants and underwear are down around his ankles. There is excrement (not the word Nat used) all over *him*, all over the *chair*, all over his *desk*, all over the *walls*. Charlie, there's Frankenstein feces all over the *ceiling* of the office. It's the most horrible thing I've ever seen in my life, and I'm sorry, but we've got to get out of here."

Now I *knew* I must be out cold and having some fever-induced nightmare from the migraine. Or I was awake and delusional, because this just wasn't happening.

"*WHAT???*"

was all I could think of to say, although I had *heard* Nat's explanation (over the wailing and crying in the background), and didn't need (nor want) him to repeat it to me again. Nat, feeling my pain, was sympathetically silent, allowing me to imagine for myself the sickening surreal scene down at Skipper's. People moaning, groaning, retching, and crying in disgust and horror; other people yelling, screaming, and cursing in anger at getting their paychecks stolen; some people doing both. And then there's Will, the eight-foot tall Frankenstein monster, unconscious or dead, in his full regalia and green glory, with his raggedy pants down around his ankles, with his bolts and his boots and his giant head, covered in his own filth.

Always wanting to be part of the solution rather than part of the problem, I then offered an idea that I thought was our only hope of getting the money owed us.

Remembering that Nat had his camera with him (he had been bringing his camera to our shows and taking photographs of the band, the dancers, etc.), and realizing that if we were in possession a photograph of local businessman Will, in his present condition, we would be able to *extort* our money via blackmail from him (if he survived) or from his next-of-kin (if he did not). I am without conscience when it comes to green and brown Frankensteins owing me money for services rendered. Seeing a way out, I told Nat to

"Take a picture of him."

Now this next sentence should be proof to you, the reader, that there are powers of Evil at work in this world that surpasses all "scientific" knowledge and understanding, especially on Halloween. Nat (an old blackmailer from way back – did I mention he was a funeral director?) replied,

"Charlie, I've already tried. My camera won't work. I don't understand it – it was working fine earlier tonight. And I thought if we at least had a picture of Will, we could, you know..."

"Never mind", I caved.

Hopelessly and utterly defeated and wishing to save my men by the only means left to me, I reluctantly ordered a full retreat,

"Just get the Hell out of there."
[Ed. note: I apologize for the use of the word "Hell" here. I don't wish to offend anyone. It is not being used as profanity or as slang; it is being used in its most literal, biblical sense]

"Skipper's" never reopened after that Halloween night. "Will" survived, but his reputation did not – thanks in part to us spreading the word. Don't tell us if you don't want it told. Afterward, we pieced together what had happened: Ol' Willie-boy knew he was going out of business after that Halloween night, and didn't tell his employees (or his band) so he could disappear and get out of paying them (and us), making his getaway with a nice chunk of change. He arranged to get the big night's big money out of the building and had planned to then skip out of Skipper's himself (sorry, I'm pun-crazy!), but he got too high to fly. Or too low to go.

On his last night in business, apparently figuring he might as well go down in flames, he decided to get drunk, take the muzzle off his DJ, and rip everyone off. Everyone, that is, except for The Insane Gynecologist. He got *his* dough. Insane??? Gynecologist??? Brother, he was neither.

Thus ends our story of a hellish Halloween, or a hallowed Helloween, or just another night at the office for Lightnin' Charlie the saloon singer. I'm just glad it's over. I am sick from writing about it (as I am sure you are sickened by reading it). But take comfort, friends that it didn't happen to you. And it doesn't happen to me anymore.

We chalked this one up in the "loss column". We lost big-time. It may be funny now, but it was not funny then. We were very serious about our money. We had to be. Having been ripped off way too many times to take it lightly, we had to adopt a zero-tolerance policy about certain things, especially our money. You can't let people push you around. If you take crap off people, they'll give you some more crap (worst pun yet!). And we never got a nickel's wages for our night's work that Halloween.

This may give you all a little perspective on the newfound joy and thanksgiving Lightnin' Charlie has now – now that he is finally out of the bars, and finally finished trying to make his music, and his living in them. Understand, rubber band? The wages of sin is death. I am still out in the world, but I'm not of the world. I'm sanctified. I'm still out there dancin', it's just that I've changed partners. Praise God – He's brought me from a mighty long way.

That's gonna do it for our Lowdown for this month, boys and girls. As I take my leave now, I'll leave you with this thought...

I've never seen Hell, but I have heard it on the telephone.

Your friend always,
Lightnin' Charlie
ex-sufferer of fools,
Hemorrhoids,
and migraine headaches

"Put on the whole armour of God, that ye may be able to stand against the wiles of the devil. For we wrestle not against flesh and blood, but against principalities, against powers, against the rulers of the darkness of this world, against spiritual wickedness in high places. Wherefore take unto you the whole armour of God, that ye may be able to withstand in the evil day, and having done all, to stand.

- Ephesians 6:11-13 KJV

NOVEMBER 2006

18

THE RE-INVENTION OF ME

"To be, or not to be: that is the question: Whether 'tis nobler in the mind to suffer the slings and arrows of outrageous fortune, or to take arms against a sea of troubles, and by opposing end them?"

- William Shakespeare "The Bard"

"To be or not to be: contemporary, that is. To be contemporary, perchance to dream (of superstardom). Ah, there's the rub, baby! To be rich and famous, to go to Hollywood parties, to be poor no more; and by fame and fortune to end the heartache and the thousand natural shocks and migraines that a starving artist is heir to; Man, oh man, 'tis a consummation devoutly to be wished."

– Lightnin' Charlie Hates-beer "The Card"

Sometimes I find myself dreaming of having huge commercial success in show business and wishing I lived the luxurious life of a major pop star (and having a big, black pompadour). But it is only a pipe dream. I know what I am. And I know I don't possess the skills needed to compete in today's world. More accurately, the skills I possess don't jive at all with what's necessary to succeed in the contemporary music scene. But still, perchance to dream...Lightnin' Charlie could *become* contemporary. I could convert and maybe get my big break. Carpe diem. But to get in the mix, I'd need a complete, personal makeover to thrive in these "enlightened" days of the 21st century.

This month's Lowdown will feature a Top Ten List, a tirade (typical of the Lightnin' Man), and a diabolical plan to reinvent myself and grab my much belated superstardom in these crazy days of wine and roses.

In my continuing effort to alienate and offend as many potential fans as possible with The Truth, this month I am going to give you a Top Ten Worst List rather than a Top Ten Best List, because, let's face it, news of an offensive, outrageous, and negative nature is really what we crave. It's what we, as present day Americans, are hopelessly addicted to. We don't want nor care about good news.

Boy scout saves twenty kids from burning school bus. – page 37

Boy scout kills twenty kids by burning school bus. – front page

But first, a tirade...

Who am I kidding – Lightnin' Charlie is an old man trying (unsuccessfully) to keep up with the constantly changing times. Just another baby-boomer trying to be a modern day hipster – a 21st century renaissance man. But it's late in the game for me. And it's going to be difficult if not impossible for me to carry the ball in today's twisted society. I've *never* been a product of my times – never been "contemporary" my whole life. In the sixties, I hated hippies. In the seventies, I despised disco. In the eighties and nineties, I just plain surrendered (to suffer the slings and arrows of outrageous society). In other words, well, I gave up. To fight against it would be the same as shoveling snow against the tide. Therefore, if Lightnin' Charlie is to become a truly contemporary artist now, in 2006, at forty-four years of age, in an industry run completely by and for kids, he's going to have to change. Big-time. Middle-aged, bald-headed, unknown ex-saloon singers aren't being catapulted to mega-stardom on American Idol, for instance. But you'll never get anywhere without a plan. And I have a plan. The journey of a thousand miles starts with a flat tire and a broken fan belt. So here's an outline of my plan for grabbing my long overdue "fifteen minutes" and finally attain the commercial glory and fan adulation I so richly deserve. But to do this, I'll have to *evolve*, to *metamorphosize* into someone worthy of idolatry in these modern times, these enlightened days. I'll have to be completely made over. Born again. I'll need to change *everything* about me.

Starting with the books I read. The first thing to go would be my books.

> *"You despise books; you whose lives are absorbed in the vanities of ambition, the pursuit of pleasure or indolence; but remember that all the known world, excepting only savage nations, is governed by books."*
> – Voltaire

The books I've always loved to read are biographies and histories – especially American history. Real people and real stories. I read everything I can get my hands on about the horror and heroism of the War Between the States, which I feel was the defining moment in our history as Americans. I love learning about the great men and women of the Second World War (The Greatest Generation), and what it took to win it. I love reading biographies about inspired (and inspiring) American Presidents like Washington and Jefferson, Lincoln and Roosevelt (Teddy and FDR), Truman and Eisenhower. I love the awesome, stranger-than-fiction dramas of pioneers like Lewis and Clark and the NASA astronauts. I love to read tales of extraordinary courage from ordinary people –

from the settlers of the American West to the survivors of the Great Depression. I love to read all about the golden age of America's Game (baseball), American music, and American musicians. Stories of everyday people who, faced with overwhelming odds, picked themselves up by their bootstraps and, with the help of Almighty God, accomplished great, great things in life.

But all that would have to go. To be a modern man, the only non-fiction books I could read would be contemporary, New York Times bestseller books. Not the right-wing propaganda mentioned in the previous paragraph. If I'm serious about this makeover, and if I'm to have any chance of getting Katie Couric to dig me, I'll have to immerse myself in those wonderfully literate, modernly monosyllabic, forward-thinking books; you know, the ones that condone terrorism and espouse socialism. The ones written by our enemies. I would only read and respect authors who:

1) hate white males
2) love third-world culture
3) appear on Oprah

Ironically, these books are almost always written by people whose ethnicity and/or "alternative lifestyles" would get them immediately beheaded in the countries whose beautiful citizens and cultures they represent as so superior to ours. But that's the old Lightnin' Charlie talking. Enough of that.

*"The man who doesn't read good books
has no advantage over the man who can't read them."* - Mark Twain

Unlike the politically correct (and fabulously wealthy) modernists, the old-fashioned Lightnin' Charlie doesn't care what race or which gender you are. I care about *who* you are and what you *do*. I agree with Martin Luther King – judge folks on the content of their character, not the color of their skin. I also agree with the ex-slave Frederick Douglass, a fearless Abolitionist and noble statesman, who vehemently opposed the concept of Affirmative Action, believing any preferential treatment towards his people would be a detriment to their progress and would ultimately be the death of them. How about Jackie Robinson, who was a lifelong Republican because they preached self-help rather than the condescending, *"Oh, let us help you poor people..."* Are Frederick Douglass and Jackie Robinson racists? Yeah? Then so am I. I believe in the unalienable right and innate ability of ALL people to accomplish unbelievable things, if the government would just get out of our way. Let the best man win.

I don't believe any particular people are somehow inferior and need a "head start" or a "ladies tee" to hit from. I believe that whole idea to be completely racist by definition – the belief that some folks can't succeed on their own without a Ted Kennedy or a Hillary Clinton (sorry – Hillary *Rodham* Clinton) to "help" them with money, housing, and jobs. I'm tired of working one day out of every four so that a crack-smoker gets food stamps. I'm just tired. Sick and tired of the insanity. All men *are* created equally, but are being treated unequally in the name of "equality". Winston Churchill said,

> *"Show me a man of twenty who isn't a liberal and I'll show you a man with no heart. Show me a man of forty who isn't a conservative and I'll show you a man with no brain."*

Lightnin' Charlie is forty-four and politically leaning a little to the right of George S. Patton. But that's got to go – I need to get my mind *right!* Oops...I mean *left!*

The next thing to be exorcized would have to be my belief in the sovereignty of the United States of America. Radio talk show host Michael Savage beats the drum loudly on this subject: preserving America's "language, borders, and culture". The old-fashioned, Neanderthal Lightnin' Man espoused those ideals, too. But the new-and-improved, enlightened and completely evolved, *contemporary* Lightnin' Man would *legislate* against that kind of "fascist thought" while applauding the teaching of Islam and Holy Jihad (Muslim genocide of all non-Muslims) in our public schools. You're aware of the "intellectuals" and collegiate bimbos responsible for this sedition, these "enlightened" THC-poisoned beatniks who bang on bongos and crow *"Kum-By-Ya"* trying to rid our society of the Ten Commandments, the Pledge of Allegiance, and Christmas trees; all in the name of "tolerance". They're everywhere. And they're oh, so successful. But these Christophobes (new word) apparently aren't enlightened enough to realize that *"Lord, kum-by-ya"* means *"Lord, come by here"* – not *"Lord, go away"*.

The ethnically sensitive modern moron (the new me) would also support legislation requiring everyone in the U.S. learn to speak fluent Spanish, making life easier and more convenient for those Spanish-speaking immigrants, both legal and illegal, who can't be bothered with learning our English language. After all, they're much too busy getting free health care.

The Enlightened Lightnin' would have to do his homework. It won't be easy. I'd have to work hard to understand the moral equivalency of the new world order. Especially as it applies to Islam – the "religion of peace", and its bearded, bloodthirsty fanatics. The central concept of this moral equivalency is the premise that there really is no such thing as right and wrong – just subjectivism. It all depends on how you look at it, how you were brought up, etc. Of course, none of these tired excuses are available for American Caucasian males, especially Southern ones. We're inherently evil no matter how we were brought up. So are all of our ancestors. We're intolerantly (and immorally) exempted from this wonderful, new moral equivalency.

For the modernist *(Homo erectus-leftus),* right and wrong, good and evil, are terms that only exist to be applied blindly (although not color-blindly) – strictly according to race and gender. Lame, circumstantial excuses for personal non-responsibility, ultra-convenient, are reserved for Palestinian mothers who strap explosives around the waists of their children and send them into skating rinks and shopping malls in Jerusalem, blowing themselves and other mother's children to bits. This poor woman wouldn't be considered to be "at fault"; she would just be *reacting* – naturally and blamelessly – to her *environment.* She must *always* be portrayed as the victim, or as a *"freedom fighter".* Never as a murdering jackal.

Another important requirement of my becoming truly "with it" and therefore being considered for invitation to trendy New York or Hollywood parties is to mock and despise the entire American experiment and to especially hate and ridicule our Founding Fathers (naturally, all mothers are exempt). The road to success is to hate the American Dream, the republic for which it stands, and capitalism, all the way to the bank.

Next thing to deal with will be my vocabulary. I realize that my verbosity identifies me as an outsider to the present day elite – a throwback. I don't have the oratory skills to succeed in the modern world. I don't talk the talk. There are certain keywords that denote this hip-ness and authority I'm jealous of. These keywords, used constantly in each and every sentence by those who have attained that level of cerebral supremacy I desire, entitle the user to automatic membership into modern day intelligentsia. Especially if you have a soul patch. These keywords and phrases, repeated like a mantra for the mindless, are:

1) "you know"
2) "actually"
3) "basically"
4) "I was like...and she was like...and then I was like...and then she was like..."
5) "I am *all* about..." and "I am *so* not..." (accent on the *"all"* and *"so")*

Thirty or forty years ago, speech like this would've identified you immediately as an idiot, and would've made you a target of ridicule. Nowadays, if you possess the verbiage of Shaggy (of Scooby Doo fame), you're automatically one of the beautiful people, and regarded as being brilliant and creative, penetrating and well informed. You know, like *smart!* Nonstop use of the word *"like"* is imperative to one's message being perceived as profound. This is not your Grandfather's simile. Repeated public use of these keywords would insure superstardom for the new

Lightnin' Charlie. Their continued use, you know, would like (just practicing) actually cause Lightnin' Charlie's original song lyrics to be celebrated at the U.N. and examined as poetry by Ivy League college professors for their depth, beauty, and wisdom – as long as the song title is misspelled with Ebonics.

All right. Onward and upward. Once my politics and vocabulary (or lack of) were in line, next I would have to change my name. I'd need something much less Anglo-Saxon than *"Lightnin' Charlie"* – something more marketable, modern and politically correct. Something folks would be *obligated* to honor and respect. Something like:

"Ramadan Carlos" or maybe...

"Ng-Jamal King Jr. Charlie" or

"Montoya El-Muhammad" has a nice, natural ring to it.

What's in a name? Everything. From now on, I am the artist formerly known as Lightnin' Charlie.

That leads us to another very important part of the makeover: my appearance. I am at a distinct disadvantage in show business, by being born a whitey. Since I can't be what I am ("tolerance" won't tolerate it), like the saying goes: if you can't beat 'em, join 'em. A white male can only be taken seriously as an artist if he is European, drug-addicted, and very angry (very redundant). I am none of these. So, of course, it would be necessary to always appear in public in blackface. I would also shave my head to look more "edgy". Bald is only beautiful when it's done deliberately. If nature does it to you, you're not edgy, just bald. I would obviously need to lie about my age, too. I'm forty-four, but I think I could pass for thirty with a slick, shiny, chocolate, chrome-dome. My plan would require me to be young enough to still be considered "sexy", but old and wizened enough to have traveled extensively through "superior" continents such as Europe, India, Africa, and Central America.

My fictional "coming of age" story will go something like this: after college, Ramadan Carlos the Romantic (or whatever I decide to call myself) backpacked and dope-smoked all over the third world seeking an antidote for America. Being disillusioned with the American way of life and, naturally full of guilt and disgrace from being American, Carlos (me) fell in love with the green grass of the other side – the primo pagan cultures, the wonderful warlords and wacko dictators, and anarchy in general. Most folks I've known (in real life) who have traveled extensively through India, Central and South America don't fall in love with these places – they fall victim in them (to malaria, dysentery, tuberculosis, assault, mugging, and imprisonment – all souveniers from Utopia).

And so my alter ego, the pinko, now full of himself and anxious to corrupt others, returned to North America, dispensing his pearls of wisdom about how much better Bangladesh is than Beverly Hills, and how superior Marrakech is to Malibu (of course, not one single Hollywood flake that preaches this stuff ever sells their Southern California estates and moves there).

Now that my name, my race, and my history have all been successfully made over, the next step in my coup would be to book a tour. Not a concert tour – a *speaking* tour: college campuses, television (swimming pools, movie stars!). UC at Berkley, NYU, Leno, Larry King, selected Starbuck's, Entertainment Tonight, anything on Al-Jezeera (it's a must to give aid and comfort to the enemy – maybe I could do an exercise video like Jane Fonda!), Letterman, Ellen Degenerate, Conan, Good Morning America, Access Hollywood, The Today Show, etc. They're all, in reality, the same entity and will come running towards my persona like a pack of hungry hounds. It will be crucial that every interview and appearance *must always* contain the following essential bullet-points:

1) Expound upon the party line – the evils of American fascist-pigs and the disgusting fuel consumption of their big SUV's (while flying from gig to gig in Al Gore's private jet and being picked up in stretch limos at the airport)
2) Hail all street thugs and prison rappers as demi-gods and modern day Shakespeares (while living in multi-million dollar gated compounds to keep out the riff-raff)
3) Pay gushing tribute to any and all females on the planet and always refer to them onstage and in interviews as "Diva", "Queen So-and-So", or "Princess" (while treating every female encountered on a daily basis as rudely as possible. They are, after all, just objects living only to serve me. Pay particular obnoxious attention towards waitresses and flight attendants)
4) Have the obligatory, bulimic, size-00 Hollywood starlet girlfriend, and recklessly adopt children from all over the third world, and then hand them over to our hired nannies to raise.
5) Bring a bunch of my blue-jeaned, billionaire Hollywood neighbors onstage to help me sing "Give Peace A Chance" (with arms upraised and "doing the wave", but without underarm deodorant – that's strictly for fascists and squares).

Next to come would naturally be the movie roles. Being black (sorry, I mean African-American), I could only be cast as a wealthy corporate attorney or a CEO, who along with his anorexic, oriental/mulatto Girl Friday, gets to shoot holes in lots of deserving white guys. Although skyscrapers, airplanes, and plenty of people are blown away in these movies, Hollywood will never show the slightest injury to a dog, a cat, or a tree. And appropriately, the Hollywood fraternity only casts leftists and pacifists for these virile, violent, vigilante roles.

Needless to say, my *Give Peace A Chance* will *never* be included in any of my movie soundtracks. I would preach pacifism to get *into* the movies, and then kill every living thing in sight *in them*. Except for bunnies and goldfish. Of course, in the movies, I would insist upon a private, closed dressing room to apply my own makeup (ala Lon Chaney), lest my secret shame (Caucasian) be revealed.

It would be necessary for me to put aside the pacifism I preach just long enough to make these ultra-violent blockbuster movies that would make me ultra-rich. I would leave my peace signs in my $50,000,000 mansion and cease my ranting about evil capitalists just long enough to make a few million bucks killing people in the movies. Then I would go back to my posh publicity party, putting down the establishment, flying around (with my staff) in my private jet, hyping my next blockbuster movie, and harping about fossil fuels. I couldn't be bothered by the hypocrisy of it all – hypocrisy would be my new religion, and I would be my new god. And at last, I will actually receive the constant attention and, you know, basically the adulation, with all due respect and sickening holy deference, from the media and fans that I've always, you know, like deserved!

Well folks, that's it. That's my plan. If you know any good Madison Avenue publicists, please feel free to give them my number. It's the perfect plan – nothing left to chance. And just because everybody's doing it doesn't mean that there's not room at the top for one more. Non-conformity is old-fashioned, too. And if this plan should fail, I could always have sex change surgery, or commit some heinous crime. Those are foolproof rockets to stardom, too.

Here is my Top Ten Worst List. These are pop culture things that, although revered by the masses, I find to be atrocious. Since I am a musician (and soon to be actor), most of these items are popular singers, songs, and movies. Keep in mind that I don't go to a lot of movies, or listen to commercial radio, so most of these things I've experienced only to see what all the fuss was about. I have included some comments and alternatives in parenthesis for you to consider in the (probably futile) hope of getting you to "see the light". I hope to offend lots of you with this. *Salute!*

10) Jimmy Buffet (horrible – try Jimmy Cliff instead)

9) The Eagles (it's not the band itself that gets me; it's their fans. Try a large dose of The Blasters and call me in the morning)

8) The country smash hit, *Long Black Train* (I had never heard it, and

after getting tons of requests for it at my shows, got curious and downloaded it. Horrendous. And the singer, Josh Turner, is even worse. It's so bad, it's bound to be around for years to come, like *Achy Breaky Heart* or toenail fungus. Antidote: immediate ear wax removal, followed by a shot of *People Get Ready* by Curtis Mayfield, with a chaser of *Mystery Train* and *Long Black Limousine* by Elvis Presley)

7) The meaningless term "Beach Music". I'll give a thousand dollars to anyone who can produce a photograph of Diana Ross and the Supremes or the Four Tops lying on a beach. Why not call it "Landlocked Music"? Because it was made by musicians from Memphis, Chicago, Detroit, etc. who probably hated the beach. I love this music but revile this baseless and brainless non sequitur (that means it's like stupid, basically)

6) Television Reality Shows (check out *The Honeymooners Classic 39* on DVD – now *that's* a reality show)

5) Television Baseball Coverage. I recently tried to watch a World Series game, but could not, due to the stupefying way that the TV cameras show you the game. See if you agree with me on this: Baseball is a sport with not a lot of action. The beauty of baseball is the non-action leading up to the action. That is the essence of baseball. The beauty of baseball is watching the pitcher shake off two or three signs from the catcher before getting the pitch he wants to throw. It's watching the batter step in and out of the batter's box before finally digging in. It's watching the pitcher step off the rubber to move the base runners back to the bags. It's watching outfielders shift their positions in expectation of where a left-handed hitter might pull the ball if the pitcher is going to throw an inside pitch. It's watching the third baseman move closer to the line to protect against an extra-base hit. It's watching the manager and third base coach give signs to the players on the field. It's watching the base runner, inch-by-inch, taking his lead off the bag, while the first baseman sneaks up behind him to try and pick him off. All that is the beauty and the essence of baseball. But I am not allowed to see any of that. All I am shown by the television cameras, especially in the ninth inning, is every single person in the stadium that's not on the field. Between pitches, we're shown every fan in the stands, biting their nails and picking their noses, screaming and waving at the camera, but mostly they are engrossed in and enjoying what I am not seeing – what is happening *ON*

THE FIELD. They're watching a baseball game and I'm watching them pick their noses and point at the camera. They then cut back to the game just in time for me to see the pitch already on its way towards home plate. I've also noticed this while watching tennis on television, where in the fifth set of the U.S. Open finals, the most important person to the TV camera crew is the tennis player's girlfriend in the stands (see "Diva" above). You know, I could stomach all the commercials and the corporate-sponsored scoreboards and the commentators' nonsense, if they would just *SHOW ME THE GAME.* Since I don't root for any particular team, city, or player anymore, and the only reason I occasionally watch at all is because of my love for the game itself, all I do in the ninth inning is scream hysterically at the TV set. If I want to sit and yell at the TV set, I'll watch CNN. It's all been taken away from us. We can't have anything. I'm mad as a hatter, and I'm not gonna *TAKE IT ANYMORE!!!* The antidote: watch Ken Burns' Series *Baseball*

4) Party Politics (Democrat vs. Republican, Liberal vs. Conservative, Patriots vs. Steelers, Black vs. White, etc.) Can't we all just get along? And maybe get something done. On Capitol Hill, that is. Can't we, as Americans, think any deeper than One vs. The Other? They don't think we can. I happen to believe that both political parties are hopelessly corrupt and their members completely criminal. 100%. At election time, we are given the choice between two crooked liars and we dutifully line up on each side like partisan fans at a high school basketball game. We put stickers on our cars and signs in our yards and argue and fight among ourselves. We're playing Cowboys and Indians, like there's a good guy and a bad guy. But they're both bad guys. It's good cop – bad cop played on a national scale, and we're schmucks for falling for it every four years. How we must look to them, wildly cheering their speeches and waiting in line to shake their hands or to have our babies kissed by them. They know what they are. But, more disastrously, they know what *we are.* We're sheep. No wonder they don't care what happens to us (after the election), they have utter contempt for us the way Lucy Van Pelt has contempt for Charlie Brown stupidly trying, again and again, to kick the football because she "promises" not to pull it out from under him this time. We're the fools who fall for the same stupid trick year after year after year. We're boobs at the fair. Or, more accurately, we're like the idiot fans at a "professional" wrestling match – going crazy for one wrestler or the other, who are pretending to fight and hate each other, but actually are actors who play golf with each other and

laugh at us all the way to the bank. Try independent thought as an alternative to being a fan (short for fanatic), and goose-stepping along to the drumbeat of either of these two political parties and the pigs in them.

3) Diversity [di-vur-si-tee] noun.
   1. the state of being diverse; difference; unlikeness.
   2. variety; multiformity.
   3. a point of difference.

Another perfectly good word, with a perfect and beautiful meaning, twisted and perverted by those with a political agenda, into meaning its exact opposite. The political agenda in this case being the one determined to make the entire population of the universe look strictly and uniformly the same. No more black people, no more oriental people, no more whites, indians, hispanics, etc. Just one big, happy family of light-browns with no disparate cultures. That's diversity? Not according to me or Webster's:

Homogeny [huh-moj-uh-nee] noun. All of the same or similar nature; corresponding in structure because of a common origin.

Why can't they call it what it is? Call a spade a spade. I prefer the divine, magnificent diversity that is ethnicity – not a world full of Stepford Wives.

2) Microwaveable Pizza, Bagels, etc. [see also number 3]. Here's a wild and innovative thought: How about real Italian food...cooked by real Italians? I know I'm old-fashioned, but you know I'm right.

And the #1 popularly prized pulp garbage on Lightnin's Top Ten Worst List is:

I Walk The Line, the movie.

I'm putting this drek at number 1 because it seems that EVERYONE loves this awful movie. And I am putting it on top of this worst list without ever seeing the entire film. I'm sorry. I can't. I bought the DVD to try and get it down gradually. I still can't. Nothing works. I've tried several times to watch the whole thing, and I just cannot. It's impossible for me. I've tried skipping through the scenes to get to something – anything – that is not pathetically bad. Simply, it's the worst slop that I have ever seen in my life. The script, the acting, and the editing are all excruciatingly horrible.

The art direction is really the pits. Art directors are the people responsible for making period pieces seem "real" and "authentic" to the viewer. For example, they show Buddy Holly playing a Gibson Les Paul guitar instead of the sunburst Fender Stratocaster that he was known for and single-handedly made world-famous (these guitars are polar opposites of one another). High school kids could do better. Guitars in a Johnny Cash movie are important props, wouldn't you say? This is, after all, a film about music and the people who made it, isn't it? Would they do a film about the life of Humphrey Bogart and give Bogie long, blonde hair, a ponytail, and a patch over one eye? Dude, it's a mess.

The screenplay (the backbone of a picture) is ludicrous at best – how about the scene where all the rock 'n' roll headliners – Cash, Jerry Lee Lewis, Carl Perkins, etc., are spending an afternoon lying drunk as dogs on the stage of the theatre they are performing at later that night, "jamming" and busting beer bottles all over the stage and the empty theatre. This ridiculous scene is interrupted when, you guessed it, Miss June Carter (see "Diva" again) comes in with her hands on her hips and straightens them all right out, by golly.

In these typical Hollywood scenes, made by dolts whose knowledge of music wouldn't fill a thimble, the dumb artist is always portrayed hanging out with other musicians and drunkenly singing their own hit songs to each other. If Cash and Jerry Lee were ever hanging out and singing together, they would've been playing other people's music (like Hank Williams or Jimmie Rodgers – their idols), and hymns (if you don't believe me, listen to the Million Dollar Quartet record of Johnny Cash, Carl Perkins, Jerry Lee and Elvis hanging out in Sun Studios in Memphis).

It's the same Hollywood halfwits who make a movie about Elvis and portray "Elvis" wearing jumpsuits and karate kicking around Graceland all night long on his nights off from work. You know what? I've changed my mind about wanting to go to parties with these people. But the worst of the worst, for me, is the typical and unrelenting overemphasis on the drugs and the women of Johnny Cash and the likewise typical minimizing and ignoring what made him a great man – his music and his Christianity. It's the same, exact, insipid movie they made about Ray Charles. Here's the plot of the award-winning motion picture, *Ray...*

drugsandwomenanddrugsanddrugsandwomenanddrugsandwomenanddrugs

Poor Elvis, same movie – different name. And Ike & Tina Turner. And Frankie Lymon. And Jerry Lee Lewis. And on and on and on. And now, for something completely different: a movie about the drugs and the women of a dead musical genius.

Is anyone else bored to tears with this? It's never about what made them great enough, and unique enough, to be the subject for a film in the first place - their *MUSIC*. Is there anything unique about a divorced guy that has a drug and alcohol problem? I guess it's because Hollywood can only talk about what they know about. In other words, he who smelt it - dealt it.

And I don't care what all the frauds at the Oscars say about this movie. Alfred Hitchcock never won an Oscar - so what do they know? I rest my case. I don't care what all my friends say, I don't care what the whole world says, this movie smells. It stinks. It's *drek auf dem teller*. That's Yiddish for "crap on a plate". That's it. And Lightnin' Charlie, an old-fashioned Child of God (and fan of Hollywood's truly great films) says Amen! Watch John Ford's *The Searchers* starring John Wayne, or Bogart in *The Treasure Of The Sierra Madre* tonight, then call me a liar.

And I smell the end of another rootin' and tootin' - rantin' and ravin' - mangy and no-good - long and lowdown - Lowdown. See y'all next time. I sure hope you enjoyed my cry for help.

Yours very truly,
Enlightened Charlie

P.S. In case any ACLU lawyers are reading this, this is SATIRE and covered by the first amendment to the Constitution (the holy document you are devoted to destroying). So stay in your hole, and I'll stay on my soapbox. Bye-bye.

DECEMBER 2006

19

DON'T WORRY, BE HAPPY

"To do is to be." - Descartes
"To be is to do." - Voltaire
"Do be do be do." - Sinatra

"We've all heard that a million monkeys banging on a million typewriters will eventually reproduce the entire works of Shakespeare. Now, thanks to the Internet, we know this is not true." - Robert Wilensky

"The truth is more important than the facts." - Frank Lloyd Wright

"It ain't the heat; it's the humility." - Yogi Berra

"The key to being a good bandleader is keeping the musicians who hate me away from those who are still undecided." - Lightnin' Charlie

I've borrowed this last bit of wit from baseball's Casey Stengel and applied it, ever so aptly, to myself and my career as a musician and bandleader. I am also a writer (of songs and this monthly diatribe you are now reading). I truly admire Stengel as a man who had such a way with words that he even coined his own language, *Stengelese*. Here's some examples of Stengelese:

"There comes a time in every man's life, and I've had plenty of them."

"Everybody line up in alphabetical order, according to your height."

"He hits from both sides of the plate - he's amphibious."

That's beautiful. The only man who can compete with Stengel for so eloquently fracturing the English language is Yogi Berra. Berra, like Stengel, is in the Baseball Hall Of Fame, and like Stengel, he played for and later managed the New York Yankees and the New York Mets (both Casey and Yogi moved to New York from their birthplace, Missouri). Here are a couple examples of Yogi-isms:

"Nobody goes there anymore. It's too crowded."

"The future ain't what it used to be."

That's the type of wit and wisdom I aspire to as a writer. That's genius. And it makes people laugh. You can have your deep, dark writers like Hemingway and Twain; I'll take Stengel and Berra. They're much more my style. Their prose uplifts people and makes them happier than they were before they read it. I don't want (or need) anyone to help me become depressed. I need the opposite. If I want to become depressed, I'll turn on the radio or watch the evening news.

It escapes me why anyone would enjoy reading the works of a suicidal alcoholic like Ernest Hemingway unless they wish to become more like him. For whom the bell tolls? It tolls for thee. And me. I know I'm going to die, so while I'm alive, I prefer to enjoy life rather than embrace death. And I believe that the sense of humor is on a much higher plane than the sense of one's mortality. Okay, the death bell tolls for thee – enough already.

Mark Twain's writings certainly contain a highly developed sense of humor, but it's always so cynical and acerbic. It's like biting into a lemon – it's never warm or light-hearted enough for me. Maybe that's why Twain and Hemingway never had a cartoon character named after them; but Yogi Berra did.

Ernest Hemingway and friend in Cuba, 1960.

Less than a year after this photo was taken, Hemingway killed himself with a shotgun blast to the head. Interestingly, this is the only picture I could find of Hemingway smiling. Come to think of it, I don't recall seeing any other photo of Castro smiling, either. I guess it's the company one keeps. Five of the Hemingway family committed suicide – his father, Dr. Clarence Hemingway, his sister Ursula and brother Leicester, Ernest Hemingway himself, and lastly his granddaughter Margaux Hemingway in 1996.

THE FOX AND THE HOUND

I met Ernest Hemingway's son at a concert my band was playing in North Carolina during the annual International Home Furnishings Market. He was in town fronting a new line of furniture that, believe it or not, was replicated from the style of chair that his Dad had blown his brains out in. Ernie's son, who was introduced to us as "The Fox", approached us during a break. Or, to be precise, his "assistant" approached us. "Assistant" is a code word Liberals use meaning, "slave". The Fox's "assistant" approached us, and asked permission to buy a round of drinks for the band. Our road manager Nat was standing there also, and Nat thanked the manservant politely but said that, since we're the band, our drinks were already on the house. Nat, the handsome ex-funeral director you'll no doubt recall from previous Lowdowns, kindly countered by offering to buy a drink for him and Mr. Hemingway (The Fox). It would be an honor to buy a drink for The Fox, and his Hound. Especially since it wouldn't cost us anything.

Hemingway's manservant (The Hound) then looked at Nat and, appearing to be very fearful of his Master, said succinctly,

"No, you don't understand. Mister *HEMINGWAY* wishes to buy *YOU* a drink. In fact, he *INSISTS* upon it."

Well, how dare us! The Hound was especially serious in his tone here, carefully enunciating every word of this directive, his bloodshot, Bohemian eyes conveying its severity by widening with each successive syllable. So what're you gonna do? Nat, trained in the ancient art of embalming, accompanied Ernest Hemingway's son's servant to the bar, and got us the round of drinks. Before taking leave of us, however, The Hound asked to buy one of our CDs for Mr. Hemingway. Nat gladly took care of him, selling him several CDs (at full retail price, I might add). The Fox apparently had excellent taste in music.

It's important to note though, that Hemingway's Hound wasn't buying the CDs *"for"* him, as one person buys a gift for another person - he was buying it *"instead"* of him, as one person picks cotton for another person.

That's another one of my pet peeves with liberals and communists that preach the doctrine of all-for-one and one-for-all. They rarely practice it once they're out of the gutter. Just as soon as they have enough money or power, they've got more slaves servicing their every whim than Carter's got little pills. Look again at the picture on the preceding page: two bearded socialists - both too good to mow their own grass. Ernest Hemingway once said his hometown of Oak Park, Illinois (a mainly Protestant, upper middle-class suburb of Chicago) was "full of wide lawns and narrow minds". That's exactly the kind of humor (or lack of) I'm talking about with these guys. Why do they always need a "target" for their jokes?

Why must their cynicism always be directed at a "whipping boy"? And why is the object of their biting wit always middle-class, working, White, Anglo-Saxon Protestants? Why is the butt of these jokes always the men who go to work every day, who go to Church on Sunday with their families, whose wives stay home and keep house and raise their kids? And the minute these wild-haired, sardonic slavers can afford it, they've got housekeepers cleaning their houses, nannies raising their children, gardeners keeping their lawns, while they're hard at work scornfully mocking the real men and women who are minding their own businesses, cleaning their own homes, and parenting their own children. These elitist holier-than-thou's are never self-effacing with their humor and sarcasm – they can't or won't poke fun at themselves. They're much too busy taking themselves much too seriously. They're always pining about how superior they are to someone else, and that's what makes them (as leftists and so-called liberals) horrible hypocrites in my opinion. And that's why Baby Hemingway (falling-down drunk, by the way – family tradition) had a Stepin Fetchit to go make his purchases for him. For whom the bell tolls? It tolls for thee.

Next stop, the sins of the father...I am adding this as a sad footnote to our story, and I apologize in advance for its gross and explicit nature (stuff like this is commonplace in my old hometown of Miami, Florida). I am going to refrain from any comment, other than to say it illustrates how Ernest's "The Sun Also Rises" should be titled "The Son Also Falls" and it provides me with a belated understanding of why Hemingway's son called himself "The Fox". This is a national news story, reported by Reuter's, from October of 2001, five years or so after our meeting in North Carolina.

The Strange Saga of Gregory Hemingway

Friday October 5 8:22 AM ET

Gregory Hemingway, Son of Writer, Dies in Miami Jail
By Angus MacSwan

MIAMI (Reuters) – Gregory Hemingway, whose troubled relationship with his late father, writer Ernest Hemingway, led him to a tormented life of drink and depression, has died in Miami, officials said on Thursday. It was another sad chapter in the story of the literary lion's family.

Hemingway, 69, died of natural causes in a Miami jail after being arrested for indecent exposure.

He was picked up last Wednesday after walking naked down the street in Key Biscayne, a Miami island community, carrying a pair of black high heels and wearing jewelry, police said.

"He had a difficult life. It's not easy to be the son of a great man," Scott Donaldson, president of the Hemingway Society, told Reuters.

Gregory, younger brother to Jack and Patrick, struggled to cope with the burden. A transvestite who later had a sex-change operation, he suffered bouts of drinking, depression and drifting, according to acquaintances.

"I don't know how it was done, the destruction," he said in a 1987 interview with the Washington Post. "What is it about a loving, dominating, basically well-intentioned father that makes you end up going nuts?"

At the time of his death, he lived in the Coconut Grove district where he was well known to its Bohemian crowd. He sometimes went by the name of Gloria and wore women's clothes.

Last Wednesday, he was reported walking naked through Key Biscayne. When an officer arrived, he was sitting on a curb trying to put on a flowered thong, the police report said.

He had a hospital gown wrapped around his shoulder but was exposing a breast and his genitals, it said. When the officer tried to arrest him, he screamed and refused to be handcuffed.

He gave the name Greg Hemingway, and then later changed it to Gloria, the report added.

Taken to the Miami-Dade Women's Detention Center, he was found dead in his cell early on Monday, spokeswoman Janelle Hall said. The cause of death was hypertension and cardiovascular disease.

He had been due to appear in court later that day on charges of indecent exposure and resisting arrest. He was booked into the women's jail because he had a sex-change operation, Hall added.

Strange and tragic deaths have haunted the Hemingway family. Ernest, the Nobel Prize-winning author who was almost as famous for his adventurous life as for works like "The Old Man and the Sea" and "The Sun Also Rises," shot himself in 1961. Ernest's father, brother and sister also committed suicide. Actress and model Margaux Hemingway, Jack's daughter, was found dead in Santa Monica in 1996 at the age of 41 after battles with alcohol, drugs and depression.

Gregory was born in Kansas City in 1931. His mother was Hemingway's second wife Pauline. He lived his early years in Key West.

"In many ways he was the most talented as a boy – he was a wonderful shooter. He won pigeon-shooting competitions down in Cuba," Donaldson said.

In the Post interview, Hemingway spoke about the pressures of trying to live up to the expectations of his macho father. He once killed 18 elephants on a safari in Africa.

"Yes, I had the most talent. I was the brightest, I could do so many of the things he loved most," he said. He also said his father knew about his cross-dressing, and added, "I've spent hundreds of thousands of dollars trying not to be a transvestite." For the most part, Hemingway lived as a man after his sex change. He had the same deep voice, and the same muscular build. Rather than adding a second breast implant, he had the first removed at some point in the 1990s.

Hemingway's apparent reluctance to let go of his male identity could be explained by many factors, among them the potential for embarrassment. But it does seem a remarkable coincidence that, in getting a sex change, Greg chose perhaps the one path most likely to pain and embarrass his father – and then went on living his life much as before.

It's also interesting to note that when he did assert his femininity, he sometimes seemed more interested in creating a spectacle than completing a process of sincere self-transformation. Perhaps the most dramatic example of that occurred in 1995, when Hemingway, then 64, boarded a Miami bus, made a series of sexual advances toward the male driver and threatened to break his jaw. When police arrived, Hemingway was standing outside an Amoco station, dressed in women's clothing and talking incoherently. Pulling up his skirt, he said to one of the officers, "Let me show you that I'm a woman." The police officer reminded him he was in public and told him to put down his skirt. Hemingway responded by kicking the cop in the groin. It took three police officers to handcuff

Hemingway, who pleaded guilty to a felony charge of battery on a police officer, but was never convicted.

Gregory Hemingway was 69.

I said I wasn't going to comment, and I won't, but boy, does that story make me homesick (emphasis on sick). Let's move on…

Mark Twain, shown here sporting the face that gave birth to the term, "Sour-Puss". Each life-breath must have been like biting into a lemon for this poor soul.

Mark Twain. Poor, pessimistic, bleak, and hopeless. That was Mark Twain, whose wry wit and snarling sarcasms (although brilliant), always leave me feeling cold, hollow and depressed (*Huckleberry Finn* being the lone exception). Reading Twain's writings, even his "humorous" offerings, usually leave me slightly sick to my stomach – like I've kicked a dead animal. Samuel Clemens was a tortured soul who suffered many losses during his lifetime, including the death of three of his children and the loss of two fortunes, and his later writings always reflect that loss and emptiness to me. Take for example his famous quote about birth and death:

"Why is it that we rejoice at a birth and grieve at a funeral? It is because we are not the person involved."

Hates life, loves death. Yeah, we get it, and that photograph shows it. Here is Twain's final writing, dismal to the end:

"Death, the only immortal who treats us all alike, whose pity and whose peace and whose refuge are for all – the soiled and the pure, the rich and the poor, the loved and the unloved."

Compare that morbid muck to what my man, Yogi Berra, has to say about death:

*"You should always go to other people's funerals.
Otherwise they won't come to yours."*

There ya' go! That's what I'm talkin' about. Where lies the true genius? Who's the Renaissance man with the right stuff? Twain or Berra? You tell me. But Berra's Hall Of Fame status wasn't only for putting the wrecking-ball to the English language. He wrecked plenty of World Series pitchers, too. Yogi Berra still holds the major league record for having the most base hits in World Series games (71). This from the man who once said,

"You can't think and hit."

And just how many hits did Mark Twain get in World Series play, hmmmm? Zero. That's because you can't whine and hit. Successfully anyway.

"Pessimists don't get hits, they get hit." – Lightnin' Charlie (hey, that's me!)

One of my favorite American presidents is also one of the all-time great optimists, Theodore Roosevelt. He was a man's man and a champion of the ideals I espouse. Walk softly, carry a big stick, and you'll go far. And like Berra, he too had a bear named for him. Yogi Berra had Yogi Bear, Teddy Roosevelt had the teddy bear.

*Theodore Roosevelt
(Looks like life tastes good to him)*

Speaking of baseball, this is what President Roosevelt had to say on the subject of hitting:

"Don't hit at all if it is honorably possible to avoid hitting; but never hit soft!"

Here's a Roosevelt quote that, unfortunately, still rings true today:

"When the roll is called in the Senate, the Senators don't know whether to answer 'Present' or 'Not Guilty'."

Roosevelt's timeless recipe for success:

"Keep your eyes on the stars, and your feet on the ground."

And my all-time favorite, the Man In The Arena speech:

"It is not the critic who counts: not the man who points out how the strong man stumbles or where the doer of deeds could have done better. The credit belongs to the man who is actually in the arena, whose face is marred by dust and sweat and blood, who strives valiantly, who errs and comes up short again and again, because there is no effort without error or shortcoming, but who knows the great enthusiasms, the great devotions, who spends himself for a worthy cause; who, at the best, knows, in the end, the triumph of high achievement, and who, at the worst, if he fails, at least he fails while daring greatly, so that his place shall never be with those cold and timid souls who knew neither victory nor defeat."

I am not a fan of cold and timid souls, the death-worshipers and the dispensers of doom-and-gloom. I prefer (and practice) the optimist's point-of-view. I believe it to be more precise, more profound, and more practical. Take this Winston Churchill gem for example:

"A pessimist sees the difficulty in every opportunity; an optimist sees the opportunity in every difficulty."

Or how about this from Richard Bach, author of Jonathan Livingston Seagull:

"That's what learning is, after all; not whether we lose the game, but how we lose and how we've changed because of it and what we take away from it that we never had before, to apply to other games. Losing, in a curious way, is winning."

Let's take a closer look at the opposite mindset and lifestyle, and see what it brings. Gather 'round, boys and girls. Here's the success story of a hopeless, pessimistic philosopher, the "father of existentialism", the revered (not Reverend) Friedrich Nietzsche. He is described in the online encyclopedia Wikipedia thusly:

"Nietzsche produced critiques of religion, morality, contemporary culture, and philosophy, centering on what he viewed as fundamental questions regarding the life-affirming and life-denying qualities of Christianity and its beliefs. Nietzsche's works demonstrated the inadequacies of normative modes of thought (that would be me). *Nietzsche's contemporaries largely*

overlooked him during his short yet productive working life, which ended with a mental collapse in 1889. But he received recognition during the first half of the 20th century in German, French, and British intellectual circles, gaining notoriety when the Nazi Party appropriated him as a forerunner. By the second half of the 20th century he had become regarded as a highly significant and influential figure in modern philosophy."

I, Lightnin' Charlie, being of unsound and inadequate mind (according to Nietzsche) do declare that I despise the writings of Nietzsche the intellectual (before his mental breakdown, that is). I am disgusted by the highly significant and influential forerunner of the Nazi Party, along with H. L. Mencken, Bertrand Russell and the rest of their ilk. I do not hate them personally, as they do me – they are just soldiers – same as I – doing the work of their father – same as I. We're just on opposite sides of the same war.

Nietzsche's tripe such as "The Death Of God" and "The Antichrist – Curse On Christianity" (his shrill attack on the morals, practitioners, and originators of Christianity), still wows the college and intellectual crowd (as it did Adolph Hitler).

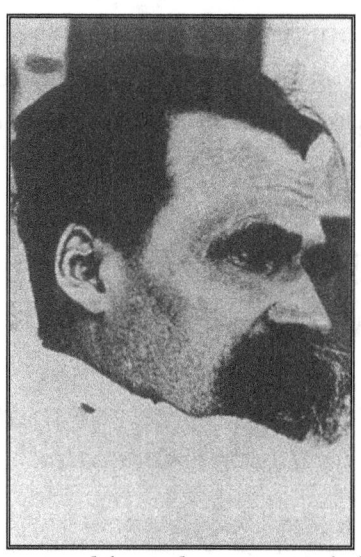

Nietzsche, shown here wrapped in a dapper strait-jacket, which is the perfect companion for a casual evening's stroll or a naughty night on the town. Free-thinking Friedrich's "in-the-mood" and looking "just right" for rollicking, stoning Christians, or crucifying the Savior. This pointy-eared demon really looks the part and even resembles his famous German soulmate and fellow Antichrist, his fan and admirer, the fun-loving Fuehrer, good old Mister H. (he would have resembled the mass-murdering Bohemian even more if his strait-jacket allowed him access to a moustache trimmer).

Listen up, as Friedrich the Fried treats us to these pearls of wisdom regarding insanity, morality, and the death of my Christian God:

> *"Insanity in individuals is something rare – but in groups, parties, nations, and epochs, it is the rule."*

> *"In Christianity, neither morality nor religion come into contact with reality at any point."*

> *"God is dead."*

Herr Nietzsche ended up a crazed syphilitic, confined to an insane asylum and not even allowed contact with society – let alone reality, unable to hold a pen, and is now quite dead. Irony though (reread the above quotes), is still quite alive and well, even if Fried Reich is not. His fifty-five Godless years on this planet, that being, according to him, all there is to life, were spent quite joyously and were very rewarding, judging by the previous photograph.

Do you remember the Twilight Zone episode where people's faces changed to look like the ugly masks they were wearing at a costume party? Whatever their particular sin of choice was – wickedness, avarice, sloth, etc., their faces changed to reflect that which was on the inside. I believe that happens to all of us, if we live long enough for it to take effect. Take a look at any elderly person and you can pretty much tell what kind of person they are, and have been. Their lives (and choices) are worn, for all to see, on their faces. Nietzsche's sure is. We all are ultimately given exactly what we want by God. Friedrich Nietzsche wanted to be without God, and my guess is that's exactly where he is today.

Let's let sleeping dogs lie and move on to another sickening soul, Bertrand Russell. This is what the Wikipedia (and most popular opinion) has to say about Bertrand Russell,

> *"Millions looked up to Bertrand Russell as a prophet of the creative and rational life. As one of the world's best-known intellectuals, Russell's voice carried great moral authority, even into his mid 90s. Among his political activities, Russell was a vigorous proponent of nuclear disarmament and an outspoken critic of the American war in Vietnam."*

Bertrand Russell   The footprint of a chicken

Bravo Bertrand! Imprisoned for four years by Britain for refusing to fight the conquering Germans during World War I, this photo of Bertrand Russell reminds me that a picture truly is worth a thousand words; that Bertrand carries the face, weak chin, and long neck (perfect for sticking his head into the sand when danger approaches) worn by cowards of all species; and just one look at him reminds me to thank God that people like him choose to sit out the wars and aren't the ones who, dutifully and honorably, have to fight and turn back the armies of the enemy, protecting our homes, our families, and our freedom. Imagine being a German soldier in WWI, and the lone defender standing between you and the conquest of Great Britain for the Motherland, is Bertrand Russell. Thank God (and you too, Bertrand) that we have our best men fighting their worst. I appreciate you removing yourself from battle, so your place on the line could be filled by a man more ready, willing, and able to fight, and maybe to die, so that you could remain free to pursue happiness and receive your many accolades and awards. You'll see some striking similarities between the views of this "Bertrand The Ethical" and the "Master Race" of Germany in a moment. But first, some horse-sense from the rear-end of the horse, the visionary, Bertrand Russell:

> *"So far as I can remember, there is not one word in the Gospels in praise of intelligence."*

> *"The human race may well become extinct before the end of the century."*

Sorry Bertrand, we're still here, but you, on the contrary, are very dead. This "Prophet of Rational Thought", revered in his day and ours as such a superior intellect, oft-quoted and of character beyond reproach, had this to say about religion and its dull practitioners:

> *"Religion is based, I think, primarily and mainly upon fear. It is partly the terror of the unknown and partly, as I have said, the wish to feel that you have a kind of elder brother who will stand by you in all your troubles and disputes. A good world needs knowledge, kindliness, and courage; it does not need a regretful hankering after the past or a fettering of the free intelligence by the words uttered long ago by ignorant men."*

Bertrand and his kind are always at-the-ready to attack the apostles of Jesus Christ, but he excuses himself when the German juggernaut of the Kaiser is burning its way through Europe. Ignorant men, Bertrand? Ignorant is as ignorant does. Check out what this "Patron Saint Of Rationality and Ethics", this coward who was awarded the Nobel Laureate "in recognition of his varied and significant writings in which he champions humanitarian ideals and freedom of thought", this "Great moral authority", this darling poster child of today's sniveling liberals and pacifists, had to say regarding the inferiority of Negroes to white men, except, of course, when working in the tropics for whitey:

> *"In extreme cases there can be little doubt of the superiority of one race to another.... It seems on the whole fair to regard negroes as on the average inferior to white men, although for work in the tropics they are indispensable, so that their extermination (apart from questions of humanity) would be highly undesirable."*

You should read that again, slowly, and ask yourself how that spittle makes Bertrand a "champion of humanitarian ideals and freedom of thought", and how that qualifies him as a Nobel Laureate. What would *The Washington Post* and PBS have to say if Billy Graham or Jerry Falwell said the same thing? Would they be hailed as "Patron Saints Of Rationality and Ethics"? Or right-wing racists? I'm disgusted and moving on...

Compare the above hateful ignorance of the "intellectuals" to the hardcore insight of my man, Yogi Berra, when he was asked for the time:

> *"You mean now?"*

Berra's compassion for those less fortunate is evidenced when he was asked what he would do if he found a million dollars:

> *"I'd find the fellow who lost it, and, if he was poor, I'd return it."*

Yogi comments on traveling through the land of opportunity:

> *"The towels were so thick there, I could hardly close my suitcase."*

Yogi's continuing efforts to broaden his horizons:

> *"You can observe a lot just by watching."*

When told he looked nice and cool in his summer suit, Yogi replied:

> *"Thanks, you don't look so hot yourself."*

Yogi Berra poses for the press on the eve of his 13th World Series. He would play in 14 over the course of his career (a major league record), and win 10.

This is what Casey Stengel said about his only living rival in malapropisms, Yogi Berra:

"They say Yogi Berra is funny. Well, he has a lovely wife and family, a beautiful home, money in the bank, and he plays golf with millionaires. What's funny about that?"

The indomitable Casey Stengel
(This is what I want to look like when I'm 80 years old)

The sagacity, wit, and goodness of Casey Stengel and Yogi Berra is much too much to try and explain or document here. But the proof's in the puddin' – it's better to illustrate than to explain. Here are some more Yogi-isms. There's a million of 'em. And like all the days of my life, each one's sweeter than the one before:

"I really didn't say everything I said."

"If you ask me a question I don't know, I'm not going to answer."

"It's deja-vu all over again."

"The only reason I need these gloves is 'cause of my hands."

"If you can't imitate him, don't copy him."

"Never answer an anonymous letter."

"A nickel ain't worth a dime anymore."

"If you come to a fork in the road, take it."

"Pair up in threes."

"I don't remember leaving, so I guess we didn't go."

"It was hard to have a conversation with anyone. There were too many people talking."

"Being with a woman all night never hurt no professional baseball player. It's staying up all night looking for a woman that does him in."

> *"No, you didn't wake me up. I had to get up*
> *to answer the phone anyway."*
>
> *"If people don't want to come to the ball park,*
> *how are you going to stop them?"*
>
> *"I knew exactly where it was, I just couldn't find it."*
>
> *"If you don't know where you are going,*
> *you will wind up somewhere else."*
>
> *"The other teams could make trouble for us if they win."*
>
> *"We made too many wrong mistakes."*
>
> *"I don't know - I'm not in shape yet."*
> (When asked what size cap he wanted)
>
> *"I want to thank you for making this day necessary."*
> (On Yogi Berra Appreciation Day, Yankee Stadium, 1947)

On this Christmas Season 2006, I wanted to let you know how I feel about life, love, laughter, and the Lord. I hope you've enjoyed this installment of the Lightnin' Lowdown, and I wish you and yours a very merry Christmas and a healthy, happy New Year. For those of you who might not agree with everything I say, that's okay - I hope you enjoy disagreeing with me. At least my cards are on the table. With me, what you see is what you get. No kid gloves here. I am too old to pull punches. Life's too short and eternity's too long to fool around with the Truth. Kahlil Gibran said,

> *"In battling evil, excess is good: for he who is moderate in announcing*
> *the truth is presenting half-truth. He conceals the other half*
> *out of fear of the people's wrath."*

I'd like to leave you with the lyrics to one of my favorite Christmas songs, written and recorded by one of my favorite singers, Marty Robbins. I've included these photographs as proof that there is a marked difference in even the physical demeanor of good people with positive outlooks and lost, lonely people without hope. I believe that is a symptom or consequence of the emotional and spiritual difference between good and evil, and that the way one chooses to live and look at life and its tragedies ultimately determines one's fate, and even one's face.

*Dear Lord, I want to thank you
For what you've done for me
For all these many blessings
In a world that's caught in grief and misery*

*No matter where I wander
I'm always in your sight
And so, my thanks, to you my Lord
Upon this Christmas night*

*If all my prayers aren't answered
Then, Lord, I'll understand
There's others more deserving
Others, Lord, who need a helping hand*

*I pray you'll guide and keep me
Ever near the right
And so my deepest thanks, my Lord
Upon this Christmas night*

Merry Christmas to all,
Charlie

JANUARY 2007

20

IT WAS A VERY GOOD YEAR

Happy New Year!

I wanted to take this opportunity to thank all of you Lightnin' Bugs for your continued love and support in what was, thanks to you, a terrific year for me and the band. 2006 was my busiest and best ever – playing 190 shows and finally turning over a new leaf. I wish I could hug each and every one of you and thank you personally for making 2006 such a wonderful, memorable, blessed, banner year for Lightnin' Charlie, the Upsetters, and Charisma. Thanks also to you loyal Lowdown readers for the quarter-of-a-million hits on my website in 2006.

In this first Lowdown of the New Year, I thought I'd make you aware of some of the marvelous things that happened for us this past year, so you would realize some of the reasons why I love you so. As 2007 rolls in, I'm sittin' on top of the world – the happiest man in show business, with the greatest, most beautiful fans in the world, my Lightnin' Bugs.

This is a "year-in-review" for Lightnin' Charlie 2006. I have reprinted most of this from my biography page on LightninCharlie.com, so please excuse the oddity of my writing in the third person.

And awaaaaaay we go...

2006 saw Lightnin' Charlie riding the wave of his brand new CD that, according to Charlie, is his "masterpiece". It featured new sidemen and special guests, big band, small ensemble, and solo acoustic cuts. The new CD, titled *A New Leaf*, received rave reviews worldwide and helped to reinvent Lightnin' Charlie. Dig this buzz, cuz'...

> "The best blues-based CD I've ever heard, including all the classic blues recordings. Every record has some deficiency, but not this one.
> Listening to *A New Leaf* from beginning to end is
> truly a musical experience."
> – Ron Baisden, Blue Rapture

> "A powerful, polished and fresh original release. Atomic-powered hybrid music, somewhere between classic rock 'n' roll and Chicago blues. Vibrant remakes and superb originals."
> – Aaron Crawford, Loafer Magazine

> "A stellar release. *A New Leaf* shines as bright and bold as autumn colors. Contains so many great cuts, it's hard to pick out one or two as standouts."
> – Joe Tennis, Bristol Herald-Courier

> "Rockin' swamp blues and rock 'n' roll just the way I like it. Lightnin' Charlie's *A New Leaf* doesn't have a weak song on it. Can't wait for his next CD."
> – Bernard Boyat, Le Cri Du Coyote (The Coyote Cry, France)

> "An authentic American original, Lightnin' Charlie, with his Stetson hat and Fender Stratocaster, has hit the mark with a FANTASTIC new CD, *A New Leaf* (Blue Chip Records). GREAT ALBUM!"
> – ROOTSTIME (Belgium)

> "Sheer magnificence. The boppin' tunes on *A New Leaf* could bring joy to watching paint dry."
> – Josh Mancuso, News & Neighbor

Lightnin' Charlie says of *A New Leaf*,

> "It's by far the best record I've ever done. It represents the band and me very well. It's us. It's the record that has taken me twenty-one years in the business to make and is the record that will take us to the next level in the business."

In 2006, Lightnin' Charlie performed 190 concerts: as a solo, with his band the Upsetters, and with his vocal group Charisma. Charisma is a three-piece vocal group that performs all the background vocals on *A New Leaf*. Charisma consists of alto, bass, and tenor, while Lightnin' sings lead and plays guitar and piano. Charlie's mother-in-law, Lynda, sings alto and her husband, Steven, sings bass. Lightnin' is most partial though to Charisma's beautiful tenor – it's his wife Beth. Lightnin' Charlie and Charisma perform a wide variety of original and traditional gospel songs and hymns. Charlie explains,

> "Charisma is the Greek word that's translated as 'gifts' throughout the New Testament. Divine gratuity – free gifts from God. That's what we are and what we do, musically. My family means everything to me, and is one of God's greatest gifts to me, so we thought Charisma was a good and proper name for the group. It all comes from God's grace and was given to us freely. And we're trying to give it back."

Lightnin' Charlie performed several unique concerts this past year as a musical triple-threat – Lightnin' Charlie acoustic/solo, Lightnin' Charlie acoustic with Charisma, and Lightnin' Charlie with the full electric band, the Upsetters.

"I've played a lot of concerts and private parties where I open the show as a solo on acoustic guitar, playing classic country and rock 'n' roll, and then bring out Charisma, playing acoustic gospel and folk songs, and then bring out the Upsetters, playing our rhythm and blues and rockabilly stuff. It's a one-of-a-kind show not to be missed, and concert promoters say they get three great acts for the price of two!"

Speaking of his musical family affair, Charlie quips,

"It's not many men who get to go to work with their wife and mother-in-law. It's not many men who'd want to! But for me, it's the greatest. We bring our kids to the shows too, if it's practical, but it's getting harder and harder to keep our four-year old Sam off the stage. He wants to be a singer! You know...*About the moon-a and the June-a and the Spring-a!*"

Charlie is currently working on a new gospel CD.

"I've been writing and working on songs for the new album, which is really going to be a lot of fun to do. And it'll be a very heavy record when God's done with it. I'm just trying to stay out of His way. It's tentatively titled *Good News*, and it's another tour-de-force CD like *A New Leaf*, but with the Ultimate in subject matter. It will be the same type of music that Lightnin' Bugs are accustomed to – rockabilly, blues, and soul, but with a Gospel message."

2006 has been a pivotal year for Lightnin' Charlie. He has gone from playing mostly in nightclubs and bars to playing prestigious performance centers, theatres, churches and nursing homes. Nursing homes?

"If you told me a year ago that I would be playing more gigs than ever, better gigs than ever, and not playing in a single bar, I would've told you to click your heels together and follow the yellow brick road home kid, 'cause this ain't Oz. You see, I play music for a living and always thought that I had to take whatever work came my way to support my family, my band, and myself. I didn't want to travel like a gypsy wildman as in the old days, and locally, bars and clubs are where live bands played. So I was stuck there and hating it.

But after *A New Leaf* came out, I decided to practice what this song preached and truly turn over a new leaf. I took a leap of faith and decided not to book bars anymore. I trusted God to put me in a better place. I figured the One who hung the stars in the sky could certainly get me gigs away from the bottle-throwing drunks and music haters, if I'd let Him.

And so, in January of '06, when a friend of mine, the activities director of a local nursing home, asked me to perform at her facility, I said yes. And that changed everything. I was amazed at the response to me and my music. Again, if a year ago, you asked me about playing nursing homes, I would've said that's a good, charitable thing to do, but not something that I would be interested in doing. After all, I'm a *professional musician* and *world-class entertainer.* A professional touring musician playing nursing homes would be someone who had really 'hit the skids', or so I thought. But how wrong I was.

The folks in these facilities, mostly folks belonging to the 'Greatest Generation', are folks born during the Great Depression, who fought and won the Second World War, and are the sweetest, strongest, most precious people I know. And they turned out to be the greatest audience for my music I'd ever played for. Ever.

What I call 'my music' is actually their music. The music from the '40s, '50s, and '60s that I've been making a living with all these years, is the stuff of their youth. The music and musicians I've loved since I was a kid is the music that they made into hits and the musicians that they made into stars in the first place. And they treated me like I was a star - they rocked and they rolled, they danced and clapped and sang along. We laughed, cried, and sang together. It was unbelievable.

I didn't have to change a thing musically either - I played the same repertoire as always - rock 'n' roll, classic country, rhythm and blues, boogie-woogie and gospel. The only thing I had to watch out for was to not play too many slow songs - they wanted to rock!

And the fact that I was being allowed to musically 'minister' to, or 'serve', this Greatest Generation, the people responsible for my kids not being Japanese or German citizens today, and have the time of my life doing it, was awesome.

Compare this holy experience to my decades of playing for drunks screaming "SKYNYRD!" and you'll understand why I feel like I'm the luckiest guy in the world. It was wonderful, it was a revelation, and it was God.

My friend the activities director then asked me two big questions: one, if she could book me (and pay me) to come back next month; and two, if it would be okay if she called the facility next door and told the activities director there about me. Two big questions with two easy little answers – YES and YES!

Now, eleven months later, I'm performing at over THIRTY health care facilities and loving it, playing good music for good people, uplifting their spirits, while they uplift mine. You can't out-give God. It's a win-win deal. Everybody wins – the residents love it, the staffs at the facilities love it, the families of the residents love it, I love it, my family loves it – I'm home before dark, and I believe God loves it because I'm using the gifts He gave me to do good for others and myself.

Having the honor to be invited into the homes of men who crawled onto Normandy Beach, who climbed Mt. Suribachi, who served with General Patton in North Africa; the heroes (men and women) who fought and won World War II, abroad and at home, is an incredible experience for me that I'll always treasure.

I see folks who, due to Alzheimer's, might not recognize their own children, but will sing every word of a Hank Williams song. I see folks who haven't responded at all to staff, therapists, other residents, or even their own family, that respond beautifully to music. That's what it's all about for me and what I believe music is for – to minister to the spirit, to calm the savage beast.

The legendary singing cowboy Roy Rogers, recalling his first trip to depression-era California in 1930, said,

> 'One night we drew a small crowd to listen to me sing with my father and cousin. They were people like us, camping out and mostly pretty hungry. You could tell most of them hadn't smiled in a long, long time. But now they smiled, listening to the music. It made them happy; kept the dark away for a little bit. That's what I learned that night: I learned what music is for.'

Well, Lightnin' Charlie finally learned in 2006, after only twenty-three years of being a professional musician, what music is for. Fredrick Buechner said,

> 'You know you're doing God's will when your greatest joy and the world's greatest need meet.'

Added to this joy is the fact that there is absolutely no work involved for me – I don't have to haul, set up, and tear down amps and a sound system. I come in playing my acoustic guitar and singing. I also play the facility's ever-present piano and sing without amplification. So I'm never too loud, and more importantly, I'm able to stroll around and sing to, for, and with my audience, rather than standing in one spot behind a microphone and singing at them. This allows me to book two, three, or even four of these one-hour shows in a single day. And I can bring my kids to work with me. What a miracle! It shows me what can happen when we let go and let God."

So nowadays, Lightnin' Charlie is busier than ever, playing concerts in churches, performing arts centers, music festivals, nursing homes and assisted living centers, private parties and reunions, on national and international television and radio, by himself, with the Upsetters, and with Charisma, playing to people who love him and his music. Charlie says, quoting James Dean from the movie *Giant*,

"I'm a rich boy – I'm a rich 'un!"

Some other notable happenings for Lightnin' Charlie in 2006 include:

* playing full gospel concerts at churches
* making the cover of *Marquee Magazine*
* being voted *Favorite Musician/Group In The Mountain South* by the readers of *Marquee Magazine*
* performing concerts at prestigious performing arts centers such as the Paramount Center For The Arts, the Niswonger Performing Arts Center, and the Lincoln Theater
* performing on national television on PBS-TV's syndicated *Song Of The Mountains* concert series
* releasing a live concert DVD *Lightnin' Charlie By Request*
* playing a concert inside a local prison
* having several songs from *A New Leaf* played on radio stations all over the world and being played regularly on XM satellite radio

Lightnin' Charlie, when asked to sum up his life and career in music, quotes Elvis, and tells it like this,

"Every dream I ever dreamed has come true a hundred times.
I learned very early in life that, without a song, the day would never end.
Without a song, the road would never bend. Without a song,
man ain't got a friend. Without a song. So I'll keep singing a song."

Well, what a year, huh? Thanks again for all your soul and support. I couldn't have done any of this without you. I'm looking forward to an even bigger and better 2007, with God's help, and I'm looking forward to hopefully seeing and hearing from all of you real soon.

Keep on the sunny side, keep hitting my website, keep signing my guestbook and writing to me, keep coming out to the shows, and most of all, y'all – keep on keepin' on. And when you're down, look up!

This is Lightnin' Charlie signing off – wishing you and yours a very healthy, happy New Year. And may God bless you as He has blessed me.

Love,
Your Action News Reporter,
Charlie

FEBRUARY 2007

21

STRANGER THAN FICTION, THE STORY OF ME

I've been asked so often about how I came to play music for a living, and there is no easy or pat answer. But I'll try to answer it here. I'll tell you about some of the circumstances that led to me becoming a musician, and some of the people who, unknowingly, influenced and inspired me greatly as a child and as an adult.

It was this month, twenty-three years ago, that I was given the vision that made me decide to pursue a career in music. The vision was in the form of an extraordinary young guitarist by the name of Stevie Ray Vaughan. Stevie Ray and his band, Double Trouble, were performing a concert in Charlotte, North Carolina, at a small nightclub called P.B. Scott's. I was at the concert and way up front – so up front that my elbows were on stage. Stevie and his guitar were within arm's reach of me for the whole concert. And it changed the course of my life. I'll try to explain the unexplainable – the effect Stevie Ray and his music had on me that snowy night in February 1984, but first, let's begin at the beginning.

"You can't be too careful what you tell a child because you never know what he'll take hold of and spend the rest of his life remembering you by."
– Frederick Buechner

According to my mother, I was singing Dean Martin's *Standing On The Corner (Watching All The Girls Go By)* on key and word-for-word (even imitating Dino's slurred baritone delivery) at age three. She says I was reading aloud the King James Version of the Bible at four. Everything I've become, at least as a "Gospel Crooner", I had started learning before Kindergarten.

Standin' on the corner watchin' all the girls go by
Standin' on the corner givin' all the girls the eye
Brother you can't find a nicer occupation
Matter of fact – neither can I
Than standin' on the corner
watchin' all the girls
watchin' all the girls

watchin' all the girls go by

Those were my first performances, given to an appreciative (although captive) audience that usually consisted of my mother and dad, brother and sister, and my Uncle Charlie and Aunt Norma, who would often come over to our house for dinner, dessert, and gin-rummy. Aunt Norma (whom I always called, "Mo-Mo", though I don't know why) and Uncle Charlie were still sweethearts after being married to one another for four decades, and would always get a big kick out of my one-song show. My Mo-Mo and Uncle Charlie were very much a part of my "raising" – they were closer than family to me and my mom and dad, and I love and miss them greatly. They were always around and we had the best times together. They were kind of like the Nortons were to the Kramdens or the Mertzes were to the Ricardos. It was my Uncle Charlie who taught me to ride a bike. My Mom and Dad and Mo-Mo and Uncle Charlie (and I) were inseparable. These dinner parties at my house, complete with my three-minute floorshow, were big fun and are still the source of many warm memories for me. Sometimes I can almost hear the sound of their laughter and cheer. Those were my good old days. You know, I saw an interesting television documentary today on the infamous Chicago Mob Boss, Sam Giancana. It seems that his nickname was also "Mo-Mo", but he bore absolutely no resemblance whatsoever, in body or spirit, to my sweet "Mo-Mo". She was a doll and never whacked anybody.

I always received payment for these performances, although not in cash (I didn't want to jeopardize my amateur status). After my concert (usually given in my soft, one-piece, terry blue pajamas with the feet built-in), I would lie down on the floor and Aunt Norma, my "Mo-Mo", would kneel down beside me and lightly scratch my back until I was in a sort of mini coma. It was terrific. I still love to have my back scratched, but I don't have Mo-Mo to do it for me. Nobody loves me like my Mo-Mo did. Hey, I just had an idea of how Mo-Mo might have gotten her nickname – maybe when she stopped scratching, I'd look over my shoulder and beg her, drunk with pleasure, (Dean Martin fashion) for *"Mo! Mo! Mo-Mo!"* Kind of my version of Oliver Twist begging Mr. Bumble for "More, please..." OK, I know. Let's move on...

My Uncle Charlie was one-of-a-kind. He wasn't my blood uncle, but he was my dad's best friend and constant companion since they were young men in Far Rockaway, New York. I always called Charlie and his wife Norma "uncle" and "aunt". He and my dad, both in their early twenties, first met at a get-together at a mutual friend's house. When another guest got unruly and out of line with the lady of the house, my dad took him outside and knocked him out in the snow. Charlie and my dad were fast friends from then on. This was back in the early

1930s (my dad was fifty-three when I was born) and my Uncle Charlie ran with some wild companions. As a young man, Charlie had made and inherited lots of money. Lots and *lots* of money. And Charlie went through it like a knife through butter. Knowing most of the "A-listers" in New York City in those days, Charlie hung out, partied, and gambled with the who's-who of the day. People like Cab Calloway, the Marx Brothers, Heavyweight Champ Max Baer and his girlfriend, Jean Harlow, and Jack "The Tin Man" Haley were among my Uncle Charlie's (and my Dad's) upper-crust circle of friends. While Uncle Charlie didn't have a great love for money, he had a great love for spending it. It burned a hole in his pocket. A manhole. Charlie had a home in New York, a home in Beverly Hills, a home in Palm Beach, and a penchant for big spending. Constant, big time spending. My Uncle Charlie was the last of the big-time spenders. King of the hundred-dollar tip. He was the guy (much to Mo-Mo's regret) who would always buy a round of drinks for the whole house whenever he entered a nightclub. He had it and he loved to spread it around. Have you heard the stories of how Elvis would fly his jet from Memphis to Denver just to get grilled peanut butter and banana sandwiches from a favorite restaurant there? Well, my Uncle Charlie routinely chartered a private plane, and flew from New York (and later from Miami and Palm Beach) to Havana, Cuba for lunch. And gambling. It was the gambling that finally swallowed up most of his fortune. And I'm talking *big money*. My mother says that when Charlie's parents passed away in the mid-1930s, Charlie inherited over three million dollars. That's Great Depression dollars. According to the Consumer Price Index, that's equivalent to around fifty million dollars today.

In later years, Uncle Charlie and Aunt Norma lived comfortably, but not richly, in a modest beachfront condo in Boca Raton, Florida ("Boca Raton" means "Rat Mouth" in Spanish, but that has absolutely no bearing on our story). This was the Charlie that I grew up knowing and loving, his jet-setting days long over. Charlie was a joy to be around – his dashing good looks, his wink, his smile, and his light-heartedness would brighten up any situation. I remember that when he laughed (and he laughed often), that his whole torso shook, and he was thin as a rail. He was wonderful. If the term "happy-go-lucky" is in the dictionary, it should have Uncle Charlie's picture beside it. His demeanor, and the way he carried himself, was what I emulated as a boy growing into a man.

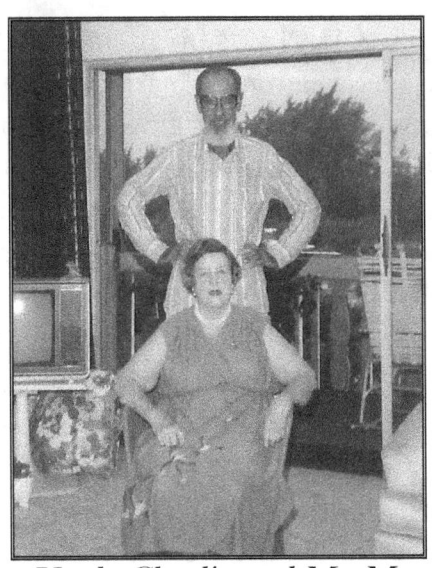
Uncle Charlie and Mo-Mo

    I have many wonderful memories of spending Saturdays with my Uncle Charlie on the beach (Mo-Mo hated the beach). Even into his sixties and seventies, he was in great physical condition. Weather permitting, he swam the ocean and walked the beach almost every day. Charlie remained in perfect health and lived to be ninety-three years old before being killed in an automobile accident in 1999. Charlie was well known and wholly adored by all the teenagers and young adults who frequented the beach at Boca Raton. He especially loved (and was loved by) the "Beach Bunnies", as Uncle Charlie called them. I, as a twelve or thirteen year-old boy, especially benefited from this relationship. When you were with Uncle Charlie, you were in with the "in-crowd". Beach Bunnies were the bronze-skinned, naturally beautiful, golden young ladies with the sun-bleached blonde hair and surfer physiques (who, without Uncle Charlie, I couldn't have gotten the time of day from). They all wanted to hang around him and thought my Uncle Charlie was the coolest. And he was. Charlie could tell uniquely marvelous stories and tall tales (most of them true) and he loved to laugh. He had been everywhere, seen everything, made and lost a huge fortune, and somehow come through it all winking and belly-laughing.

    A real class act, my Uncle Charlie was the consummate gentleman, the most completely likeable person I've ever known, and one who had the rare quality of being liked by both women and men. Nobody met Charlie that wasn't instantly charmed by him. And he was unforgettable. If I have a public persona today as "Lightnin' Charlie", I learned it as a child from watching my Uncle Charlie. The way he carried himself in public, well-dressed and distinguished, but also sporty and down-to-earth, Charlie was always dignified without ever being snobbish, jovial and a cut-up without ever being vulgar. He was a man's man. That's what I wanted to be when I grew up. And you know, on my best day, I ain't even close.

My Aunt Jeannette, my mother's baby sister was a ball of fire. Never married and with no kids of her own, she was like a second mother to my brother, my sister, and me. And we were like the children she never had. Extroverted, cheerful, and extremely loving, Jeannette ran several restaurants through the 1960s and '70s in the sunny, funny playground of the rich and famous, Miami Beach. She was a lot of fun to be around, always laughing, always "up", and always there for us. She had pet names for my sister, brother, and me – we were her "bubeleh's" and her "Shaineh-Yingeleh's". These were her nicknames for us always. In case you don't know, these are Yiddish words, and my Aunt Jeannette, like the rest of us, was an English-speaking, Southern Baptist from Tennessee. But anyone living and working in Miami Beach in the 1960s and 1970s would invariably pick up lots of Yiddish. It was part of the culture there and is the most colorful, imaginative language I know of. I still use a lot of Yiddish words today – sometimes it's the only word that "works". Yiddish, for those of you who might not know, is a sort of "slang" form of the more proper Hebrew language. My brother Billy, my sister Kathy, and I – are forever our Aunt Jeannette's "bubeleh's" ("babies") and her "Shaineh-Yingeleh's" ("beautiful dolls").

During the early '60s, when I was a baby, Aunt Jeannette had a very famous boyfriend. Leo Durocher and my Aunt Jeannette dated for years after his highly publicized divorce from Hollywood actress Laraine Day. Jeannette and Leo were sweethearts throughout the early '60s when Leo was with the Los Angeles Dodgers and spending the winters and springs in South Florida. I wasn't old enough to remember the two of them together, Leo and Jeannette, but my guess is that there was never a dull moment. I only know what an effervescent character my Aunt Jeannette was. And Leo's character is a matter of record.

Leo "The Lip" Durocher is legendary, in and out of baseball. He's in the baseball Hall Of Fame, making his mark as a manager rather than as a player. His record for most managerial ejections still stands today, hence his nickname, "The Lip". During his career, Durocher was a teammate of Babe Ruth (whom Durocher hated, after Ruth accused Leo of stealing his watch!), was manager to Jackie Robinson, Willie Mays, and Ernie Banks (to name a few), and coined the phrase "Nice guys finish last". Durocher also had the distinction of managing the 1951 New York Giants, famous for the "shot heard 'round the world" – the most celebrated home run in baseball history. Bobby Thomson's famous blast won the pennant for the Giants, beating their cross-town rivals, the Dodgers (who had fired Durocher as manager the previous year), and broke every beating heart in Brooklyn.

You know how everyone has a story of a car or a guitar or some other future collectible that, if they hadn't sold it for peanuts or given it away, would be worth a bundle today? Well, dig this: Leo once gave my big brother a baseball signed by the entire 1956 pennant-winning Brooklyn Dodgers, a team that included Jackie Robinson, Sandy Koufax, Duke Snider, Pee Wee Reese, Don Drysdale, Roy Campanella, et al. The '56 Dodgers had, by my count, at least fifteen future Hall Of Famers on the squad. My brother, being a kid and not knowing any better, played with the ball in the street and probably left it in a schoolyard someplace. It's long gone. God only knows what that baseball would be worth today, but my guess is it would be somewhere up there with my Uncle Charlie's inheritance!

Leo left baseball, Miami Beach, and my Aunt Jeannette in 1964 and moved back to Los Angeles where he starred in television episodes of *The Munsters* and *Mr. Ed,* then returned to baseball, managing the Chicago Cubs from 1966 to 1972, before finally retiring. But back to our story of how my Aunt Jeannette inspired me to become a musician. That story – my story – doesn't stem from her love affair with "The Lip" of baseball fame. Our story stems from her meeting another famed lip – an even more famous lip – a curled one belonging to a former truck driver in Memphis, Tennessee.

In 1957, Jeannette was sixteen, going to high school, and living with her mother, dad, and brothers in Greeneville, Tennessee. Her mother (my grandmother) was a seamstress and her father (my grandfather) was a policeman. My mother (Jeannette's older sister) had already moved south to Florida, and this was five years before I was born. The story goes like this:

Once upon a time, half a century ago, in a quiet little hamlet nestled in the shadows of the Smoky Mountains of East Tennessee, my grandmother wrote a love song. Now, to my knowledge, this was the only song my grandmother (who didn't sing or play a musical instrument) had ever written, before or since. Positive that this song would be a hit if the right singer sang it, my grandmother decided Elvis Presley should be the one to record it. Despite the fact that money was very tight, and despite the fact that they didn't know a soul in Memphis, and despite the fact that Elvis was, well... *Elvis*, my grandmother, not deterred by the facts, bought Jeannette a bus ticket from Greeneville to Memphis to deliver it. Crazy, huh? Growing up around my grandmother and knowing her to be a very down-to-earth, sensible, stable, working woman, none of this makes any sense, and is therefore *especially* crazy-sounding to me. I couldn't make it up. But once again, reality strangles invention. So this whole crazy story begins with three very crazy assumptions: one, that my grandmother was suddenly a songwriter; two, that Elvis Presley would even consider recording her song; and three, that her teenage daughter should make the four-hundred-and-fifty mile bus trip to

Memphis, alone, to somehow deliver this song to Elvis personally. If this story sounds incredible to you as you're reading it, believe me... I am sitting here scratching my head in disbelief as I am writing it. I can only tell you that it is incredible, it is unbelievable, and it is true. So my sweet grandmother, Bessie, put a very reluctant Jeannette on a Greyhound bus bound for Graceland with instructions not to give the song to anyone but Elvis himself. Sure, that makes sense.

Once in Memphis, Jeannette's only chance to see Elvis was to hang around all day outside the now-famous gates of Graceland along with dozens of other fans. She explained her mission to the friendly gatekeeper, who introduced himself as "Travis Smith". Travis, taking a liking to Jeannette (and probably feeling more than a little sorry for her as well), invited her to eat dinner with him and his wife and kids. Jeannette gratefully accepted and when Travis' shift was over, he put her into a golf cart and drove up the driveway towards Graceland. "Going to his car", Jeannette thought. But at the top of the hill, at a house trailer beside the house, Travis got out of the golf cart and told Jeannette to *"come on!"* Jeannette, perplexed, said, "I thought we were going to your home for supper". Travis laughed and replied, *"This is my home. I live here. Elvis is my nephew."* Travis Smith, the gatekeeper, was Elvis' uncle, and he and his wife, Lorraine, lived adjacent to the main house with their two sons (Elvis' first cousins), Bobby and Billy. After eating supper, they took a stunned Jeannette over to the house and introduced her to their famous nephew.

Jeannette says that she wasn't a huge fan of Elvis before her trip to Memphis. She says that she enjoyed his records, but didn't understand what all the "fuss" was about. But that night she saw him, half-naked and in the flesh, and all bets were off. Inside Graceland, upstairs, Elvis had apparently just gotten out of the shower. His hair was wet, and he was standing in a doorway, wearing slacks and shoes, but no shirt. My Aunt Jeannette was walking through the hallway when she saw him,

*"He was just breathtaking! He literally took my breath away –
he was sooo beautiful!"*

Clumsily trying to tell him how much better he looked in person, Jeannette stammered,

"Y-y-you're not very pho-to-gee-nic".

To which Elvis replied, politely correcting her nervous mispronunciation,

"Photo*genic.*"

Ironically, the song, the original purpose of her trip, was never even mentioned to Elvis, and no copy of it survives today. Jeannette went out on the town with

Elvis and his gang of cousins and friends, in awe of the whole crazy deal. She was suddenly a friend of the family's, hanging out with the biggest star in the world. Elvis rented a roller skating rink the first night and a movie theater the next, and then Jeannette returned home to East Tennessee and normalcy. Vernon and Gladys (Elvis' dad and mom) invited Jeannette to return and stay with them, whenever she had a long weekend from school, which she often did. But unfortunately, longevity did not run in the Presley family. Gladys Presley passed away in 1958, her brother Travis in 1964. Travis and Lorraine's son Bobby also died very young, of congenital heart disease at age twenty-eight.

Jeannette remained good friends with Elvis' Aunt Lorraine for the rest of her life, and saw Elvis for the last time at Graceland on his homecoming from the Army in 1960. That same year, my Aunt Jeannette, along with my grandparents and my four uncles, all left Greeneville, Tennessee and moved to Miami, to join my mother and hoping for better-paying jobs. Kind of an east-coast version of *The Beverly Hillbillies*.

Aunt Jeannette

Aunt Jeannette's stories of being a part of the inner sanctum of the young Elvis Presley would leave quite an impression on me. She never tired of talking about her visits to Graceland, which she saw for what it was in those days – Elvis' parents' home, always filled with music and fun, family and friends. But she also saw, first-hand, some of the burdens of having fame like Elvis suddenly had, and the price Elvis paid for the blessings of his success. Destiny had taken him from the abject poverty of the Lauderdale Courts Housing Projects, to this beautiful Graceland mansion in two years. And he brought his entire, extended family with him. In spite of all the fun, and in spite of being around Elvis, which was unreal, Jeannette said she was always ready to go home after her two or three day visit.

Since everything revolved around Elvis, and since Elvis slept until three or four in the afternoon, Jeannette (and everyone else, according to Jeannette) spent most of their time sitting around waiting for Elvis to get up. Then they'd go mess around Memphis with Elvis all night, running from people, then sneak back into Graceland at dawn and go to bed. After a couple of days (and nights) of this, Jeannette would be exhausted. She said it was like being in prison. A gilded cage is still a cage, and in those days, Memphis and the fans still allowed Elvis to go out and about to some degree. And at that time, it was still new (and fun) to Elvis. But not for long. Jeannette forever after loved to talk to me about Elvis because I loved him so much. She never forgot the truly humble, shy, nice person he was and she would always shake her head and laugh in disbelief when talking about the way he *"looked"*...

"Nobody looked like him, kiddo. Nobody!"

To have this personal connection with the biggest star, certainly of the 20th century, and probably of all time, would change my life. Although I didn't play in bands growing up (I didn't play in a band until I was grown), I played guitar all the time. By myself, for myself, in my bedroom, and Elvis was the inspiration for that. I didn't "perform" for family or friends anymore (being the "baby", I got my back scratched whenever I wanted!).

I learned to play the guitar by ear, and learned EVERY song Elvis ever recorded (there's about three million of them). I learned to play and sing virtually every hit song from the 1950s, along with more contemporary songs by the Beatles, Creedence Clearwater Revival, etc.

But, for me, Elvis was (and still is) very different from all the rest. Not only did I memorize every *syllable* of every Elvis song, I wanted to learn every song and singer that Elvis *listened* to. I felt such a strong connection to Elvis, the man, that I wanted to learn what his musical likes and dislikes were. I wanted to know the music and musicians that influenced *him*. That's what led me to discovering gospel greats like Mahalia Jackson and Sister Rosetta Tharpe. Sensational quartets like Hovie Lister and the Statesmen (with their fantastic lead singer Jake Hess - Elvis' favorite singer), the Soul Stirrers (featuring the unbeatable twin leads of Paul Foster and Sam Cooke), the Harmonizing Four (with Jimmy Jones' brutal bass), the jumpin' jubilee sound of the Golden Gate Quartet, and the fabulous Dixie Hummingbirds were (and still are) some of my faves. I learned classic R&B songs by The Clovers and Ivory Joe Hunter. I learned every song (although I couldn't sing them!) by Elvis' favorite vocalists, people like Roy Hamilton and Clyde McPhatter. Country artists like Marty Robbins and Hank Williams were favorites of Elvis and are still favorites of mine today. I went for the pop singers that Elvis loved, like Bill Kenney of the Ink Spots, and Nat

"King" Cole. Elvis' love of the blues and blues singers sent me off in search of the likes of Arthur Crudup, Lowell Fulson, Big Bill Broonzy, Junior Parker, and Jimmy Reed.

As a teenager, I loved all of this, and wanted to copy and *"be"* all these artists, at an age when I was most impressionable, and most willing and able, to soak up all these influences. These were very illogical musical choices – eclectic to a fault – but led to my blending of all my favorite music into the style that would later become "Lightnin' Charlie".

Ironically, it is the exact same potpourri of music that had, in the late '40s and early '50s created what became "Elvis" and "rock 'n' roll". I don't think Elvis was necessarily the greatest *singer* in the world – I don't think Elvis is even the greatest singer in the preceding paragraphs – but what Elvis could *communicate* through his singing is what I wanted a piece of, and is what makes him "the greatest" in my book. His singing still has that "X-factor", that Spirit of Communication, that creates gold and platinum records and number one hit songs, even thirty years after his death. Name another singer that can do that.

Without Elvis leading me to these great artists and their repertoire, I never would have dug deep enough to find these gems. Remember, I was a middle-class, white kid growing up in Miami, Florida during the 1970s. I'll bet no one in my high school had ever even heard the song *Baby What You Want Me To Do* – let alone be able to play the guitar part. But I could, thanks to my Aunt Jeannette.

No one person "invented" rock 'n' roll, but what Elvis did, before and to a greater degree than anyone else, was to combine gospel with rhythm and blues, country with pop, and blend it all together to make a sound purely unique, and never before heard. The music that he heard and loved as a kid all came together in him to become the musical persona that was "Elvis". When you hear Elvis singing all these different styles of music, you don't hear all the different styles or ingredients, you hear Elvis.

Elvis was pop culture's first "Great Emancipator", and in my opinion, was the single-handed precursor to Martin Luther King and the civil rights movement of the 1960s. Before you laugh at me and disregard the validity of what I just said, consider this: Elvis Presley put previously segregated musical styles together and, consequently, brought previously segregated *people* together – people of all colors and creeds, that beforehand, were not *allowed* together – sacred and secular, black and white. He blended more disparate cultures together than all the "sit-ins" and marches of the 1960s combined. It's one thing to change laws, and it's another thing to change hearts and minds. Elvis Presley changed the *people* of this country, forever.

I've been told after performing a concert that includes gospel, blues, rock, and country, that somehow, it all just "sounds like Lightnin' Charlie". That's quite a compliment. And that's the key. It is this peculiar blending of eclectic American musical styles which is my formula. It is the formula that has created my career and allowed me to appeal to such a wide range of people today. For me to say that Elvis *influenced* my career is quite an understatement. Elvis Presley virtually *invented* my career.

I don't know if Elvis would have impacted me so, if not for having the personal connection through my Aunt Jeannette. But I believe that it was my looking back, *beyond Elvis*, to these great artists who influenced him, which was the vehicle for my future success. And this surely came as a result of my wanting to know Elvis, the man (rather than just "Elvis", the image), as my Aunt Jeannette had.

But there's still another thing that Elvis did for me. The Greatest Thing. And that was to lead me, through his gospel music, to Calvary, to the Christ that died for me, and to a lifelong love affair with the Lord.

I would not be where I am or who I am today, without my grandmother Bessie's song, without my Aunt Jeannette, and without Elvis Presley. I know I wouldn't be a singer today if not for that crazy trip my Aunt Jeannette took to Memphis fifty years ago. And it was my singing, my *"sound"*, which first captured the heart of a beautiful young Virginia girl who would become my wife, my best friend, and the mother of our two precious sons. Allow me to again quote one of my favorite verses of scripture:

> *"And we know that all things work together for good to them that love God, to them who are the called according to His purpose."*
> - Romans 8:28 KJV

I don't have any sense of humor about certain subjects. If you want to "walk on the fightin' side of me", make an ignorant, crude joke about my family, my country, my Lord, or my main man, Elvis Presley. I'm the number one fan of the man from Tennessee.

My biggest fan is my wife Beth. As if my life story needed more irony, my Aunt Jeannette's first name was "Elizabeth" ("Jeannette" was her middle name), and so my wife has the same first name as my Aunt Jeannette, and has the same nickname as my Grandmother ("Bessie"). Some coincidence, huh? Well, I believe "coincidence" is actually God working anonymously.

Once upon a time, long before I ever saw her, Beth says that she already "loved me". She had heard my first CD, and was instantly enchanted...

> *"I had never heard anything like it before – I loved it. And, somehow, I loved you! I really did. I started going to as many of your shows as I could, which caused a lot of fights between my boyfriend and me at the time. I really loved you, but he didn't like you at all!"*

Sounds to me like her boyfriend must've been some kind of imbecile. Never having "the nerve" to come up and introduce herself to me, Beth says that every time she was en route to one of my shows, she would give herself a pep-talk...

> *"Tonight's the night, I'll just go up to him and introduce myself and say 'I love your music and I love Muddy Waters and I'd love it if we could just hang out sometime and listen to music...' but it never happened. Every time I saw you, you were surrounded by all the women and I just couldn't – I was too shy."*

Nice work if you can get it, huh boys?

But one summer night, at a club in Claypool Hill, Virginia, I found my thrill. Yes friends, I found my thrill on Claypool Hill. The band was between sets and I sat down at a table, talking with some friends. And Beth was there, sitting across the table from me. I was mesmerized. She was the most beautiful girl I had ever seen in my whole life. Enchanted would be a huge understatement – it was literally *IN* love-at-first-sight for me. Her friends at the table, feeling uncomfortable, were telling her, *"He's staring at you Beth!"* And I was – I couldn't take my eyes off her. Still can't. Although we had not spoken one word to each other, I knew right then that she would be my wife.

So meanwhile, back on Claypool Hill, her friends, thinking that I must be some kind of predator, all got up to leave. They got just outside the club, when Beth stopped, turned around, and gathering her nerve, came back in, telling her friends that she "wanted to get a CD". We made small talk for a minute, introducing ourselves (even though we had known each other forever), and then I walked her to the door. She wrote her phone number on my hand before she said goodnight, and the rest, as they say, is history. We're currently growing old together, celebrating our tenth wedding anniversary next month, and two kids later, we're still honeymooners.

Beth shares the image she has of me in her memory from those days...

> *"You're onstage in a packed-out little club, sounding great – like nobody else I had ever heard, you're thin as a rake, in a white dress shirt soaked through with sweat, playing to a dance floor filled with beautiful girls."*

She says that she doesn't remember there ever being men on the dance floor – just women. Ah yes, it's good to be king! Beth remembers that when I would play the guitar behind my head...

"People would go wild – women and men".

All this sounds very familiar to me. Almost parallel. It sounds a lot like the image I have in my memory of seeing a peerless young musician named Stevie Ray Vaughan, a night that would change me, my ambitions, and my future, forever.

I was twenty-two years old when I met the guy who turned my life around. That's the same age Beth was when she met the guy who turned hers around: me! Irony abounds in the Lowdowns, doesn't it? I was in my fourth year of college at East Tennessee State University, but nowhere near graduation (I had changed my major three times and nothing seemed to be "clicking" for me academically). As far as my music was concerned, I was still in the same bag as when I was a pre-teen – I was playing guitar and singing along with songs on my stereo, but had never – at no time – *ever* considered the possibility of playing music as a career. I had never been one of those stereotypical kids with a loud garage band and aspirations of rock stardom.

Then one day, the phone rang. It was my buddy Taro, whom I worked with at a local record store (he was a full-time employee, I worked part-time, doing inventory, just so I could get the employee discount – 25% off of records!). Taro, a college student from Kyoto, Japan, and I shared a love for blues music, and guitar in particular. One of Taro's record store perks, was that he could take promo copies of albums he liked home, and listen to them, tape them, and bring them back to the store the next day. He would sometimes "turn me on" to different music he found, but since most of the music I liked was not coming out on newly released records, it never amounted to anything for me. But this time was different. Very different. I don't remember what I ate for dinner last night, but I remember that phone conversation verbatim, word-for-word, from twenty-three years ago. It went exactly like this. Feel free to read this aloud, adding a Japanese accent to Taro's part.

   Me: *"Hello"*
   Taro (laughing): *"You're not gonna believe this, man..."*
   Me: *"What?"*
   Taro (laughing harder): *"This guy – Stevie Ray Vaughan!"*
   Me: *"Who?"*
   Taro: *"Stevie Ray Vaughan, man! He's un-be-lieve-able!"*
   Me (unimpressed): *"Who is he?"*
   Taro: *"He's a blues guitarist from Texas, man. Un-be-LIEVE-able!!!"*
   Me (still unimpressed, having no faith that anybody could play the blues

like my heroes, the long-established giants of deep blues guitar, B.B. King, Freddy King, Magic Sam, and Lightnin' Hopkins): *"Who does he sound like?"*

Taro (laughing again, even harder now): *"He sounds like ALBERT KING...and Jimi HEN-drix, man!!!"*

Me: *"What???"*

Taro (still laughing): *"Yeah man!!!"*

This is where I went silent, my mind unable to process the impossible. This was in the days of *Footloose* and *Men At Work*. My initial reaction was typical of shock victims. First, utter disbelief; followed by cynical skepticism; then, thinking I must not be hearing this correctly, asking him to repeat what he had just said; followed finally by just being silently dumbfounded.

I wonder if the Mercury astronauts of the early '60s reacted the same way to JFK's pledge that we (they) would walk on the moon by the end of the decade, before we had put even a monkey into orbit. Albert King? Jimi Hendrix? It was simply nonsense.

Me (hearing the music playing in the background): *"Albert King and Jimi Hendrix???"*

Taro (in a state of bliss): *"Yeah man!!!"*

Me (still in denial): *"Lemme hear it."*

Taro (holding the phone in front of his speakers): *"Okay man, here you go!!!"*

Taro played for me, over the phone, three songs, which I learned later were the first three cuts from SRV's debut album, namely "Love Struck Baby", "Pride And Joy", and "Texas Flood". In these three songs, Stevie Ray managed to combine every style of music I had loved since I was a kid, and what came out sounded brand new. And *phenomenal*. Taro came back on the phone, still laughing, and I couldn't say a word. I was speechless. Completely blown away. It's impossible to realize the impact of an event, outside the relative context of time. To help you understand my initial cynicism, here's a few of the top records of 1984:

Karma Chameleon by Culture Club (Boy George)
Time After Time by Cyndi Lauper
Wake Me Up (Before You Go-Go) by Wham!
Like A Virgin by Madonna

You get the picture?

I finally regained enough consciousness to speak into the phone.

Me (mumbling): "Who IS this guy???"
Taro: "Stevie Ray Vaughan!"
Me: "Where's he from?"
Taro: "Texas!"
Me: "A black guy?"
Taro: "No, he's white, man!"
Me (thinking again I had heard wrong): "He's white? What's he look like?"
Taro (laughing again and describing at the album cover): "He's holding a Strat (guitar), he's wearing a poncho and a big bolero hat! He looks like Clint Eastwood, man!!!"

Well, that shut me up again. *Clint Eastwood? Poncho* and *bolero hat?* Once again, I was cold-cocked by the facts. God is the greatest dramatist.

SRV

So went our baptism by Stevie Ray. Soon after, Taro and I got tickets to see Stevie and his band, Double Trouble in concert in Charlotte, North Carolina. We made the four-hour drive, anxious and excited, but really not knowing what to expect. His record was mind-boggling, but what would he be like live?

We arrived at the club very early. The opening act hadn't started, and the place was almost empty. Perfect. Taking my place on the dance floor at the front of the stage (even Taro thought I was crazy), I was stationed and ready – the area secured. Just because the place was empty now, didn't mean that it wasn't going to be slammed later, and I was not moving from that spot. I was *"like a tree that's planted by the water, I shall not be moved"*. The small club was laid out like this – there was the stage, then a dance floor, then cocktail tables and chairs, and a bar in back. There was also a second-level balcony that ran around the club's perimeter. We were the only people on the floor – me at the stage, and Taro at a table. A few patrons were sitting at the bar like normal people. But me? I was standing at the edge of the stage. I was dug in. I didn't go to the bar, I didn't go to the bathroom, I didn't dare budge from that spot – *my spot* – right in front of SRV's microphone stand. Not for the whole night. Anybody else wanting to see Stevie Ray Vaughan that night would be seeing him from behind me.

A half-hour or so later, the opening band took the stage, and a few more folks started arriving. Naturally, they took seats at the dozens of empty tables in fine view of the stage. The opening act was unknown at the time, but was soon to become very big in the blues world. They were the Robert Cray Band, and would also figure quite prominently, years later, on the night of Stevie's death. Well, they thought I was a psycho. Here's this big empty room, with plenty of places to sit and enjoy the show, and I'm standing by myself, at stage front, with my elbow and my drink on the foot of the stage, which was about three feet high, or waist level. The whole band thought I was some kind of a nut, and never took their eyes off me. The fact that I thought Cray was great didn't ease their minds, either, because the more I clapped and hollered, the more concerned they got for their safety. As their set was finishing up, the club had gotten full. Now it was break time and Stevie was next. I was in position, dead-smack center; with his mic stand a mere eighteen inches away from my elbow.

The closer it got to show time, the more crowded the place became. The dance floor had begun to fill up behind me, and even Taro joined me up front, thinking that maybe I wasn't so crazy after all. Then the house lights went down, and they introduced the band,

"And now, ladies and gentlemen, from Austin, Texas,
Stevie Ray Vaughan and Double Trouble!"

They played two smokin' instrumentals before Stevie came to the mic for Hendrix's *Voodoo Chile (Slight Return)*, and my life, as I knew it, was over. I would never be the same again.

He was like a musical meteor. Technically, he was beyond brilliant. Dynamically, he was incredible – he'd break it down from a torrent to a whisper then back up again. His tone was unbelievable. People were going crazy. He played and sang with so much soul, I couldn't believe what I was seeing. Nobody could. I've seen a lot of truly great blues musicians, but this was like another *planet* in comparison. Everyone who saw Stevie in person during his tragically short career would know exactly what I am talking about. Those who didn't can only imagine. He didn't seem to be "playing" the music – the music was playing him. He seemed to be the "vessel" through which this outrageously beautiful music freely flowed. And the music was, in my opinion, straight from God. It even sounded like God's personality – it was brutal and soft, loving and dangerous, angry and sweet. Stevie Ray Vaughan was the vehicle, but God was the driver.

I am at such a loss to try to describe in words what Stevie's music was like. It was so far beyond the physical realm, such a Spiritual Experience for me, that mere words fail me. For thousands of years, poets have been trying, unsuccessfully, to describe love. But the *effect* it had on me...that I can easily describe. I knew right then and there, and without a doubt, *THAT* was what I wanted to do. I had never seen "it" done before, and I haven't seen "it" done on that level since. I didn't know, before seeing Stevie that "it" *could* be done. The fact that I was seeing it from two feet away was mind-blowing. The result of the concert was the *knowledge* that I was going to play in a blues band, and I would pursue a career in music. Period. It seemed obvious, all of a sudden, that that was my destiny. Like every day of my life up till then had the sole purpose of bringing me there to that spot. I had never even considered playing music "professionally" before. It came to me that night like an Epiphany. And like a true Epiphany, I had to be *shown*.

> Epiphany – the manifestation of a god.
> [From the Greek, *epi* – "to"; *phainein* – "show"]

I gave a newspaper interview right after Stevie died, and the reporter asked me about seeing him in person, what it was like, and about the multitude of Stevie Ray imitators out there at that time. It was a very emotional interview for me, and the subject of Stevie Ray's death is something I can't talk about even today. It's just too sad.

> "It was like I had been to the mountaintop. I had seen the Promised Land. Of guitar playing. You just couldn't get any better than that. Stevie had it all – every gift a guitarist could possibly have. There is a level of musicianship that one cannot go above. And the ones that are at that level, you can't say one is 'better' than another. Just different. It becomes a matter of style.
>
> Can you say that Frank Sinatra is 'better' than Mahalia Jackson? Or that Louis Armstrong is 'better' than Hank Williams? Was Moses was a 'better' prophet than Isaiah? The term 'better' doesn't apply to these guys. Their musicianship is on an infinite, spiritual level that one cannot even describe in finite terms, or with mere language. And there are a lot of guys,

in my opinion, on the very top of the blues guitar heap. Freddy King and B.B. and Lonnie Johnson and Magic Sam. But there's never been, and never will be, a guitarist that can say that they're 'better' than Stevie Ray Vaughan. He's tops.

You know, there are guys by the bushel out here now, copying his every lick, note-for-note. They've got his amps and their guitars set up like his. They wear their hair like him and have hats and stage clothes like him and make faces like him. And they miss the whole point. They're like Elvis impersonators. Have you ever heard an Elvis impersonator that was even a tenth as good as Elvis? And there's not one of 'em that's even CLOSE to sounding like Stevie. Nor will there ever be.

Why is that? Well, I'll tell you friend, that's when you know you're dealing with something that's not of this world, when man can't copy it. Edison invented the electric light bulb – a great accomplishment. But his work can be copied exactly by any 4th grader doing a science project, and you can't tell the difference. It's easy to simply copy the culmination of someone's lifework. You've got the blueprint. But reciting the Gettysburg Address doesn't make you Lincoln. No one will ever be able to copy what Stevie Ray was. It's impossible. Someone may equal it, by letting God speak through them and their music to such an extent that it's no longer them, but God. I thank God for Stevie Ray. And I thank Stevie Ray for letting go and letting God *use him*. And I thank God for bringing me to the front of that stage that first night in Charlotte, North Carolina."

After Stevie's show, I waited outside the stage door, in the snow, for about an hour, in hopes of getting to speak to Stevie. I spoke with the very sweet Tommy Shannon (Stevie's bass player), for a little while, and then Stevie came out carrying his guitar case. I got to speak briefly to Stevie and shake his hand, but I don't remember exactly what was said. It was too surreal. I think I said something feeble like, "Unbelievable show!" He said, "Thanks", we shook hands and he was gone.

But one thing stuck out to me then, and it sticks out to me now, and that was a bumper sticker (all puns intended) on the guitar case Stevie was carrying (which contained his now-famous "Number One"). It illustrates, in one word, what I have been trying to convey in this Lowdown about "style". That night in Charlotte, I wouldn't have thought Stevie Ray Vaughan was into anything but the very best instrumentalists and greatest guitarists ever born, and that much of the music I loved would be a joke to him. But there's more to music than meets the ear, and there's more to an artist than meets the eye. Every human being is a culmination of all that has gone before him. The bible says,

"There is nothing new under the sun."

My style, being the combination of so many old styles, is nothing new. It's just me. Hopefully, whatever it is that is "me" comes out through my music sounding fresh and original. What was this great big idea about "style" and "originality" on Stevie Ray Vaughan's guitar case? A surprising (to me) little sticker with one big word on it:

"ELVIS"

The greatest fruit to come from that Stevie Ray Epiphany is not a band, but a band of gold - that is, meeting my wife, Beth. Would we have ever met if I had continued to sing and play guitar only in my bedroom? I believe so, but I don't know how - we lived over a hundred miles apart from each other, so I don't know how we would've gotten together. One thing I do know is that we are meant to be together. I'm sure of that. And I know that God would've made a way. But I'm glad This Way worked.

His Way was made through the people and events I've discussed here. Without my Stevie Ray Epiphany, there would be no band. Without my band, there would've been no CDs. Without my CDs, there would be no Beth. Without Beth, there would be no Sidney and no Sam, our six and four year-old boys, who are laughing and playing and pestering me as I write this.

Who would I be without my Mother and Dad, my two dearest ones, who raised me with the purpose to "be my own man", and taught me that whatever I decided to do in life, to be happy doing it, and to always do my best doing it.

Where would I be without Uncle Charlie and Aunt Jeannette? What would I be doing? All I know is, I wouldn't be who I am or what I am today. And I wouldn't be doing what I'm doing with whom I'm doing it. I'm successful and I'm happy and I'm blessed with a wonderful family. I have "made it". I'm a "made man". But I'm in no way a *self*-made man. A multitude of people and events helped make me and shape me - *build* me into the man I've become. I wish I could thank them all.

But there's one Man who's above all others, who bled and died so that someday, I'd be the man He always knew me to be. I thank Him most of all.

His truly,
Charlie

photo by Bill W. Bryant

MARCH 2007

22

THE SQUEAKY WHEEL

Maybe it's cranky old age creeping in, maybe it's due to my going a bit "stir-crazy" this winter, or maybe it's the fact that customer service is quickly becoming a thing of the past in business today, but lately I've been writing a lot of complaint letters to companies, expressing my dissatisfaction with their service and/or product.

I believe this is more indicative of lousy products and rotten service rather than me being in a foul mood with nothing else to do but email complaint letters. Often these letters, addressed to customer service departments (who promise complete satisfaction), are either ignored completely, or answered with a "form letter" that doesn't address any of my problems.

The worst thing, for me, is to be taken advantage of and then ignored. Can I get a witness? This is where righteous indignation enters in and I admit I can become a bit obsessive. My wife would disagree. She'd say a lot obsessive. Although I really don't have the time to fool with any of this, I am too stubborn to let it go, especially when my hard-earned money is at stake and I know I'm right. Are you with me? But I've learned that more flies are drawn with sugar than with vinegar – if I can make them laugh at my situation, then I've got them. I've learned to rant and rave with a sense of humor, much like a lot of the stories here in the Lightnin' Lowdown. If you just rant and rave, they laugh at you, and then ignore you. But if you rant and rave with a sense of humor, they're more likely to laugh with you, and maybe even address your situation.

> Service (them) – an act of helpful activity; help; aid.

> Righteous indignation (me) – retribution, retributive justice; anger and contempt combined with a feeling that it is one's right to feel that way; anger without guilt.

Here's some sad (but true) facts: firstly, most corporate businesses today, especially the service industries, would rather lose your trade forever than to have someone on salary to deal with your problem; secondly, most "managers" at the store level don't have the necessary skills to be on a junior high school yearbook committee – let alone deal with customer complaints in a pragmatic and responsible fashion; and lastly (and sadly), they just don't care – not about the customer and his or her dissatisfaction, not about their company and the future loss of revenue and business, and, most importantly, not about themselves and the impression they make on other people. And if you think I am mistaken, spend half an hour in a mall this Saturday and then call me a liar. Or try getting some tech support from your Internet provider (in English). Or try getting help from a customer service representative from your friendly credit card company. You'd think a 28% interest rate would entitle you to some service, right? To quote Muhammad Ali from the second Leon Spinks fight,

"Not here and not today!"

In this Lowdown, I'll tell you about three of these episodes that demonstrate the fact that it's the squeaky wheel that gets the grease, but it's the humorous squeaks that get the response. Big business counts on the fact that most disgruntled customers won't take the time and effort to pursue the matter. They'll ignore you (and the situation) if they can. Bullies bank on the notion that once the little guy is bullied, that he'll just go away. But I'm their worst nightmare. I'm the Jake LaMotta of the Internet! I'll just keep comin' at 'em. I refuse to lose. And my definition of winning sometimes is simply getting acknowledged. I exist and I am somebody! I hope you enjoy – have fun...

<u>Part One</u>

After an absolutely dreadful family birthday dinner at a local chain restaurant, and after getting no satisfaction from the "management team" there, I emailed their corporate office, full of rage and righteous indignation (not to mention indigestion). Let's call the restaurant "O'Bobby's" (not its real name, but terribly close).

In my letter, I told O'Bobby's about our nightmare experience, which was the worst dining experience I've ever had in my lifetime, and is the worst restaurant experience that anyone I've told it to has ever HEARD OF in their lifetime. I'm not going to relive (and put you through) the torment of all the gory details from that night, but it was total meltdown. Please understand that I am not one of those horrible people who nit-pick and complain about everything in restaurants. I've worked in (and eaten in) enough restaurants to despise those people. I'll quietly suffer a cold baked potato or an overcooked steak rather than risk being mistaken for one of them. I am the opposite. I hate to complain and hardly ever send anything back to the kitchen. Having worked in lots of restaurants, I know what happens to much of the food that gets sent back to the kitchen.

But this particular night was so abysmal and so outrageously over-the-top (and our complaints to restaurant "management" fell on deaf ears – they actually hid from us) that I immediately shot a furious email to O'Bobby's corporate customer service department. I love the Internet – thanks Al Gore!

I told them my tale of woe in detail and promised them that although this was my first telling of this tale, it would not be my last. I swore that, with practice, I would get good at telling it. I also told them that I was a full-time musician/entertainer, and if they didn't make this right, not only would I tell the story to everyone and anyone – every time I heard the name "O'Bobby's" mentioned, for as long as I lived, or as long as they were in business (which, if this was the way they conducted business, that I should outlast them by a hundred years), but I would make this horror story a regular part of my stage act.

At that time, I was playing a "house gig" (playing the same room five nights per week) in a hotel convention center [see Chapter 1], located on the same block as O'Bobby's. I could tell and retell my misadventure, on stage, to large audiences of their potential customers, forever. The story really was that extraordinary – it would make a terrific comedic screenplay – people love to laugh at the misfortunes of others. And this was belly-laugh material, as long as it was not happening to you.

I received a phone call the next day from a lady at the O'Bobby's corporate office, saying how sorry they were, how unacceptable this was, etc. She said that they would speak to the store "managers", and that they were prepared to do anything to keep me as a customer. I think they just wanted to make sure this story didn't wind up in my act (I hope they're not reading this – I'm probably violating a gag order of some kind). She said I could expect a call from their regional manager later that day. She also said that they had passed my email around their office, due to its fantastic comedic value, and that everyone was getting a big kick out of it ("Don't get me wrong – what *happened* to you and your family is not funny and is totally unacceptable, but the *way you tell the story...*"). She closed by telling me that (based upon my letter-writing ability), I must be some fine entertainer. I realized that it was my letter-writing ability, and not my injuries, that got me the call back. I was onto something.

The regional manager called me as promised, and dig this: he refunded my money completely and in cash, sent each of my guests $25 gift cards (we were a party of thirteen), and sent me two $50 gift cards for my trouble. My email letter yielded several hundred dollars. But the bad news was that the gift cards were only redeemable at O'Bobby's. Oh well, can't win 'em all.

Part Two

Dealing with rejection has been as much a daily part of my show business experience as guitar strings. I've made thousands of phone calls and sent hundreds of press kits (CDs, promo materials, etc.) to clubs and promoters in hopes of getting a positive response. I don't think I've ever gotten a favorable response from contacting someone "cold" – that is, they don't know me, don't know what I do, and haven't asked me to contact them.

But the thing that upsets me most is when someone asks me to call them or send them materials, and then won't respond. I'll call, and they're "in a meeting". I'll call back, and "they're out". I'll call back, and they're "on the other line". Of course I'll leave messages, and of course, they don't call me back. This makes me crazy. I would much prefer a simple "NO!" so I could go on with my life. I've got other people waiting anxiously to reject me. I could move on. And I would stop calling them and wasting their time, too. I would rather have someone tell me, "Sorry man, you stink" or "We don't have anything for you right now", than to say "Try back tomorrow morning". What ever happened to the good old days of "Don't call us – we'll call you"? That's much too direct and honest for folks these days.

Once in these situations, I usually obsess and, full of righteous indignation [see above], vow to get someone to take my call and tell me something. Anything. And since I'm not going to get the gig anyway, I make it a point to ingratiate myself on them, until at least I know they'll remember my name. After all, they're the ones who saw me or heard me – they gave me their business card and told me to call them so we could do business. And then all I get from them is the runaround, when a one-syllable "No!" would be a real timesaver for both of us. This has been the case more often than not, and must result in one either getting a sense of humor about it or getting out of the business.

One particular instance of this I remember well because I really wanted the gig. While in Memphis, Tennessee playing the Memphis In May Music Festival, I was approached by a gentleman who said he was opening a new club on Beale Street. He said he saw my performance and that he thought that I would be "perfect" to play at his club when it opened. He asked if I would like to see it, as it was truly one-of-a-kind, and when he told me what the name of the club was, I jumped at the chance. It was called "Elvis Presley's Memphis" and was located at Second and Beale in the old Lansky's building, where a young Elvis (along with every other Memphis musician shopped for "cat clothes"). Elvis Presley's Memphis was owned by Lisa Marie, Priscilla, and EPE (Elvis Presley Enterprises), and was filled with unbelievable Elvis items from his Palm Springs home such as his white Story And Clark baby grand piano, a gigantic crystal chandelier that was hanging over the front of the stage, and the pool table that the

Beatles played pool on with Elvis while visiting him at his California home in August of 1965.

My private tour of the club was awe-inspiring for me, having only read about and seen pictures of these items, and the décor inside the club was equally unbelievable. The front doors were gold with huge handles: "E" on the left-hand door and "P" on the right. There were white-carpeted stairs leading up to where the piano and pool table were located (the piano was behind a "movie theatre rope" and was supposedly off-limits, but the pool table would be available for patrons to play on, for an hourly fee. *What? Hello?)*

The stage was magnificent (with the chandelier at the front), and the booths were circular and covered in white and beige suede. Needless to say, I was dumbstruck at the beauty of the club and its furnishings and asked the manager what he expected to happen when drunks and tourists (redundant) filled the place. White carpeting and suede booths? Allowing the public access to a museum piece like that pool table for $10 an hour? All this, and a full bar, seemed (to me) to be the recipe for disaster, but what do I know?

The highlight of this VIP tour for me was getting to sit down at Elvis' piano and playing and singing the gospel song, *I Believe.* On *ELVIS' PIANO!!!* This made everything that was to follow worthwhile.

I was having a coronary at the prospect of playing this place, on that stage, among all this stuff, but I retained a cool, collected exterior. I needed the manager to be more excited about the prospect of getting Lightnin' Charlie than me showing my excitement about playing the gig of my life. But, on the inside, my heart was galloping. I felt that I was born to play this room. It was my birthright. Like Sinatra reading the script of *From Here To Eternity* and knowing that he was born to play Maggio, I knew that this was rightfully mine.

The manager explained that Jewel (a friend of Lisa Marie's) was booked to play the grand opening, but that my mix of blues, rock 'n' roll, and my king-sized (love them puns!) repertoire of Elvis tunes would be "a perfect fit" for this room. He told me he would "love" to talk to me about booking a weekend there with my band. I thanked him and told him I would definitely be in touch and left, making it about a half a block up Beale before starting to stagger.

[Ed. note: staggering up Beale Street is no longer an option, it's required]

I waited the obligatory week before calling him, and was told he was "out", and would I like to leave a message? I did, and after a few days went by without a return call, I called back. And back. And back again. Three weeks went by, and I left messages each time. I remember asking if he still worked there. The reality was dawning on me. I was brokenhearted and wildly upset. Why would he take the time (his time) to give me a private tour of the club, tell me to call him to book a show, and then not take or return my calls?

I thought that he must have not been getting my messages, so I took to sending him letters. Lots of letters. These were also unanswered.

Pathetically, I became determined to get a response – any response. My dreams were being crushed here, and I just wanted to know why (sob-sob). I felt jilted, I didn't understand, and I was tired of being pushed around. And I wasn't gonna TAKE IT ANYMORE!!! Hell hath no fury like a musician scorned.

After dozens of polite, professional phone calls, and several down-to-earth business letters, I started writing poems. Funny, sarcastic poems. I remember saying to my wife,

"At least they'll know who Lightnin Charlie is after they read this!"

I was ready for the Jerry Springer Show. I can see myself: screaming at the club manager, mascara streaming down my cheeks, my shirt torn off...

"I just want you to say it to MY FACE!!!"

I was dealing with some serious emotional trauma, and I just needed closure. I remember writing one little ditty about Lisa and Michael Jackson, and one about Priscilla and Mike Stone (the karate instructor she cheated with while married to Elvis; the guy Elvis famously wanted his Memphis Mafia to kill). Look how beautifully I proposed that, if I changed my name to Michael, would that get me a call back?

My name is Lightnin' Charlie
Not Billy, Frank, or Jack
But if I changed my name to Michael
Then you'd surely call me back

This was quickly followed by...

It seems that only wheels
Named Stone and Jackson get your grease
If you'll respond to Lightnin' Charlie
I'll move on, desist and cease

These four-line poems were uproariously funny (to me), and allowed me to finally "let go" and "move on". I wish I had a copy of some more of these (there were dozens), but none survive, except for these few that I remember. Here's another one of the earlier, more polite ones (they went from bad to worse). Remember, these were only intended to elicit a response. Any response. It went like this...

Elvis had Lincolns
Cadillacs and a Harley
Why not pick up the phone
and book Lightnin' Charlie?

[Ed note: these poems are sick, but are nonetheless copyright protected by LC Enterprises 2001]

I know, it's pretty sad. But it got me what I wanted – they finally responded with a form letter thanking me (yeah right!) for my

"...interest in Elvis Presley's Memphis. Although we do not have any openings for entertainment at this time, we will retain your information for our records, and will possibly contact you in the future.
Thank you and best wishes."

In other words, we have forwarded your politically incorrect poetry to local law enforcement, and we want you to cease and desist. Leave us alone! Hallelujah, that's all I wanted to hear.

I never bothered them again, and a year or two later, the club closed its doors. Friends of mine in Memphis told me that they went out of business "due to terrible management". Tell me something I don't know!

Ironically, Elvis' motto in business was "Takin' Care Of Business - In A Flash", hence his TCB logo with the lightning bolt. But obviously, it skips a generation. Or an ex-wife.

Part Three

The last little diatribe I'll leave you with is my most recent. Many of you are aware of the online movie rental services like Netflix and Blockbuster. I was a member of Netlix for four years and constantly had trouble with their service.

As you probably know, with these services, there are no due dates for movies to be returned – you keep them as long as you want. You keep a list (or queue) of movies you want. When you return one, the next one in your queue will ship. Netflix advertised that they ship your next movie in "one business day" Sounds good. But Netflix was recently forced to settle a lawsuit on this fraud and added the words "usually" and "about" to the above pitch, saying now that they ship your next movie "usually in about one business day".

They go on to say in the fine print on their advertisements that "most people live within a one-day shipping radius of one of their distribution centers".

Apparently I am not "most" people, and live three or four days away from their distribution centers. Since they only ship your next movie upon receiving your old one, this three or four day turnaround time (each way) severely affects the value of the service. It sure did mine.

And when I would receive broken or incorrect DVDs, that would also cause me to cry "foul". After reporting the damaged DVD (and demanding compensation), I would get form emails back from their customer service department assuring me that their crack team (pun intended) of quality control experts diligently inspected every DVD prior to leaving their distribution centers, insuring that their customers receive the best of service.

These form letters never mentioned any compensation for my lack of service (see definition above). They just told me what a good job they were doing.

I started regularly receiving scratched, unplayable DVDs, some broken completely in half. I began to receive DVDs I did not order, other DVDs never arrived at all. I understand that things might occasionally get damaged or lost in the mail, but when things continually go wrong with a service, through no fault of mine, that I am paying for, and is not what is advertised, and I can't get a response from customer service (nor any compensation), I get mad.

Once, after complaining about the turnaround time, Netflix even suggested that I use an address closer to their distribution center (sell my house and move closer to Netflix?), or if I'm on a rural route (I'm not), I should consider using a post office box. Now that's a customer service department. Unbelievable.

You want to get my goat? Lie to me, take my money, and then when I complain about it, ignore me. That'll get it every time. Can I get an "Amen"?

Here's a funny and satisfying (for me) little dialogue between Netflix and myself, after I had cancelled my membership. When they had my monthly subscription fee in their grubby, little hands, they were totally unconcerned with the speed of service. Notice how differently they act when they've shipped three DVDs, and then I cancelled my membership. To quote my man, W. C. Fields, *"Even the worm turns!"*

On 2/21/07, Netflix wrote:

> *Netflix Membership Cancelled*
>
> Dear Charles,
>
> Per your request, your Netflix membership has been cancelled, effective 02/20/2007.

Please return the following titles by their specified due dates:

Due Date   *Title*

02/27/2007   Frank Sinatra: The Man and His Music
02/27/2007   The Sound of Music
02/27/2007   The Hee Haw Collection: Vol. 3

We hope you enjoyed the service (!) and will consider returning some day.

-Your Friends at Netflix

On 2/21/07, I wrote back:

To My Dear Friends at Notflix,

I will gladly and promtly return the DVDs (usually in about one business day), but what's your hurry? Why the big rush all of a sudden? "The Sound Of Music" is being shipped today – so you can expect to receive it within one business day as advertised, unless your distribution center is located outside of my one-day shipping radius. The other two DVDs I have not yet received, but will return them immediately after watching them (usually within one business day). These were shipped during the month of service I paid for, and so don't expect me to send them back to you without viewing them (if they're not broken, that is).

Part of my ongoing problem with Notflix (and my reason for cancellation) is the lousy service: your no-fault customer service department professionals, poor quality control, and slow turnaround time, so now that the "shoe's on the other foot", you can expect the same delays that I've dealt with for my 4 years as a customer.

Be advised that I don't ship on Sundays, evenings, holidays, Martin Luther King Day, Secretary's Day, John Travolta's Birthday, Groundhog Day, etc.

You shipped two of these DVDs Tuesday the 20th, so I might receive them Thursday the 22nd, but maybe not until Friday the 23rd or Saturday the 24th. If I watch them Friday or Saturday, they will be processed and shipped Monday the 26th. And you expect them back the next day???

You are being more than a bit optimistic, demanding to receive them by Tuesday the 27th. You realize, after the lawsuit you lost in California (the one I was never compensated for as promised in your settlement, by the way), that the one-day turnaround time you advertise is a mythic legend and should be filed in your fantasy/sci-fi section. One-day turnaround time has never been the case with me during my years of membership – how naïve of you to expect it to be the case now. You have been watching too many of your own commercials if you believe that.

And if you should receive them, and they're broken in half or otherwise horribly damaged, please rest assured that my team of quality control experts have diligently inspected each of these discs prior to shipping, insuring that they are in tip-top shape prior to leaving my distribution center.

Your satisfaction is my number one priority. If (due to circumstances out of my control) you receive them damaged (or late), you should consider using another mailing address, such as a post office box or non-rural route, or moving your distribution center to another location more convenient to me. Because it's not my fault. Most folks I send mail to receive my correspondence within one business day (usually). Sound familiar?

Do not respond to this email as it was generated by a robot on an expired working visa.

- Your friend at Blockbuster,
Charlie Dolinger

On 2/22/07, Netflix Customer Service wrote in response:

Dear Charles,

Thanks for your message. I have confirmed your account was cancelled on 02/20/07.

All outstanding rentals must be received by Netflix within 7 days of cancellation or we will automatically charge a replacement fee for the unreturned DVDs.

If you have any further questions or concerns, please feel free to contact us.

Thanks,
Jo-lynn
Netflix Customer Service

Los Gatos, California

Not a word addressing the issues, right? Customer service representatives and politicians make strange bedfellows.

On 2/23/07, I saw the light, and wrote back thusly:

Dear Jo-lynn,

Thanks for responding to my previous letter, although you did not address any of the issues I raised. But that's okay – I realize firsthand that English must be tough as a second language. The important thing is for you to keep trying!

Anyway Jo-lynn, I've got good news – I received the DVDs yesterday and they will be ON THEIR WAY BACK TO YOU TODAY!

The reason I am returning them immediately (without watching them) is not because of you threatening to charge me, it's because the Netflix envelopes were full of RED ANTS!!! No kidding.

I was so glad to receive them (the DVDs) yesterday (giving me some ray of hope that I wouldn't be charged for them), that I immediately opened the first DVD envelope and was shocked to see a bevy (is that the right word?) of RED ANTS streaming out of the envelope and onto my middle finger!

I was standing at my mailbox, at the street in front of my house (I don't live on a rural route!), with my middle finger outstretched and held out from my body. This caused several drivers and passengers in passing cars to do the same. They didn't know my middle finger was a gangplank for this horde of genuine California Red Ants!

I examined the second envelope and saw that it too had a stream (band? gaggle? host?) of RED ARMY ANTS coming out from the little address window.

Well, Jo-lynn, I was certainly surprised! Although at this point of my membership, nothing should shock me about the condition or expediency of my incoming Netflix DVDs, but RED ANTS??? This was a first.

Thankfully, this was not my first picnic (so to speak), so I didn't panic and recoil, possibly hurting the ants on my finger, and possibly dropping and damaging your DVD. I am very well acquainted with red ants and remained cool. I even had an ANT FARM when I was a kid!

My first thought was how I was going to get these red ants BACK into the Netflix envelope promptly, so I could avoid being charged a late fee. Luckily I had a little backwash of coca-cola in a cup nearby and I quickly dribbled a little dab of it on the inside of the paper flap of the envelope – no charge, I was glad to do it.

I was also very careful not to get any on the disc for fear of your crack team of inspectors getting their inspecting-hands sticky, after all – that's how they make their living! (Do they wear rubber gloves when inspecting the DVDs? Just wondering...)

Anyway, Jo-lynn, don't you know those red ants U-TURNED, and MARCHED RIGHT BACK INTO THE ENVELOPE?!? Jo-lynn, it's a joy watching them work together (we could learn a lot from RED ANTS!).

Then (making sure no ants were under the self-stick seal of the envelope before I closed it), I marched (!!!) the two DVDs down to the post office and they are now on their way back to you.

And most importantly, I can assure you, Jo-lynn, that NO RED ANTS WERE HARMED IN THE RETURNING OF THESE MOVIES.

Although I didn't get to view the DVDs (one I didn't even open), I feel no animosity toward you or your company. I love to WATCH ANTS!

I know, from being a loyal customer for four years, that Netflix is a company that values its customers and welcomes new and innovative ideas from them. This being said, I have an idea! Maybe you could forward this on to your friends (amigos) in the research and development department.

Since you are already shipping these little critters without charging us (your customers) any extra fee, I thought that there would be others (like myself) who would enjoy watching insects working and playing as a TEAM and would gladly pay for the privilege. I know I'm not alone in this – remember the success of the ANT FARM!!!

Jo-lynn, I got more enjoyment from watching that ARMY of red ants (I think that's the correct verbiage) march round and round than I got from the last three or four broken DVDs Netflix sent me combined! Really.

My idea is this: why not start a DVD rental service that includes insects with the DVD? Kind of like "dinner and a movie". It would be beneficial to the insects as well, because as you know, most folks enjoy eating sweets of some kind while viewing the movie, and this would be good for the insects. Chocolates and lots of coca-cola are my personal favorites – great for ants – red or black (no offense).

Hopefully you wouldn't be violating any laws by sending ants (some underage) across state lines. With people that's called the Mann Act, but I don't know what it's called when it's ants.

This would be a problem in many states, but probably not in California. I realize (after my many correspondences with your customer service department) that the immigration laws in California are pretty lax.

GOD BLESS GOVERNOR SCHWARZENEGGER!

He's a guy who respects ants (and people too!) of all colors.

Of course you would have to charge an extra fee for including the insects (ants, beetles, silverfish, whatever) with the movie rental, but I think this would really enhance the viewer's pleasure – I know it did mine!

You could call this service "PET-TRIX", cleverly rhyming it with "NETFLIX"!

But the name is totally up to you. Netflix probably has a staff of professionals, dedicated to research and development, which only deal with name-creation. Your online movie categories like "Foreign", "Children", "Gay and Lesbian", etc. make it obvious to me that I am dealing with professionals who know what they are doing!

Thanks so much, Jo-lynn, for letting me talk to you about this red ant situation, and you can rest assured that they will be back home in Los Gatos (isn't that Spanish for "The Cats?") before you can say "Blockbuster!"

Please let me know what you think of my red ant idea – I'm not looking for credit or compensation of any kind. Helping my dear friends at Netflix AND giving my friends THE INSECTS a free vacation (with free meals) is all the thanks I need. It really is a win-win deal for everyone. Thanks Jo-lynn and tell everybody there I said, "Buenos Dias!"

Yours respectfully,
Charlie Dolinger

P.S. I have always enjoyed Dolly Parton's beautiful rendition of "Jolene". From now on, whenever I hear that song, or look at red ants, I'll think of you and all of my dear friends at Netflix.

Well, I used to have to wait days for a response from Netflix customer service, and sometimes got none at all, but... later that SAME DAY, 2/23/07, Netflix replied, and I love this guy. This is what makes it all worthwhile for a sicko like me with too much time on his hands:

> Dear Charles,
>
> Thanks for your message. We appreciate you taking the time to provide us with your feedback and comments.
>
> I truly apologize for any inconvenience or frustration this experience may have caused. We are continually striving to improve our service
>
> (now with 100% less RED ANTS!)
>
> and to ensure your concerns are properly addressed.
>
> We sincerely appreciate your patience and understanding.
>
> Thanks,
>
> Jason
>
> Netflix Customer Service

There! That's it! Jason gets it, and whether he really cares or not is beside the point – I'm not naïve, I just want to know that I'm not invisible. He at least took the time to insert a parenthetical, personal response into the usual form letter. Apparently, the robots at Netflix didn't have a category for automatically generating a response to queries about red ants in their movies!

Well folks, the squeaky wheel gets the grease. And today, more than ever, it's important to not take anything or anyone too seriously. Especially yourself. My advice to you is don't sweat the dumb stuff. Keep smilin', keep the faith, keep fightin' the good fight, and never give up when you're in the right. You may not receive the justice you deserve, but maybe, if you're lucky, you'll get a laugh out of it. And that's what it's all about. If you can't laugh at life, you're in big trouble. No one gets out of here alive. Live, laugh, and love. And tell 'em Lightnin' Charlie sent ya'.

Later,
LC

APRIL 2007

23

AL ROKER AND THE MIRACLE CURE

Ol' Lightnin' is running way behind this month and apologize for being so late getting the Lowdown up for April. Lucky for me that I am my own boss and I cannot fire me for missing the April 1st deadline. I think I might lay myself off for a couple of weeks though. With pay. Just to teach me a lesson.

With no further ado, what do you say we start a brand new monthly feature in the Lowdown?

Lightnin' Charlie's Official Pet-Peeve-Of-The-Month

These will be petty, paltry, insignificant things that, although petty, paltry, and insignificant, never fail to rub me raw. Part of what galls me is that I am generally helpless to do anything about these peeves, thereby qualifying them, by definition, as "peeves". A peeve can only become a peeve by virtue of being chronic and unavoidable. They are considered my "pet" peeves because probably, deep-down, I secretly love and care for these things, cherishing them, even clinging to them, and relishing the righteous outrage [see last month's Lowdown] they stir up in me. Perhaps putting these peeves, pet or no, down in writing will be both therapeutic for me and amusing for you.

Maybe I can start an Official Pet Peeve Of-The-Month Club for all my Lightnin' Bugs. You can share your pet peeves with me and we can commiserate. Though neither of us will feel any better about it, having wasted our time commiserating about pet peeves.

I've done top ten lists here before (favorite books, movies, CDs), but I'm learning that it's what aggravates me – not what makes me happy – that you, my loyal reader, demand from me and are growing more and more accustomed to. I'm spoiling you rotten with this. And like a wealthy man can forever spoil his children with lavish, extravagant gifts, never having to worry about running out of "dough-re-mi", I possess an unending wealth of aggravations, exasperations, and petty annoyances, and have the repertoire and resources to lavish you with them for centuries to come. I realize (or try to) that all of these personal vexations of mine come as a result of my many, many blessings. If I didn't have all these things, I wouldn't have so many things to go wrong.

It has come to my attention that the Lowdowns detailing and describing my various and sundry irritations (and the accompanying hopelessness) seem to be some of my best work. Or at least my most popular. Writing these Lowdowns every month is a job that requires both pride and pathos, and to quote Baloo the bear from *Jungle Book*,

"I'm loaded with both!"

Is it still considered "pathos" when the laments and sufferings of one create laughter and solace in another? Well, whatever it is, baby I've got it, and it's not for me to ask what or why. It's up to me to deliver it. Respond to popular demand. I'll hit you where I hurt.

The need for video documentation in today's visual, virtual world is a pressing one for me. Since I started to post the Lightnin' Lowdown (and long before), I've been accused of taking poetic license with the truth, embellishing the facts, and even making up funny names for people. These accusations are hurtful and are all untrue (except for the funny names) and those who know me know that I don't *have* to make anything up.

A 24/7 video cam on Lightnin' Charlie would provide me with all the proof I need, and the resulting video footage could probably promote Lightnin' Charlie to a whole new audience, as well. As the popularity of the whiniest Lowdowns will attest, my pain and suffering are much more publicly palpable than my music is, or ever will be. And video of these mishaps could make Lightnin' Charlie much more commercially viable than ever before.

I've noticed that hearing (or seeing) my troubles always cheers others up. I admit I don't understand this, but it's true. My last broken tooth (on Christmas Day) had everyone in my family in stitches! I see myself as a kind of modern-day Dick Van Dyke – an everyman who, more than half the time, trips and falls over his own ottoman.

It's important in show business to know your audience. And I've grown to know my audience. The more I get knocked down, the more my audience cracks up. Folks today don't want to hear good music sung well and performed honestly, they want to see guys falling down stairs and getting hit between the legs with line drives. And I do all that, and more, on a daily basis. All I am missing is the ability to show my fans (and the rest of America) this rare talent I possess, namely: giving people pleasure with my personal pain.

I need clean, close-up, digital video of me violently stubbing my toe or banging my baldhead into doors and things. I could post these on my website. Fans of me and my website ("Lightnin' Bugs") would love it. Now *there's* a DVD that would sell like hotcakes! Imagine a

"LIGHTNIN' CHARLIE BANGS HIS HEAD!" video series!

That would probably outsell my concert video a thousand to one, because people would naturally respond to me doing what I do best. I could have a whole series of Lightnin' Charlie disaster films. I could be the Irwin Allen of gospel singers! I could have a

"LIGHTNIN' CHARLIE – ROAD RAGE!" series,

and a

"LIGHTNIN' CHARLIE GOES TO THE DENTIST!" holiday series.

The possibilities are endless. Picture this:

"LIGHTNIN' CHARLIE – FILM NOIR"

a stark, black-and-white, tragicomedy consisting entirely of long, Ingmarr Bergman-style, extreme and shadowed close-ups of my facial expressions while preparing my taxes.

The problem lies in my not being able to preserve (not to mention license and distribute) these precious moments often enough. Where's a camera or a cop when I need one? Someone once said, "All my greatest successes have been in private and all my greatest failures have been in full public view." But my talent of failing so regularly and so successfully, and to always be funny failing, is truly unique, irresistible, and (most importantly) hugely marketable.

That's where my wife, and constant companion, Beth comes in. I'll make her a partner. Beth needs to quit her job (or give up watching "American Idol") and singularly devote herself to following me everywhere I go with a video camera. She's even got one on her phone, for Heaven's sake, so there's no excuse for her missing a close-up of my face, the next time I get semi-electrocuted by putting my wet lips onto an ungrounded microphone, for example. Nothing like a couple of thousand watts per lip to really put the Lightnin' into Lightnin' Charlie! Audiences, young and old, always cheer for that one.

It's necessary for me to have a full-time videographer to capture these gems, and I won't have to pay Beth a salary – I can pay her out of the profits. And deduct it from my taxes!

Likewise, the pain portrayed herein has to be spontaneous and real for it to work. We've all watched enough *America's Funniest Home Video* shows to know that you can't fake the real stuff. People who set up and stage the "pain shots" are never funny – they're pathetic, and make a liar out of Darwin. And besides, Lord knows I've got enough of these petty pains that I don't have to resort to staging them. I am the master of disaster. My wife Beth will verify this. She realizes the enormity of my gift – the rare talent that I have of turning personal abuse into public entertainment. She's my biggest fan – no one laughs longer and harder at me then she does.

If only she could catch on video the next time a playful wrestling match with my kids ends with me rolling on the floor, neutered, and writhing in hilarious, groin-mashed, Eggs Benedict-induced, agony. I grin just thinking about it. And with a little luck (and the right camera angles), this kind of cinema could make me instantly more of a success on YouTube than I could ever hope to become by simply *singing*.

> "Nature gave men two ends – one to sit on, and one to think with. Ever since then, man's success or failure has been dependent on which one he used most."
>
> – Robert Bloch

> "An American monkey, after getting drunk on brandy, would never touch it again, and thus is much wiser than most men."
>
> – Charles Darwin

Speaking of Darwin, I am reminded that I have seriously digressed here. Several paragraphs ago, I promised you a pet peeve of the month for April 2007. I'll bet some of you wondered if you'd get to hear it by May. You May never. But seriously, the fallacy in Darwin's famous theory of evolution is beautifully illustrated by my long-awaited, pet peeve of the month for April 2007. And my Official Pet Peeve Of The Month for April 2007 is what I call:

"Rokermania"

"Rokermania" is when huge crowds of people, seeing a TV camera, insanely shriek the only syllable in their vocabulary – the grossly simian, pre-wheel, Cro-Magnon wail (in falsetto):

"Wooooooooooohhh!"

Anyone who thinks (as Darwin did) that the human race is *e*-volving, *pro*-gressing, and getting smarter with each passing generation, should watch the morning news shows on network television.

Live from New York City, the most cosmopolitan city in America, where people press themselves (and their children) against the outside windows in the rain, waving hysterically at the cameras inside the studio. Watch the weatherman's report from the streets outside the studio. That's where they're truly taking their life in their hands. Oh, those New Yorkers are *so sophisticated!* People herded, bovine-style, behind barricades (can't allow the masses to get close to the *weatherman!),* going berserk at the sight of a live camera, throwing fits and frantically waving homemade signs:

"We Love You *place weatherman's first name here*"
"Hello Ethel!"
"Get Well Soon Misti!"
"Happy Birthday Tyler!"
etc., etc., etc.

These cretins probably had to arrive at the barricade at four o'clock in the morning to get a place in front.

"Wooooooohhh!"

This happens, rain or shine, sleet or snow, five days a week, or whenever and wherever there's a camera. And it's common knowledge in show business that a New York audience is the "toughest audience in the entire world". Case in point:

Roker (or whoever): "It's going to reach the low 90s today in the Deep South."
New York Audience: *"Wooooooooh! Wooooooohhh! Woooooooooooohhhh!"*

Whew, that's a tough crowd! One morning, ashamed of my association with humanity, I changed the channel to the Discovery Channel. There I saw a group of wild orangutans fighting over a piece of flesh from a nearby carcass. Their arms were upraised; mouths wide open, waving sticks and fists at each other, shrieking:

"Wooooooohhh!"

No difference. Except the wild apes were carrying on in order to get food for survival, not to get their faces, agape and contorted, on television for one second. Comparing people to apes is not fair to the apes. Maybe Darwin had it backwards.

"Rokermania" is not to be confused with other popular manias such as "Beatlemania", or "Elvismania". After all, in those cases, people (teenage girls) were going wild for...well, *Elvis* and the *Beatles* - not talk show hosts and weathermen. And today, it's young and old alike that display this disease of the mind. Two generations ago, the "less developed" folks of Darwin's theory didn't scream hysterically for Ed Sullivan, they applauded politely for him and waited to go crazy for Elvis. They had discretion and control of their mania. They could *selectively* go berserk, to use a term of Darwin's. Why this *de-*volution and *di-*gression of the species?

I would like to offer an alternate diagnosis, one I believe is closer to the truth. Maybe this is not "Rokermania" at all, but a highly aggressive, malignant form of "Me-mania". If it is the camera, rather than the superstar (weatherman) that induces pandemonium, this would suggest "Me-mania" – that it's not about Al Roker at all – it's all about

"Me".

It does seem that the same effect occurs, with or without Letterman, as long as there's a camera present. Maybe the real "superstar" in the mind of the screaming banshee is the banshee him or herself. Perhaps the object of their worship and adulation is not the talk show host, or the TV camera, but they themselves.

For a point of reference, watch the opening scene of Stanley Kubrick's *2001 - A Space Odyssey* where the prehistoric "ape-men" are fighting, jumping up and down, arms raised over their heads, fists clenched, and with mouths wide open, screaming:

"Wooooooooh!Wooooooooh!Wooooooooh!"

Compare that to Conan O'Brien's studio audience or an NFL receiver when he makes a first down. The modern-day ape-man (apologies again to the apes) believes that *he* or *she* is the superstar, and is in the throes of self-worship when captured squealing wide-eyed at TV cameras. These poor, empty souls are demonstrating their delusion the only way, and with the only syllable, they can: with fists in the air and a hearty...

"Wooooooooooh!"

This depraved, falsetto shriek with upraised arms and fists clenched are both sure signs and definitive symptoms of "Me-mania".

I think this theory holds up, and would offer "The Jerry Springer Show", "American Idol", "YouTube", and "Girls Go Wild - Daytona Beach" as evidence. This ain't your father's Oldsmobile, and we *sure* ain't in Kansas anymore, Dorothy.

Would Darwin change his mind after viewing any of these "evolutions"? Would Martin Luther King, if he visited a crack house in a Miami housing project today, rewrite his "I Have A Dream" speech as "I *Had* A Dream"? If Dr. King found himself in a modern-day crack house, he probably wouldn't live long enough to change the tense – he'd be shot to death (again) in seconds. This time for his pinky ring. Would America's Founding Fathers rewrite the Constitution if they could observe the folly and felony that is today's Capitol Hill? I believe the answers to these questions are:

"Yes", "Yes", and "Yes".

The only known cure for "Me-mania" can be found in Scripture. "Me-mania" has been an epidemic ever since Eden, and its Antidote has only been available for two thousand and seven years. This Miracle Cure, obtained from a spotless Lamb, was first seen flowing from a Prisoner's pierced side on a hill that was called "Skull", in a land that is now war-torn Palestine. Just ask your Doctor for the Blood. That's all you have to do. The Blood will do the rest. There is no charge – you just have to admit you're sick, and ask for help. Your insurance company won't be billed, there is no co-pay, and the Lamb's Cure is freely available for all. This Wonder drug has no expiration date and, contrary to popular belief, is completely ineffective in generic form. Ask your Doctor for the "Lamb's Blood from Calvary". The Cure is to be taken only on an empty stomach, with equal measures of repentance and commitment. Side effects include freedom, gladness, purpose, and immortality. Don't ignore the warning signs for too long – they're telling you something is wrong. See your Doctor at once, before it's too late.

By the way, I was in church this Resurrection Sunday, and can report seeing a lot of folks completely cured of "Me-mania" and now exhibiting the symptoms of "Him-mania". They (and myself) have been given a clean bill-of-health, and are now, miraculously, brand new. We were terminally ill before and it took a Miracle to make us well again. Rather than arms raised threateningly overhead with clenched fists as before, these patients I observed had their hands raised skyward and open, with eyes filled with tears of gratitude and joy. We are all very thankful to the One responsible for our health and our new lease on life. Unfortunately, "Me-mania" is still rampant, and is reaching pandemic proportions worldwide. It's up to us (the cured) to get busy dispensing information about the Cure.

And what would the Founding Fathers, Martin Luther King, and Charles Darwin have to say about this? I believe they would say:

"Amen!", "Hallelujah!", and *"Huh?"*

Well, two out of three ain't bad.

Till we meet again,
Charlie

"There are only two ways to live your life. One – as though nothing is a miracle. The other – as though everything is a miracle."
– Albert Einstein

"If a man is called a streetsweeper, he should sweep streets even as Michelangelo painted, or Beethoven composed music, or Shakespeare wrote poetry. He should sweep streets so well that all the hosts of heaven and earth will pause to say, here lived a great streetsweeper who did his job well."
– Martin Luther King Jr.

"I don't deserve this award, but I have arthritis and I don't deserve that either."
– Jack Benny

24

TAKING THE FIFTH...
COMMANDMENT, THAT IS

Of all the Ten Commandments, there's only one that contains a promise. That's the fifth.

"Honor your Father and your Mother, *so that you may live long* in the land the Lord God is giving you." [italics added]

May and June contain two of my favorite holidays, Mother's Day and Father's Day, which celebrate two of my favorite people of all-time, my Mom and my Dad. I think it's about time I wrote a Lowdown about the two most important and influential people that the Lord God has given me in my life – my parents.

My mother was born in the Great Depression, in Greeneville, Tennessee, into a family of seven children – five brothers and one sister (one brother, Tommy, died as a baby). Her mother was a seamstress and her father a policeman.

*My Uncles Glen and Jack,
and my Mother Barbara*

My mother, Barbara Ann, was raised in the Southern Baptist church, learned to play piano, sing in the choir, and developed a strong, personal relationship with the Lord, all at a very early age. By the time my Mother was nine years old, she felt the call to preach the gospel. Having an amazing grasp on scripture, she began delivering sermons in many churches and revivals in and around East Tennessee.

Mother, age 10

Her reputation spread rapidly, and was soon recruited by churches as far away as Washington D.C. and Ohio. Over the next four years, she traveled extensively throughout eight states. She was such a sensation that soon she had her own Saturday morning radio program in East Tennessee. Barbara's sudden popularity, and the need for gasoline to travel to these programs, coincided with World War II and domestic gas rationing. My Mother remembers needing a judge's permission to buy extra fuel. After being turned down by the local office, which considered her traveling hundreds of miles to preach frivolous (they were turning down men wanting extra gas to travel to second jobs), my Grandmother took Barbara before an appellate judge. This judge said he had heard about my Mother, had heard about the large numbers of people she drew to her meetings, and, most importantly, had heard about the souls saved at her revivals. He said he was only able to grant such permission for causes that were emergencies and truly necessary. But, in the midst of the darkest days of the Second World War, he felt that hearing (and responding to) the good news of the Gospel of Jesus Christ met both of those criteria, and gave her his blessing and the gas card. Desperate times call for desperate measures.

MISS BARBARA ANNE WEEMES
"Evangelistic Preacher"

GREENEVILLE, TENNESSEE

TEL. NO. 243-W   444 W. MAIN ST.

*My Mother's first business card 1943
"Evangelistic Preacher"*

The bible tells us not to premeditate what we say in the last days, but to trust and rely upon the Holy Spirit to give us our words. My Mother, at nine, ten and eleven years of age, would not always have a message planned for her sermon, and would trust in the Spirit to guide her and give her the words and the wisdom to deliver the message. She would sometimes go up into the pulpit, her bible in hand, and let it fall open to the pages that she would preach from. The fact that this was done in front of huge audiences didn't seem to make a difference to my Mom. She wasn't concerned about the congregation, the message, or herself – she was focused only on Him. And He never let her down.

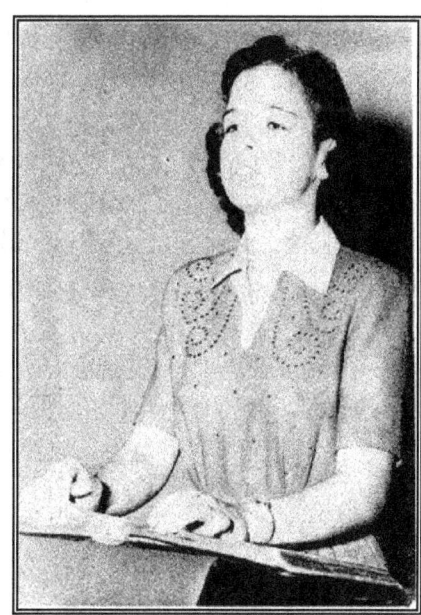

Mom at 10   *In the pulpit at 12*

Once, while visiting a church in Johnson City (my future home), the pastor approached my Mother and said that though he had tried and tried, he had not been able to come up with a sermon for that evening's service. Having met her previously, he asked if she would preach the service for him. My Mother agreed and went up into the pulpit, unprepared, her bible falling open to Matthew 25 and Jesus' Parable of the Ten Talents. After she delivered the message on this parable, the pastor took her aside and said he wanted to show her something. He reiterated that he had drawn a blank for that evening's service, and all he had managed to plan for his sermon was the subject. And then he showed my Mother a piece of paper from his bible. He had written his intended subject across the top for the sermon he never gave. His subject? The Parable of the Ten Talents.

The next phase of my Mother's life was one of her hardest. She married young, and soon had two children of her own – a boy and a girl, born four years apart. Her soldier husband Bill, after getting out of service, grew to find the role of provider distasteful. He was soon jobless and staying home all day.

My Mother's typical day would begin at dawn. She would get the babies up and dressed, cook a big breakfast, do the dishes, then, along with the two babies, ride the bus to the babysitter's house (Bill refused to watch the kids while she worked). After dropping them off there, she would ride another bus to her job as a waitress in a drugstore luncheonette. Then, after her shift was over, she would catch the bus to the babysitter's house, collect the children, and catch the next bus home, where her duties would be waiting for her – namely, clean up all the day's mess, do all the laundry, and get a full-course supper on the table. This was before washing machines, dryers, microwave ovens, automatic dishwashers, permanent press clothing, and disposable diapers.

My Mother suffered this for eleven years. She says that Sundays (the day of rest) were the hardest because, in order to take her two children to church for Sunday School and worship service, she had to start cooking by dawn, fixing the full breakfast and dinner her husband demanded. She had to prepare two full meals before she left the house at nine o'clock; the full breakfast eaten before church, and pre-cook the full dinner he insisted be ready at 12:30 sharp when the bus dropped her off at the house. These are some of the duties and hardships that shaped the character of the "Greatest Generation" that my saintly Mother is a member of.

Barbara and her family moved to Miami, Florida in September of 1955, where her husband Bill had finally taken a construction job the previous June. He had started work on a brand new, exquisite hotel on Miami Beach's Collins Avenue. It was located right next to the Fountainbleu and was to be called the Eden Roc. This decision to move to a place they had never been and didn't know a soul in was based purely on economics – this construction job would be full-time, at a good wage, so she loaded up the kids, and moved to Miami.

They arrived on Labor Day weekend, just in time for my brother Billy to start the first grade, and just in time for Mom to have emergency surgery in early October. She would recover and take a waitress job at the newly opened Eden Roc in January of 1957.

My Brother Billy, Mother, and Sister Kathy

Barbara leaving Tennessee for far away Florida was terribly traumatic for my Grandmother, as she did not like being separated from any of her children. For her entire life, my Grandmother (whose first name was Eula, but was always called her by her middle name, Bessie) always wanted her kids close to her, if not living in the same house with her. At this time, my Grandmother Bessie, and my Grandfather E. J. had one son home from the service and working, one son still in the service, and two younger sons and one daughter at home. So in the summer of 1958, times being tough in Tennessee, my Grandmother and Grandfather, along with my three uncles and one aunt, all packed up their things and moved to Miami too.

Meanwhile, my Mom's marriage to Bill was hitting rock bottom. Bill had been working steadily, for the first time in their marriage, until the Eden Roc was finished. But then, with plenty of construction jobs pending, he quit the construction company and never worked a steady job again. That, along with other problems, led Barbara to finally take the children and leave him in December of 1958, moving in with her Mother and Daddy. She waited a year, futilely hoping that Bill might change, but it wasn't to be. She finally filed for divorce in the winter of 1959.

In the fall of 1960, my Father Sidney was the night-manager of the brand new Eden Roc's coffee shop, which was a favorite late-night hangout for frisky folks like Frank Sinatra, Dean Martin, Sammy Davis Jr., Jerry Lewis, etc. My Dad's cafe, the Villa d'Este, was the scene of many an after-show jam and cut-up session for the Rat Pack, who often performed next door at the Fountainbleu. Elvis Presley's first appearance after returning home from the Army was at the Fountainbleu on Sinatra's TV Show, filmed there in 1960. It's awfully ironic that my Mom's ex-husband built the hotel where her and my Dad's paths would cross.

Eden Roc, Miami Beach

2A THE MIAMI NEWS, Thursday, June 2, 1960

Beauty of the Day is Barbara Livesay. She is a waitress in the Villa d'Este Coffee Shop of the Eden Roc Hotel on Miami Beach.

Sid and Barbara met at work (Dad worked nights, Mom worked days) and hit it off immediately. They began a whirlwind romance, painting Miami Beach red through the wee hours of the night.

Sid didn't get off work until 2 AM, so they would typically begin their evening (at 2:30!) by meeting for dinner at the Old Forge on Arthur Godfrey Road or The Place For Steak on 71st Street. Then they would be off to Murray Franklin's on South Beach to catch a show or hit a piano bar like Bill Jordan's Bar Of Music.

Sidney was a good singer and had a rich, crooning baritone. He loved to sit at the piano in piano bars, making requests and singing along with his favorites like *Make It One For My Baby (And One More For The Road)*, *All The Way*, and his all-time favorite song, *You're Nobody Til Somebody Loves You.*

They would usually top the night/morning off with some scrambled eggs and coffee at the International House Of Pancakes on Collins Avenue. Then, parting company, my Mom would run home in time to shower, put some ice cubes on her eyelids, and change into her waitress uniform – she had to be at work at 7 AM! My Dad would go home and sleep all day – he didn't have to be at work until 6 PM.

How my Mom endured this, throughout her nine-month courtship with my Father, is beyond me. It was like she knew time was short, and she was trying to squeeze the most out of every moment. And she was having the time of her life.

During this time, Miami Beach was enjoying its heyday. The "Sun and Fun Capital Of The World" was at its peak. Movies and TV shows were regularly being filmed there, and in 1960, movie mogul Howard Koch *(The Manchurian Candidate, The Odd Couple, Airplane!)* used my Mom as an extra in a scene from his movie, *Miami Undercover*. She was filmed coming off of a plane and walking through the terminal at the Miami International Airport.

Unfortunately, *Miami Undercover* was never released, but there are lots of great shots of the Eden Roc in Jerry Lewis' *The Bellboy* (1960) and James Bond's *Goldfinger* (1964), as well as countless others.

Needless to say, I love watching the many movies filmed in Miami Beach during the late '50s and early '60s, and on location shots, I get real close to my TV screen, always trying to catch a glimpse of my Mom or my Dad in the background.

My Dad and my Uncle Charlie [see February '07 Lowdown] were at the first Cassius Clay-Sonny Liston heavyweight championship fight at the Miami Beach Convention Center, when Clay (Muhammad Ali) won the title and *"shook up the world!!!"*

Every time I watch that fight on videotape, I'm searching the stands for them, although I've not seen them yet (Beth honey, if you're reading this, I need a bigger TV set – preferably plasma).

On June 6, 1961 (D-Day), Sidney and Barbara were married. I was born nine months later.

My Mom tells a funny story about going to a fortuneteller with my Grandmother in the summer of '58, prior to moving to Florida. This was more than a year before her divorce from Bill, and three years before I was born. This fortuneteller, eerily named Mrs. Smith, lived in Blountville, Tennessee, and was a favorite of my Grandmother's. Mrs. Smith, telling my Mom's fortune, told her that she was going to have a baby and it would be a boy. Mama told her,

"If I have a baby, I'm dead! My husband's had a vasectomy!"

Mrs. Smith said no, my Mother would remarry, that she did not know her future husband yet, but that she would meet him at work, and that they would have a son.

Wedding Day, Beach Tower Hotel
Miami Beach, D-Day 1961

Mom's baby shower, pregnant with me, and holding guitar over her belly (me!). It worked! Due to health reasons, the doctor told my Mother not to gain more than ten pounds during her pregnancy. She gained nine, and I weighed eight. See? She started sacrificing for me even before I was born.

That's my Dad at the fights, front and center, looking like a fashion plate as usual

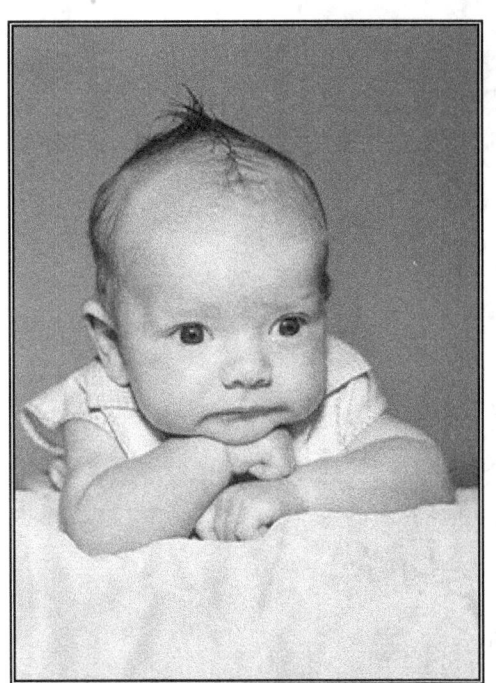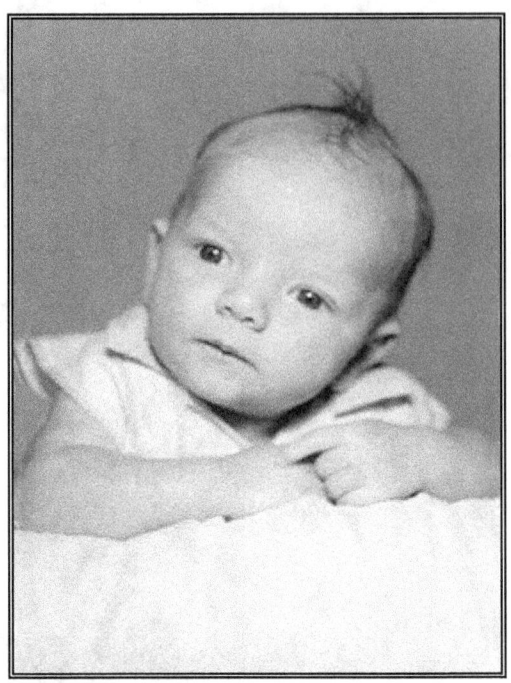

Here I am, sporting the same hairstyle I have today!

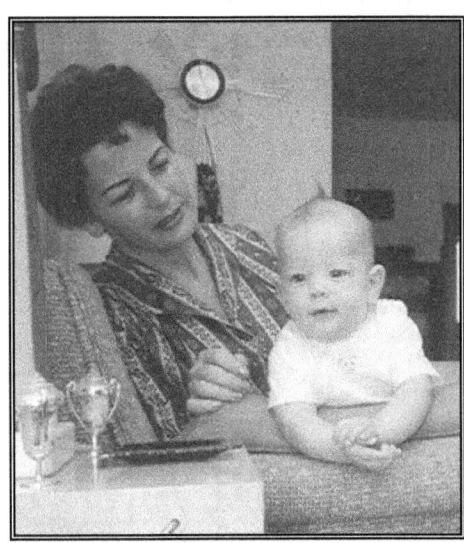

Reception Planned

The Women's Committee of the Florida Symphony will sponsor a champagne reception following the movie premier of "Johnny Tiger" on April 21. Making plans for the reception to be held at the Quality Court Motel are, from the left, Mrs. Craig Linton, Sid Dolinger and Mrs. B. J. Hardwick.

After marrying my Dad, Mama was able to quit working outside the home and be a housewife. She was very happy, staying home and taking care of me and my brother and sister for the first time in her life. But it wouldn't last long. My Mother would soon go back to work and it would be a good thing she did. It would save my Father's life.

In 1969, with my brother and sister grown, and me in school, my Mom went to work for my Dad at Flagler Dog Track in Miami. He was the food and beverage director there, and he hired my Mom as hostess in the clubhouse dining room. My Dad was working so many hours that he put an army cot in his office so he could catch a nap now and then.

SID Dolinger, who spells Dolinger with one "l" to avoid any confusion with the name Dillinger, is a generous guy.

That goes double for the establishment he manages, the House of Beef at the Quality Courts Motel.

They've done a rare thing.

On discovering a tremendous surplus of fish and seafood in the freezer, Dolinger had a brainstorm. Why not donate it to a worthwhile cause and what is more worthwhile than the Salvation Army?

As a result, the Salvation Army soup kitchen has never had it so good. Dolinger, on behalf of the House of Beef, has donated au jus

Sen. Robert Kennedy   Sid Dolinger

about every kind of fish: four cases of rainbow trout, four cases of red snapper filets, six cases of lobster tails, eight boxes of halibut steaks, five boxes of swordfish steaks, one case of grouper.

Needless to say, Major Sid Lynch of the Salvation Army was tickled to "pisces" to receive this hearty donation.

WONDER why Larry, the indomitable showman, Sunbrock mailed me a check for $2 made payable to Sen. Robert Kennedy and earmarked for his "haircut fund only?"

Don't be a dumb bunny, J. Y., although it is the season. The answer is simple. Larry wants you to write

FASHION WITH A FLING... The theme for the Welcome Wagon fashion show Mar. 17 at the Civic Center. Above Mrs. Sidney Dolinger models an aqua formal with white fox shrug.

One night, my Dad had gone into his office to lie down. My Mom was in the dining room taking dinner reservations when, suddenly she got the feeling that something was wrong. She told the maitre d' that she needed to go check on Sid, that something was wrong. She went to his office, found him there on the cot, in terrible pain, sweating profusely, and holding his chest. She called for an ambulance and he was rushed to the hospital.

My Dad had suffered a massive coronary, and his doctor said that if he had been thirty minutes later getting to the hospital, he would've been dead. My Mother's intuition had saved my Dad's life. Or, more accurately, her obedience to the same Spirit that was saving souls when she was a little girl had now saved the life of her husband and my Father.

My Dad recovered, but was told that he wouldn't be able to work a job that was very demanding on him, schedule and stress-wise. So he took a job managing a restaurant in Orlando with the stipulation that they would hire an assistant manager to help him take care of business. Well, we packed up and moved again (we moved constantly – I didn't go to the same school two years in a row until high school) and my Dad started the job, but with no assistant. After four months, and still no assistant, and after experiencing more chest pains, the doctor told my Dad to either quit working, or else the next time he saw him, it would be in the hospital or the morgue.

So we moved back to Miami (again) and my Mother started working and being the family's sole provider. History has a strange way of repeating itself.

Me and my Dad

I should stop here for a moment and tell you about the relationship I had with my parents, growing up. To say they are the world's greatest Mother and Dad would be an understatement. They managed to give me every single thing I needed to make the best out of me and to make the best out of life and all its twists and turns. They did all of this while life was twisting and turning all around them, too. They are the two strongest and most wonderful people I've ever known and we love each other dearly.

But while my Mom and Dad are two very terrific people, they're two very different people, especially in their roles with me as a child. My Dad spoiled me rotten. As it often happens with older parents (my Dad was fifty-three when I was born), I was the apple of my Father's eye and he refused me nothing. He always told me he loved me "too much". It was almost like grandparents do with their grandchildren – how they get to spoil 'em and then give 'em back. Well, that's what my Dad did with me – spoil me silly and then give me back...to my poor Mom.

My Mother, by default, had to be the disciplinarian. She was the one who had to set limits and say "no". She was the spanker. Although I deserved hundreds, if not thousands, of spankings, I only received three or four, and always with her flip-flop shoe. And Mama could take care of plenty business with a flip-flop. A couple good whacks across my
bottom with one of those, and not only would I be cured forever of the misbehavior I was being spanked for, it cured me forever, from ever wearing a pair of those damnable
things. I still hate them. I cringe every time I see them. The rubber ones. I don't even like my wife wearing them. She's got a couple pair of the fancy ones. They're just as scary-looking to me with rhinestones on 'em as not. Lord knows I'm already afraid of my wife enough as it is, without the threat of those weapons on her feet.

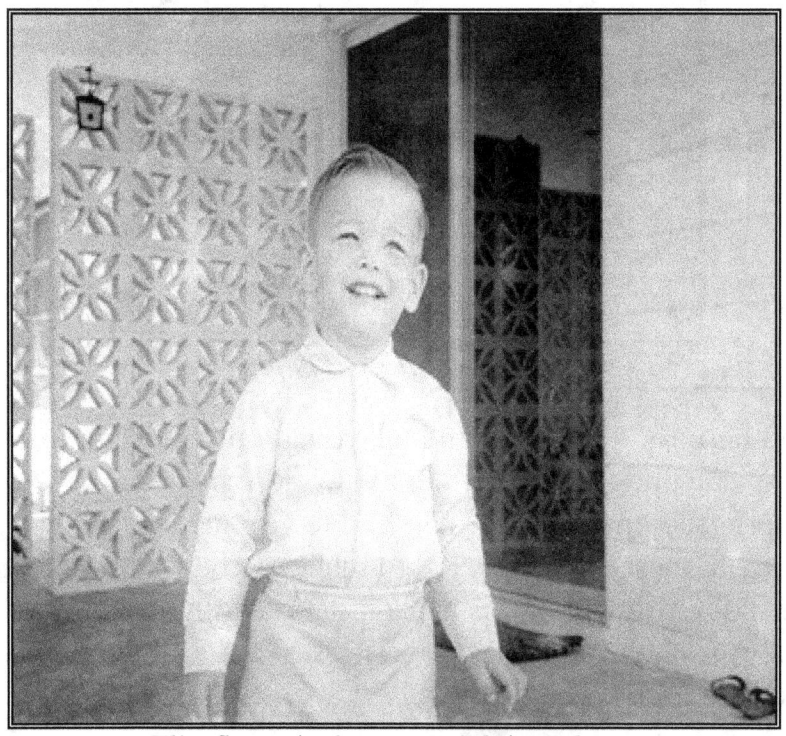

Flip-flops (at bottom right) and me, their unsuspecting victim!

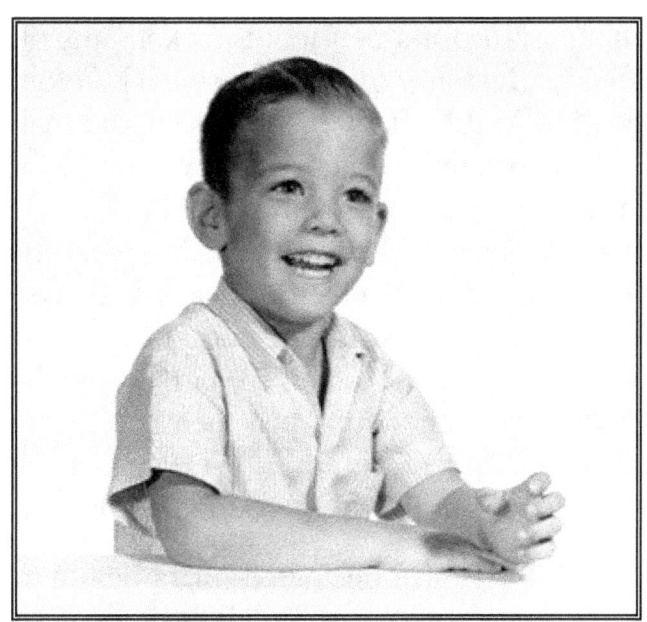

Young Lightnin' Charlie
[notice my left hand, already making an F-chord!]

With my Mom working to support the three of us, we didn't have a lot of money, but my Dad had an awful time denying any of my heart's desires. My wish was his command. And since he wasn't able to work and was left home alone with me all day, it was like shooting fish in a barrel for me.

Peanuts, Me, Dad, & Mom
[Peanuts was the only sweet-hearted Pekingese dog ever.
His full name was Prince Penalt!]

One time I remember asking for a new tennis racket – my old one wasn't good enough anymore. After all, I was *on the tennis team*. Therefore I needed the one Jimmy Connors used. The Wilson T-2000. My Mom said that she was sorry, but we just couldn't afford a new tennis racket right now, but maybe for Christmas. So that night, when my Mom got home from work, I not only had the brand new Wilson T-Two Grand tennis racket I wanted, I had *two of them!* My Dad and I explained to her that a tournament level tennis player like myself required more than one racket, in case of a broken string, or in case one just didn't *feel right*. That was my Daddy. But unlike most kids who get most anything they want and, in return, completely disrespect and embarrass their parents, I adored my Dad and wanted to spend every moment with him. We were inseparable. My poor Mother says she often felt like a fifth wheel around my Dad and I.

One dull afternoon, my Dad and I decided it might be fun to try and scare Mom to death. So we made a fake corpse on the floor to surprise her when she got home from work. Good clean fun, that. We stuffed some t-shirts into a pair of my pants for legs and stuffed a shirt for a torso, and used a big stuffed, brown ball for the head (that was the hardest part – finding something to match my brown hair). It couldn't be just *any anonymous* corpse – it had to look like *my* corpse to get the desired effect from my Mother. So once we had the corpse, we had to have a murder weapon. A big kitchen knife stuck into the middle of its back (complete with fake blood) did the trick nicely.

With everything ready, and it time for Mama to get home, my Dad and I backed into the jalousied closet to watch. Let the fun begin!

When Mom came through the front door and saw what looked like my dead body sprawled out on the floor with a knife in my back, *she went nuts! Woohooo!* But when Dad and I fell out of the closet laughing hysterically, she didn't think it was too funny. She just didn't share our sense of humor, that's all. Thank God she wasn't wearing flip-flops, or she would've killed both of us. The police would've found the real me on the floor with a flip-flop sticking out of my hind end. It's a wonder we didn't cause her to drop dead right there.

Because of my Dad's health, he wasn't able to do a lot of the usual things that fathers do with their sons. But Mom took up the slack. She would agree to about anything where I was concerned. She's still that way.

Besides "normal" activities like taking me to the beach or to a movie, Mama (after working all week) would go with me horseback riding and roller-skating. And I don't mean just *taking me there* and comfortably watching *me* do it, she would put on the skates, or get up on the horse, and *go!* She did her fighting from the trenches, buddy! And she wasn't a spring chicken anymore either – when I was fifteen, Mama was forty-five. I'm forty-five now, and you couldn't pay me to roller-skate around with a bunch of teenagers.

Mama isn't the tomboy type that would enjoy those sorts of things either – she's the complete opposite. I know now that she was trying to make up for me not getting to do those kinds of things with my Dad.

I remember going to one of those gigantic metal slides with her. The ones you slide down, sitting on burlap sacks. You climb about ten thousand steps to get to the top (in Miami heat), then you sit down on the burlap sack, and then *away you go!* It was about a thousand feet to the bottom. The slide had lots of big dips in it, so your butt would come flying off the slide, and then slam back down again.

Yes folks, butt on burlap, coming down onto hot metal. And she did it over and over again with me. These adventures always left her so sore the next day that she could barely go to work. But she had to. She was all we had.

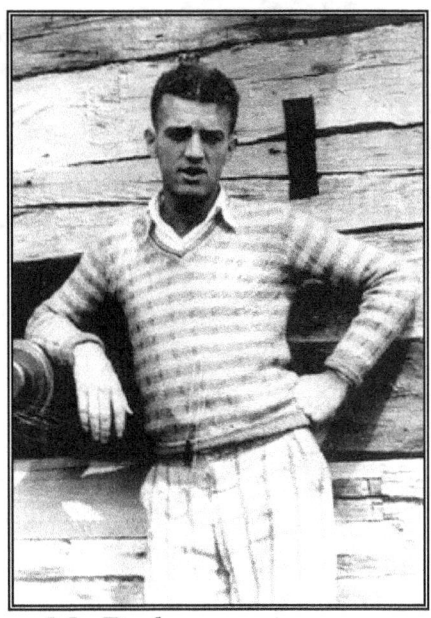 

My Dad as a young man   *My Mother as a young teen*

And she's the same way today with my two sons. We went to Disney World and Sea World in Orlando last summer, and I know we walked ten miles or better each day; on concrete in ninety-eight degree heat and one hundred percent humidity. And she rode every ride the kids did. She's something else. And this October, Mama will be seventy-five years young. What a lady.

As a kid, I had loads of everything. I had all the toys I wanted, all the affection and guidance and support a kid could ask for, and most of all, lots and lots and lots of love. The only thing I didn't have a lot of was time.

About three years after his heart attack, when I was ten, my Dad found out that he had prostate cancer. My Mother and Dad didn't tell me about it until I was twelve. By then, the cancer had spread to the bone, and my Father's agony couldn't be kept a secret from me anymore. He underwent radiation and chemotherapy, but it spread anyway.

I remember constantly praying for two things: firstly, for God to take the pain away from my Dad and give it to me; and secondly, for the Lord to please send His angels to watch over my Mother, keeping her safe from all harm. For if something were to happen to my Mother, I'd be left an orphan. God answered both prayers – one with a "no" and the other with a "yes".

It's impossible to overstate the effect all this had on me as a child. My Father's death, when I was fifteen years old, forced me to look at life, and love, much more deeply than I would've wished. As much as I prayed for God to take this away, I realize now that the heavy burden of my Father's illnesses led me nowhere but straight to the Cross. The biggest crisis of my life led me to a personal relationship with the Savior, and it led me, directly, to everything I've become since then.

The last picture I have of us together.
Christmas 1976

Where could I go but to the Lord? I've learned (the hard way) that the very things we beg God to take away from us are the very same things that make us into the people He wants us to be. The best we can be. My Dad used to say,

"Whatever doesn't kill you, makes you stronger."

That's the truth. That's the hard truth. I am in no way grateful for any of the pain and suffering my precious Father went through, but I am truly grateful for all the pain and suffering I went through. It's what I had to endure as a child that made me into the man I am today.

I hope when I get to heaven, the first thing I see is all my family – especially my Dad – gathered 'round the feet of Jesus, so I can fall, rejoicing and remaining there, for at least a million years. I've got a lot of lost time to make up for.

There isn't an hour that goes by that I don't think of my Dad. I miss him more with each passing day. But each day that passes brings me closer to my reunion with him.

There is also never an hour that passes that I am not thankful to the Good Lord for providing me with a strong and saintly Mother to pull us through. She's got to be the eighth wonder of the world. And she's still going strong.

My Mother's 75th surprise birthday party (2007)

These pictures are from my Mom & Dad's thirteenth Wedding Anniversary in 1974. I was twelve. I withdrew all my money out of my savings account, surprised my parents with a big gift certificate from a local department store, bought my Mother an orchid corsage, and took them out for a fancy dinner at a fine restaurant, complete with strolling violinists! I'm so glad I did this (and I'm glad they let me), because time was short. Remember the woman who poured the expensive perfume on Jesus' head and was scolded by the disciples for wasting all that money that could have been given to the poor? This was done two days prior to Jesus' Last Supper and three days prior to his death. I think it's important to note what Jesus said to them:

> *"Why are you bothering this woman? She has done a beautiful thing to me. The poor you will always have with you, but you will not always have me. When she poured this perfume on me, she did it to prepare me for burial. I tell you the truth, wherever this gospel is preached throughout the world, what she has done will also be told, in memory of her."*

Mom and Dad's 13th Wedding Anniversary 1974

It's Memorial Day weekend, and as I am writing this, my wife and I, along with my Mom, are in Gatlinburg, Tennessee, attending a 3-day Gaither Homecoming gospel concert called *Family Fest*. The greatest singers on the planet are all gathered under one roof singing the greatest story ever told. I'm having a wonderful time, being with my two favorite girls, my Mother and my wife. And not a flip-flop in sight! I should remind you that my wife's first name is Beth, but everyone's called her "Bessie" since she was a little girl. So do I. The more things change, the more things stay the same.

Me, Mom, Beth, and Joe (Beth's big brother)
"The Hole-in-the-Head Gang" Gatlinburg, Tennessee 2007

Mama and Me (1973)

What a shirt (it was pink!), and what a chest!
What was I thinking? Mother and Me (1977)

Our two sons are staying with their maternal Paw-Paw and Nanny in Virginia for the weekend, acting out the life of Huckleberry Finn, walking across swinging bridges and exploring the nooks and crannies in and around the Clinch River. It's paradise there for a boy – throwing rocks into the river and shooting targets with a BB gun.

What a joy it is for me this Memorial Day weekend, living in freedom, singing songs of freedom, with two women that mean more than the whole world to me. One gave life to me and the other gave life to mine.

If only I was poetic enough to convey the feelings of love and appreciation I have for them both. To my Mother, my rock, the one who has never, ever let me down...I love you always. And to my wife, my lover, and my friend, the Mother of my children, the one who always lifts me up, I'll be loving you, too. Always. You are my sweethearts.

Mother & Me (2006)

Mama still doing anything I ask her to [here posing like Ma Barker with toothpick and 12-gauge!]

Happy Mother's Day and Happy Father's Day to you all, and by the way, I don't have a Pet Peeve Of The Month this time. We'll pick that up again next month. I just can't think of anything to complain about.

I'm truly the luckiest guy in the world. Because having two of the best parents God ever gave anyone is cause for celebration. My only "peeve" this Mother's Day and Father's Day is that some children are born to parents who don't deserve to have children. And some children, who are blessed with a great Mother or a great Father, and some kids who are lucky enough to have both, don't appreciate them nearly enough. Or they wait until it's too late to tell them.

If you read this and have a Mom or a Dad that you can look at and hug, or call and say "I love you", for God's sake and theirs, do it. Do it right now. If your parents are no longer with you, but loved you, get on your knees and thank God for giving them to you. Don't waste any opportunity to tell those you love how much you love them. Our time ain't long.

> To happiness,
> Charlie

P.S. I love you!!!

25

KISSIN' COUSINS
- OR -
I'M MY OWN GRANDPAW
- OR -
IT'S ALL RELATIVE

What's buzzin' cousin? Gather around kiddies, and let me tell you a killer story. Rather, a story about a killer. *The* Killer. Well, the Killer's daughter. And his first cousin. And his cousin's daughter. You see, the Killer's daughter is also his second cousin. And that's who this story is about. The Killer's wife and first cousin, and their daughter and/or second cousin. It's all so confusing. There sure is a whole lot of shakin' goin' on! And oh, what a tangled web we weave when first we practice to conceive...with a cousin, that is. Anyway, here goes. And look out - mad dogs are using this family tree!

In May of 1993, Lightnin' Charlie and the Upsetters went to Memphis, Tennessee to appear in an international blues festival and talent competition. The annual event was held on world-famous Beale Street at the renowned Daisy Theater. We were one of hundreds of bands, coming in from all over the world, competing in the three-day fest, organized by the Blues Foundation, a hack-pack of lawyers and thieves (redundant) who are responsible for "blues preservation". Instead, they have helped to kill it. This competition was (and is) a very high-profile gig where aspiring blues bands (suckers) travel to Memphis, and play for free, hoping to get some high-end exposure and maybe land a record deal.

Regional blues societies hold local talent competitions and their winning bands go to Memphis for these international finals. Bands could also come on their own and compete as wild-cards in the first day's judging to try and win a spot in the second day's finals.

But first, some background. In 1992, after winning the Piedmont Blues Preservation Society's annual competition in Greensboro, North Carolina, Lightnin' Charlie and the Upsetters went to Memphis and got busy tearing up the

Daisy Theater. One local entertainment magazine, the *Memphis Metro*, reported that:

"The cheesiest band present won first-place."

The *Memphis Metro* then went on to say:

"If you want to see who should have won [the Blues Foundation's Annual Blues Talent Contest], check out Lightnin' Charlie and the Upsetters, who hail from East Tennessee. They played the best set in the contest Saturday and then held court for over an hour in the after-show jam on Sunday, nearly burning down the house."

You see, we didn't win, we didn't come in second, and we didn't come in third. Even though one of the four judges, a well-known blues and jazz singer (and the only judge out of the four who was a musician), came backstage to tell us that our set was the highlight of the day and that we were, by far, the highest scoring band on her card.

But the fix was in. The other three judges just happened to be regional blues society presidents, who had sent their own regional winners to Memphis to compete in the finals. One judge was president of the Miami Blues Society, another was president of the Kansas City Blues Society, and the third was president of the Blues Society of Memphis.

Strangely, the bands that won that year were as follows: first-place was the blues society group from Miami [see *"cheesiest"* above], who were awarded a big record deal, the second-place winner was the blues society band from Kansas City, who won a block of recording studio time, and the third-place group was the blues society band from Memphis, who won some gift certificates, t-shirts, and assorted crap.

Imagine that – Miami, K.C., and Memphis – one-two-three – right down the line. Like most crooked politicians (redundant again), these nepotistic "judges" didn't even feel the need to be clever about their treachery. They just gave it to their own, apparently throwing out the fourth judge's card (the one who loved us); her opinion on the blues was probably deemed irrelevant anyway – she being both black and a musician.

In a newspaper interview I gave upon returning home, I spoke of the sham perpetrated in the name of the blues in Memphis, and foretold the death of the blues, if the industry was left in the hands of these Philistines. How much more corrupt could a contest be? I said it was like having a beautiful baby contest, and having the mothers of the babies be judges. It was a joke. But we got to perform with B. B. King, Bobby Blue Bland, Albert Collins, and many other Real Blues Greats. So, as usual, life was good until the lawyers got involved.

But the following year, in May of 1993, being gluttons for punishment and always eager for the chance to develop more calluses on our hearts and heads, we returned to Memphis to try to win our way into the finals again – this time as one of the hundreds of wild-card entries.

The wild-card competition was held on Friday, and the finals on Saturday and Sunday. Hoping for the best, but expecting the worst, we smartly booked a gig for Saturday afternoon at a little club on Beale Street to try and cover some of our travel expenses. If we didn't get through Friday's wild-card competition, we would have Saturday off anyway. And if we did get through to Saturday and Sunday's finals, chances are our performance times at the Daisy wouldn't conflict with the three afternoon sets at our other gig. The club we booked was located on the historic corner of Second and Beale (across the street from B. B. King's blues club) and has been featured in loads of music documentaries and was even in a scene in the Tom Cruise movie, *The Firm*. Hereafter, I'll just refer to it as "the club" so as not to give this pit any more publicity it doesn't deserve.

But the fact of the club's prominence didn't affect how they paid their bands. They took full advantage of their prime location on Beale Street and starved their bands to death. They don't call Memphis the "home of the blues" for nothing. What they paid us for the gig there ($200) was less – much less – than we would've agreed to play for at a salad bar back home. But we were in need of money (nothing new to blues bands), and were at a serious bargaining disadvantage. There were hundreds of bands within walking distance that would gladly take this gig – any gig – if we didn't want it. And in case of a miracle – that we won the wild-card division and advanced to the finals on Saturday, we would just have to deal with having two gigs on the same day.

The club had also agreed to provide us with a hotel room for the weekend. This is standard practice when booking bands from out-of-town. But what wasn't so standard was the kind of hotel they put us in.

Now, after traveling extensively for three decades, I could write a book just on horrible hotel stories, but this was probably...no this was *definitely* the weirdest hotel experience I ever had. You see, due to the huge number of tourists in town for the weekend, there weren't any rooms to be had in Memphis. *Hotel* rooms, that is. But the fine folks at the club had procured us lodging as promised. They got us a room in Baptist Memorial Hospital. That's right, in the hospital! This is the same Memphis hospital where Elvis often stayed in the last years of his life, and where he was ultimately pronounced dead.

They rented us a room in a wing of the hospital that was used for patient's families staying overnight, folks awaiting surgery, terminal cases, etc. So there we were, carrying guitars and dressed in purple suits and big black hats, riding the elevator alongside patients lying on gurneys and stretchers going into surgery, dialysis, or God knows where. It was a nightmare. For them as well as us. The looks on their faces! Those were the longest elevator rides of my life. I know that most of those poor patients, doped out of their minds, must've thought they had died on the operating table and now they were going to the bad place. And we were the devils with pencil-thin moustaches and sideburns, in purple suits and black hats, taking them down...down...down. Those elevator rides probably caused many real spiritual conversions and Christian recommitments. Hallelujah! The Lord does work in mysterious ways.

We performed well in Friday's wild-card competition, and out of hundreds of bands, earned one of the two spots available in the finals. The trouble started when we couldn't find out when we were to perform on Saturday.

God love the lawyers, they didn't even make out a rough schedule for the fifty or so bands that were performing on Saturday, they just said to be there, waiting for your name to be called. All day. Take turns getting food, going to the bathroom, etc. There were so many bands that it was probably impossible to keep to a schedule, but for God's sake (and the bands' sakes), at least make out a schedule and then try to keep as close to it as possible.

There were drums, amps, keyboards, and mics already set up on stage that all the bands played through so there was a minimum of set up time. You just carried your guitar, bass, horn, or whatever on stage and plugged in. And your set times were very strictly enforced. I think you had fifteen minutes. And if you went one second over the fifteen minutes, you were automatically disqualified. Yeah, that's the blues. So rather than make a schedule that might be off by half an hour at the end of the nine-hour day, the shyster powers-that-be ruled that all bands needed to be present all day. From 10:00 in the morning till 7:00 at night, waiting for their name to be called. Just like in court.

This "policy" was equally unfair to the fans. They were supposed to sit in the theater all day also. Busloads of blues society members had traveled to Memphis with their bands to support them. This "support" was usually in the form of cheering wildly for their babies, while remaining stoically silent while every other band performed. These "lobbyists" would talk to all in earshot of how great their band was, and how awful all the other bands were. These folks really had a handle on how to "preserve the blues", all right. They wouldn't know the blues if the blues bit 'em.

Having no clue (and no intention) of preserving the *music* that is (was) the "blues", they were really gifted at preserving and promoting the personal misery and poverty that is popularly known as "the blues". And these Philistines forged, full-steam ahead, into the 21st Century, teaming with club-owners and pathetically bad "blues musicians", and successfully making a corpse out of the majestically beautiful American art form known as "Blues".

Back in our room Friday night, we reasoned that we would do our best to go back and forth between the club and the Daisy Theater on Saturday, but that our first responsibility was to the club that was paying us (and putting us in this terrific room where we could ring for a nurse if we wanted).

After two days and two nights in the hospital,
Charlie took a turn for the nurse!
[My apologies to Groucho Marx]

This was the deal: We were supposed to play three forty-five minute sets at the club, so we would simply run up Beale, from the club to the Daisy at the end of our sets, and see if we were "up". We had a thirty-minute break between each of our three sets, so we could easily (!) run the two blocks up Beale Street, our guitars around our necks, and put in our fifteen-minute set at the Daisy when called. If we got there and our name had already been called, and we missed it, then we missed it. So what? We knew the deal from last year anyway. But we would do our best to get there. We would be able to wait at the Daisy for two or three hours in the morning, before we had to go to our club gig, and we could come back immediately after our gig was over, so there was a good chance that we would be called either before or after our other gig, Murphy's Law notwithstanding. So, feeling good about our chances to at least perform in the finals, we pushed the button lowering the back of our electric beds down, put the side rails up, said our prayers, and went to sleep.

The next morning, I was up at 6:00 and, after a brisk walk to the bathroom, was back in bed by 6:05. We all got up a bit later, showered and got dressed, and rode the elevator down. Wearing a bright red sport-jacket, black slacks, and black Stetson hat, I think I made quite an impression on the semi-conscious but wide-eyed gentleman on his way down to O.R. He kept trying to say something to me, but I couldn't understand him, so I just nodded and smiled.

On Beale, we each took turns waiting at the Daisy while the other two of us were setting up our equipment at the club. We did get to see ourselves on the news on the TV behind the bar. The midday news story opened with a close-up shot of my two-tone snakeskin shoes, tapping the beat, and then slowly panned up and out to us rocking Slim Harpo's *Shake Your Hips*. Wow, that was cool – we made the Memphis news! Then they showed an interview with the Blues Foundation president, a dry, female attorney with the obligatory hyphenated last name, who delivered a carefully scripted "State Of The Blues" speech.

The staff at the club, seeing the news story, seemed happy that they were getting the benefit of their $200 Saturday afternoon band being featured on network television. For the ridiculously small amount of money they were paying us, driving one thousand miles round-trip, this was a nice, unexpected bonus for them, and us.

We were not (naturally) called at the Daisy before our club gig started, and so after our forty-five minute first set at the club, we unplugged, and leaped off the stage (literally), our guitar and bass still around our necks, and, drumsticks in hand, raced up the two blocks to the Daisy Theater, where we asked the stage manager, huffing and puffing and pouring sweat, if we had been called. I should also mention that the temperature in Memphis in May was in the mid 90s with 100% humidity, and we were running up the street in suits, felt hats, and snakeskin shoes.

Do you remember the Batman television series from the 1960s? Remember the animated shot of Batman and Boy Wonder (Robin) running toward the screen, arms and legs churning, as they were racing to the Batmobile or the Batboat to fight crime and foil the bad guy? Well that's what the three of us must've looked like, dressed in our wild suits, running as fast as we could, through the drunken throng on Beale Street, with the tools of our trade in our hands. I can hear the Batman theme song in my head as I think about how we must have looked...

Na-na-na-na-na-na-na-na-na-na-na-na-na-na-na-na
LIGHT-NIN'!!!

We were not called up at the Daisy Theater during either of our two breaks between sets (naturally again), but we made it back and forth between venues without a scrape. We finished our third and last set at the club, even doing an encore, and I immediately dispatched our bass player Leroy up to the Daisy to wait for our call (he was our fastest runner), while my drummer and I broke down our equipment from the stage, making room for the next band to set up. We then ran to the Daisy where we met Leroy halfway. He told us they just gave our stage call – we were on next! Without a chance to have even a sip of water, up we went. We blazed through our fifteen minutes, and got a thunderous ovation from the crowd. Even some of the blues lobbyists were cheering before they caught themselves.

As an anti-climactic footnote to all of this, we came in third-place in the finals, winning a bunch of crap. But we have the satisfaction of being the only wild-card band to ever get through all the politics and place in the finals in the twenty-four years of the contest. Maybe some of the lawyers read the press we got for not winning the year before. But enough about all of this – I know you must be wondering where the "Killer" part of this story is.

The manager of the Beale Street club we were playing that Saturday afternoon happened to be the daughter of Jerry Lee Lewis. Yep, The Killer himself. Her name is Phoebe Allen Lewis and she was the result of the unholy matrimony between Jerry Lee and his first cousin Myra. I'm sure you all know the infamous story of Jerry Lee marrying his thirteen year-old cousin Myra Brown (Jerry Lee lied to the press at the time, saying Myra was fifteen and adding, *"I married the girl, didn't I?"*). Yeah, Jerry Lee was never a master of damage control.

Myra was the daughter of Jerry Lee's bass player/uncle, J.W. Brown. The fact that The Killer wasn't divorced from his second wife, Jane, when he married Myra only added bigamy to the cradle-robbing and incest charges. But Jerry Lee hadn't been divorced from his first wife, Dorothy, when he married Jane (his second), either, so at least he was consistent.

Let's briefly examine the family tree of the woman I'm working for in Memphis. Try to stay with me on this, y'all. It's very confusing, but it's all relative.

Jerry Lee and Myra's forbidden union produced two children/second cousins, one son and one daughter. Phoebe is the daughter. She's also her Daddy's second cousin. Her brother, Steve Allen Lewis, drowned suspiciously in the family pool at age three. I'll detail in a moment some of the tragedies associated with Jerry Lee, many of which give credence to his nickname, "The Killer".

But first, let me describe the tragedy that was Phoebe Lewis. Phoebe was not a happy camper. Upon meeting her at the club Friday morning, I told her what a huge fan of her Father's music I was, and how much we were looking forward to playing her club. She just sneered at me, not responding to either compliment, and then barked the set times and house rules at me. These house rules included everything from no drinks on stage, to no guests, to no excessive volume, etc. etc. etc. Her second cousin, The Killer, also known to her as "Daddy", sure couldn't have played there. I thought for a second about breaking this "reading of the riot act" tension by cracking a little joke *("I promise not to set the piano on fire either!")*, but thought better of it. Phoebe Lewis didn't seem to have much in the way of a sense of humor. So I just nodded, agreeing to her list of rules, and wondering to myself if she might have a third earlobe somewhere or webbed feet. A little levity, even to oneself, goes a long way in times of stress.

Her physical appearance was making me a little uncomfortable as well. Phoebe looked just like her Daddy/Cousin. She was very thin and had long, blonde hair, a sick, sallow complexion, and her black, beady eyes were set way too close together. This gave her angular face a strange "possum" look to it. She was also quite "top-heavy". The cumulative effect of all this on a young and fairly inexperienced musician like me was a bit distressing, to say the least. Having the offspring of incest bark orders at me was, at that time, something rather unusual. But thanks to a career in music, dealing with this kind of thing would become less unusual and more commonplace. Routine even.

Learning to expect the unexpected is necessary for one's survival out on the road. If you don't believe me, ask any old possum. Ask George Jones – he'll tell you. And speaking of the road and road-kill, let's get back to Phoebe, the buxom, blonde opossum. Allow me to describe Phoebe's looks in these terms: if there is ever an episode of *The Simpsons* where various road-kill and marsupials are partying in their own strip club, Star Wars-style, the bitter, blonde, and busty, pole-climbing possum would be Phoebe Lewis.

*Jerry Lee, responding to
the previous paragraph*

Let's look at some of the demonically inspired events in Jerry Lee's life, just to give some context to this story and some relevance to his ever so apt nickname, "The Killer". Now would be a good time for all of you to take a deep breath and hold on to something – this ain't gonna be pretty. Okay, here we go…

Jerry Lee's father, Elmo Lewis Sr., was a convicted moonshiner and alcoholic. When Jerry Lee was three, his eight-year old brother Elmo Jr. was run over and killed by a drunk driver in front of the family's house. The driver probably purchased the booze that had helped to kill Elmo Jr. from Elmo Sr. Thirty-four years later, The Killer gives his firstborn son, Jerry Lee Jr., a new Jeep for his nineteenth birthday, and a year later, Jerry Lee Lewis Jr. was killed when he totaled it (police said alcohol was "definitely a factor"). Big surprise there.

Jerry Lee's second son (Phoebe's brother and third cousin, Steve Allen Lewis) drowned in their swimming pool at age three. Myra and Jerry Lee were both inside the house at the time, obviously making drugs and alcohol a factor in his death, too.

Jerry Lee has been married six times, divorced four times and widowed twice. Both wives' deaths occurred under highly suspicious circumstances.

One wife, Jaren Elizabeth, after giving birth to a daughter named Lori Leigh Lewis, also drowned in their swimming pool. Drug and alcohol related, perhaps? Take three guesses.

One year later, his fifth wife, Shawn, died of what was ruled a "methadone overdose" by authorities, although her body, found in the couple's bedroom, was severely bruised and beaten.

> *"Your sister's dead",* Jerry Lee said to Denise Stevens (Shawn's sister) the day after Shawn's bruised and bloodied corpse was discovered, *"and she was a bad girl."*

Eight months later, in 1984, Jerry Lee, not being prone to long bouts of grief, married his sixth wife, Kerrie. They remained husband and wife for twenty years and had a son, named Jerry Lee III, until they divorced in 2004. But Jerry Lee did take a little time out from this marriage to have an affair with Bonny Lee Bakley.

Bonny Lee was a notorious groupie/stalker who had moved from New Jersey to Tennessee just to get closer to Lewis, whom she was obsessed with. Before long, she was intimately involved with him, and his family.

Bonny Lee and Jerry Lee's sister, Linda Gail Lewis, went into business together, selling nude photos of Bakley and sending them to customers through the mail. Bakley and Linda Gail were indicted on federal mail and pornography charges, but the charges were later dropped.

Bonny Lee and Jerry Lee did manage to produce yet another gift to the world – a daughter named Jeri Lee. Amid all the murder and mayhem, incest and adultery, drugs and booze (Lewis once estimated he had spent $500,000 on Demerol alone), one can excuse Jerry Lee's lack of imagination when it came to naming all these little fruits of his loins.

Bonny Lee Bakley later gained national notoriety by marrying actor Robert Blake and then getting shot to death by him.

I am going to digress for a moment here to inject (hey! pun intended) a little bit of levity. We could use some about now. Here's two guys talking:

"My first wife passed away"
"Oh, I am sorry. How did it happen?"
"Food poisoning. She ate some poisoned mushrooms."
"Oh, that's terrible. Did you remarry?"
"Yes, but my second wife, she passed away."
"Gee, that's terrible. How did it happen?"
"Food poisoning. She also ate some tainted mushrooms."
"That's just awful. Have you remarried?"
"Yes, but my third wife, she died too."
"Food poisoning?"
"No. Skull fracture. She wouldn't eat her mushrooms!"

In 1976, at Jerry Lee's forty-first birthday celebration, Lewis "accidentally" shot his bass player, Butch Owens, in the chest with a .357 magnum (Owens miraculously recovered).

Two months later, "The Killer" was arrested at Graceland, waving a pistol and telling the security guard he was there to kill Presley. Elvis dropped the charges. Lewis, who often referred to the Beatles as "that English band", was most jealous of the fame accorded Elvis Presley.

"I was glad [when Presley died]", Jerry Lee once said. "Just another one out of the way. I mean, Elvis this, Elvis that. All we hear is Elvis, Elvis, Elvis. What the [expletive deleted] did Elvis ever do except take dope that I couldn't get ahold of?"

My Aunt Jeannette remembers Jerry Lee coming, uninvited, to Graceland once when she was there [see February '07 Lowdown]. She said the gatekeeper called up to the house, saying Jerry Lee was at the gate and wanted to come up. Elvis asked,

"Is he drunk?"
"No, just drinking", the gatekeeper answered.

So Elvis reluctantly let him come up. Jeannette said Jerry Lee came riding up the driveway in the back of a convertible, perched on top of the back seat with his arms crossed in front of his chest and yelling to all at Graceland,

"The Killer's here and is now available for autographs!"

Jeannette said nobody could've cared less that Jerry Lee was there and that Elvis couldn't stand having him around either, drunk or sober.

Another time, Jerry Lee showed up at the gate, characteristically drunk and pilled out of his mind, demanding to come up to the house, and Jeannette said Elvis told the gatekeeper to,

"Put Jerry Lee out back with the rest of the trash."

I read a recent interview with Jerry Lee, where he was asked about his arrest for wildly crashing his Continental into the gates at Graceland and threatening to kill Elvis. Let's let Jerry Lee pick up the story. Lewis reminisced,

"Elvis had called me and asked me to come over to the house, saying he wanted to talk to me about something. When I got over there, I just nosed that Lincoln into the gates real easy, and it looked like those guys [the figures with guitars on the iron gates] *were rockin' and rollin', so I just pushed down on 'em a little more, and watched the show. Then the law came and said 'Are you here to hurt Presley?' so I said, 'Of course I'm here to hurt Presley'. If someone asks me a stupid question, I'll give 'em a stupid answer."*

Stupid is as stupid does, Jerry Lee. The really disturbing thing about this Demerol-sponsored explanation is that Lewis probably believes it, as he probably believes his wife Shawn beat herself to death. But it's light years from the truth.

Verily I say unto you, Jerry Lee Lewis would be the last person on Earth that Elvis Presley would call up and ask to have a private chat with. If Elvis were ever looking for advice, a friend, or a confidante, Jerry Lee would be at the very bottom of those lists.

The Killer was never criminally charged with anything worse than misdemeanors: driving while intoxicated, drunk in public, driving without a license, etc. He was sued for failure to pay child support (to Kerrie and Jerry Lee III), but he was never more than questioned regarding the trail of corpses in and around his house and swimming pool. Jerry Lee Lewis was the first person inducted into the Rock And Roll Hall Of Fame, and deservedly so, but, in my opinion, he has never been given his due concerning the morbid reality of his well-earned nickname, "The Killer".

*The Killer and The Undead
(Myra at age thirteen was one
of the few to get out alive)*

I've got to stop for a moment to say something about these eyes. In 1995, Phoebe's eyes were set so close together that she had virtually no bridge of the nose. At least the bridge of her nose was not where it was supposed to be. It could've been hanging from her armpit for all I know. And Jerry Lee's eyes, when he was young, were close-set also. But I've seen Jerry Lee a few times recently, and I swear his eyes (socket and ball) are moving outward, toward the sides of his head. I found a recent picture on the Internet (thanks again, Al Gore!) of Jerry Lee and Phoebe and Myra, and Phoebe's eyes are not nearly as close together as they were twelve years ago. This freaked me out. She is also at least sixty or seventy pounds heavier now than before. I don't suppose hard drugs had anything to do with her being so thin then. Or so heavy now.

Look closely at this "Three Flew Over The Cuckoo's Nest" picture of Phoebe, Myra, and Jerry Lee below, and notice how Myra (center) looks like she's smartly resisting being dragged to the family swimming pool for some Demerol and a "dip". Notice too how Jerry Lee's eyeballs are bulging and are almost on opposite sides of his head. He didn't used to look like that. I don't know if it's the dope, the demons, or the incest, but I think the whole family is mutating into goldfish. Seriously. And as the Good Book says,

"The eyes are the windows to the soul."

Amen to that. Now let's move on.

Daughter Phoebe Lewis (on left), with her second cousins, Mama & Daddy.

Well, when we last left our hero, Lightnin' Man, he was having a whale of a weekend in Memphis. Having played the gig at Phoebe Lewis' dirty little dive on Beale Street, and having obeyed all of her Gestapo "house rules" (not drinking while on stage meant no drinks, not even water), having slept in a hospital room, and having helped to "preserve the blues" for the Philistine Lawyers of the Blues Foundation, it was time to take care of business with Phoebe for our afternoon performance.

Exhausted from running up and down the street in the Memphis heat (not to mention performing four sets without the benefit of a glass of water), I slowly followed Ms. Lewis upstairs to get paid. She led me into a seedy, dark, little office and sat down behind her desk. She didn't offer me a seat, nor did she say anything complimentary about our sets (although we drew large crowds that were very enthusiastic and stayed for all three sets, which is unheard of on Beale Street, where there are bands playing in every nook and cranny, and bands are lucky to get people to stay for one whole set, let alone three). I stood, waiting silently, while she counted out our money on her desk. Then she looked up at me and said,

*"You were supposed to start your third set at 4:45,
and you didn't start your third set until 4:47."*

I looked at her, waiting for the punch line, or a chuckle, forgetting for a moment who/what I was talking to. Realizing the seriousness and severity of her tone, I said tiredly,

"So we were supposed to start our third set at 4:45, and we didn't start until 4:47. So? We still played the full 45 minutes. Actually we played longer."

Another of Phoebe's "house rules" required the bands to sign in and out, when going on and off stage. This time card was closely monitored for discrepancies by Ms. Lewis' female (?) stage manager, a fat, butchy, bar-bull who would've looked right at home in a SS uniform.

When I signed off after our third set (and Leroy was hauling bass up to the Daisy), I remarked to the bull-butch what a great crowd we had. They stayed for the whole show and, demanding an encore, we had actually played overtime by several minutes. The stage manager, probably Phoebe's cousin/sister/lover (which is triply-redundant among the Lewis family), simply stared back at me blankly. Another goldfish.

Meanwhile, back in the office, Phoebe sternly repeated herself to me,

*"You were supposed to start your third set at 4:45,
and you didn't start your third set until 4:47,
and so I am docking you for the two minutes you were late."*

Well, I was flabbergasted. The fact that someone as mentally and genetically challenged as Ms. Lewis was going to go to the trouble, without a calculator, of multiplying the 45-minute sets by three, giving a total of 135 minutes, then dividing our fee of $200 by 135, coming up with a rate of $1.48 per minute, then multiplying $1.48 times two (for the two minutes late), getting a total of $2.96 for punitive damages, then subtracting this from $200, and deriving $197.04 as our payment was just too much for me to handle.

I stood watching this, incredulously, and was equally amazed by the way her fingers (I counted four, and one thumb) wielded the pencil with a lobster-like grip, madly scrawling in the dark, with her oily brow furled up like a pack of hotdogs (this bringing her black, beady eyes even closer together), and by the astonishing fact that I was being docked at all.

This was, and is, the only time in my twenty-four year career, that I have ever been docked any money. I've been robbed lots of times, been paid zero by promoters and managers who skipped out, had hundreds of dollars mysteriously "missing" from our fee, but never have I experienced someone meticulously and surgically removing pennies from my pay. Not before or since.

Watching this mean-spirited, top-heavy, carny freak scribble away $2.96 of our hard-earned money was an experience I will never forget, and one that finally gets me my money's worth by its inclusion in the Lightnin' Lowdown. It's a story that deserves to be told.

As does my final, three-word response to Ms. Lewis. I must've had a look of total disbelief on my face because when Phoebe pushed my peanuts across her dirty desk, she leered up at me with this twisted, belligerent scowl which is typical of inbreds, and said,

"You got anything to say?"

I stuffed the money into my pocket and shrugged,

"When cousins marry!"

That was all I said. And that says plenty. And then I split! I turned and made my way down the stairs, looking back over my shoulder a couple times to make sure she wasn't coming after me with a loaded syringe and a pair of swimming trunks.

I can imagine the authorities finding me the next morning, floating in her swimming pool after taking an "overdose" of Demerol and going for a midnight swim. While they dragged my bloated and bruised corpse from the pool, as they did with William Holden in the macabre, final scene in *Sunset Blvd,* I can imagine the haunting strains of Jerry Lee singing in the background,

"You have left me.......BREATHLESS!!!"

So many folks in Jerry Lee's life leave him just that way – breathless, beaten, and dead.

*Jerry Lee and friend, both looking stuffed
(a picture truly is worth a thousand words)*

I see on the Internet that Phoebe is now living in Nashville, pursuing a career in country music, and acting as manager and blog-writer for her second cousin and Paw, Jerry Lee Lewis. That's rich.

The Killer has, in my opinion, at the very least, contributed to the deaths of several people. These are just deaths that we know about. God only knows what else he has done that nobody knows about. He's probably got more skeletons in his closet than Tony Soprano. So the fact that my association with this filthy, inter-breeding bunch of junkies only cost me $2.96 is pretty fortunate. Associating with The Killer and his Klan has cost many people their lives.

Until we meet again, I leave you with this happy little ditty, an ode to the blues, and dedicated to Phoebe Lewis. Sing this to the tune of Otis Redding's *Dock Of The Bay*.

*Sittin' in a mess of the blues
gettin' tired of payin' these dues
Workin' for this freaky fool
Did someone pee in her gene pool?*

Now you're just...

Sittin' there dockin' my pay
I'm watchin' an inbred take it away
Ooooh, play the blues and dues you'll pay
wastin' time...

I left my home in the mountains
headed for ol' Memphis town
And I've done nothin' but run y'all
tearin' up Beale Street and racin' back down

And you're just....

Sittin' there dockin' my pay
I'm watchin' an inbred take it away
Ooooh, play the blues and dues you'll pay
wastin' time...

Looks like a possum on a pole
everything's wrong – there ain't no soul, but
I can't do what these pit-people tell me to do
But at least I'll go home whole

Sittin' there mean as can be
and your Cousin is your Da-a-a-ddy
One thousand miles I flee
Just to play for pennies

Now you're just...

Sitting there dockin' my pay
I'm watching an inbred take it away
Ooooh, play the blues and dues you'll pay
wastin' time...

Hope you've enjoyed this light, breezy little tale. It ain't nothin' but the blues. And the blues is truth. And the truth is, I'm out of here.

After while, crocodile,
Lightnin' Charlie

26

REDNECKS, SPANDEX, AND CAR WRECKS
- OR -
GET OFF MY ALLEY, PALLY

Hello out there from Lightnin' Land! This month I am going to catch up on some pet peeves. In the April 2007 Lowdown, I promised you a monthly

Official Lightnin' Charlie Pet Peeve Of The Month

But things have been going so extraordinarily well, that I've found myself unable to complain or nitpick about anything. Really. If you don't believe me, ask my wife. But a promise is a promise, and since I promised you some senseless whining, I'll just have to force myself.

My wife, kids, and I live on what used to be a quiet, two-lane road that winds around the foothills of Buffalo Mountain in East Tennessee. Mountain roads apparently are an attraction for redneck litterbugs who drive much faster than their ability to think, and bicycle riders who, dressed in spandex wet suits, travel in packs and take up an entire lane of traffic. These two detriments to modern society, when allowed to roam freely on the same two-lane blacktop, create danger and havoc for all. And as usual in America, it's too bad for the majority – the folks like me who are simply and soberly driving the speed limit, carefully minding our business, and going to or from our homes, churches, and schools with our families.

Let me elaborate here on the term "redneck". "Redneck" does not accurately describe the genetics and soul-lessness of the thugs I'm discussing here. I used it earlier in the title purely for the purpose of rhyme. Originally, "redneck" was a derogatory term Northerners and Elitists (present-day Democrats) used for Southern white males who, after working the fields and farms all day in the hot sun, had a sunburned, or "red" neck. These men, being hard-working, and in love with the land – their land – are most definitely not the scum-of-the-earth I'm referring to here. The empty beer can-flinging vermin are the polar opposite of a workingman. They have probably never worked one day in their life, thanks to the welfare system in this country. If they worked hard, they would have some respect for the hard work of others, and wouldn't litter the land – their land – with trash. So what shall we call these loathsome, ignorant, drunken creatures? Certainly they're not "rednecks" in the true sense of the word. Today, many respectable, working-class Southern men are proud to refer to themselves as "rednecks". And the fact that they work for a living, take pride in themselves, their homes, and families, makes them altogether different than this donkey we're trying to pin a tail on. To call them "animals" would be unfair to the animals. Even pigs won't defecate where they eat and sleep.

To call them anything but what they are would be less than fair. Let's judge this tree by its fruit. Let's call 'em what they are. Let's use their well-earned and most-apt nickname: "trash". There are several terms that are commonly used with the term "trash". "Drunken trash" is one. This is seriously redundant. Trash is always in some state of drunkenness. They're either drinking, drunk, or recovering from a previous drunk [see "drinking"]. The term "White Trash" is overused also, and it misses the mark by attacking only one of the many ethnic varieties of this soul-sickness. There is, in my experience, equal amounts of trash in Black, Latino, and other communities, why bother with a qualifier like "white"? The obvious answer is because it's the most convenient and it's the only race we're allowed to ridicule. But trash transcends all color lines. Trash is as trash does.

One qualifier that does help, descriptively, is to preface "trash" with where the trash comes from. Tennessee Trash have a look, smell, and feel all their own, and they're a bit different than Florida Trash, or Texas Trash. But we will confine our ethnography to the Tennesseans who are trashing Tennessee.

There was a famous public service television campaign here in Tennessee that dealt with our litter problem. A filthy fat guy, swilling beer while driving, was shown throwing empties and piles of garbage out of his car. I always cracked up at the end when he stops at a lake and his rear bumper falls off the car, amid piles of trash. The name of the campaign was "Tennessee Trash". In the Tennessee Trash public service announcement, Mr. Trash sported a heart-shaped tattoo on his arm that simply said *"TRASH"*. They even had a song that went with it, sung by Ed Bruce,

"Lord, there ain't no lower class than Tennessee Trash"

The man who portrayed "Tennessee Trash" in this PSA was Irving Kane. The Tennessee Trash PSA made him a household name in Tennessee, but he was also a composer of classical music, who conducted the Nashville Symphony playing his compositions in Tennessee and at Carnegie Hall! It pays not to judge a book by its cover. The Tennessee Trash PSA came out at about the same time as another well-known PSA featuring a Native American rowing his canoe through lots of filth. The "money shot" at the end of this one had a close-up of a teardrop coming from the Indian's eye, from what was being done to his land (I can relate). And the actor portraying the Indian, Iron Eyes Cody, was Italian!

Trash, being unimaginative to the extreme, is also pathetically predictable. Nowadays, Tennessee Trash invariably drives one of two types of late model, rusty-dusty automobiles – either old pick-up trucks or beat-up "muscle cars". This is a source of shame for all the decent people who drive pick-ups or muscle cars. My first car was a 1970 Camaro, but that was a different time and a different place. And a different species of driver.

The problem I have with Tennessee Trash is twofold. One, he/she/it drunkenly and carelessly throws their garbage out onto the street, my lawn, and the lawns of my neighbors. This is filthy, unnecessary, and gross. But so are they. It is an absolute irony that these people – oh excuse me...this trash, pollutes and disrespects the very land they claim to be so proud of. They'll fight you over abstractions like "Tennessee" or the "South", while they're busy trying to make my beautiful countryside look like a ghetto in Newark. Adding to the irony here is the fact that Tennessee Trash is, by definition, racist. And racism, by definition, decrees one's clear superiority to another. Tennessee Trash (the white ones) especially dislikes all Blacks. Conversely, black trash hates all whites. But Tennessee Trash's hatred of Jews and Yankees (redundant? *Oh come on...I'm joking!)* transcends all color lines, thinking them dirty, inferior, and no-good. That's rich, ain't it? The pot calling the kettle dirty, inferior, and no-good.

I happen to love Tennessee. I love living here. I love the beauty, culture, and work ethic of the Southern United States and its people. More than just loving the "South", I love beauty – wherever I find it. And Tennessee happens to be majestically beautiful. The street where I live is beautiful, nestled in a little green valley looking up toward Buffalo Mountain and the lower Appalachian Mountains. Therefore, I have nothing but contempt for those who go out of their way to destroy that which is beautiful. Either you're with me or you're agin' me. It used to be the Cowboys and the Indians, and now it's us and them.

But Tennessee Trash doesn't care a thing about beauty. Just look at them and you'll agree. Tennessee Trash doesn't care about Tennessee either. Just look at my front yard on any Sunday morning and you'll agree again. But unfortunately, there's just too darn many of 'em for me to shoot.

My other complaint has to do with how recklessly fast trash drives in front of my house. It's out of control. My neighborhood is residential and the speed limit on all the streets nearby is 30 mph. Most of my neighbors have children of various ages. Mine are six and five and like to play outside. This causes us much consternation when pick-ups and broken-down Firebirds are flooring it in front of our house. We are forced to keep to our fenced-in back yard. Two stop signs, about 200 feet apart, on connecting streets at opposite sides of my house, do little to slow trash down. Trash must get all four or five gears in between the two stop signs, to feel like men. What this kind of driving does to their gas mileage one can only imagine. But I guess if you don't have to work to buy it yourself, what does it matter? It's my taxes that are paying for their gas and food (beer) stamps. Talk about biting the hand that feeds you. I should note that, although the female trash population is plentiful here, and are tireless breeders, the reckless, dangerous, stupidity of the maniac-driver is exclusively male.

Just so you don't accuse me of overreacting, here's a little resume of some of the experiences I have had with T.T. (Tennessee Trash), in and around my front yard. I have had vehicles spin-out into my yard, vehicles run through my yard, vehicles plow through our flower beds, vehicles do "360s" in the middle of the street (several have crashed into my neighbor's fence). My mailbox has been hit six or seven times in the five years we've lived here. A guard rail was installed in front of my other next-door neighbor's house last year – it has been crashed into so many times, it now resembles the crushed beer cans Tennessee's finest are so gaily chugging and chucking. Needless to say, mowing and weed-eating the edge of lawn at the street is often a near-death experience for me. I should put a sign up in my yard that says,

"LITTERBUGS AND RECKLESS DRIVERS WILL BE SHOT. SURVIVORS WILL BE SHOT AGAIN"

Speaking of "gaily", this leads me to another curiosity. I've noticed that when I am outside, walking to my car, working in the yard, getting my mail, etc., T.T. steps on it even more. I don't get it. Are they "puffing up" and putting on this display of machismo, faced with another rival male of the species? Are they showing off how cool they are, gunning their hundred-dollar rust-buckets up the hill to the next stop sign? Does this make them feel somehow superior in their primered pick-up trucks with no bumpers (although they're in full view of my vintage Cadillacs and Lincoln Limousine)? Who knows what makes these ticks tick? Like the song says,

"I really don't want to know."

I should mention that I've long since stopped yelling, glaring, or otherwise giving any attention to them when they speed by. I assume that attention is part of why they do it, and any attention they get just encourages them.

Even more disturbing, for me, is the fact that if I am working in the yard shirtless, T.T. shows off all the more. Originally, I thought that this was just coincidence or my imagination, but it has become so consistent as to be scientific even. I have a theory of why T.T. does this. It is because Tennessee Trash (the male ones) must be closet homosexuals, one and all, and are uncontrollably attracted to me – especially when I am bare-chested and weed-eating. And who could blame them for that? That's perfectly understandable. But my honest (and less facetious) opinion is that the tattooed Tennessee trash – subconsciously, at least – recognizes me as their immortal enemy.

To paraphrase Jesus, they're about their father's business, and I'm about the business of mine, and our fathers have been at war with each other since before Eden. I believe T.T. has discernment of spirit (even though they can't discern when it's time for a bath or a trip to the dentist) and they view me, correctly, as their adversary and their immortal and spiritual foe. This would explain the extreme lack of courtesy I receive in convenience stores and in Wal-Mart, as well.

Spandexed mountain bikers pose another problem – this one, ironically, caused by a lack of speed. But these persnickety pedal-pushers are in harmony with their T.T. cousins in that they have no regard or consideration for anyone else but themselves. Having to use the roads, I am in constant conflict with these weirdos, dressed in leotards and helmets, looking like a cross between Jacques Cousteau and the cast of *Cats*.

The two-lane roads around where I live are extremely hilly and curvy, resulting in very limited visibility. Drivers cannot see oncoming traffic when going over hills and around curves, and hills and curves are about all there is around here. Hills, curves, and bikies (let's call them "bikies", to be fair to real "bikers", who wouldn't be caught dead in spandex).

Everyday as I'm driving, I top a hill, or round a curve at my safe and sober 30 mph, only to throw on my brakes because of the bikies. Mountain bicycles, and their Twinkie pilots fill the lane. There are usually at least three or four in a pack, sometimes as many as ten or twelve, and they never ride single-file. They spread out across the lane of traffic, so they can converse with each other about the new Michael Moore movie, their favorite power bars, etc. Only after following behind them for a half-mile or so, will they reluctantly consent to single-file status (I think deferring to an automobile that outweighs them by half a ton must be damaging to their self-esteem).

But to get around them, even when they're riding single-file at the right side of the lane, one must swerve out into the center of the street, and prayerfully "gun it" past them. This maneuver is a risky one, to say the least, due to the very limited visibility. If a car happens to be coming toward you when you're swerving out and around these Twinkie-Nymphs, you're in a world of hurt. Thus begins the terrible vehicular disaster commonly known as the "head-on collision". There are no shoulders on these roads – they're narrow, country roads that are just wide enough for two vehicles to pass one another. Generally, there is a grassy ditch that runs beside the road. This is the destination I desperately desire for these inconsiderate quiffs, when I am trying to get around them and also trying to avoid sudden death.

Should cars slow down to 5 mph and just coast along behind the Twinkies until the opportunity presents itself for safe passage? Am I the only one who doesn't have an hour to spend, riding behind a bunch of poofs too proud to pull off to the side and let someone pass? Aren't there laws about what is allowed to travel on the public roads and about maintaining a flow of traffic? Can I go walking, or, better yet, crawling on all fours, or push a baby stroller down the middle of the street, and expect everyone else to kill themselves getting around me?

The fact that these "men-in-tights" believe they have the right to use our roadways to pedal around at their leisure, while giving cars dirty looks, amazes me. They show no fear of, nor even a healthy respect for, automobiles. On the contrary, they show utter contempt for our horseless carriages and are clearly bothered by the nuisance the *cars* create for *them*. Of course, if one of these Twinkie-Bikies were to wobble into the side of my car and get struck, I'm sure the liability would be mine.

There are some of these numbskulls that take stupid to a new level by having their infants and toddlers on the back of their bikes (death-traps) with them. Let's call this "Birth Control for Dummies". Now look, there's nothing wrong with the desire to bicycle around or ride through a scenic part of the mountains, but why not use a roadway with a bike path that's safe for everybody, or drive up to the mountains in a car before using one of the many bike paths provided there? Beautiful bike paths that were built with my tax dollars, I might add.

So what am I (and the rest of Mister Charlie's neighborhood) to do about these two scoops of scourge? Well, the obvious solution would be for the Tennessee Trash and the Mountain Bikies to simply destroy each other. Wipe each other out. Oh, happy day. How this hasn't already occurred is a mystery to me, due to the fact that these two hordes, the Twinkies and the T.T.'s, traveling together on a two-lane road, would seem to be mutually exclusive of one another. Consider for a moment that the former is going 3 to 5 mph in a wobbling clump, filling the lane, and the latter is flying blind, over hill and over dale, in drunken abandon. Whence shall the twain meet? Soon and often, I hope.

And I hope that this trip down Lightnin' Charlie Lane has been fun for you. That's my Official Pet Peeve Of The Month for September. Twinkies and T.T.'s. For someone who was in such a good mood, I managed to force out quite a respectable tirade, I think. I can really work myself into a lather over some of the cretins I am forced to share the world with. At least I have the calm assurance of knowing that the feeling between us is mutual.

"It is lamentable, that to be a good patriot
one must become the enemy of the rest of mankind."
- Voltaire

"The Public - a thing I cannot help looking upon as an enemy,
and which I cannot address without feelings of hostility."
- John Keats

"Guys, you're gonna annoy the enemy.
Tease them, and the more the better."
- Knute Rockne

"Hospitality in the prairie country is not limited.
Even if your enemy passes your way,
you must feed him before you shoot him."
- O. Henry

Well, it seems like my feelings put me in good, strong company. I rest my case. Tennessee Trash and Twinkies - can't live with 'em, can't shoot 'em.

That's all, folks! See you next time.

Your friend and child of God,
LC

OCTOBER / NOVEMBER 2007

27

LIGHTNIN'S LOG CABIN ON THE HILL

Dear Lightnin' Bugs and 'fraidy cats. In honor of Halloween, our creepiest "holiday", this installment of the Lightnin' Lowdown tells a creepy story – one that I'm sure many of you will find difficult to believe. I know I wouldn't believe it either. Except that I saw it. Saw it with my own beady, little, green eyes. So sit back, relax, and leave the gabbing to me. No need to thank me. It's my job. It's what I do.

Way back in ancient times, when I was in college, I found a real cool place to hang my hat for the summer. I moved into a log cabin. Yes folks, a real log cabin. This party pad was well-known by partiers around here, and called simply, "The Log Cabin".

So young Lightnin' Charlie, following in the footsteps of young Abe Lincoln (except for the latter's celebrated wisdom, academic excellence, and presidency), moved into a decrepit, old, log cabin to party and rock the summer away (hence the former's famous folly, academic anemia, and musicianship). And just like Honest Abe, I too had a lot of tall, black hats to hang. Ah yes, a very young LC living in a very old LC (Log Cabin, that is). Very nice, very nice. Should make interesting reading...

The Log Cabin was a pretty good deal for me at the time. It fulfilled all my real estate needs. It was big, it was cheap, it had no neighbors, and every party girl in town knew their way there. It was what we called a "hippie house". A "hippie house" was generally an inexpensive rental property, occupied by a group of poor, shiftless students or musicians (Communists), low in self-respect, who were poor due to the fact that they refused to work (unless you consider class-skipping, keg-renting, and party-planning "work"). We only required the most basic of shelter. The log cabin fit that bill. Certainly, it could only be called a "house" in the most primitive sense, and was already called "home" by five of my runnin' buddies. I could move in with my friends, have real cheap rent (split six ways), have a large enough place to rehearse the band, and get the party started. Or, to be more precise, keep the party going (the party at The Log Cabin started way before I moved in, and continued long after I moved out).

Allow me to divulge some of the reasons that The Log Cabin was so cheap. First, it had no air conditioning and no heat. This was not one of those pre-fab "log cabin" homes sporting gas fireplaces, central heat and air, and a Jacuzzi. This was an authentic log cabin, made out of real logs. Old logs. *Real, real* old logs. Built in the 1780s, The Log Cabin should long ago have either been torn down, or turned into a historical landmark. We, the hippie tenants of The Log Cabin, were busily trying to accomplish both (tearin' it up, and makin' some history of our own). But back to the issue of heat and air.

I moved in during the summertime, and planned on using a fan and a "window-unit" air conditioner in my bedroom. But my roommates, veterans of several years in The Cabin, warned me that winter was a completely different story. In the wintertime, you just could not heat the inside of the house. Even though there were huge fireplaces (the main source of heat in 1780) in every room downstairs, it was still impossible to heat.

"What about propane heaters?" I naively asked.
"We use propane heaters, and we burn fires in the fireplaces constantly," my commie-roomies replied, *"but it's still freezing".*

And when they said "freezing", they meant freezing. Literally. This was due to the fact that The Cabin's two hundred year-old logs were so separated from each other, that one could actually see through the spaces in between them. One could even stick one's hand through the gaps in some of them. When the wind would blow, one could feel the breeze from the inside of the house. One never knows, do one? It was basically an "open-air" hippie house.

This was before the plague of "Entitlement" swept across our nation, and back then, for the most part, poor people lived poorly. The Cabin's lack of insulation (understatement) was bearable in the summertime, but in the winter, my roomies said that water left in the kitchen sink would be a solid block of ice by morning, and that a coca-cola left on your night table when you went to sleep at night would be frozen when you woke up. This chilling news didn't stop me from moving in, but prompted me to make plans to move out by late fall. After all, I had only lived in Tennessee for five or six years, and was still just a transplanted Floridian. I had never ice-fished, and didn't intend to learn from my bedroom.

Another little tidbit about The Cabin (that the realtor didn't mention) was the rats. The Log Cabin was on a large wooded lot, probably five or six acres, and there was a big field behind the house that was grown over and a mess (Communists don't mow). This field seemed to be Rat Mecca (redundant). And they sure grew 'em big out there. We had rats the size of Mini Coopers. It was incredible.

I'd watch them through my bedroom window at night, gigantic rats running up and down trees, then across limbs onto the roof and gutter of the house. *That's entertainment!* And since we didn't have cable TV, and we couldn't have a keg party with a live band *every* night, some nights we would spend simply. Watching rats. Yes brothers and sisters, it's reminiscent of Norman Rockwell's America, a simpler time, when folks, after supper, would sit around as a family, and watch rats. Lord have mercy, how they would pour up and down those trees; hundreds of them at a time! I had never seen rats this size before (never wanted to), and never knew rats could climb trees either (never needed to).

I remember telling my bass player, Kevin (who was from a Tennessee town so small, that the bowling alley only had one lane), about these huge rats, running up and down our trees. He laughed and said, ala Gomer Pyle,

"Gaa-ah-leee Florida Boy, haven't you ever seen a squirrel before?"

Squirrel indeed. This coming from a guy whose hometown's only claim to fame was for executing an elephant for murder. Seriously.

In 1916, a circus elephant named Mary accidentally killed her handler, and Mary was brought to trial, charged with murder. I'm not making this up. She was convicted (by a jury of her peers?) and sentenced to death. The judge probably didn't realize when he passed sentence on Mary that the official method of capital punishment in this bright, cheerful, little town was death by hanging. So the town fathers had to come up with a way to carry out the execution. Just how were they going to hang a five-ton elephant by the neck until dead?

They settled on putting a chain around Murderous Mary's neck, and lifting her up into the air with a train derrick. This is just one of several stories in this Lowdown that simply could not be made up. I dare you to try. And it sheds some more light on the company I was keeping.

Murderous Mary

Sorry to digress (again). We would watch these king-sized, mungo rats from very close range, maybe three feet away, separated (thank God) by a window. But suffice it to say we were close enough to know we weren't looking at squirrels.

At first, it was pretty cool watching them do their do, and we irrationally felt separated from them, watching them through glass, as one can safely look at poisonous snakes through terrarium glass.

But the novelty of rat-watching soon wore off, and was replaced with the realization that if there were that many rats outside, that they were certainly inside too. Although I had never seen a rat inside The Cabin, they had surely seen me. None of us liked the idea of rats being inside our home, so we began shooting them.

One of my first-floor roommates had a good vantage point from his bedroom window. His window looked out at the base of one of the trees on the rats' regular route. A small hole, cut into the plastic webbing around his window's air conditioner, was perfect for the barrel of his 22-caliber pellet rifle, and turned his ordinary window into a rat shooting gallery!

Wasting rats replaced watching rats as our entertainment flavor-of-the-week for a while, and soon, word spread through the rat battalion of the heavy losses they were taking, and they moved on. Let's do the same.

I was aware of some of The Log Cabin's history, as well as its infamy, before moving in, but that didn't deter me. Weird, wild and crazy tales the guys and their girlfriends would tell of seeing ghosts and other apparitions didn't bother me. These stories were common knowledge. I personally did not believe in "ghosts", and neither did I believe the guys and their girlfriends. Consider the source.

These were party people, living in a party house, and living to party. I'm not being judgmental here, that was their job, and that's what party people *do*. But their stories were pretty remarkable. There were so many Log Cabin stories of seeing foggy phantoms and ghostly figures gliding around the house and up and down the stairs, that they became routine to those of us "in the loop".

But most of the ghosts seemed to regularly appear to the craziest among us, which, relatively speaking, was mighty crazy. Everyone I knew seemed to be of one opinion or the other, regarding the Log Cabin Ghosts. And the two opposite opinions were: either you thought it pure fantasy, or pure fact. And that opinion was dependent upon whether you lived there or not.

Everyone who lived there (or spent the night there) seemed to take each other very seriously when reporting what he or she had "seen". But I didn't live there (yet) and neither did I believe them (yet). Perhaps they were severely stretching the truth just for kicks. Or perhaps they, themselves, were severely stretched; their Bolshevik brains burnt and stretched beyond repair by the never-ending party.

Let's face it; the bulk of their lives could be divided into two basic parts: one, avoiding work; and two, intentionally altering their sense of sight, of smell, and of mind (use Rod Serling voice here). Perhaps what they and their spaced-out girlfriends were "seeing" was merely a product of their own polluted imaginations. At least that's what I told myself. They weren't lying intentionally or maliciously; they were just being fooled by their own psychedelicized senses. Add to this the potent power of suggestion, where a midnight walk across the dark room to turn over the Jimi Hendrix record would include watching for the "ghost" that someone else had "seen" the night before.

There was also the fact that people, once inside The Log Cabin, always appeared "smoky" and "hazy" anyway, due to all the smoke and haze inside The Log Cabin. I might not have been smart enough to graduate college, but I was smart enough to realize that.

Eyewitness accounts of the paranormal in The Log Cabin, though, were nothing new. Due to the unusual amount of alleged ghost sightings there, professors at East Tennessee State University sanctioned a group of parapsychologists (ghostbusters) to set up shop inside The Log Cabin for a couple nights in the winter of 1970. They spent the night there, trying to catch a ghost on film. But they didn't catch anything (besides the flu).

So by the time I came around in the mid-1980s, The Log Cabin was already fairly famous, at least among our fractured, fraternal fringe of society. The reputation of The Cabin, and its residents (both dead and alive), preceded me.

But during the summer of my tenure, its prodigal tenants were definitely wanted, dead or alive. Wanted, at least, by local members of the fairer sex. Lots of college girls would come out to parties at The Cabin who, otherwise, would never have graced us. They knew they would be entertained, at the least, with *stories* of the supernatural, and if they were brave enough to stay past midnight (nudge-nudge, wink-wink), they might even get the chance to *behold* the supernatural. Not that they were beholding to me in any way, I just be holdin' out and holdin' on! Till fall, that is. Behold, I be cold, y'all! Sorry about all that, but like I said before, this place, haunted or not, suited young LC to a large "T".

But there was one Log Cabin story that was different from all the rest I'd heard, and it really "bugged" me. This was the story of "The Fly Room".

One of the things that differentiated The Fly Room Story from their other run-of-the-mill ghost stories was that the guys didn't like to tell it. They didn't like to talk about it, and seemed to get truly uncomfortable if and when anyone mentioned it. I guess it "bugged" them, too (sorry). This was in stark contrast to every other ghost story from The Log Cabin, which was always told colorfully and with much animation and gusto, never fearfully. The other thing that made The Fly Room Story different from all the other tall tales from The Log Cabin was that I couldn't imagine anyone making it up. Stephen King couldn't make it up.

The story of The Fly Room went like this. About five years before I moved in, two of the older residents of The Log Cabin had just taken up residence there. Let's call them Greg and Tim (because that really was their names). Greg and Tim (let's call them "Grim" for short, because you know by now that I'm a sucker for the cheap pun) were looking around the place, exploring this room and that. Remember, this house is two hundred years old, and there were lots of interesting nooks and crannies in it, and many antique, original accoutrements.

Well, in an upstairs hallway, "Grim" came upon this little door that was only about three feet tall. Grim couldn't guess what this room was. The doorway was too small to walk through, and they agreed it must be some kind of pantry or closet. But none of the rooms had closets (they didn't build closets in 18th century bedrooms), and why would there be a pantry or cupboard in an upstairs hallway. Also, wouldn't a cupboard door be up off the floor? This was a hinged entry door, with doorknob, that was hobbit-sized.

Adding to Grim's curiosity was the strange sound coming from behind the door. A drone. A buzzing sound.

Kneeling down in front of the door, Grimly (not Gimli the dwarf from Tolkien's "Lord Of The Rings", but Greg and Tim!) nervously opened the door and cautiously stuck their heads inside to see.

What they saw was a small room, dwarf or hobbit-sized, maybe eight or ten foot square, too small for a bedroom, but much too large for a pantry or closet. And there was nothing inside that identified the mysterious room's purpose. There was no shelves, no table, no chair, no window – the room was completely bare. Barren of everything...except flies.

The walls, floor, and ceiling were covered in houseflies. Live, buzzing houseflies. This undulating, buzzing mass of vermin by the thousands (resembling the audience at a Rolling Stones concert) was as thick as black carpet on the floor, walls, and ceiling. Maybe there were tens of thousands of them. Or hundreds of thousands. Who knows how many there were? It would be an interesting math problem to calculate how many houseflies it would take to entirely cover every inch of space in a ten square-foot room.

Grim said that the flies were so thick, covering every bit of wall and floor space in there, that you would not have been able to touch the walls, ceiling, or floor with the eraser end of a pencil without touching flies.

Another extraordinary thing (and something that just didn't sound "made up") was Grim saying that all of the flies in "The Fly Room" were alight. All ten thousand, or twenty thousand, or five hundred thousand of them, whatever their unholy number, were all sitting or standing (or whatever it is that flies do when they're not flying), and that none of the flies – not one – was *flying*.

This is the creepiest part of The Fly Story for me: that they were just sitting there. The scariest part of Alfred Hitchcock's *The Birds* wasn't the scenes when the birds were flying around, attacking Tippi Hedrin and the poor school kids. The worst scenes, for me, were the ones that showed the hundreds of birds, just sitting there. Waiting. Watching. Premeditating. That's more terrifying than the sight of them flapping around, wildly pecking out eyeballs. And the sight of all those black houseflies, buzzing-in-place, must've been the most horrible thing Grim ever saw. So, justifiably horrified, Grim slammed the little door shut, and scurried in a hurry.

Once outside, they stopped running. Then, shuddering, asked each other if they had really seen what they thought they had just seen. Greg and Tim agreed that yes, they had each just looked into a ten square-foot closed room, which was completely covered in live flies.

After taking a few minutes to summon up the necessary courage, Grim went back upstairs, this time armed with large cans of bug spray (which were always kept on hand in The Log Cabin).

Grim crept up to the door of The Fly Room, Raid in hand, and taking a deep breath, slowly opened the door.

What they saw freaked them out worse than their previous horror. For inside The Fly Room there was nothing. No flies. Not one. There wasn't a single fly inside that room.

Where had the thousands upon thousands of flies gone? There wasn't a window, there wasn't a vent; there wasn't any escape route that Grim could see (which also begs the question, how did they get *in* there in the first place?). And a space large enough to accommodate the exit of all those vermin would have been clearly visible, as there was nothing in this little, square room to hide any such exit from view.

The Fly Room didn't have logs (with gaps) on the inside. It wasn't "open air" like the downstairs – all of the walls in the upstairs rooms were sheet rocked, which accounts for the residents with seniority taking the upstairs bedrooms, and the new kids on the block (like me) getting the downstairs rooms which turned artic in the wintertime.

And supposing there was some crack in the wall that thousands of flies had entered the room through, and exited the room through, could they all be gone in a matter of minutes? Who was their commander, Dwight D. Eisenhower? How could a single fly not be left out of thousands? Or a single dead fly. The Normandy Invasion didn't go that precisely.

I remember one bloodshot-eyed houseguest, upon hearing The Fly Room Story for the first time, suggesting that the flies must have been United States Marines, because,

"They never leave a man behind!"

This cute joke didn't go over with Grim, though. I never saw them laugh or be flip about The Fly Room, and needless to say, The Fly Room was never used for storage or anything else. I would sometimes open that strange, little door, peer in, and look around, imagining what it must've looked like covered in flies. And then imagining it, not ten minutes later, to somehow be completely barren again. Unbelievable.

But boys and girls, this was no Grim's Fairy Tale (nyuk-nyuk!). This was real. To Greg and Tim it was. And to me, too. It had to be real. I don't think anyone could invent this story. Not Grim. Not anybody. Just the bit about none of the flies *flying* makes a strong case for the story's overall veracity. If I were making up a story about a room with ten thousand flies in it, I would automatically say that they were *flying*. So would you. No need to agree with me, ma'am, it's just what flies *do*.

Well, enough about the pre-LC history of The Log Cabin. Our story begins on the night Lightnin' Charlie moved into The Log Cabin. Shall we begin?

My bedroom was located on the ground floor of the house, and featured a huge rock fireplace and hearth, and ancient hardwood floors. The rickety, old windows and the refreshing breeze blowing through the log and mortar walls reminded me that I had to be out of there by Thanksgiving. I don't remember why I was moving in at night, but I do remember it being dark out.

I was carrying in my meager belongings by myself from my car, with no help from any of my buddies (remember they were allergic to work). They were sitting around, smoking, and listening to real hippies (from the 1960s) on the stereo singing about "helping your fellow man", "give him a helping hand", etc. But they obviously didn't take these lyrics in a literal sense, because they didn't budge from the sofa.

I've heard it said that it's a good friend that'll help you move, and it's a real good friend that'll help you move the body. I had neither.

After watching me make several trips back and forth, carrying things, they must've felt guilty (or thirsty), because they got up and left, saying they were going to go get some beer. So I was left alone. Or so I thought.

There were some items in my new room, which I'll describe to you, due to the fact that they figure prominently in the rest of our story. One is an acoustic guitar I didn't have a case for, and consequently, I had leaned it up against a wall in my bedroom. Another is a small, metal table that I used as a bedside or night table. I had set my electric alarm clock on top of the table, and it was sitting, safely out of the way, beside my bed. The last item of note was already there when I moved in: a beautiful, tiffany-style shade that was attached to the overhead light fixture. It was the type of tiffany shade that hangs over pool tables, only square.

I was carrying the last of my things into my room. As I set down a box and turned to go back out, my acoustic guitar, leaning against a wall on the other side of the room from me, slid out from the bottom and fell down.

Ka-bongggg!!!

I thought nothing of it, I simply assumed that by walking on the hardwood floor, the vibrations had caused the bottom edge of the guitar to slide out, and the guitar fell onto its back. No big deal.

I walked the fifteen feet or so over to where it lay, picked it up, and placed it flat across my bed (so it wouldn't fall again), when the unexplainable happened.

I was standing at the foot of my bed, facing the headboard, and had just laid the guitar down. The nightstand, beside the bed's headboard, was about six feet in front of me, when it suddenly and violently overturned, smashing the clock on the floor.

I stood there for a moment, frozen, trying to explain to myself what had just happened. Did I just see that? It didn't just lightly tip over and fall either. It slammed to the floor with force, like it was thrown down.

How could a table, with four sturdy, metal legs, suddenly capsize and crash onto the floor with nothing or nobody within six feet of it? Not being able to come to any logical conclusion, I stood there, staring, with the classic body language that represents universal disbelief. My mouth was hanging wide open and my arms were extended slightly out in front of me, with palms up. You know, the classic pose that says,

"What the..."

I know for certain what position my arms were in, because at the very next instant, while I was standing in the center of the room at the foot of my bed, the tiffany shade came down off the ceiling fixture and fell right into my open arms.

Wham, bam, thank you ma'am!

Then I remember it being very quiet and surreal in that moment, like I was suspended in a dream, and the next thing I did made as little sense as the three things that had just occurred. I didn't scream. I didn't faint. I didn't run.

What I did was sit down on the bed with the shade in my lap. And wait. For what, I don't know; the next shoe to drop? Or table to flip? But everything was very still. I felt sure (understatement) that something was in that room with me, but somehow, I didn't feel afraid. I don't know why I didn't take off running like Jesse Owens with his keester on fire out of that house, but I didn't. I just sat down on the bed and, after a minute or two, said out loud,

"Okay, you're here. And I'm here.
How are we gonna get along and live together?"

And that was it. I didn't see any ghostly figures or misty apparitions; I didn't hear any moaning or rattling of chains, on that night or ever again. But I felt positive that whatever or whoever was in my room wanted me to know that he was there, and more importantly, that he was there first. It was *his* room, not mine.

And once I acknowledged that, aloud, that was the end of it. Come to think of it, The Fly Room incident happened to Greg and Tim immediately after they moved in, too. This must've been a proprietary ghost, and he was very territorial. Don't mess with his toot-toot.

I should point out to all you rational-minded people that The Log Cabin is located in East Tennessee, and is not on a fault line where an earthquake could cause things in a house to suddenly tumble and fall. Also, there were no dogs or cats in the house. Or kids.

But I'm open to suggestions and would welcome any logical explanations. I could easily explain the guitar falling down, if it were the only thing. But in the time it took me to walk over and pick the guitar up and lay it on the bed (maybe five or six seconds), the nightstand table went down like Dick Butkis had hit it. Then, as I'm standing there dumbfounded (maybe two seconds), the tiffany shade fell into my arms. All this took ten seconds.

BAM-BAM-BAM!

This I can't "logically" explain. Neither would I believe you if you told it to me. But I saw it with my own eyes, and I've never forgotten it. It's the truth, the whole truth, and nothing but the truth, so help me God (except I might've exaggerated the part about the college girls a little).

I have been very selective about telling this story through the years, because I don't want people to think I'm a total nutcase. So I was a bit apprehensive about putting it up on the Internet for all eternity, to be read and re-read by my legions of fans, potentially numbering in the hundreds.

But those of you who know me, the real me, know I'm not *too* far "out there". Yes, I once was in a room with a ghost, or a doppelganger, or a table-banger, or whatever you wish to call it. And I hung out with Gregg Allman backstage once (that's twice!).

I have never, to my knowledge, been abducted by aliens (unless you count the time I was hitch-hiking in Texas and was picked up and rolled by a vanload of Mexicans). I have never contacted Janis Joplin or Harry Houdini in a séance or seen the Wolfman running beside my car at 90 mph. I have never seen a flying saucer. But since my website is now being hit by literally dozens of people per month, I thought that including some wacko keywords in this last paragraph might help me get some much needed, and well deserved hits.

Really, I'm a businessman. And millions of people are bound to be Google-searching things like:

"Houdini and Wolfman in flying saucer"
"Janis Joplin's ghost abducted by aliens"
and
"Mexican séances in Texas"

So maybe they'll surf in to LightninCharlie.com and buy a CD or a t-shirt from someone who has had a real-life ghost experience. After all, crazy people buy CDs too. If you don't believe me, look at this week's top-selling CDs on Billboard. That is all.

Good night and good luck,
Lightnin' Charlie

DECEMBER 2007

28

LIGHTNIN'S QUOTATIONS FOR A HAPPY LIFE

I recently wrote a song for my two sons called *Wisdom*. Most of it is taken from King Solomon's beautiful book of wisdom in the bible, Proverbs. It starts out with the lines:

My son, this world is wicked
life is so unfair.
There's one thing I want most for you
to save you from the snare.

If only one gift I could give you
to serve you your whole life.
Enrich you and preserve you
and see you through all strife.

Dear Lord let it be
the gift of wisdom.

In the struggle of life, it's the gift of wisdom that gets us through it, determines *how* we get through it, and ultimately, allows us to survive it. I want my sons to grow up with the wisdom to work hard, to love one another, to trust in God. Wisdom teaches us to love, laugh, and not take life too seriously. Wisdom, very different from knowledge, begs us to simply live and be happy.

Happiness and success is, oftentimes, our choice. Having the wisdom to make the right choices in life, and avoiding the pitfalls of the wrong ones, is what I want most for my children. I want them to be smarter than I was. I want them to be equipped to handle the storms of life. Because when trouble calls, we need to be armed and ready. When we get knocked down, we need to be helped back up. I wish for them the wisdom to get through those hard times, with a wink and a smile.

When life seems to be out to get us, guess what? It is. The enemy is at our door, and we cannot face him all alone. If all we bring to the fight is our intellect and our wealth, our pride and our *selves*, we're dead. Life will kick seven kinds of you-know-what out of us, and that's for sure. How we face, and react to, trouble is what the battle hinges upon. And wisdom is our defense.

It's wise to realize that wisdom does not come from within us. Wisdom comes from God. My favorite scripture, oft-quoted in the Lowdown, is Romans 8:28, which says:

> *"And we know that all things work together for good to them that love God, to them who are the called according to His purpose."*

What makes this verse my favorite is the word *'all'*. But it's conditional. All things work for good *when we love God*. And all means all. All things. Bad things. Senseless things. Tragic things. Yes, even sinful things can, and will, become good in our lives if we have the wisdom to trust Him, and get back in the race. He has taken some of the worst defeats in my life, and turned them into victories. I was broken. He touched me, and made me whole. You know, Jesus' first job on earth was carpenter. He fixes things. Broken things. Builds great things from scraps. And builds them into wonderful things we could never imagine. We only need the wisdom to love Him, and hear His call.

As a father, I want my kids to grow up healthy, happy, and successful. What do you suppose our Heavenly Father wants for us? In The Sermon On The Mount, Jesus says,

> *Blessed are the meek, for they shall inherit the earth.*

There are two words here that, I believe, have been translated poorly. The word that is translated in the King James Version here as "Blessed" is the Greek word, 'makarios', which means 'happy' (not 'eulogetos', which means 'blessed', and is used only of God).

> *Happy are the meek.*

Secondly, the word translated as 'meek' is from the Greek word, 'praus', which means 'mild, gentle, humble'. Unfortunately, the word 'meek' in English has some negative connotations that, I believe, Jesus did not intend here. I prefer any of the three definitions above for the Greek adjective, 'praus'. 'Mild', 'gentle', or 'humble' would be more faithful to the original text than 'meek'. 'Makarios', then, means 'happy' – not 'blessed', and 'praus' means 'mild', 'humble', or 'gentle'. I am going back to the original Greek text here to try and illustrate how different the meaning of this verse would be if it were translated thusly:

> *Happy are the gentle, for they shall inherit the earth.*

I think we forget how happy God the Father wants us to be, in the now. "Meek", in this verse, implies a weak and defenseless victim, waiting to be blessed with a far-off, future inheritance. This is not the idea I believe Jesus is conveying. He wants us to be filled with joy. Right now.

Consider this: the French bible translates this verse using the word 'debonair' rather than 'meek'.

> *Happy are the debonair, for they shall inherit the earth.*

Now there's an idea that makes more sense to me. 'Debonair' implies carefree, light-hearted, happy living. That's who inherits the earth. And that, according to Jesus himself, is the reason why He came. Jesus says:

> *Let not your heart be troubled.*

> *You shall know the truth, and the truth shall set you free.*

> *These things I have spoken to you, that my joy might remain in you, and that your joy might be full.*

> *I am come that they might have life, and that they might have it more abundantly.*

> *Look! I am making all things new.*

> *Happy are the debonair, for they shall inherit the earth.*

The world belongs to the debonair. The light-hearted, joyful, abundant, full, happy life of freedom; that's the life for me. That's the life I want for my children. That's the life the Lord wants for all of us. And that truth is at the core of all the wit and wisdom contained in these quotations. Some are more light-hearted than others, but I think you'll get the idea. I hope you enjoy them and take them to heart. Wisdom seeks wisdom.

TRUTHS, MAXIMS, & WILL ROGERS

Do the best you can, and don't take life too serious.
Will Rogers

If everything isn't black and white, I say, 'Why the hell not?'
John Wayne

There are no extraordinary men... just extraordinary circumstances that ordinary men are forced to deal with.
Admiral William F. "Bull" Halsey

The difference between reality and unreality is that reality has so little to recommend it.
Allan Sherman

Confucius say: crowded elevator smell different to midget.
Redd Foxx

You've got to go out on a limb sometimes because that's where the fruit is.
Will Rogers

Even if you're on the right track, you'll get run over if you just sit there.
Will Rogers

Everything is funny, as long as it's happening to somebody else.
Will Rogers

Get someone else to blow your horn and the sound will carry twice as far.
Will Rogers

People who fly into a rage always make a bad landing.
Will Rogers

What the country needs is dirtier fingernails and cleaner minds.
Will Rogers

Don't gamble; take all your savings and buy some good stock and hold it till it goes up, then sell it. If it don't go up, don't buy it.
Will Rogers

EVIL

The devil sleepeth not, neither is the flesh as yet dead; therefore cease not to prepare thyself for the battle, for on thy right hand and on thy left are enemies who never rest.
Thomas a Kempis

It is the image of God reflected in you that so enrages hell; it is this at which the demons hurl their mightiest weapons.
William Gurnall

Live as though your life is at stake, and the enemy is waiting to outwit you.
Jesus Of Nazareth, Matthew 10:16

The thief comes only to steal and kill and destroy; I have come that they may have life, and have it to the full.
Jesus Of Nazareth, John 10:10

We and the world, my children, will always be at war. Retreat is impossible. Arm yourselves.
Leif Enger

Enemy-occupied territory...that's what this world is.
C. S. Lewis

THE HEART OF MAN

Where your treasure is, there your heart will be also.
Jesus Of Nazareth, Luke 12:34

Don't worry about your heart, it will last you as long as you live.
W. C. Fields

Man looks at the outward appearance, but the Lord looks at the heart.
I Samuel 16:7

All I can do is be me, whoever that is.
Bob Dylan

No man, for any considerable period of time, can wear one face to himself and another to the multitude without finally getting bewildered as to which may be the truth.
Nathaniel Hawthorne

Esse quam videri (To be, rather than to appear)
Cicero

I've done a lot of things and I've been a lot of people, but now I've come to realize who I am.
Bobby Darin

The tragedy of life is what dies inside a man while he lives.
Albert Schweitzer

He begins to die, that quits his desires
George Herbert

The heart of a man is like deep water.
Proverbs 20:5 NKJV

Are you there?
Say a prayer for the Pretender
Who started out so young and strong
Only to surrender.
Jackson Browne

It ain't what they call you, it's what you answer to.
W. C. Fields

The greatest loss I had known was the loss of my heart. While I was in love I was the happiest man on earth; but no one can love who has not a heart.
The Tin Woodman – L. Frank Baum's *The Wonderful Wizard Of Oz*

A man is a god in ruins.
Duke Ellington

If I had my life to live over, I would want to be a man.
Little Richard

A man who views the world the same at fifty as he did at twenty has wasted thirty years of his life.
Muhammad Ali

Man is the only kind of varmint that sets his own trap, baits it, then steps in it.
John Steinbeck

Trust in the Lord with all your heart, and lean not on your own understanding.
Proverbs 3:5

Love the Lord your God with all your heart and with all your soul and with all your strength.
Deuteronomy 6:5 (Jesus called this the greatest of all the commandments – and notice that the heart comes first.)

These people honor me with their lips, but their hearts are far from me.
Jesus Of Nazareth, Matthew 15:8

Above all else, guard your heart, for it is the wellspring of life.
Proverbs 4:23

The heart – the largest muscle in the human body.
Beth Dolinger, LPTA (my wife)

You are never a great man when you have more mind than heart.
Beauchene

I pray also that the eyes of your heart may be enlightened.
The Apostle Paul, Ephesians 1:18

I am concerned with a certain way of looking at life, which was created in me by the fairy tales, but has since been ratified by the mere facts.
G. K. Chesterton

Be your own man.
Sidney Dolinger (my Dad)

LIFE & HAPPINESS

The glory of God is man fully alive.
Saint Irenaeus

Happiness can be found neither in ourselves nor in external things, but in God and in ourselves as united to Him.
Pascal

Narrow the road that leads to life, and only a few find it.
Jesus Of Nazareth, Matthew 7:14

We shall not cease from exploration
And the end of all our exploring
Will be to arrive where we started
And know the place for the first time.
T. S. Eliot

We have sailed too close to shore, having fallen in love with life, we have lost our thirst for the waters of Life.
Sir Francis Drake

O God, you are my God,
  earnestly I seek you
My soul thirsts for you,
  my body longs for you,
in a dry and weary land,
  where there is no water.
Psalms 63:1 NIV

DREAMS & DESIRE

Blessed are those who hunger and thirst.
Jesus Of Nazareth, Matthew 5:6

Hold fast to dreams
  for if dreams die,
life is a broken-winged bird
  that cannot fly.
Hold fast to dreams
  for when dreams go,
life is a barren field
  frozen with snow.
Langston Hughes – *Dreams*

We are never living, but hoping to live.
Pascal

It seems to me we can never give up longing and wishing while we are alive. There are certain things we feel to be beautiful and good, and we must hunger for them.
George Eliot

Everybody's got a hungry heart.
Bruce Springsteen

*And my desires, like fell and cruel hounds,
E'er since pursue me.*
William Shakespeare

The problem with desire is, you want everything.
Paul Simon

Want in one hand and [BLEEP] in the other. See which one fills up first.
E. J. Weemes (my Grandfather)

TROUBLES, TROUBLES, TROUBLES

If it weren't for the rocks in its bed, the stream would have no song.
Carl Perkins

The best way out of a difficulty is through it.
Will Rogers

After you start learning all about the mechanics of piloting a riverboat, you stop seeing all the pretty sunsets and you start thinking about the weather.
John Hartford

Those who sow in tears will reap with songs of joy. He who goes out weeping, carrying seed to sow, will return with songs of joy, carrying sheaves with him.
Psalms 126:5-6 NIV

The way through the world is more difficult to find than the way beyond it.
Wallace Stevens

There comes a time in the affairs of man when he must take the bull by the tail and face the situation.
W. C. Fields

Therefore we do not lose heart. Though outwardly we are wasting away, yet inwardly we are being renewed day by day. For our light and momentary troubles are achieving for us an eternal glory that far outweighs them all. So we fix our eyes not on what is seen, but on what is unseen. For what is seen is temporary,

but what is unseen is eternal.
The Apostle Paul, 2 Corinthians 4:18-19

See! The winter is past,
   the rains are over and gone.
Flowers appear on the earth,
   the season of singing has come.
Song of Solomon 2:11-12 NIV

MARRIAGE & FAMILY

Do you know what it means to come home at night to a woman who'll give you a little love, a little affection, a little tenderness? It means you're in the wrong house, that's what it means.
Henny Youngman

Why do Jewish divorces cost so much? They're worth it.
Henny Youngman

Why do Jewish men die before their wives? They want to.
Henny Youngman

Some people ask the secret of our long marriage. We take time to go to a restaurant two times a week. A little candlelight, dinner, soft music and dancing. She goes Tuesdays, I go Fridays.
Henny Youngman

My wife dresses to kill. She cooks the same way.
Henny Youngman

My advice to you is get married: if you find a good wife you'll be happy; if not, you'll become a philosopher.
Socrates

I never knew what true happiness was until I got married, but by then it was too late.
Dean Martin

Women don't want to hear what you think. Women want to hear what they think – in a deeper voice.
Bill Cosby

I take my wife everywhere, but she keeps finding her way back.
Henny Youngman

You want to fall in love with a shoe, go ahead. A shoe can't love you back, but, on the other hand, a shoe can't hurt you too deeply either. And there are so

many nice-looking shoes.
Allan Sherman

Oh, I just wish someone would try to hurt you so I could kill them for you.
Frank Sinatra

Nothing I've ever done has given me more joys and rewards than being a father to my children.
Bill Cosby

If evolution really works, how come mothers only have two hands?
Milton Berle

I was married by a judge. I should have asked for a jury.
Groucho Marx

Alimony is like buying hay for a dead horse.
Groucho Marx

Marriage is a wonderful institution, but who wants to live in an institution?
Groucho Marx

Marry me and I'll never look at another horse!
Groucho Marx

Ah, the patter of little feet around the house. There's nothing like having a midget for a butler.
W. C. Fields

Always end the name of your child with a vowel, so that when you yell, the name will carry.
Bill Cosby

Human beings are the only creatures on earth that allow their children to come back home.
Bill Cosby

You're not a parent until you have more than one child, because if you only have one child, you'll always know who did it.
Bill Cosby

I haven't spoken to my wife in years. I didn't want to interrupt her.
Rodney Dangerfield

I looked up my family tree and found three dogs using it.
Rodney Dangerfield

No matter how much cats fight, there always seem to be plenty of kittens.
Abraham Lincoln

On Groucho Marx's 1950s TV show, *You Bet Your Life*, Groucho, lighting his ever-present cigar, asked a nervous lady contestant if she had any children. *"Yes Groucho, fourteen",* she said. When Groucho (and the live audience) reacted with surprise at the enormity of her reply, she added defensively, *"My husband and I love each other very much."* Groucho then uttered this gem: *"Well I love my cigar, but I take it out of my mouth every once in a while."* A classic.

MEMORIES

If I make the lashes dark,
  and the eyes more bright
And the lips more scarlet,
  or ask if all be right
From mirror to mirror
  no vanity's displayed:
I'm looking for the face I had
  before the world was made.
Yeats – *Before the World Was Made*

Only be careful, and watch yourselves closely so that you do not forget the things your eyes have seen or let them slip from your heart as long as you live.
Deuteronomy 4:9

I will always remind you of these things, even though you know them and are firmly established in the truth you now have. I think it is right to refresh your memory.
The Apostle Paul, 2 Peter 2:12-13

POLITICS

Everything is changing. People are taking their comedians seriously and the politicians as a joke.
Will Rogers

Suppose you were an idiot, and suppose you were a member of Congress; but I repeat myself.
Mark Twain

A fool and his money are soon elected.
Will Rogers

Diplomacy is the art of saying "Nice doggie" until you can find a rock.
Will Rogers

This land is your land and this land is my land, sure, but the world is run by those that never listen to music anyway.
Bob Dylan

Democrats never agree on anything, that's why they're Democrats. If they agreed with each other, they would be Republicans.
Will Rogers

Politics, n: A strife of interests masquerading as a contest of principles. The conduct of public affairs for private advantage.
Ambrose Bierce

Conservative, n: A statesman who is enamored of existing evils, as distinguished from the Liberal who wishes to replace them with others.
Ambrose Bierce

Politics, n: from the Latin word 'poly', meaning 'many', and 'ticks', meaning 'blood-sucking vermin'.
Lightnin' Charlie

Left wing, chicken wing, it don't make no difference to me.
Woody Guthrie

Always be sincere, even if you don't mean it.
Harry S. Truman

The only thing new in the world is the history you do not know.
Harry S. Truman

My choice early in life was either to be a piano-player in a whorehouse or a politician. And to tell the truth, there's hardly any difference.
Harry S. Truman

The world will never have lasting peace so long as men reserve for war the finest human qualities. Peace, no less than war, requires idealism and self-sacrifice and a righteous and dynamic faith.
John Foster Dulles

An election is coming. Universal peace is declared and the foxes have a sincere interest in prolonging the lives of the poultry.
T. S. Eliot

Those who stand for nothing fall for anything.
Alexander Hamilton

The ballot is stronger than the bullet.
Abraham Lincoln

My brother Bob doesn't want to be in government – he promised Dad he'd go straight.
John F. Kennedy

I am not a crook.
Richard M. Nixon

I did not have sex with that woman.
Bill Clinton

A zebra does not change its spots.
Al Gore

How many legs does a dog have if you call the tail a leg? Four. Calling a tail a leg doesn't make it a leg.
Abraham Lincoln

If I had eight hours to chop down a tree, I'd spend six hours sharpening my ax.
Abraham Lincoln

If I were two-faced, would I be wearing this one?
Abraham Lincoln

Important principles may, and must, be inflexible.
Abraham Lincoln

In great contests each party claims to act in accordance with the will of God. Both may be, and one must be wrong.
Abraham Lincoln

In the end, it's not the years in your life that count. It's the life in your years.
Abraham Lincoln

It is better to remain silent and be thought a fool than to open one's mouth and remove all doubt.
Abraham Lincoln

When I do good, I feel good. When I do bad, I feel bad. That's my religion.
Abraham Lincoln

A house divided against itself cannot stand.
Abraham Lincoln (quoting Jesus, Mark 3:25)

When I hear a man preach, I like to see him act as if he were fighting bees.
Abraham Lincoln

Sir, my concern is not whether God is on our side; my greatest concern is to be on God's side, for God is always right.
Abraham Lincoln

For NASA, space is still a high priority.
Dan Quayle

I love California, I practically grew up in Phoenix.
Dan Quayle

I was recently on a tour of Latin America, and the only regret I have was that I didn't study Latin harder in school so I could converse with those people.
Dan Quayle

The future will be better tomorrow.
Dan Quayle

The loss of life will be irreplaceable.
Dan Quayle

This President is going to lead us out of this recovery.
Dan Quayle

Unfortunately, the people of Louisiana are not racists.
Dan Quayle

We are ready for any unforeseen event that may or may not occur.
Dan Quayle

We expect them (Salvadoran officials) to work toward the elimination of human rights.
Dan Quayle

We have a firm commitment to NATO, we are a part of NATO. We have a firm commitment to Europe. We are a part of Europe.
Dan Quayle

What a waste it is to lose one's mind. Or not to have a mind is being very wasteful. How true that is.
Dan Quayle

What you guys want, I'm for.
Dan Quayle

A low voter turnout is an indication of fewer people going to the polls.
Dan Quayle

Bank failures are caused by depositors who don't deposit enough money to cover losses due to mismanagement.
Dan Quayle

Bobby Knight told me this: 'There is nothing that a good defense cannot beat a better offense.' In other words a good offense wins.
Dan Quayle

We're going to have the best-educated American people in the world.
Dan Quayle

Welcome to President Bush, Mrs. Bush, and my fellow astronauts.
Dan Quayle

I don't make jokes. I just watch the government and report the facts.
Will Rogers

BEAUTY AND THE BEAST

Beauty is not only a terrible thing, it is also a mysterious thing. There God and the Devil strive for mastery, and the battleground is the heart of men.
Fyodor Dostoyevsky

Beauty may be skin deep, but ugly goes clear to the bone.
Redd Foxx

Joe Frazier is so ugly that he should donate his face to the US Bureau of Wildlife.
Muhammad Ali

I never forget a face, but in your case I'll be glad to make an exception.
Groucho Marx

She got her looks from her father. He's a plastic surgeon.
Groucho Marx

I was so ugly my mother used to feed me with a slingshot.
Rodney Dangerfield

I worked in a pet store and people would ask how big I would get.
Rodney Dangerfield

I told my dentist my teeth are going yellow – he told me to wear a brown tie.
Rodney Dangerfield

I had plenty of pimples as a kid. One day I fell asleep in the library. When I woke up, a blind man was reading my face.
Rodney Dangerfield

My mother had morning sickness after I was born.
Rodney Dangerfield

My psychiatrist told me I was crazy and I said I want a second opinion. He said okay, you're ugly too.
Rodney Dangerfield

My wife was afraid of the dark... then she saw me naked and now she's afraid of the light.
Rodney Dangerfield

When I played in the sandbox, the cat kept covering me up.
Rodney Dangerfield

When I was born I was so ugly the doctor slapped my mother.
Rodney Dangerfield

MUSIC

Music is a moral law. It gives soul to the universe, wings to the mind, flight to the imagination, and charm and gaiety to life and to everything.
Plato

All music is folk music. I ain't never heard a horse sing a song.
Louis Armstrong

I have to be modest – if I told you how good I really am, you'd call me a liar.
Bob Wills

Men profess to be lovers of music, but for the most part they give no evidence in their opinions and lives that they have heard it.
Henry David Thoreau

Its language is a language which the soul alone understands, but which the soul can never translate.
Arnold Bennett

He who sings scares away his woes.
Cervantes

If you play more than two chords, you're showing off.
Woody Guthrie

By the time I figured out that I had no talent at all, I was already too famous to quit.
Roger Miller

If you have to ask what jazz is, you'll never know.
Louis Armstrong

There is two kinds of music, the good, and the bad. I play the good kind.
Louis Armstrong

There are only two kinds of music, good and bad. I play a mixture of both.
Lightnin' Charlie

Don't be a blueprint. Be an original.
Roy Acuff

I was eating in a Chinese restaurant downtown. There was a dish called Mother and Child Reunion. It's chicken and eggs. And I said, 'I gotta use that one'.
Paul Simon

If you play a tune and a person don't tap their feet, don't play the tune.
Count Basie

But of course it's different now, the blues is no longer blues, it's green now.
Ruth Brown

Now I can say loudly and openly what I have been saying to myself on my knees.
Duke Ellington

I merely took the energy it takes to pout and wrote some blues.
Duke Ellington

I think popular music in this country is one of the few things in the twentieth century that has made giant strides in reverse.
Bing Crosby

There is no truer truth obtainable by man than comes of music.
Robert Browning

Old men need applause too.
Don Everly

PEOPLE

People are like dirt. They can either nourish you and help you grow as a person or they can stunt your growth and make you wilt and die.
Plato

Some people walk in the rain, others just get wet.
Roger Miller

Who are these people? (To a tour guide at Monticello after seeing busts of George Washington and Ben Franklin)
Al Gore

You have your heads in your Bibles constantly because you think you'll find eternal life there. But you miss the forest for the trees. These scriptures are all about me! And here I am, standing right before you, and you aren't willing to receive from me the life you say you want.
Jesus Of Nazareth, John 5:39-40 *The Message*

Don't matter how much money you got, there's only two kinds of people: there's saved people and there's lost people.
Bob Dylan

Be kind, for everyone you meet is fighting a hard battle.
Plato

Some white people hate black people, and some white people love black people, some black people hate white people, and some black people love white people. So you see it's not an issue of black and white, it's an issue of Lovers and Haters.
Eden Ahbez

Horse sense is the thing a horse has which keeps it from betting on people.
W. C. Fields

You can fool all the people some of the time, and some of the people all the time, but you cannot fool all the people all the time.
Abraham Lincoln

You can fool some of the people all the time, and those are the ones you want to concentrate on.
George W. Bush

SUCCESS & FAILURE

Failure is impossible.
Susan B. Anthony

If at first you don't succeed...so much for skydiving.
Henny Youngman

The worst thing that happens to you may be the best thing for you if you don't let it get the best of you.
Will Rogers

You build on failure. You use it as a stepping stone. Close the door on the past. You don't try to forget the mistakes, but you don't dwell on it. You don't let it have any of your energy, or any of your time, or any of your space.
Johnny Cash

If at first you don't succeed, try again. Then quit. No use being a damn fool about it.
W. C. Fields

I don't measure a man's success by how high he climbs but how high he bounces when he hits bottom.
George S. Patton

You always pass failure on the way to success.
Mickey Rooney

Success is the ability to go from one failure to another with no loss of enthusiasm.
Winston Churchill

If you want to be successful, it's just this simple. Know what you are doing. Love what you are doing. And believe in what you are doing.
Will Rogers

I don't know the key to success, but the key to failure is trying to please everybody.
Bill Cosby

Failure is simply the opportunity to begin again, this time more intelligently.
Henry Ford

My great concern is not whether you have failed, but whether you are content with your failure.
Abraham Lincoln

Failure seldom stops you. What stops you is the fear of failure.
Jack Lemmon

Develop success from failures. Discouragement and failure are two of the surest stepping stones to success.
Dale Carnegie

Nothing except a battle lost can be half so melancholy as a battle won.
Duke of Wellington

If we don't succeed we run the risk of failure.
Dan Quayle

I couldn't wait for success... so I went ahead without it.
Jonathan Winters

KNOWLEDGE & WISDOM

Knowledge speaks, but wisdom listens.
Jimi Hendrix

Common sense is not so common.
Voltaire

Life is hard; it's harder if you're stupid.
John Wayne

Everybody is ignorant, only on different subjects.
Will Rogers

The man who doesn't read good books has no advantage over the man who can't read them.
Mark Twain

The man who reads nothing at all is better educated than the man who reads nothing but newspapers.
Thomas Jefferson

I can't tell you if genius is hereditary, because heaven has granted me no offspring.
James Whistler

By three methods we may learn wisdom: First, by reflection, which is noblest; second, by imitation, which is easiest; and third by experience, which is the bitterest.
Confucius

There is a wisdom of the head, and a wisdom of the heart.
Charles Dickens

The greatest thing you'll ever learn is to love and be loved, just to love and be loved.
Eden Ahbez

I find television very educational. Every time someone switches it on I go into another room and read a good book.
Groucho Marx

You teach a child to read, and he or her will be able to pass a literacy test.
George W. Bush

It's clearly a budget. It's got a lot of numbers in it.
George W. Bush

DEATH

Death is very often referred to as a good career move.
Buddy Holly

I have never killed a man, but I have read many obituaries with great pleasure.
Clarence Darrow

Give me liberty, or give me death.
Patrick Henry

Health nuts are going to feel stupid someday, lying in hospitals dying of nothing.
Redd Foxx

O death, where is thy sting?
The Apostle Paul, I Corinthians 15:55

Drown in a cold vat of whiskey? Death, where is thy sting?
W. C. Fields

I intend to live forever, or die trying.
Groucho Marx

Death is no more than passing from one room into another. But there's a difference for me, you know. Because in that other room I shall be able to see.
Helen Keller

Either he's dead or my watch has stopped.
Groucho Marx

TECHNOLOGY

The computer can't tell you the emotional story. It can give you the exact mathematical design, but what's missing is the eyebrows.
Frank Zappa

Any sufficiently advanced technology is indistinguishable from magic.
Arthur C. Clarke

It has become appallingly obvious that our technology has exceeded our humanity.
Albert Einstein

Television: A medium. So called because it's neither rare nor well done.
Ernie Kovacs

Telephone, n: An invention of the devil which abrogates some of the advantages of making a disagreeable person keep his distance.
Ambrose Bierce

The Internet is a great way to get on the net.
Bob Dole

Technology is the knack of so arranging the world that we don't have to experience it.
Max Frisch

Humanity is acquiring all the right technology for all the wrong reasons.
R. Buckminster Fuller

The newest computer can merely compound, at speed, the oldest problem in the relations between human beings, and in the end the communicator will be confronted with the old problem, of what to say and how to say it.
Edward R. Murrow

Men have become the tools of their tools.
Henry David Thoreau

I invented the Internet.
Al Gore

The day I made that statement, about the inventing the Internet, I was tired because I'd been up all night inventing the Camcorder.
Al Gore

If Al Gore invented the Internet, I invented spell check.
Dan Quayle

JUSTICE

Military justice is to justice what military music is to music.
Groucho Marx

Parents are not interested in justice; they're interested in peace and quiet.
Bill Cosby

Punishment is justice for the unjust.
Saint Augustine

I don't know if capital punishment stops someone from killing, but I'm sure it stops them from killing again.
Elvis Presley

I tremble for my country when I reflect that God is just; that his justice cannot sleep forever.
Thomas Jefferson

THE FRENCH

The thing that's wrong with the French is that they don't have a word for entrepreneur.
George W. Bush

Hors D'oeuvre: A ham sandwich cut into forty pieces.
Jack Benny

When told that eating pigeons was the only thing that kept the French people from starving to death during the Nazi occupation of France, my friend Danny Julian replied:

"There's another reason to hate pigeons."

VICES

Be at war with your vices, at peace with your neighbors, and let every New Year find you a better man.
Benjamin Franklin

It has been my experience that folks who have no vices have very few virtues.
Abraham Lincoln

If I had my life to live over, I'd live over a saloon.
W. C. Fields

I like whiskey. I always did, and that is why I never drink it.
Robert E. Lee

My only aversion to vice is the price.
Victor Buono

I prefer a pleasant vice to an annoying virtue.
Moliere

The foolish and wicked practice of profane cursing and swearing is a vice so mean and low that every person of sense and character detests and despises it.
George Washington

Her virtue was that she said what she thought; her vice was that what she thought didn't amount to much.
Peter Ustinov

I drink therefore I am.
W. C. Fields

I never drink water because of the disgusting things that fish do in it.
W. C. Fields

I never drink water; that is the stuff that rusts pipes.
W. C. Fields

I cook with wine; sometimes I even add it to the food.
W. C. Fields

Always carry a flagon of whiskey in case of snakebite and furthermore always carry a small snake.
W. C. Fields

I never trust a fighting man who doesn't smoke or drink.
Admiral William F. "Bull" Halsey

He has all of the virtues I dislike and none of the vices I admire.
Winston Churchill

Part of the $10 million I spent on gambling, part on booze and part on women. The rest I spent foolishly.
George Raft

Italians come to ruin most generally in three ways, women, gambling, and farming. My family chose the slowest one.
Pope John XXIII

I know a man who gave up smoking, drinking, sex, and rich food. He was healthy right up to the day he killed himself.
Johnny Carson

My rule of life prescribed as an absolutely sacred rite smoking cigars and also the drinking of alcohol before, after and if need be during all meals and in the intervals between them.
Winston Churchill

When I read about the evils of drinking, I gave up reading.
Henny Youngman

YESTERDAY, TODAY, & TOMORROW

Don't let yesterday use up too much of today.
Will Rogers

I, not events, have the power to make me happy or unhappy today. I can choose which it shall be. Yesterday is dead – tomorrow hasn't arrived yet. I have just one

day – today, and I'm going to be happy in it.
Groucho Marx

Tomorrow is the most important thing in life. Comes into us at midnight very clean. It's perfect when it arrives and it puts itself in our hands. It hopes we've learned something from yesterday.
John Wayne

If you're going to do something tonight that you'll be sorry for tomorrow morning, sleep late.
Henny Youngman

In the entire history of the universe, let alone in your own history, there has never been another day just like today, and there will never be another just like it again. Today is the point to which all your yesterdays have been leading since the hour of your birth. It is the point from which all your tomorrows will proceed until the hour of your death. If you were aware of how precious today is, you could hardly live through it. Unless you are aware of how precious it is, you can hardly be said to be living at all.
Frederick Buechner

Since this Lowdown is dedicated to my children, and since this holiday season we're celebrating our Heavenly Father sending us His Son, I'll leave you with my father's favorite poem, *If,* by Rudyard Kipling. Dad had the whole poem committed to memory, and I remember him reciting it to me when I was a kid. It is the beautiful wish of a father for the future of his son. Now that I'm a Dad, I understand, first-hand, a father's desperate desire for a life of wisdom and happiness for his children. I think it speaks too, of our Heavenly Father's wish for His children.

> *If you can keep your head when all about you*
>   *are losing theirs and blaming it on you;*
> *If you can trust yourself when all men doubt you,*
>   *but make allowance for their doubting too;*
> *If you can wait and not be tired by waiting,*
>   *or, being lied about, don't deal in lies,*
> *Or, being hated, don't give way to hating,*
>   *and yet don't look too good, nor talk too wise;*
> *If you can dream – and not make dreams your master;*
>   *if you can think – and not make thoughts your aim;*
> *If you can meet with triumph and disaster*

*and treat those two imposters just the same;
If you can bear to hear the truth you've spoken
    twisted by knaves to make a trap for fools,
Or watch the things you gave your life to broken,
    and stoop and build 'em up with worn-out tools;*

*If you can make one heap of all your winnings
    and risk it on one turn of pitch-and-toss,
And lose, and start again at your beginnings
    and never breath a word about your loss;
If you can force your heart and nerve and sinew
    to serve your turn long after they are gone,
And so hold on when there is nothing in you
    except the Will which says to them: "Hold on";*

*If you can talk with crowds and keep your virtue,
    or walk with kings – nor lose the common touch;
If neither foes nor loving friends can hurt you;
    if all men count with you, but none too much;
If you can fill the unforgiving minute
    with sixty seconds worth of distance run
Yours is the Earth and everything that's in it,
    and – which is more – you'll be a Man my son!*

In closing, I would like to wish you all a very merry Christmas and lots of blessings and health in the New Year. Thank you for all your love and support in '07.

Your debonair reporter,
meek and mild,
Lightnin' Charlie
God's child

JANUARY / FEBRUARY / MARCH 2008

29

FAMOUS LAST WORDS

Well folks, this is it. Famous Last Words will be the last word for me. I am going to take a much-needed hiatus from writing our beloved Lightnin' Lowdown to fully concentrate on finishing my new CD. Over the last three years, I have relished writing these rants, and I hope you have enjoyed reading them.

The Lightnin' Lowdown has been a lot of hard work, but a real joy for me. A labor of love. There's something special about sharing laughter with others, and I hope the Lowdown has made you laugh. Out loud. Maybe some have even made you cry. This has been my intent from the beginning. My intent as a writer has been the same as my intent as a musician, and that is, simply, to make you *feel*. Not necessarily to make you laugh, or cry, or get angry, but to *communicate*; to convey *feeling*. Strangely, we humans need this to constantly remind ourselves of our shared humanity. And I hope that, in sharing my beliefs, my loves, and my life with you, that you think of me now, in this our final chapter, as a brother and a friend. Lightnin' Bugs, I believe we are here to help others, but I am not sure what the others are here for.

Singer and harmonica player extraordinaire, Sugar Ray Norcia has a song on his new record called *The Last Words Of A Fool,* in which he playfully tells of an assortment of idiots, all violently deceased, saying *"watch this!"* just before they go. The various causes of death are popping wheelies on bikes, crushing cans against their heads, and going over Niagara Falls in a barrel. Their last words as living beings are *"watch this!"* Here is a bit of it:

He said, "Hey Man, watch this!"
  As he crushed a can upon his head
He must've hit a soft spot
  For now the fool is dead
That something could go wrong
  To him never did occur
It all ended there
  With those famous last words

"Hey Man, watch this!
  Look what I'm about to do!"
People don't you know?
  These are the last words of a fool

I have collected a great mess of last words, some from famous people, and some from fools. Some are poignant and some are preposterous. Some are very wise and others are hilariously stupid. There are last words of Presidents, and last words of condemned criminals. I've always been fascinated by reading the last words of people, some of whom knew they were dying and others who had no idea. Where there is a difference of opinion as to the exact last words of a person, due to differing accounts and recollections of those present, I have included the one that is the most appropriate to the source and the most poetic, if you will. One thing I've learned in writing the Lightnin' Lowdown is that, when in doubt, go for the laugh. Here goes...

Abimelech, Judge of Israel (Judges 9:50-55)
"Draw your sword and kill me, so they can't say, 'A woman killed him.'"
Abimelech said these words to his armor-bearer during the siege of Thebez after a woman dropped an upper millstone from the wall onto his head, cracking his skull. The armor-bearer complied, killing him with his sword.

John Adams (1735-1826)
"Thomas Jefferson still survives."
John Adams, the 2nd United States President, died on the 50th anniversary of the Declaration of Independence. Following his presidency, Adams retired to his farm and began a lengthy correspondence with Thomas Jefferson that would last over twenty-five years. Although in his nineties and gravely ill, he resolved to live until the 50th anniversary of the Declaration of Independence on July 4, 1826. That morning, Adams was awakened by his servant who inquired, "Do you know what day it is?" "Oh, yes," Adams replied, "It is the glorious fourth of July. God bless it. God bless you all." He then lapsed into unconsciousness. Later that afternoon, he awakened briefly to mumble "Thomas Jefferson still surv . . . " before dying. Actually, Thomas Jefferson had died earlier that day.

John Quincy Adams (1767-1848)
"This is the last of Earth! I am content."
John Quincy Adams, sixth United States President (1825-1829), collapsed on the floor of the U.S. House of Representatives, of a stroke. He died two days later, with his wife and children at his side, in the Speaker's Room inside the Capitol Building. Adams had become a U.S. Representative from the 11th District of Massachusetts after his presidency.

Alex the African Grey Parrot
"You be good. See you tomorrow. I love you."
Alex was used in comparative psychology research at Brandeis University. Spoken to his handler, Dr. Irene Pepperberg (Dr. Pepperberg???), when she put him into his cage for the night; Alex was found dead the next morning.

Alexander the Great (356 BC-323 BC)
"To the strongest!"
Alexander the Great was one of the most successful military commanders in history, and was undefeated in battle. By the time of his death, he had conquered most of the world known to the ancient Greeks. These last words were in response to his generals asking the heirless Alexander to whom the empire would belong to after his death.

Ethan Allen (1738-1789)
"Waiting, are they? Waiting, are they? Well, let 'em wait!"
Ethan Allen was an early American revolutionary and guerilla leader during the American Revolution. After being shot, a doctor told him, "General, I fear that the angels are waiting for you."

Marie Antoinette (1755-1793)
"Pardon me, sir. I did not do it on purpose."
As she approached the guillotine, convicted of treason and about to be beheaded, she accidentally stepped on the foot of her executioner.

Archimedes (287 BC-212 BC)
"Don't disturb my circles!"
Archimedes was a Greek mathematician, physicist, engineer, inventor, and astronomer. This was said in response to a Roman soldier who was forcing him to report to the Roman general after the capture of Syracuse, while he was busy sitting on the ground proving geometry theorems. The soldier killed him despite specific instructions not to.

Lady Astor (1879-1964)
"Am I dying or is this my birthday?"
Lady Astor was the first female Member of Parliament. Noted for her biting wit, she occasionally got into verbal spats with Winston Churchill. She spoke her last words when, on her deathbed, she momentarily awoke to find herself surrounded by her entire family.

Jane Austen (1775-1817)
"I want nothing but death."
Jane Austen was a British novelist whose realism, biting social commentary, and masterful use of free indirect speech, burlesque, and irony have earned her a

place as one of the most widely-read and best-loved writers in British literature. Early in 1816, due to what is now thought to be Addison's disease, Austen's physical condition began a long, slow, and irregular deterioration culminating in her death the following year.

Phineas Taylor "P. T." Barnum (1810-1891)
"How were the receipts today at Madison Square Garden?"
Entrepreneur P. T. Barnum was an American showman who is best remembered for his entertaining hoaxes, and for founding the circus that eventually became the Ringling Bros. and Barnum & Bailey Circus. Just before his death, he gave permission to the *Evening Sun* to print his obituary, so that he might have a chance to read it. After reading his own obituary, he asked about the box office receipts for the day; a few hours later, he was dead.

L. Frank Baum (1856-1919)
"Now I can cross the Shifting Sands."
As author of *The Wizard Of Oz,* Baum was referring to the Shifting Sands, the impassable desert surrounding the Land of Oz.

Todd Beamer (1968-2001)
"Let's roll."
Passenger on United Flight 93, Todd was killed on September 11, 2001. These are his last recorded words, coming at the end of a cell phone call before Beamer and others attempted to storm the doomed airliner's cockpit to retake it from hijackers who were part of the 9/11 terrorist attacks. Heroes Beamer and the others caused the plane to crash in a field near Shanksville, Pennsylvania, rather than into the terrorists' intended target, The White House.

Thomas Becket (1118-1170)
"If all the swords in England were pointed against my head, your threats would not move me."
Thomas Becket, the Archbishop Canterbury, to his killers. He is venerated as a saint and martyr.

Henry Ward Beecher (1813-1887)
"Now comes the mystery."
Henry Ward Beecher, brother of Harriet Beecher Stowe, was a fervent abolitionist and one of the most influential American clergymen of the 1800s. His down-to-earth sermons and outspoken moral earnestness helped make him "the most famous man in America."

Lawrence Beeter
"Maybe they only had one rocket..."
A World War II British soldier, Beeter was taking cover in a bunker alongside

other soldiers. After an enemy artillery blast barely missed them, Beeter said these last words to his comrades. A second volley destroyed the bunker and Beeter was killed.

Ludwig van Beethoven (1770-1827)
"Pity, pity . . . too late!"
Ludwig van Beethoven, a German composer, was one of the world's greatest musical geniuses, despite losing his hearing. Beethoven spoke his last words from his deathbed when told of a recent gift of twelve bottles of wine. Some sources have listed his last words as, "I shall hear in heaven", but this is almost certainly myth. Likewise, the popular belief that his last words were: *"Plaudite, amici, comedia finita est"* ("Applaud, my friends, the comedy is over"), the typical conclusion to performances of Italian stage tragedies.

Humphrey DeForest Bogart (1899-1957)
"I should never have switched from Scotch to Martinis."
Humphrey Bogart was an Academy Award-winning American actor and film star. In 1999, the American Film Institute named him the Greatest Male Star Of All Time. Some of Bogart's most notable films include *The Maltese Falcon* (1941), *Casablanca* (1942), *To Have And Have Not* (1944), *The Big Sleep* (1944), *Key Largo* (1948), *The Treasure of the Sierra Madre* (1948), *The African Queen* (1951), *The Caine Mutiny* (1954), and many more. He married co-star Lauren Bacall. Bogie's illustrious career spanned seventy-five motion pictures during the heyday of Hollywood.

John Wilkes Booth (1838-1865)
"Tell my mother I did it for my country . . . (looking at his hands) Useless, useless."
John Wilkes Booth was an American stage actor who, as part of a conspiracy plot, assassinated Abraham Lincoln, the 16th President of the United States, at Ford's Theatre in Washington, D.C. on April 14, 1865. Lincoln died the next day from a single gunshot wound to the back of the head, becoming the first American president to be assassinated. Booth was chased into Virginia by a detachment of Union soldiers. He was cornered in a barn and the barn set afire. Booth came out, but was fired upon — whether orders to shoot were given is uncertain — and was fatally wounded in the neck. Booth was dragged from the barn and died three hours later, at age 26, on the porch of the Garrett farmhouse. The bullet had severed his spinal cord, paralyzing him. In his last dying moments, he reportedly whispered, "Tell my mother I did it for my country," and asked for both his hands to be raised to his face so he could see them. He looked at them and uttered his final words, "Useless, useless," and died as dawn was breaking.

Dominique Bouhours (1628-1702)
"I am about to . . . or I am going to . . . die. Either expression is correct."
Dominique Bouhours was a French grammarian, at it till the end.

John Brown (1800-1859)
"I, John Brown, am now quite certain that the crimes of this guilty land will never be purged away but with blood. I had, as I now think vainly, flattered myself that without very much bloodshed it might be done."
John Brown was a white American abolitionist who advocated and practiced armed insurrection as a means to abolish slavery. He led the unsuccessful raid at Harper's Ferry, VA in 1859 where slaves refused to join with him or aid him. He was captured and tried for treason against the state of Virginia and was hanged, but his behavior at the trial seemed heroic to millions of Americans. Southerners alleged that his rebellion was the tip of the abolitionist iceberg and represented the wishes of the Republican Party, but those charges were vehemently denied by the Republicans. Historians agree that the Harpers Ferry raid in 1859 escalated the tensions that a year later led to secession and the eventual War Between the States. John Brown's last words were not spoken, but written on a note and handed to a guard right before his execution.

James Buchanan (1791-1868)
"Whatever the result may be, I shall carry to my grave the consciousness that at least I meant well for my country."
James Buchanan was the fifteenth President of the United States (1857-1861). To date he is the only President from Pennsylvania and the only President never to marry. Historically, Buchanan has taken a beating due to his refusal to act decisively regarding the pre-war insurrection in "Bloody Kansas" and the impending secession of Southern states.

Aaron Burr (1756-1836)
"On that subject I am coy."
Aaron Burr, Jr. was an American politician, Revolutionary War hero, and adventurer. He served as the third Vice President of the United States under Thomas Jefferson (1801–1805). He was also a longtime political rival of Alexander Hamilton. Taking umbrage at remarks made by Hamilton at a dinner party and angered by Hamilton's subsequent failure to account for the remarks, Burr challenged Hamilton to a duel on July 11, 1804, at the Heights Of Weehawken in New Jersey (where Hamilton's son Philip was mortally wounded). Hamilton agreed. Arguably the most famous duel in U.S. history, it had immense political ramifications. Burr, who survived the duel, was indicted for murder in both New York and New Jersey (though these charges were either later dismissed or resulted in acquittal), and the harsh criticism and animosity directed towards

him brought about an end to his political career in the East, though he remained a popular figure in the West and South. Burr was a notorious atheist. His last words were a response to the efforts of his friend, Reverend P. J. Van Pelt, to get Burr to acknowledge that there was a God.

Julius Caesar (100 BC-44 BC)
"Et tu, Brute?"
Translation: *Even you, Brutus, my son?*
Attributed to him by Shakespeare's famous play; his real last words are unknown. There is actually a little more to the quote. The full quote is: "Et tu, Brute? Then fall, Caesar." The entire quote means "Even (And) you, Brutus? Then all hope is lost and I shall fall." He thought Brutus would be on his side, but discovering Brutus has stabbed him, gives up all hope of salvation.

Caligula (12-41)
"Vivo!"
Translation: *I live!*
Caligula (Gaius Julius Caesar Augustus Germanicus), Roman Emperor, as he was being murdered by his own soldiers.

Giacomo Casanova (1725-1798)
"I have lived as a philosopher, and die as a Christian."
Casanova was a Venetian adventurer and author. His autobiography is regarded as one of the most authentic sources of the customs and norms of European social life during the 18th century. So famous a womanizer was the Italian-born libertine Giacomo Casanova that, a full two centuries after his death, his name remains synonymous with the art of seduction.

Charlie Chaplin (1889-1977)
"Why not? After all, it belongs to Him."
Many consider Chaplin to be cinema's greatest comedian. When the priest, who was attending him on his deathbed, said, "May the Lord have mercy on your soul," Chaplin quickly replied, "Why not? After all, it belongs to Him."

Charles I (1600-1649)
"I go from a corruptible to an incorruptible Crown, where no disturbance can be, no disturbance in the world. Remember!"
Charles I was King of England, King of Scotland, and King of Ireland until his execution by beheading in 1649. King Charles spoke these words with his head on the executioner's block. It was common practice for the head of a traitor to be held up, and exhibited to the crowd, with the words "Behold the head of a traitor!" Although Charles's head was exhibited, the words were never used. In an unprecedented gesture, one of the revolutionary leaders, Oliver Cromwell,

allowed the King's head to be sewn back on his body so the family could pay its respects. Sew there!

Robert Childers (1870-1922)
"Take a step or two forward, lads. It'll be easier that way."
Robert Erskine Childers was an author and Irish Nationalist who was executed by the authorities of the newly independent Irish Free State during the Irish Civil War. His last words were spoken to his firing squad. Before his execution, in a spirit of reconciliation, Childers obtained a promise from his then 16-year-old son, the future President Erskine Hamilton Childers, to seek out and shake the hand of every man who had signed his father's death warrant. The condemned Childers did shake hands with each member of the firing squad that was about to execute him. His last words, spoken to them, were (characteristic of Childers) in the nature of a joke: "Take a step or two forward, lads. It'll be easier that way."

Fredric Chopin (1810-1849)
"The Earth is suffocating. Swear to make them cut me open, so that I won't be buried alive."
Chopin was a Polish virtuoso pianist and piano composer of the Romantic period. He is widely regarded as the greatest Polish composer and one of the most influential composers for piano in the 19th century.

Christine Chubbock (1944-1974)
"In keeping with Channel 40's policy of bringing you the latest in blood and guts and in living color, you are going to see another first . . . attempted suicide."
On July 15, 1974, during technical difficulties during a broadcast, 30-year-old anchorwoman Christine Chubbock said these words on-air before producing a revolver and shooting herself in the head (While she drew the gun on camera, the technicians quickly cut the video feed, but the gunshot could be clearly heard). She was pronounced dead at the hospital fourteen hours later.

Sir Winston Churchill (1874-1965)
"I'm bored with it all."
Known chiefly for his leadership of Great Britain during World War II, he served as Prime Minister of the United Kingdom from 1940 to 1945 and again from 1951 to 1955. A noted statesman, orator, and strategist, Churchill was also an officer in the British Army. A prolific author, he won the Nobel Prize in Literature in 1953 for his historical writings.

Cleopatra (69 BC-30 BC)
"So here it is!"
Cleopatra was the legendary Hellenistic ruler of Egypt, originally sharing power with her father Ptolemy XII and later with her brothers/husbands Ptolemy XIII and Ptolemy XIV; eventually gaining sole rule of Egypt. Brothers/husbands?

Sounds like an ancient version of the Jerry Lee Lewis family tree to me. As Pharaoh, she consummated a liaison with Julius Caesar that solidified her grip on the throne, and, after Caesar's assassination, aligned with Mark Antony, with whom she produced twins. In all, Cleopatra had four children, one by Julius Caesar and three by Mark Antony. Then she moved to New York, became a senator, and ran for the Presidency of the United States! *Whoops* . . . sorry, honest mistake. Anyway, her unions with her brothers produced no children. Her reign marks the end of the Hellenistic Era and the beginning of the Roman Era in the eastern Mediterranean. She was the last Pharaoh of Ancient Egypt (her son by Julius Caesar, Caesarion, ruled in name only before Augustus, Caesar's other son, had Caesarion, his step-brother, executed, saying famously, "Two Caesars are one too many."). And we've got a salad named after these people? After Antony and Cleopatra was defeated by their rival (Cleo's stepson and Caesar's legal heir and son, Gaius Julius Caesar Octavian, who later became Augustus, the first Roman Emperor), Cleopatra committed suicide. She accomplished this feat, her last seduction, by enticing an asp (snake) to bite her. This is all much too much for me, and is the reason that I am not a registered Democrat today. Cleopatra's last recorded words were upon seeing the asp. So much for advanced civilizations.

Del Close (1934-1999)
"Thank God. I'm tired of being the funniest person in the room."
Improviser, teacher and comedian, Del Close influenced and tutored many up-and-coming comedians during his tenure at Second City and Saturday Night Live, such as John Belushi, Bill Murray, Gilda Radner, Mike Myers, John Candy, Chris Farley, etc. Before passing away, Close requested that his skull be given to the Goodman Theatre for use in their *Hamlet* productions, on the condition that he/his skull should receive credit in the program as Yorick. However, in 2006 it was revealed that an alternate skull was given to the Goodman instead. There's a theater with good taste.

Sam Cooke (1931-1964)
"Lady, you shot me!"
Sam Cooke, my favorite singer of all time, was shot and killed by an ex-convict hotel night clerk named Bertha Franklin and a prostitute named Elisa Boyer. Miss Franklin claimed Sam Cooke was attacking her, and was going to rape her, and she shot him three times with her 22-caliber pistol. Then Sam spoke his last words. But Sam Cooke wasn't the first man Bertha Franklin had shot at the Hacienda hotel. Bertha had a history of shooting men at the Hacienda that were trying to "attack her", and one look at her picture below should prove her irresistibility to everyone.

On the night of December 11, 1964, Sam Cooke was introduced to an attractive young woman named Elisa Boyer at Martoni's, an upscale Italian restaurant on Sunset Blvd. in Hollywood. After Sam and Elisa hit it off, and after stopping for a few drinks at PJ's on Santa Monica Blvd, they left in Sam's Ferrari, apparently seeking a place for romance. But instead of stopping at any of the hundreds of hotels in Hollywood, Sam drove 17 miles to a dumpy, $3 per night hotel in South-Central Los Angeles called The Hacienda. Locals knew the Hacienda Hotel as a notorious hangout for pimps and prostitutes. Sam and Elisa arrived, checked in, and went to their room in the back. A few minutes later, Sam appeared back at the office, looking furiously for Miss Boyer, and trying to get Bertha Franklin to call the police. Instead, Bertha Franklin shot him three times in the chest. When he didn't die quickly enough to suit her, she beat him in the head with a broom handle.

When police arrived, Sam Cooke was dead, minus his pants, credit cards, and the wad of cash witnesses from PJ's say was well over $1000. Elisa Boyer told police that Sam had abducted her, taking her to this hotel despite her repeatedly "begging him to take me home". Once inside the room, he began assaulting her and tried to violently rape her. She managed to escape though (along with Sam's pants and cash), and as Sam was pursuing her, good old Bertha Franklin shot and killed him. Just another night at the office for Miss Boyer and Miss Franklin.

A typical night's work for professional rollers like Miss Boyer consisted of meeting men in some swanky bar, luring them to a particular hotel, and while they're in bed or in the bathroom, take their pants, shoes and money, and beat it. This is standard practice for hookers. Men call it getting "rolled". Prostitutes call it "grab and dash". But, on the night of December 11, 1964, it was grand theft and first-degree murder. Most victims of "rollers" can't or won't pursue their assailant, since he's guilty of being with a prostitute, plus he's without pants and shoes. In this case, the hotel clerk was there to make sure she got away. Miss Franklin's part in this filthy enterprise was to provide a safe haven for the prostitute to lure her victim to, and then, most importantly, to see to it that the prostitute escaped with the cash.

On the night of the murder, Bertha Franklin and Elisa Boyer were both questioned and released by the LAPD investigators. No one was ever charged with Sam's murder, and his tragic death remains a mystery. Elisa Boyer, who during her frightful escape from Sam the rapist, somehow managed to take possession of his pants and wallet, told police she had inadvertently taken Cooke's clothing in her rush to get out of the room. This, of course, made perfect sense to investigators who believed their stories, and no arrests were made.

Exactly one month later, on January 11, 1965, after being "kidnapped, assaulted, and almost raped" by Sam Cooke, Elisa Boyer was arrested at, you guessed it, Bertha Franklin's Hacienda Hotel, for, you guessed it again, offering to have sex with an undercover officer for $40. This time, she was arrested and charged with prostitution. And if $40 seems cheap, keep in mind that the price she quoted really didn't matter since Elisa and Bertha were going to get away with the victim's entire wallet and pants anyway. But wait. Poor Miss Boyer claimed she was "entrapped" by police, and was, of course, again set free by the Los Angeles "Justice" System, and charges were, naturally, dropped.

After a public outcry about the murder of Sam Cooke, the district attorney and the LAPD held an official inquest to look deeper into the matter. At the inquest, Elisa Boyer claimed that Sam Cooke had kidnapped her, drove her to the motel against her will (although she accompanied Sam into the hotel office to register as "Mr. and Mrs. Sam Cooke", and even Miss Franklin testified that Boyer didn't appear to be in the midst of an abduction), and once inside the room, Sam began yelling at her, ripping off her clothes, and tried to forcibly rape her. But she was able to escape when he "went to the bathroom." Do rapists generally stop to relieve themselves when in the middle of a violent crime? I ask this now, but it was never asked of Miss Boyer. According to their testimony, Sam Cooke then ran outside to the motel office, wearing his jacket and a towel wrapped around him, attacking and presumably intending to forcibly rape the ugly-as-an-ape Miss Franklin. Their assertion that the rich, famous, thirty-three year old superstar Sam Cooke kidnapped and attempted to rape one woman, then was shot, beaten, and killed while assaulting and attempting to rape the fat, fifty-five year old pig, Bertha Franklin, apparently made perfect sense to the sharp-as-nails LAPD and district attorney, and neither Bertha Franklin nor Elisa Boyer were even cross-examined by the D.A. at the inquest.

No charges have ever been filed in the death of Sam Cooke. Bertha Franklin, the murderess, seeking justice and reparations, successfully sued Sam's estate for $200,000 in compensation for injuries sustained that night. She was eventually awarded $30,000. Naturally. In 1979, Elisa Boyer was found guilty of second-degree murder in the shooting death of her lover, Louis Reynolds. She claimed Reynolds had "attacked her with a chair". She received an indeterminate sentence of two to five years in the California Institution for Women at Frontera; classic case of too little, too late. I have provided a photograph of each of the two mongrels that murdered Sam Cooke, the singer's singer. In these photos of hellhounds Boyer and Franklin, taken at the time of Sam Cooke's murder, note the smug, smiling face of Bertha Franklin who had just silenced one of the greatest voices in the history of popular music. Doesn't she look proud? Pride in one's profession is a beautiful thing. Well, pride goeth before a fall. She was found dead in a Michigan hooker house eighteen months after Sam's murder. Alas, too little, too late.

Elisa Boyer   *Bertha Franklin*

Lou Costello (1906-1959)
"That was the best ice-cream soda I ever tasted!"
One half of the very successful comedy team of Abbott and Costello, remembered most for their *Who's On First?* routine, said these words just before collapsing from a massive heart attack. But what a way to go!

Joan Crawford (1905-1977)
"Damn it! Don't you dare ask God to help me."
Joan Crawford was an Academy Award-winning American actress, but not exactly a joy to be around. The American Film Institute named Crawford among the Greatest Female Stars of All Time, ranking her at number 10. I wonder what Miss Crawford's rank would be as a human being. Crawford's angry last words were directed towards her housekeeper who began to pray aloud.

Bing Crosby (1904-1977)
"It was a great game, fellers."
Bing Crosby had just sunk his final putt during a game of golf at La Moraleja golf course near Madrid, Spain, when he turned to the spectators and acknowledged their applause by saying, "It was a great game, fellers." As he turned to walk to the clubhouse, he collapsed and was carried inside by his three golfing partners. There, a physician unsuccessfully tried to resuscitate him.

George Armstrong Custer, General (1839-1876)
"Hurrah Boys! Let's get these last few Reds, then head on back to camp! Hurrah!"
Custer was a cadet at West Point, graduating last in his class, then a U.S. Army officer and cavalry commander in the War Between the States and later in the Indian Wars. He was defeated and killed at the Battle Of Little Bighorn in 1876, being surprised by a huge army of enemy Sioux, Cheyenne, and Arapaho

warriors, led by Crazy Horse and Sitting Bull. This battle is popularly known in American history as *Custer's Last Stand.*

Leon Czolgosz (1873-1901)
"I killed the President because he was the enemy of the good people, the good working people. I am not sorry for my crime . . . (through clenched teeth) I am sorry I could not see my father."

An anarchist from the cradle, Czolgosz assassinated President William McKinley, and was executed in 1901. He said the second line as he was being strapped to the electric chair. The case of Czolgosz illustrates my firm belief that we, as a nation, should not allow anyone to enter that has two non-consecutive 'Z's in their last name. That's asking for trouble.

Jeffrey Lionel Dahmer (1960-1994)
"I don't care if I live or die. Go ahead and kill me."

Convicted of murdering seventeen men and boys between 1978 and 1991, with the majority of the murders occurring between 1989 and 1991, Dahmer's crime spree was highly publicized and particularly gruesome, involving rape, necrophilia, and cannibalism. Fellow prisoner, Christopher Scarver, who beat Dahmer to death with a "preacher bar" (part of a weight machine), reported that these were his last words. It's such a shame that Dahmer was never allowed to enjoy the benefits of rehabilitation and a chance at being returned into society.

Salvador Dali (1904-1989)
"Where is my clock?"

Dali was a very popular and influential Spanish surrealist painter.

Georges Jacques Danton (1759-1794)
"Show my head to the people. It is worth seeing."

Danton was the acknowledged leader of the French Revolution. Sentenced to death by guillotine, he said these words to the executioner as he placed his neck in the guillotine.

James Dean (1931-1955)
"That guy's got to stop . . . he'll see us."

In his new Porsche, James Dean and a stuntman sped off to a weekend racing event in Salinas, California. They were soon stopped by a patrol car near Bakersfield, and Dean received a ticket for speeding. Two hours later, still speeding along a dark, two-lane highway, Dean saw a car begin to turn onto the road ahead and spoke his last words. The other guy, of course, did not stop and Dean's Porsche slammed into the other vehicle, killing Dean instantly. His passenger was seriously injured when thrown from the car. The driver of the other vehicle, a 23-year-old college student, suffered only minor injuries.

Emily Dickinson (1830-1886)
". . . the fog is rising."
Emily Dickinson was one of the greatest and most prolific American poets, yet she published only seven poems, all anonymously, during her lifetime. She was born and died in the same house in Amherst, Massachusetts. In between, she left her hometown only a handful of times, and after 1872, she seldom ventured out her house or yard. A rather outgoing young girl, she retreated into a tighter circle of family and friends, as she grew older, and communicated primarily through cryptic letters and fragments of poetry. Even during her terminal illness, Bright's disease (a old term that included a variety of kidney problems), she only permitted her physician to perform examinations by watching through a partially closed door. She died on May 15, 1886, after lapsing in and out of consciousness for several days. It is possible that her last words referred to a poem she wrote nearly twenty-five years earlier, *I've Seen A Dying Eye.*

Denis Diderot (1713-1784)
"But how the devil do you think this could harm me?"
Denis Diderot, French encyclopedist, upon being warned by his wife not to eat too much.

Isadora Duncan (1878-1927)
"Farewell, my friends. I go to glory."
Isadora Duncan was an American dancer who, although never very popular in the United States, entertained throughout Europe, performing shows featuring a new style of dance she invented that was based on the figures found on Greek vases. She flaunted traditional mores and morality, and her private life was subject to considerable scandal, especially following the tragic drowning of her children in the Seine River. One evening, after a party in Nice, Duncan hopped into a Buggati with a new male friend and shouted farewell to her friends standing nearby, "Adieu, mes amis. Je vais la glorie." She did not notice that her long scarf, which was her trademark, had fallen under one of the vehicle's rear wheels, and the cloth simultaneously tightened around her neck and wrapped around the axle. Duncan was yanked violently from the car and dragged for several yards before the driver noticed what had happened. She died almost instantly of a broken neck.

George Eastman (1854-1932)
"My work is done, why wait?"
George Eastman, the American inventor, first became interested in amateur photography while working at a bank in Rochester, New York. He developed a process that not only simplified the method of making photographic plates, but also allowed them to be mass-produced with relative ease. Realizing that there

was a large market for his plates among other photographers, he went into business for himself, eventually introducing flexible film in 1884 and the first mass-produced camera for amateurs, the Kodak box camera, in 1888. As his company thrived, Eastman made a fortune and donated vast sums to universities, dental clinics, and musical institutions. At the age of 77, plagued by a painfully debilitating spinal disease, Eastman put his affairs in order, wrote a note, and committed suicide.

Thomas A. Edison (1847-1931)
"It's very beautiful over there."
In the spring of 1929, Thomas Edison traveled from his home and laboratory at Menlo Park, New Jersey, to Dearborn, Michigan, to celebrate the 50th anniversary of his invention of the electric light as well as the opening of both the Ford Museum and Greenfield Village. After being introduced by President Hoover, Edison delivered a brief banquet speech and then collapsed. The president's physician quickly rushed to Edison's aid and determined that he was suffering from severe pneumonia. Edison returned to Menlo Park but never fully recovered. He collapsed again in August 1931, and was bedridden for the last two months of his life. He sank into semi-consciousness, and his second wife, Mina, remained by his side. On Edison's last day, she leaned close and asked, "Are you suffering?" to which he replied, "No, just waiting." Edison then looked out of his bedroom window and softly spoke his last words.

Albert Einstein (1879-1955)
"? ? ?"
The famous German-born American physicist, whose theories of relativity revolutionized physics, won the Nobel Prize in 1921, was named "Person Of The Century" by *Time* magazine in 1999, and was considered so extraordinary an intellect, that, after his death, his brain was preserved for scientific study. The rest was cremated and his ashes scattered. We will never know what wonders Albert Einstein revealed on his deathbed, because his last words were spoken in German, and the only other person in the room was a New Jersey hospital nurse who didn't speak German, so Einstein's last words remain a mystery. Verily, a chain is only as strong as its weakest link! We can only assume that his last words were brilliant. Einstein's wit was also legendary, and I am including some quotes from Albert the Great on varying subjects. Enjoy.

<u>On Wireless Telegraph:</u>
"The wireless telegraph is not difficult to understand. The ordinary telegraph is like a very long cat. You pull the tail in New York, and it meows in Los Angeles. The wireless is the same, only without the cat."

<u>On Gravity:</u>
"Gravitation can not be held responsible for people falling in love."

<u>On Fame:</u>
"With fame I become more and more stupid, which of course is a very common phenomenon."

<u>On Creation:</u>
"God does not play dice with the universe."

<u>On how World War III will be fought:</u>
"I don't know, but I know how World War IV will be fought . . . with sticks and stones."

<u>On the Theory of Relativity:</u>
"Put your hand on a hot stove for a minute, and it seems like an hour. Sit with a pretty girl for an hour, and it seems like a minute. That's relativity!"

<u>On Science and Religion:</u>
"Science without religion is lame, religion without science is blind."

<u>On Infinity:</u>
"Two things are infinite: the universe and human stupidity; and I'm not sure about the universe."

<u>On Common Sense:</u>
"Common sense is the collection of prejudices acquired by age eighteen."

<u>On God:</u>
"I want to know God's thoughts; the rest are just details."

<u>On Failure:</u>
"Anyone who has never made a mistake has never tried anything new."

<u>On Science:</u>
"Science is a wonderful thing if one does not have to earn one's living at it."

<u>On Creativity:</u>
"The secret to creativity is knowing how to hide your sources."

<u>On Understanding:</u>
"You do not really understand something unless you can explain it to your grandmother."

<u>On Intellect:</u>
"We should take care not to make intellect our god; it has, of course, powerful muscles, but no personality."

<u>And finally, ex-football player and sports commentator, Joe Theisman, commenting on genius:</u>

*"Nobody in football should be called a genius.
A genius is a guy like Norman Einstein."*

Dwight D. Eisenhower (1890-1969)
"I've always loved my wife, my children, and my grandchildren, and I've always loved my country. I want to go. God, take me."
Dwight Eisenhower was the 34th President of the United States, but he is perhaps even more famous as a military officer. During World War II, Eisenhower led the Allied invasions of North Africa, Italy, and France as the Supreme Allied Commander. Afterward, he served a tour as the Army Chief of Staff and finished his career as the first military commander of NATO. Following his presidency, Eisenhower retired to his farm in Gettysburg. He died at Walter Reed Army Medical Center in 1969.

Elizabeth I, Queen of England (1533-1603)
"All my possessions for a moment of time."
Elizabeth I, the daughter of Henry VIII and Anne Boleyn, was the Queen of England from 1558 until her death in 1603. Her reign is famous for the glamour of her court as well as the success of her policies. By the end of her life she had outlived all of her friends, suitors, and enemies. She spent most of her last days in partial consciousness in a pile of pillows on her chamber floor but finally consented to be placed in her bed just before she died.

Sir William Erskine, Major General, 1st Baronet (1769-1813)
"Now why did I do that?"
Major-General Sir William Erskine began his military career with a brilliant feat of arms, served as a member of Parliament, achieved important commands in the Napoleonic Wars under the Duke of Wellington, but ended his service in insanity and suicide. These were the General's last words, after he jumped from a window in Lisbon, Portugal in 1813.

Douglas Fairbanks, Sr. (1883-1939)
"Never felt better."
Douglas Fairbanks, Sr., was the premier swashbuckling star of early Hollywood. In December 1939, after returning from the USC-UCLA football game, Fairbanks became ill. He skipped work the following morning with chest and arm pain. A doctor prescribed total bed rest, a restricted diet, and professional nursing care. Fairbanks slept on and off through the morning and awakened in the afternoon asking his attendant to open the window. "How are you?" the attendant asked. Fairbanks answered with a grin, rolled over, and went back to sleep. He died later that night with his dog, a 150 lb. mastiff, named Marco Polo, curled up at the foot of his bed.

Marquis de Favras (1744-1790)
"I see that you have made three spelling mistakes."
The Marquis de Favras was caught by the radicals of the French Revolution as he plotted to help Louis XVI escape. Convicted of treason after a two-month trial, he was handed his official death sentence by the court clerk as he was led to the scaffold, and uttered this gem.

Franz Ferdinand, Archduke of Austria (1863-1914)
"It's nothing . . . it's nothing . . ."
Whispered to Count Harrach as the Archduke fell unconscious after being shot in Sarajevo; he died shortly after without ever regaining consciousness. His assassination precipitated the Austrian declaration of war. This caused countries allied with Austria, Hungary, and Serbia to declare war on each other, starting World War I.

William J. Fetterman (1833-1866)
"Give me 80 men and I'll ride through the whole Sioux nation."
In November 1866, Captain William J. Fetterman reported in to the 18th U.S. Infantry at Fort Phil Kearney. At the time, the regiment was tasked with containing Red Cloud and his band of Sioux. Its commander, Colonel Carrington, found Fetterman to be a troublesome officer despite an exemplary Civil War combat record. Several times during December, the Sioux launched forays against settlers and grazing herds in hopes of baiting the soldiers into a hot pursuit and subsequent ambush. Each time, officers commanding patrols sent out in response by Colonel Carrington recognized the traps before they could be sprung. The Sioux set the stage once more on December 21 when they pinned down a supply train not far from the fort. Carrington assigned another officer to lead the 80 man relief column, but Fetterman, although inexperienced in Indian warfare, demanded the assignment based upon seniority, and said his last known words. Carrington acquiesced but gave Fetterman emphatically explicit instructions not to pursue any Indians. A second patrol sent out later in the day found the bodies of Captain Fetterman and all 80 of his men stripped of their clothing and horribly mutilated.

John Field (1782-1837)
"I am a pianist."
John Field was a British pianist and composer whose works were said to have a major influence on Chopin. As he lay dying, his friends thought a minister should be summoned. However, no one had ever heard Field mention his religion. One friend whispered to Field, "Are you a Papist or a Calvinist?" "I am a pianist," Field answered.

W. C. Fields (1880-1946)
"Looking for loopholes!"

A friend, visiting Fields on his deathbed, was surprised to find Fields reading a Bible. The friend asked Fields why he was reading a Bible. "Looking for loopholes!" Fields answered wryly.

Adolf Fischer (1859-1887)
"This is the happiest moment of my life."

Adolf Fischer, a German anarchist, was a principal leader in the Chicago branch of the International Working People's Association, better known as the Black International. After organizing a walkout at the McCormick Harvester Works, gunfire broke out between anarchist supporters and police. Immediately, the Black International distributed circulars urging workers to "arm themselves, assemble at Haymarket Square, and take revenge". At the rally, Fischer and seven other anarchist leaders addressed the three thousand workers who showed up. After several hours of rather boring political oratory, the crowd became restless and most began to go home. Shortly thereafter, a police detachment arrived and ordered those who remained to disperse. The anarchist speakers objected, and someone tossed a bomb into the middle of the police ranks, killing one man and injuring about sixty others. The surviving police opened fire, as did a number of anarchists and workers; another sixty men were injured or killed. The person who threw the bomb was never captured, but the anarchists who spoke at the rally were arrested and charged as accessories to murder. All were convicted. One was sentenced to fifteen years, the others to death. Fischer was hanged in November 1887. The Haymarket rioters have long-since become martyrs and heroes of international communism and anarchy, and leftist interpretations of the event abound.

Lavinia Fisher (1793-1820)
"If any of you have a message for the Devil, give it to me, for I am about to meet him!"

Lavinia Fisher was hanged for murder on February 18, 1820, while wearing her white wedding gown. She is widely considered to be America's first female serial killer.

Arthur Flegensheimer, AKA Dutch Schultz (1902-1935)
"Mother is the best bet."

Dutch Schultz was born in the Bronx around the turn of the century and quit school in the fourth grade to take up burglary. A murderous sociopath, Schultz became New York's "king of beer" during Prohibition and ran the Harlem numbers racket as well. Intensely disliked by other gangsters, Schultz finally went too far when he threatened the life of a federal prosecutor, and future

Presidential candidate, Thomas Dewey. Lucky Luciano feared Schultz's instability would bring too much heat upon all of organized crime, so he contracted with Murder, Inc. to have Schultz eliminated. On October 23, 1935, Schultz, along with three of his henchmen, was massacred at a Newark, New Jersey restaurant. Schultz took three machine gun rounds in the stomach as he left the toilet and died two days later. Schultz babbled incoherently to the police as he lay dying. His last words have also been recorded as "Hey, Jimmie! Chimney sweeps, talk to the sword! Shut up, you got a big mouth! Please come help me up, Henny. Max come over here...French Canadian bean soup...I want to pay, make them leave me alone", etc. But I feel "Mother is the best bet" is best.

Errol Flynn (1909-1959)
"I shall return!"
Errol Flynn was famous for his many romantic swashbuckler roles in Hollywood films and his flamboyant, excessive lifestyle. Numerous legends surround Flynn's death. At a party, on October 14, 1959, with Flynn regaling guests with stories and impressions, Flynn suddenly felt ill, and retired to a bedroom to rest, announcing, "I shall return!" A half hour later, he was dead from a massive coronary. His friends later stole his body from the morgue, and propped him up with a cocktail at the Hotel Georgia lounge. He shares coffin space with six bottles of whiskey, a parting gift from his drinking buddies.

James Forrestal (1892-1949)
"Frenzy hath seized thy dearest son,
  who from thy shores in glory came
The first in valor and in fame;
  Thy deeds that he hath done
Seem hostile all to hostile eyes . . .
  Better to die, and sleep
the never waking sleep, than linger on,
  and dare to live, when the soul's life is gone."

James Forrestal was the Secretary of the Navy during World War II. After the war, President Truman appointed him as the first Secretary of Defense. Forrestal became extremely frustrated when the other branches of Service, especially the Air Force, resisted his proposals. He became ineffective and depressed by their, and the press, continually criticizing his every decision. After Truman relieved him of his duties, he became paranoid as well. He told anyone who would listen that he was victim of a vast conspiracy, and he searched closets everywhere, thoroughly convinced that enemies were hiding within. On April 2, Admiral Forrestal was admitted to the distinguished visitor suite on the 16th floor of

Bethesda Naval Hospital for observation. He appeared to be recovering, but on May 22, after tying one end of his bathrobe belt around his neck and the other to a radiator pipe, he jumped out the window. The belt snapped, and Forrestal fell, crashing onto a passageway roof thirteen floors below. The noise immediately alerted the nursing staff, which found him dead when they arrived at the scene. Earlier that evening, when an attendant checked on Forrestal during his rounds, he found Forrestal copying verse from a book. It turned out to be the suicide note, a poem from *Chorus from Ajax* by Sophocles.

Benjamin Franklin (1705-1790)
"A dying man can do nothing easily."
One of the most important and influential Founding Fathers of the United States of America, Franklin was a leading author and printer, satirist, political theorist, politician, scientist, inventor, civic activist, statesman, and diplomat. As he lay dying, his daughter suggested that if he lay on his side, he could breathe easier.

Sigmund Freud (1856-1939)
"This is absurd! This is absurd!"
The father of psychoanalysis, and a heavy cigar smoker, Freud endured more than 30 operations during his life due to mouth cancer. In September 1939, he prevailed on his doctor and friend Max Schur to assist him in suicide, saying, "My dear Schur, you certainly remember our first talk. You promised me then not to forsake me when my time comes. Now it is nothing but torture and makes no sense any more." Schur administered three doses of morphine over many hours that resulted in Freud's death on September 23, 1939.

Rajiv Gandhi, Indian Prime Minister (1944-1991)
"Don't worry, relax!"
Said to his security staff minutes before being killed by a suicide bomber attack.

George Gipp (1895-1920)
"Win one for the Gipper!"
George Gipp was a football player who led the University of Notre Dame to unbeaten seasons in 1919 and 1920. In December 1920, he contracted pneumonia after a serious throat infection and died at the height of his college football fame. On his deathbed, he told his coach, Knute Rockne, that "Someday, when things look real tough for Notre Dame, ask the boys to go out there and win one for the Gipper." Then he died. Eight years later, at the end of a terrible season, Notre Dame was about to play the Army team. Trailing at half time, Rockne gathered the players and for the first time ever, related Gipp's last words in an attempt to inspire the team. Notre Dame went on to beat Army by the score of 12 to 6. President Ronald Reagan had been a radio sports broadcaster long before he became a movie actor. The Gipp story had always

fascinated Reagan, and when he heard that Warner Brothers was planning a film on the life of Knute Rockne, he lobbied hard to play the part of "The Gipper". Reagan did, of course, win the role, and spoke the famous words that are today part of movie history.

Crawford Goldsby, AKA Cherokee Bill (1876-1895)

"No! I didn't come here to make a speech. I came here to die."

Cherokee Bill, convicted of murder, was standing on the gallows with the noose around his neck, when he was asked if he had any last words. He replied, "No! I didn't come here to make a speech. I came here to die."

Ulysses S. Grant (1822-1885)

"Water."

U. S. ('Unconditional Surrender') Grant was the Commanding General of all Union Forces at the end of the War Between the States, and became the 18th President of the United States (1869-1877). Bankrupted by bad business deals and suffering from throat cancer (another heavy cigar smoker), Grant and his family were left destitute. At the time, retired U.S. Presidents were not given pensions, and Grant had forfeited his military pension when he assumed the office of President. It was not until 1958 that Congress, feeling it quite inappropriate that a former president or his wife might be poverty-stricken, passed a bill granting (no pun intended) a pension to such individuals, a practice that continues to this day.

Joseph Henry Green (1791-1863)

"Congestion. Stopped."

Joseph Henry Green was a distinguished 19th century British surgeon. On his deathbed, he is said to have remarked, "Congestion," after taking an especially raspy breath. He then checked his own pulse, announced "Stopped!" and died.

Frank "Tight Lips" Gusenberg (1893-1929)

"Nobody shot me."

Tight Lips, an American mobster, was one of Bugs Moran's gangsters murdered in the 1929 St. Valentine's Day Massacre in Chicago by Al Capone's henchmen, who were dressed as policemen. When Gusenberg was asked by arriving police who had shot him, he replied, "I'm not gonna talk – nobody shot me!"

Charles Gussman (1913-2000)

"And now for a final word from our sponsor . . ."

Gussman was a television writer for the soap opera Days of Our Lives.

Edmund Gwenn (1875-1959)

"Dying is easy. Comedy is difficult."

Edmund Gwenn was an English stage actor, originally discovered by George

Bernard Shaw, who became a Hollywood star in his middle age. Twice nominated for an Academy Award, he won an Oscar as the Best Supporting Actor for his portrayal of Santa Claus in *Miracle on 34th Street*.

Nathan Hale (1755-1776)

"I only regret that I have but one life to lose for my country."

Nathan Hale was an officer for the Continental Army during the American Revolutionary War. Widely considered America's first spy, Hale volunteered for an intelligence-gathering mission, but was caught by the British. He is best remembered for his speech before being hanged following the Battle of Long Island.

Albrecht von Haller (1708-1777)

"My friend, the artery ceases to beat."

Albrecht von Haller was a Swiss physician, scientist, and poet. He was instrumental in the founding of the University of Gottengin where he served as the chairman of botany, surgery, and anatomy. Haller's last words have also been recorded as "It's beating...beating...beating...it's stopped."

Richard Halliburton (1900-1939)

"Southerly gales, squalls, lee rail under water, wet bunks, hard tack, bully beef, wish you were here . . . instead of me!"

This is the last known communication from Richard Halliburton on the Chinese junk *Sea Dragon* at sea, March 23, 1939. Halliburton was an American traveler, adventurer, and author. His final adventure was an attempt to pilot a traditional Chinese sailing ship eastward across the Pacific Ocean; the *Sea Dragon* radioed mid-way that it was laboring in a typhoon, and Halliburton and the crew were not heard from again.

Alexander Hamilton (1755-1804)

"This is a mortal wound, doctor . . . (And then, to his wife) *. . . Remember, my Eliza, you are a Christian."*

Alexander Hamilton was an Army officer, lawyer, Founding Father, politician, statesman, financier, and political theorist. One of America's first constitutional lawyers, he was a leader in calling the Philadelphia Convention in 1787; he was one of the two chief authors of the anonymous Federalist Papers, the most cited contemporary interpretation of intent for the United States Constitution. Soon after the gubernatorial election in New York—in which Morgan Lewis, greatly assisted by Hamilton, defeated Aaron Burr, a newspaper published a letter recounting a dinner party in upstate New York during which Hamilton said he could reveal "an even more despicable opinion" of Colonel Burr. Burr, his honor insulted, and still stinging by the political defeat, demanded an apology. Hamilton refused. Following an exchange of three testy letters, and despite the attempts of friends to avert a confrontation, a duel was nevertheless scheduled for July 11, 1804, along the west bank of the Hudson River in Weehawken, New Jersey, a common dueling site at which, three years earlier, Hamilton's eldest son, Philip, had been killed. At dawn, the duel began, and Vice President Aaron Burr shot Hamilton. Hamilton's shot broke a tree branch directly above Burr's head. A letter that Hamilton wrote the night before the duel states, "I have resolved, if our interview [duel] is conducted in the usual manner, and it pleases God to give me the opportunity, to reserve and throw away my first fire, and I have thoughts even of reserving my second fire", which asserts an intention to miss Burr. The circumstances of the duel, and Hamilton's actual intentions, are still disputed. But one thing's certain – Burr certainly intended to shoot Hamilton. And he did. Hamilton died on the scene after speaking these words to his doctor and wife. Politics were a lot more fun in those days.

George Harrison (1943-2001)
"Love one another."
Ex-Beatle guitarist, George Harrison, was on his deathbed dying from cancer, spoken to his family, on November 29, 2001.

Wallace Henry Hartley (1878-1912)
"Gentlemen, I bid you farewell."
Wallace Hartley was a violinist and bandleader on the RMS *Titanic* on its maiden voyage. He became famous for leading the eight-member band in *Nearer My God To Thee* as the ship sank on April 15, 1912. These words were spoken to his bandmates as the Titanic sank into the Atlantic Ocean. One survivor who clambered aboard a lifeboat reported that she distinctly heard Hartley say these words before he and the band was swept off the deck, into the sea.

Rutherford B. Hayes (1822-1893)
"I know that I am going where Lucy is."
Rutherford B. Hayes, speaking of his late wife, was an American politician, lawyer, military leader, and the 19th President of the United States (1877–1881). Hayes was elected President by one electoral vote after the highly disputed election of 1876. Losing the popular vote to his opponent, Samuel Tilden, Hayes was the only president whose election was decided by a congressional commission.

Georg Wilhelm Friedrich Hegel (1770-1831)
"Only one man ever understood me . . . and he didn't understand me."
Hegel was a German philosopher and one of the representatives of German idealism.

Heinrich Heine (1797-1856)
"God will forgive me. It's his profession."

Heinrich Heine was a German poet who spent the final years of his life in Paris where he was a key figure in radical political journalism. By 1845, he had contracted a spinal disease that confined him to bed until his death. He faced death calmly, and shortly before he died he told his visitors "God will forgive me. It's his profession."

O. Henry (1862-1910)

"Turn up the lights! I don't want to go home in the dark."

O. Henry was the pen name of American writer William Sydney Porter. Porter's 400 short stories are known for their wit, wordplay, characterization and his trademark was his clever use of twist endings.

Abram S. Hewitt (1822-1903)

"And now, I am officially dead."

Industrialist. teacher, lawyer, iron manufacturer, U.S. Congressman, and Mayor of New York, Hewitt had just removed the oxygen tube from his mouth in the hospital.

Conrad Hilton (1887-1979)

"Leave the shower curtain on the inside of the tub."

Conrad Hilton was born in San Antonio, New Mexico, and began his career by renting out rooms in his adobe home. He took a job as a local bank cashier and was so successful that he soon purchased a bank of his own. In 1919, he assumed control of a small hotel in Cisco, Texas and, over the next sixty years, built an international hospitality empire. On his deathbed, just before he died, Hilton was asked if he had any last words of wisdom for the world. Hilton quietly gave us this pearl of wisdom, a classic, and is far more profound than anything his not-so-great granddaughter Paris, has uttered in her lifetime.

John Henry "Doc" Holliday (1851-1887)

"This is funny."

Doc Holliday was a dentist before turning his talents toward gambling and gunfighting, and is usually remembered for his associations with Wyatt Earp and the Gunfight at the O.K. Corral. As one of the consummate gunfighters of the American Old West, Holliday always figured he would die honorably, in a fight. Die with his boots on. But Doc died in a hotel bed from tuberculosis. These last words were uttered on his deathbed after seeing his feet with boots off.

John Holmes (1812-1899)

"John Rogers did."

This is a gem. John Holmes was a U.S. lawyer and the brother of Oliver Wendell Holmes. After he had lain absolutely quiet and motionless on his deathbed for an extraordinarily long period of time, those assembled in the room suspected that he had died. A nurse checked his pulse, found none, and announced that she would feel his feet to see if they were warm, saying, "If they're warm, he's alive. Nobody ever died with warm feet." "John Rogers did!" came Holmes' reply. John Rogers was a Protestant martyr who had been burned at the stake!

Harry Houdini (1874-1926)
"I'm tired of fighting. I guess this thing is going to get me."
One of Harry Houdini's many stage tricks was to tighten his stomach muscles and invite strong men to punch him in the stomach, and he would easily withstand the blow. While reclining on his couch backstage after a performance, relaxed and having an art student sketch him, Houdini was asked by a young man if he was really able to withstand such a blow. Houdini replied yes and was promptly punched in the midsection several times. As Houdini wasn't expecting the punches, he hadn't tightened his abdominals, and the blows burst his appendix. Houdini died seven days later, on Halloween, of peritonitis from a ruptured appendix. He was fifty-two.

Samuel Houston (1793-1863)
"Texas, Margaret! Texas!"
Sam Houston was a 19th century statesman, politician, and soldier, and was a key figure in the history of Texas, including serving as President of the Republic of Texas, Texas Senator (after Texas had joined the United States), and finally as Governor of Texas. His last words were spoken to Margaret, his wife.

Victor Hugo (1802-1885)
"Now day and night are locked in combat. I see black light."
Hugo was a famous French poet, playwright, and novelist. He was perhaps the most influential exponent of the Romantic Movement in France. His best-known works are the novels *Les Miserables* and the *Hunchback of Notre Dame.*

Aldous Leonard Huxley (1894-1963)
"LSD, 100 micrograms."
A British writer, Huxley was best known for his novels and his personal advocacy of hallucinogenic drugs. On his deathbed, he wrote these last words in a note to his wife, a love letter of sorts. She obliged and he was injected twice before dying. Aldous Huxley's grandfather, Thomas Huxley, was the inventor of the term 'agnosticism', which is to doubt the existence of God. Dare I say . . . Doubting Thomas? At any rate, it sure is a beautiful family legacy.

Henrik Johan Ibsen (1828-1906)
"On the contrary!"
Ibsen was a major Norwegian playwright, often referred to as the "father of modern drama". This was his response to a nurse who told a visitor he was feeling a little better.

Washington Irving (1783-1859)
"I have to set my pillows one more night? When will this end already?"
Washington Irving, American author, aggravated at having to ready himself for bed, said this to his niece, then suffered a massive stroke, and died.

Andrew Jackson (1767-1845)
"Oh, do not cry – be good children and we will all meet in heaven."
Andrew Jackson was the 7th President of the United States (1829-1837). Jackson was also Military Governor of Florida, commander of the American forces at the Battle Of New Orleans (*In 1814, we took a little trip...along with Colonel Jackson down the mighty Misissip...*), and was a polarizing figure that dominated American politics in the 1820s and 1830s. Nicknamed "Old Hickory" because he was renowned for his toughness, Jackson was the first President primarily associated with the frontier, as he based his career in good ol' Tennessee. But Jackson's legacy is much-sullied (and with good cause) due to his signing of the Indian Removal Act of 1830 which resulted in the infamous Trail of Tears. Relocated Native Americans from the southeastern United States died by the thousands, including 4,000 Cherokee.

Thomas "Stonewall" Jackson (1824-1863)
"Let us cross over the river and sit under the shade of the trees."
Stonewall Jackson was one of the premier Confederate generals in the American War Between the States. He was mistakenly shot by his own men on May 2, 1863 during the battle of Chancellorsville, and his left arm had to be amputated. General Robert E. Lee decided that Jackson should recuperate in a safe refuge and ordered that Jackson be transported to Guinea Station about 30 miles from the front lines. Jackson endured the ambulance ride well and was expected to eventually recover. Pneumonia set in, however, and by Sunday, May 10, it became clear that Jackson would not last through the day. When told of this prognosis, Jackson calmly remarked to his physician, "I have always wanted to die on Sunday". After lapsing into delirium, Stonewall Jackson uttered these last words before dying at 3:15 PM, "Let us cross over the river and sit under the shade of the trees." Jackson's chaplain, B. Tucker Lacy, who attended to the general at Guinea Station, reported that during the ordeal General Lee spoke to him of what Jackson meant to him as a commander, "He has lost his left arm, but I have lost my right."

Alfred Jarry (1873-1907)
"I am dying. Please, bring me a toothpick."
Alfred Jarry, writer and playwright, obviously kept his sense of humor till the end.

Thomas Jefferson (1743-1826)
"This is the Fourth?"

The principal author of the Declaration of Independence (1776), and one of the most influential Founding Fathers for his promotion of the ideals of Republicanism in the United States, Jefferson achieved distinction as, among other things, a horticulturist, statesman, architect, archaeologist, paleontologist, author, inventor and founder of the University of Virginia. When President John F. Kennedy welcomed forty-nine Nobel Prize winners to the White House in 1962 he said, "I think this is the most extraordinary collection of talent and of human knowledge that has ever been gathered together at the White House — with the possible exception of when Thomas Jefferson dined alone." Major events during his presidency include the Louisiana Purchase (1803) and the Lewis and Clark Expedition (1804-1806).

Both Thomas Jefferson and his old friend and rival John Adams died on the 50th anniversary of the Declaration of Independence. On the evening of July 3, 1826, Jefferson, the 3rd President of the United States, roused from semi-consciousness on his deathbed and asked an attendant, "This is the Fourth?" To comfort Jefferson, the man replied that it was. Jefferson smiled with satisfaction and returned to sleep. He died just after noon on the following day.

Jesus Of Nazareth
"Father, into thy hands I commend my spirit." [Luke 23:46]
"It is finished." [John 19:30]
"Eloi, Eloi, lama sabacthani?" ("My God, My God, why have you forsaken me?") [Mark 15:34 & Matthew 27:46]

Joan of Arc (1412-1431)
"Hold the cross high so I may see it through the flames!"
Joan was the youngest of five children of Jacques d'Arc, a peasant farmer from Domremy. She began to hear "voices" when she was thirteen that told her she was to serve the Dauphin and save France. Joan was repeatedly rebuffed in her attempts to join the French army until she successfully predicted its defeat at the Battle of Herrings in 1429. Afterwards, a local commander sent her to the Dauphin. When she recognized the heavily disguised Dauphin hiding in a group of courtiers, he sent her to be examined by group of theologians at Poitiers. After three weeks of questioning, they proclaimed that her voices were genuine. The Dauphin then sent her to serve with the Army as it fought to lift the siege of Orleans. There, clad in a suit of armor, she led her men and saved the city by capturing several English forts. Later that year, she led the French army to an even more important victory at Troyes. This allowed the Dauphin to be crowned Charles VII at Reims, and Joan stood at his side during the ceremony. She continued to lead the army until Burgundians at Compiegne captured her and turned her over to the English. Charles made no effort to save her, and in fact,

some have suggested that he helped arrange her capture as part of a secret deal with the Burgundians. Joan was tried in a religious court for heresy and witchcraft, and although she defended herself well, she was forced or tricked into denying her "voices" and promising never again to wear men's clothes. Later, she once more dressed as a man and was declared a heretic. She was burned at the stake in the Rouen marketplace, and her ashes were thrown into the Seine. Twenty-five years later, Pope Callistus III reopened her case, and she was found innocent. Joan was canonized by Pope Benedict XV in 1920.

James Augustine Aloysius Joyce (1882-1941)
"Does nobody understand?"
James Joyce was an Irish expatriate writer, one of the most influential writers of the 20th century. He is best known for his landmark novel *Ulysses* and its highly controversial successor *Finnegan's Wake*.

Terry Kath (1946-1978)
"Don't worry...it's not loaded."
Kath was a singer, guitarist, and founding member of the popular rock band *Chicago*. In 1978, after attending a party at his roadie's home in Los Angeles, Kath, a gun enthusiast, took a .38 revolver and put it to his head, pulling the trigger several times on the empty chambers. Then picking up an automatic 9mm pistol, Kath showed the empty magazine to his friend, put the gun to his temple and pulled the trigger, infamously saying, "Don't worry, it's not loaded." However, one bullet remained in the chamber, and the gun fired, killing him instantly.

George Kelly (1887-1974)
"My dear, before you kiss me good-bye, fix you hair. It's a mess."
George Kelly was an American playwright and the uncle of Grace Kelly. On his deathbed, he was visited by another niece, who leaned forward to kiss him farewell.

John F. Kennedy (1917-1963)
"That's obvious."
John Kennedy was the 35th president of the United States. He was assassinated by Lee Harvey Oswald as he was traveling by motorcade through the streets of Dallas. JFK was visiting Dallas to help prepare for his coming election campaign. Although unpopular in the South, many citizens were lining the streets to watch the procession as it passed. Kennedy had just responded to Texas Governor John Connolly's wife's comment, "Mr. President, you can't say that Dallas doesn't love you!" when the first of Oswald's bullets struck him in the head.

Tom "Black Jack" Ketchum (1863-1901)
"I'll be in Hell before you start breakfast! Let her rip!"

Black Jack Ketchum, notorious train robber and member of the infamous Hole In The Wall gang, sprung up the gallows steps to his execution, and said these words to his executioner. Unfortunately for all present, the rope was too long, and Black Jack was decapitated.

John Maynard Keynes (1883-1946)
"I should have drunk more Champagne."
John Maynard Keynes was a British economist, whose ideas, called Keynesian economics, had a major impact on modern economic and political theory.

Martin Luther King Jr. (1929-1968)
"Make sure to play Take My Hand, Precious Lord tonight. Play it real pretty."
King, a Baptist minister, was one of the pivotal leaders of the American civil rights movement in the 1960s. In 1964, King became the youngest person to receive the Nobel Peace Prize, given for his efforts to end segregation and racial discrimination through civil disobedience and other non-violent means. King was assassinated on April 4, 1968, in Memphis, Tennessee. King's last words on the balcony were spoken to musician Ben Branch, who was scheduled to perform that night at an event King was attending: "Ben, make sure you play *Take My Hand, Precious Lord* tonight. Play it real pretty." Reverend Samuel "Billy" Kyles, whose house King was on his way to visit, remembers that upon seeing King go down he ran into a hotel room to call an ambulance. Nobody was on the hotel switchboard, so Kyles ran back out and yelled to the police to get one on their radios. It was later revealed that the hotel switchboard operator, upon seeing King shot, had suffered a fatal heart attack and could not operate the phones. King was pronounced dead on arrival at St. Joseph's Hospital. The assassination led to a nationwide wave of riots in more than 100 cities. At King's request, his good friend Mahalia Jackson sang his favorite hymn, *Take My Hand, Precious Lord* at his funeral.

James Earl Ray, an escaped convict who had broken out of the Missouri State Penitentiary a year before the assassination, was arrested at London's Heathrow Airport while trying to leave the U.K. on a false passport. Ray was quickly extradited back to Tennessee and charged with King's murder. He confessed to the assassination on March 10, 1969, and then recanted this confession three days later. Ray was sentenced to 99 years in prison.

On the advice of his attorney, Ray took a guilty plea to avoid a trial conviction and the possibility of receiving the death penalty. Ray later fired his attorney, claiming that a man he met in Montreal, Canada, using the alias "Raoul" had been deeply involved, as was his brother Johnny, but not himself, further asserting that although he didn't "personally shoot Dr. King," he may have been "partially responsible without knowing it," hinting at a conspiracy. He spent the remainder of his life attempting (unsuccessfully) to withdraw his guilty plea and secure the trial he never had.

On June 10, 1977, Ray and six other convicts escaped from Brushy Mountain State Penitentiary in Petros, Tennessee. They were recaptured on June 13, and returned to prison. One more year was added to his previous sentence to total 100 years. Shortly after, Ray testified that he did not shoot King.

In 1997, Martin Luther King's son Dexter met with Ray in prison, and publicly supported Ray's efforts to obtain a retrial. A restaurant owner in Memphis named Loyd Jowers was brought to civil court and sued by King's family as being part of a conspiracy to murder Martin Luther King. Jowers was found liable, and the King family was awarded $100 in restitution to show that they were not pursuing the case for financial gain. Dr. William Pepper (Dr. Pepper???), a friend of King's in the last year of his life, later represented Ray in a televised mock trial in an attempt to get Ray the trial that he never had. Dr. Pepper then represented the King family in a wrongful death civil trial against Loyd Jowers. To this day, the King family does not believe James Earl Ray had anything to do with the murder of Martin Luther King. Ray died in prison in 1998, at the age of 70, from complications related to kidney disease, caused by hepatitis C. Ray contracted hepatitis as a result of a blood transfusion, given after he was stabbed inside Brushy Mountain State Pen. He was stabbed by an inmate who believed neither in Ray's innocence, nor in King's doctrine of non-violence.

Stan Laurel (1980-1965)
"I wish I was skiing." [Nurse: "Oh, Mr. Laurel, do you ski?"] *"No, but I'd rather be skiing than doing this!"*
Stan Laurel was an English-born, American comic genius, writer and director. Famous as one half of the comedy team Laurel and Hardy, Stan delivered this classic shtick before dying of a heart attack on February 23, 1965.

Saint Lawrence (225-258)
"Turn me. I am roasted on one side."
Saint Lawrence is one of the most celebrated Roman martyrs. A church deacon during the time Emperor Valerian was vigorously persecuting Christians, Lawrence also served as the keeper of the church's treasures. He was arrested and told that to save himself, he must give the church treasures to the government. Lawrence readily agreed and told the official that it would take at least eight days to assemble them. On the eighth day, Lawrence returned to the Emperor and presented him with hundreds of poor and disabled men, women, and children. "These," Lawrence said, "are the riches of the church." The enraged Emperor then ordered Lawrence to be stripped, tied face down on a gridiron suspended over a bed of burning coals, and slowly burned to death.

Lawrence maintained a cheerful appearance throughout the horror and, when asked if he had any last request, responded with these, his last words. His behavior was said to have been so impressive that several Roman senators converted to Christianity on the spot, and hundreds of citizens did the same on the following day.

Robert E. Lee (1807-1870)
"Strike the tent!"
Robert Edward Lee was a career United States Army officer, engineer, brilliant tactician, and the most celebrated general of the American War Between the States. Prior to the war, Lee opposed the secession of his home state of Virginia, and rejected President Abraham Lincoln's offer to command the Union forces. But when Virginia did secede from the Union in April 1861, Lee chose to follow his home state. He took command of the Confederate forces in the East, which Lee himself renamed the Army Of Northern Virginia. The war, the deadliest in American history, caused 620,000 soldier deaths, plus a huge, undetermined number of civilian casualties, ended slavery in the United States, restored the Union by settling the issue of secession, and strengthened the role of the Federal government. The social, political, economic, and racial issues of the war continue to shape contemporary American thought, and I agree with filmmaker Ken Burns, who said, "The Civil War, to a much greater extent than even our Revolutionary War, defines us as Americans." Historian and author, Shelby Foote adds, "Before the war, the United States of America was regarded, even grammatically, as a plurality; a group of individual states. After the war, the United States of America was forever changed to a singular idea. Before the war, we said, 'The United States *are*...' After the war, we say, 'The United States *is*...' The war changed that."

Just a note here on why I feel the term "Civil War" is far from accurate in describing the war fought between the American North and South. The war grew out of deep-seated differences between the social structure, economy, and culture of North and South. At the time, Southerners felt they were fighting for the very same ideals that the American Revolution was fought over, and most Southerners considered the "War for Southern Independence" or the "War Between the States" as a continuation of that same struggle for independence from an oppressive federal government. I feel either of these names to be much more accurate than "civil war", although much less tidy for Northerners. A civil war is, by definition, two or more factions, fighting for control of the central government. The South wanted no part of the U. S. central government, but wanted the exact opposite, independence from it. I still do, especially at tax time.

Meriwether Lewis (1774-1809)
"I am not a coward, but I am so strong. It is hard to die."
Following his return from his legendary expedition to the Pacific Ocean, Meriwether Lewis was appointed the first governor of Upper Louisiana by Thomas Jefferson. He was a poor administrator and decided to travel to Washington to get reimbursed for some expenses that had left him deep in debt. He departed Saint Louis, with $200 in his pockets, for New Orleans, where he planned to finish his journey by boat. En route, he suffered a breakdown near what today is Memphis, Tennessee. He recuperated there for several weeks and again set out, this time overland. While stopped just south of Nashville, at the home of Mrs. Robert Grinder, whose husband was away, Lewis was said to have become very agitated about his personal affairs. Mrs. Grinder later reported that, during the night, she heard a gunshot followed by a cry of "Oh, Lord!" This was followed by a second shot. A few minutes later, a bleeding Lewis staggered to her door and pleaded, "Oh, madam! Give me some water and heal my wounds." Good old Mrs. Grinder, too frightened to open the door, ignored Lewis until morning when she sought out Lewis's servants. They found him alive and in horrible pain, his skull shattered and brain exposed. Mrs. Grinder claimed that Lewis begged her to kill him, but she refused. Lewis's death was never investigated, and while many believed it to have been a suicide, an equal number suggested that he was killed while being robbed by his servants, Mrs. Grinder, her husband, or others. Lewis's $200 was never found.

Abraham Lincoln (1809-1865)
"They won't think anything about it."
Lincoln, the 16th President of the United States, was reassuring his wife, Mary, that it would be all right for them to hold hands, just before John Wilkes Booth sneaked into their box and shot him from behind. I am reluctant to provide any more detailed biographical info here, as any attempt to put the life story of Abraham Lincoln into a single paragraph would be futile, to say the least. Someday, I'd like to write a book on which I consider to be the greatest life story of any American in history.

John Winston Lennon (1940-1980)
"Yeah."
John Lennon, the assassinated Beatle, was dying in the back of a police car on the way to the hospital. The officers asked him if he was John Lennon, and then one of the greatest songwriters in rock 'n' roll history spoke his last word on Earth.
She loves you yeah, yeah, yeah, yeah.

Huey P. Long, Jr., AKA The Kingfish (1893-1935)
"I wonder why he shot me."

Huey P. Long was a Democrat politician who, while governor of Louisiana from 1928 to 1932, created a powerful political machine and ruled the state as a dictator. He was sent to the Senate in 1932, where he promoted a "share-our-wealth" program that promised to take money from those who had it and redistribute it to those who did not. Long developed considerable support among the poor and was seen as a possible third-party threat to the Roosevelt presidential campaign. He was shot and killed by the son-in-law of a former political opponent. Long's story was fictionalized in the 1947 novel, *All the King's Men*. It was made into a movie two years later, and Long's character, Willie Stark, was played by Broderick Crawford.

Joseph Lucas (1834-1902)
"Never drive at night."
Lucas, known as "The Prince of Darkness", was the founder of Lucas Industries, manufacturer of automotive electrical components such as alternators, headlights, etc. which were renowned for their unreliability in the early days of automotive engineering.

James Madison (1751-1836)
[Niece: "What's the matter, Uncle James?"]
"Nothing more than a change of mind, my dear. I always talk better lying down."
James Madison, Jr. was the 4th President of the United States, (1809–1817), and one of the Founding Fathers of the United States. Madison was the last of our Founding Fathers to pass away.

Gustav Mahler (1860-1911)
"Mozart! Mozart!"
Gustav Mahler was a Bohemian-Austrian composer and conductor, whose last words were reported by his wife, Alma.

Antonio Mancini (?-1941)
"Cheerio!"
Gangster Mancini's last words, standing on the gallows at Pentonville Prison in London, just before the trapdoor was sprung. Cheerful chap.

Robert Nesta "Bob" Marley (1945-1981)
"Money can't buy life."
Bob Marley, Reggae musician and Rastafarian, to his son Ziggy, as he lay dying from cancer. Marley was buried in a crypt in Jamaica along with his Gibson Les Paul guitar, a soccer ball, a large bud of marijuana, a bong, a ring that was given to him by the Prince of Ethiopia, and a Bible. If I may quote Colonel Kong (Slim Pickens) from *Dr. Strangelove*, "Shoot. A man could have a pretty good weekend in Las Vegas with all that stuff!"

Karl Marx (1818-1883)

"Go on, get out! Last words are for fools who haven't said enough!"

Karl Marx was the German economist, philosopher, and revolutionary who, with the aid of Friederich Engles, produced his gift to the world, the theory of modern socialism and communism. As Marx lay in bed shortly before his death, his housekeeper foolishly asked if he had any last words.

William Barclay "Bat" Masterson (1853-1921)

"We all get the same amount of ice. The rich get it in the summer. The poor get it in the winter."

Bat Masterson was a figure of the American West. His adventurous life included stints as a buffalo hunter, U.S. Army scout, avid fisherman, gambler, frontier lawman, U.S. Marshal, and sports editor and columnist for a New York newspaper. He was the great-grandfather of Robert Ballard, the marine scientist who discovered the wreck of the *SS Titanic* in 1985. *Bat Masterson* was an NBC television program, running from 1958 – 1961, starring Gene Barry. Bat Masterson collapsed from a heart attack at his desk after penning his final column for the *New York Morning Telegraph*. Masterson's last words were the last bit of column he had been typing at the moment of his death, found on his typewriter. Here are a few of his other, non-interrupted, quotes.

> *"Every dog has his day, unless there are more dogs than days."*

> *"If you want to hit a man in the chest, aim for his groin."*

> *"When a man is at the racetrack, he roars longer and louder over the twenty-five cents he loses through the hole in the bottom of his pocket than he does over the twenty-five dollars he loses through the hole in the top of his pocket."*

William B. McKinley (1843-1901)

"We are all going."

William McKinley, the 25th U.S. President, was the last Civil War veteran to be elected. He was assassinated by an anarchist, Leon Czolgosz, at the Pan American Exposition in 1901. McKinley died after lingering painfully for several days. At his bedside, his wife cried, "I want to go too, I want to go too!" McKinley answered her plea before he expired.

Ernest McSorley (1912-1975)

"We are holding our own."

McSorley was captain of the ill-fated, 729-foot, Great Lakes freighter *SS Edmund Fitzgerald*. McSorley died, along with the other 28 members of his crew, when the *Fitzgerald* sank suddenly and mysteriously in Lake Superior, on November 10, 1975. The *SS Anderson*, who was trailing behind the *Fitzgerald*, asked

McSorley how they were doing. Moments after McSorley radioed these last words to the *Anderson,* she suddenly sank. No distress signal was ever received, and a short ten minutes later, *Anderson* could neither raise *Fitzgerald* nor detect her on radar. All twenty-nine men aboard were killed. Despite losing his ship in a storm, McSorley was respected throughout his career as a superb bad-weather ship handler. The saga of the *Fitzgerald* and her crew was immortalized in Gordon Lightfoot's ballad, *The Wreck Of The Edmund Fitzgerald.*

Wilson Mizner (1876-1933)
"Why should I talk to you? I've just been talking to your boss."
Wilson Mizner was a U.S. writer and gambler. On his deathbed, he briefly regained consciousness before dying and found a priest standing over him. Mizner waved the priest away saying, "Why should I talk to you? I've just been talking to your boss."

Eric Morecambe (1926-1984)
"I'm glad that's over."
Eric Morecambe, English comedian who, together with Ernie Wise, formed the comedy team of Morecambe and Wise. After his show had ended, and Morecambe had left the stage, the musicians returned and picked up their instruments for an encore. Eric Morecambe rushed back out onto the stage to join them and energetically played various instruments. He then left the stage again, only to return moments later. All in all, he made six curtain calls. Finally, he said, "That's your lot!", waved to the audience, and left the stage. He walked into the wings and joked, "Thank goodness that's over", before collapsing with a fatal heart attack.

Wolfgang Amadeus Mozart (1756-1791)
"The taste of death is upon my lips . . . I feel something, that is not of this earth."
Mozart was a hugely prolific and influential Austrian composer of the Classical era. Mozart is among the most enduringly popular of classical composers, and many of his works are part of the standard concert repertoire.

Andrew Mutton
"Well, this is certainly a pleasant surprise."
A Chicago mobster whose car was always having starter problems, Mutton made this cheery remark to his associate when his car started successfully on the first try. Moments later, a bomb rigged to the ignition exploded, killing Andrew and wounding his associate.

Ramon Maria Narvaez (1800-1868)
"I do not have to forgive my enemies. I have had them all shot!"
Ramon Narvaez was a Spanish general who served repeated terms as prime minister during the mid-18th century.

Nostradamus (1503-1566)
"Tomorrow, I shall no longer be here."
Nostradamus was a cryptic prophet whose verse has been credited by some as foretelling future events despite its vague language and lack of any chronological reference. His predictions achieved local recognition after he claimed to have discovered a cure for the plague. Word of one of his prophesies eventually reached Catherine de Medici, the superstitious wife of Henry II, who believed it was about her husband: "The young lion will surpass the old one in national field by a single duel. He will pierce his eyes in a golden cage two blows at once, to die a grievous death." After Henry was killed in 1559 during a tournament when a lance, yielded by a younger opponent, pierced his eye, Nostradamus achieved true fame. One evening, in 1566, Nostradamus's assistant found him writing at his bench and bid him good night saying, "Tomorrow, master?" After Nostradamus replied, "Tomorrow, I shall no longer be here", the assistant left the room. When he returned the next day, he found Nostradamus dead and a note on the desk: "Upon the return of the Embassy, the King's gift put in place, nothing more will be done. He will have gone to God's nearest relatives, friends, blood brothers, found quite dead near bed and bench."

Laurence Olivier (1907-1989)
"This isn't Hamlet, you know. It's not meant to go into the bloody ear."
Sir Laurence Olivier, revered English Shakespearean actor of stage, film, and television, said this to his nurse who, attempting to moisten his lips, missed and dripped water into Olivier's ear. Note: In Shakespeare's play *Hamlet*, the title character's father is killed when poison is dripped into his ear while asleep.

Eugene O'Neill (1888-1953)
"Born in a hotel room, and damn it, died in a hotel room."
Eugene O'Neill, thought by many critics to have been the most important American dramatist, earned one Nobel and four Pulitzer Prizes during his lifetime. He was born in a New York City Broadway hotel room, the son of an Irish-American actor. For much of his life, he suffered from a debilitating Parkinson's-like disease. When he died in 1953, it was, much to his chagrin, also in a hotel room.

William "Buckey" O'Neill (1860-1898)
"Sergeant, the Spanish bullet isn't made that will kill me." (See also John Sedgwick)
Buckey O'Neill was an Arizona lawyer, miner, cowboy, gambler, newspaperman, sheriff, and congressman. He was also one of the most important members of Teddy Roosevelt's Rough Riders during the Spanish-American War, having recruited many of the volunteers and supervised their training while in San

Antonio waiting to be deployed. Just prior to the famous charge up Kettle (not San Juan) Hill, O'Neill was standing up, smoking a cigarette, and joking with his troops while under withering fire from the ridge. One of his sergeants shouted to him above the noise, "Captain, a bullet is sure to hit you!" to which O'Neill shouted back his reply. O'Neill then calmly turned to another officer. As he started to speak, a bullet struck him in the mouth. Private Tuttle, who was standing nearby, later recalled, "I heard the bullet. You usually can if you're close enough, you know. It makes a sort of 'spat.' He was dead before he hit the ground."

Lee Harvey Oswald (1939-1963)
"I will be glad to discuss this proposition with my attorney, and that after I talk with one, we could either discuss it with him or discuss it with my attorney, if the attorney thinks it is a wise thing to do, but at the present time I have nothing more to say to you."
On November 22, 1963, Lee Harvey Oswald shot and killed President Kennedy from a window of the Texas Book Depository in Dallas. Later that afternoon, he shot Officer Trippit of the Dallas Police and was shortly thereafter apprehended inside the Texas Theater. Two days later, well aware of his rights, he addressed his last words to Inspector Thomas Kelly of the U.S. Secret Service just before he was shot and killed by Gangster Jack Ruby.

Pablo Picasso (1881-1973)
"Drink to me!"
Pablo Picasso was a Spanish painter, sculptor, and ceramist, who developed Cubism, one of the most influential modern painting styles.

Marco Polo (1254-1324)
"I have not told half of what I saw."
Marco Polo was a Venetian explorer, who gained fame for his worldwide travels, recorded in the book *The Travels Of Marco Polo*.

Jeanne-Antoinette Poisson Pompadour (1721-1764)
"Wait a second."
Madame de Pompadour was a lady of the French court and mistress to Louis XV. She was a major influence on French politics of the mid-18th century. As she died, Madame de Pompadour called on God to "Wait a second." When He did, she quickly applied rouge to her cheeks.

Elvis Presley (1935-1977)
"Okay, I won't."
Those were his last words to fiancée Ginger Alden, who told him not to fall asleep reading in the bathroom. He died there of a massive heart attack. In his

last press conference, after a life lived in the press, Elvis' last words to the press were, "I hope I haven't bored you."

Sir Walter Raleigh (1554-1618)
"Strike, man, strike!"
Sir Walter Raleigh, a poet, historian, explorer, philosopher, and soldier, was the epitome of a Renaissance man. Unfortunately, Raleigh's anti-Spanish privateering infuriated King James I who charged him with treason in 1603. Raleigh was held, under sentence of death, in the Tower of London until 1616 when he was finally granted a reprieve. The reprieve was revoked in 1618 after Raleigh sailed to South America and attacked a Spanish camp near the Orinoco River. Upon his return to England, Raleigh was beheaded. Before his execution, Raleigh refused to be blindfolded and touched the ax, saying, "Doest thou think that I am afraid of it? This is that which will cure all sorrows." He then placed his head on the block and noting a hesitance on the part of the executioner said, "What dost thou fear? Strike, man, strike!" It took two blows to sever his head, which his wife embalmed and kept in a red leather bag until her death 29 years later.

George "Superman" Reeves (1914-1959)
"I'm tired. I'm going back to bed."
George Reeves was an American actor most famous for playing Superman on the classic 1950s television series. Although Reeves had been a respected actor for years (one of his first important roles was as one of the Tarlton twins in *Gone With The Wind*), he became so typecast in his Superman role that he couldn't find work after the series ended in 1957. Late one night, while he was living with his finance and another friend, two other friends came to visit. Reeves became angry that he had been awakened and announced that he was going back to bed. He went back upstairs to his bedroom and shot himself in the head with a 30-caliber luger.

Frederic Remington (1861-1909)
"Cut 'er loose, Doc!"
Frederic Remington was the premier artist of the American West. In 1909, he developed an acute case of appendicitis. He spoke his last words to the surgeon just before his emergency appendectomy and died of peritonitis and other complications following the operation.

Cecil John Rhodes (1853-1902)
"So little done, so much to do."
Cecil Rhodes immigrated to South Africa from England for health reasons and made a fortune from gold and diamond mining. He died from heart disease, beset by personal scandals and discredited for his role in fomenting the Boer War. A colleague, sitting at his bedside, heard Rhodes murmur his last words.

Franklin Delano Roosevelt (1882-1945)
"I have a terrific headache."
Franklin Roosevelt was the 32nd president of the United States and greatly expanded the role of the federal bureaucracy in attempting to manage economic and social issues. As president, he also led the nation through most of World War II. In February 1945, Roosevelt met with Winston Churchill and Joseph Stalin at Yalta to plan the final months of the war and decide upon the organization of the post-war world. Bested by Stalin at the conference and exhausted by the negotiations, Roosevelt returned to the United States and took Lucy Page Mercer Rutherford, his long-time mistress and his wife's former secretary, with him to relax at his private getaway in Warm Springs, Georgia. There, while having his portrait painted, he remarked to the artist that he had a terrible headache, collapsed, and died of a cerebral hemorrhage. Of course, Mrs. Rutherford was spirited away before Roosevelt's wife, Eleanor, arrived.

Arnold Rothstein, AKA Mr. Big (1882-1928)
"Me mudder did it."
Arnold Rothstein was the notorious gangland money man who made a fortune on the 1919 World Series fix. Rothstein, a partner of Meyer Lansky, was shot while playing poker at Park Central Hotel in New York City on November 4, 1928. He was taken to Polyclinic Hospital where despite intensive police questioning he refused to name his killer. He appears as the fictional character, Meyer Wolfshiem, in F. Scott Fitzgerald's novel, *The Great Gatsby*.

George Herman "Babe" Ruth (1895-1948)
"I'm going over the valley."
Babe Ruth was one of the all-time greatest American baseball players. On June 13, 1948, he returned to Yankee Stadium in New York City to celebrate its 25th anniversary despite being gravely ill from throat cancer. He was admitted to the hospital a little over a week later but recovered enough to attend the premier of *The Babe Ruth Story* in late July. He became so weak during the screening that he departed before the movie finished and was readmitted to the hospital. On August 16, Ruth told a visitor, "Don't come back tomorrow. I won't be here." Later that evening, he left his bed and began to wander about his room. A doctor noticed him and asked where he was going. Ruth answered, "I'm going over the valley." Ruth returned to his bed and lapsed into a coma and died within the hour.

Hector Hugh Munro, AKA Saki (1870-1916)
"Put that damned cigarette out!"
Spoken to a fellow soldier while in a trench during World War I, for fear the cigarette smoke would give away their positions. A German sniper who had heard

his remark then shot him. Munro, better known by his pen name Saki, was a British writer, whose witty and sometimes macabre stories satirized Edwardian society and culture. He is considered to be a master of the short story. At the start of the war, although forty-three and officially over age, Munro joined the Army as an ordinary soldier, refusing a commission. More than once he returned to the battlefield when officially still too sick or injured to fight. He was sheltering in a shell crater in France in November 1916, when the German sniper killed him. Below are some delicious quotes from Saki stories.

> *"A little inaccuracy sometimes saves a ton of explanation."*

> *"I always say beauty is only sin deep."*

> *"Hors d'oeuvres have always had a pathetic interest for me. They remind me of one's childhood that one goes through, wondering what the next course is going to be like, and during the rest of the menu one wishes one had eaten more of the hors d'oeuvres."*

> *"There are more ways of killing a cat than by choking it with cream, but I'm not sure that it's not the best way."*

> *"Forbidden fizz is the sweetest."*

> *"He is one of those people who would be enormously improved by death."*

> *"Think how many blameless lives are brightened by the blazing indiscretions of other people."*

> *"Every reformation must have its victims. You can't expect the fatted calf to share the enthusiasm of the angels over the prodigal son's return."*

George Sanders (1906-1972)
"Dear World. I am leaving you because I am bored. I feel I have lived long enough. I am leaving you with your worries in this sweet cesspool. Good luck."
George Sanders was a British actor whose film career spanned four decades and included *Rebecca, Foreign Correspondent,* and *All About Eve,* for which he won an Oscar. The screen's epitome of a cad, Sanders was married four times in real life; his wives included two of the Gabor sisters, Zsa Zsa and Magda. In April 1972, Sanders checked into a hotel in Barcelona, wrote a short suicide note, and took an overdose of sleeping pills.

William Saroyan (1908-1981)
"Everybody has got to die, but I have always believed an exception would be made in my case. Now what?"
William Saroyan was a Pulitzer Prize winning writer of plays, short stories, and novels whose works were noted for their sentimental optimism. Before his death in 1981, Saroyan telephoned his final words to the Associated Press.

Jannetje Johanna "Hannie" Schaft (1920-1945)
"I shoot better than you!"
Hannie was a Dutch resistance fighter during World War II. *The Girl With The Red Hair* was the title of a subsequent book and film about Hannie's life and death. The Nazis occupying her native Holland arrested her as a spy and, although there was an agreement between the Nazis and the Dutch not to execute women, she was shot dead three weeks before the end of the war by the Nazi occupiers. Well, consider the source. Two German soldiers took her to the infamous dunes of Bloemendaal, and one shot her there at close range. But he only wounded her. Then she brazenly said to her executioners: "I shoot better than you". Then they emptied their machine guns into her, killing her. After the war, in these dunes, the remains of 422 resistance people were found, 421 men and one woman, Hannie Schaft.

Jean Seberg (1938-1979)
"Forgive me. I can no longer live with my nerves."
Jean Seberg was an American actress, starring in thirty-four films in her career. Because of her support of the Black Panther Party, her private life became closely observed by FBI Director, J. Edgar Hoover. In 1970, when Seberg was seven months pregnant, the FBI leaked a story to the press that the child she was carrying was not fathered by her second husband, French author Romain Gary, but by a member of the Black Panther Party. Hoover turned out to be half-right. She gave birth to a girl, but the infant died two days later. Seberg publicly contended that the FBI's surveillance and slander of her had brought upon her premature labor, and subsequently, the death of her child. The child was proven to have not been fathered by a Black Panther, but was proven to have been fathered by someone other than her husband, a man named Carlos Navarra. *Oops!* After the loss of her child, she sank deeper into depression and became suicidal. She had a long history of alcoholism and prescription drug dependence, certainly not the best pre-natal care, with or without the FBI. Over the next few years, and two more husbands, she made several attempts to take her own life including throwing herself under a train on the Paris Metro. In August 1979, she was found dead in the back seat of her car in a Paris suburb. The police report stated that she had taken a massive overdose of barbiturates and alcohol. A suicide note ("Forgive me. I can no longer live with my nerves") was found in her hand, and suicide was ruled the official cause of death. I wonder if Hannie Schaft [see previous] ever felt nervous. Everyone gets nervous, but it's how one deals with it that matters.

General John "Uncle John" Sedgwick (1813-1864)
"They couldn't hit an elephant at this distance."

General John Sedgwick was a corps commander in the Army of the Potomac during the War Between the States. At the battle of the Wilderness, while inspecting his troops, he approached a parapet and peered out over the surrounding countryside. His officers and men urged him to take cover from small arms fire, but Sedgwick scoffed at their concerns, "What! What men! This will never do, dodging from single bullets!" Sedgwick's Chief of Staff recorded that shortly thereafter Sedgwick saw another soldier drop to the ground as a sharp-shooter's bullet passed by with a long shrill whistle. Again, Sedgwick repeated his remark about the elephant, and the soldier replied that he'd been dodging bullets all day and that if he hadn't, one of them surely would have taken off his head. Sedgwick replied, laughingly, "All right, my man, go to your place." No sooner had the words left his mouth then the general fell to the ground, blood spurting "in a little fountain" from a hole in his cheek, just under the left eye.

Ayrton Da Silva (1960-1994)
"The car seems OK..."
Ayrton Da Silva, Brazilian racecar driver, and triple Formula One World Champion, a few seconds before his steering column broke and his car hit the wall at the San Marino Grand Prix, killing him instantly.

Frank Sinatra (1915-1998)
"I'm losin' it."
Frank Sinatra was a singer, actor, and American music icon. These last words are according to his daughter Nancy, as told to *Variety* magazine.

Michael J. Smith (1945-1986)
"Uh oh . . . "
Michael J. Smith, crew member of the ill-fated Space Shuttle Challenger 51-L mission, his last statement was recorded on the spacecraft's cockpit recorder, immediately before the shuttle exploded, killing all aboard.

Robert Weston Smith, AKA Wolfman Jack (1938-1995)
"Oh, it is so good to be home!"
Veteran rock 'n' roll radio personality and inductee to the Rock and Roll Hall of Fame, Wolfman Jack died of a heart attack in Belvidere, North Carolina, on July 1, 1995, at age fifty-seven. The night before his death, after finishing the broadcast of his last live radio program, a nationally syndicated weekly program from Planet Hollywood in Washington D.C., Wolfman Jack said, "I can't wait to get home and give Lou a hug; I haven't missed her this much in years." He had been out on the road, promoting his new autobiography *Have Mercy!* When he got home, he entered his house, hugged his wife, said "Oh, it is so good to be home!", then suffered a coronary and died in her arms.

Jack Soo (1917-1979)
"It must have been the coffee."
This was a reference to the running gag of Soo's character Nick Yemana from the TV show *Barney Miller* having the reputation for making horrible coffee. According to friend and fellow cast-member Hal Linden, these were Soo's last words before being taken into surgery for cancer of the esophagus. He died, never regaining consciousness.

Henry John Temple (1784-1865)
"Die, my dear doctor, that's the last thing I shall do!"
Henry John Temple was a British statesman who served twice as Prime Minister of the United Kingdom in the mid-19th century.

Dylan Marlais Thomas (1914-1953)
"I just had eighteen straight scotches. I think that's the record! After thirty-nine years, this is all I've done."
Welsh poet Dylan Thomas was regarded by many as one of the 20th century's most influential poets.

Henry David Thoreau (1817-1862)
"One world at a time."
Henry Thoreau was an American author, naturalist, transcendentalist, tax resister, and philosopher, best known for *Walden*, a reflection upon simple living in natural surroundings, and his essay, *Civil Disobedience*, an argument for individual resistance to an unjust state. In a discussion with his aunt, while on his deathbed, his aunt asked, "Have you made your peace with your God?" Thoreau replied, "I never quarreled with my God." The aunt continued, "But aren't you concerned about the next world?" Thoreau countered, "One world at a time."

Herbert Khaury, AKA "Tiny Tim" (1932-1996)
"No, I'm not!"
American ukulele player Tiny Tim suffered a heart attack while playing his only hit (thank God) "Tiptoe Through The Tulips" at a Gala Benefit. His wife asked him if he was okay and he said, "No, I'm not!" He then collapsed and later died at a hospital in Minnesota.

Timothy Treadwell (1957-2003)
"Get out here . . . I'm getting killed!"
Timothy Treadwell to his girlfriend, Amie Huguenard, as he was being mauled to death by a bear. Huguenard was also killed. Treadwell was an American bear enthusiast, environmentalist, amateur naturalist, and documentary filmmaker. He lived among the coastal grizzly bears of Katmai National Park in Alaska for approximately thirteen seasons. At the end of his thirteenth season in the park in 2003, he and his girlfriend Amie Huguenard were devoured and killed by one or

possibly two grizzly bears. An audio recording of the attack survived, leaving us with his last words. Treadwell's life, work, and death were the subject of the 2005 documentary film titled *Grizzly Man*.

Vincent Willem van Gogh (1853-1890)
"The sadness will last forever."
Vincent van Gogh was a Dutch Post-Impressionist artist, pioneer of what came to be known as Expressionism, whose paintings and drawings include some of the world's best known, most popular and most expensive pieces. At the age of thirty-seven, after a life of depression and sadness, Vincent walked into a field and shot himself in the chest with a revolver. He then returned to his room at the Ravoux Inn, in Auvers-sur-Oise, France, where he died in his bed two days later. His brother Theo had hastened to be at his side and reported his last words.

Titus Flavius Sabinus Vespasian, Emperor (9-79)
"Woe is me, I think I am becoming a god."
Vespasian was a Roman emperor who rose from humble origins as a result of his military accomplishments. He was pronounced Emperor to resolve potential conflict following the death of Nero, and he worked hard to improve the life of the common Roman citizen.

Francisco "Pancho" Villa (1878-1923)
"Don't let it end like this. Tell them I said something."
Pancho Villa was a Mexican bandit, revolutionary, and folk hero. He conducted a guerilla war against the national government for many years until he was granted amnesty and a hacienda in return for laying down his arms. He retired in Chihuahua, Mexico, but was assassinated by supporters of his long-time enemy, General Alvaro Obregon. Villa made his last request to newspaper reporters as he lay dying.

Leonardo da Vinci (1452-1519)
"I have offended God and mankind because my work did not reach the quality it should have."
Leonardo da Vinci, the illegitimate son of a Tuscan notary and a peasant girl, was an Italian scientist, mathematician, engineer, inventor, anatomist, painter, sculptor, architect, botanist, musician, and writer.

Leonardo has often been described as the archetype of the "Renaissance Man" or universal genius, a man whose seemingly infinite curiosity was equaled only by his powers of invention. He is widely considered to be one of the greatest painters of all time and perhaps the most diversely talented person ever to have lived.

It is primarily as a painter that Leonardo was and is renowned. Two of his works, the *Mona Lisa* and *The Last Supper* occupy unique positions as the most famous, most reproduced, and most parodied portrait and religious paintings of all time.

As an engineer, Leonardo conceived ideas vastly ahead of his own time, conceptualizing a helicopter, a tank, concentrated solar power, a calculator, and the double hull, and many, many, many others. Relatively few of his designs were constructed or even feasible during his lifetime, but some of his smaller inventions, such as an automated bobbin winder for sewing machines, and a machine for testing the tensile strength of wire, entered the world of manufacturing unheralded.

As a scientist, he greatly advanced the state of knowledge in the fields of anatomy, civil engineering, and hydrodynamics. And with his dying breath, he says, "I have offended God and mankind because my work did not reach the quality it should have." C'mon Lenny, don't you think you're being a little hard on yourself? And today, after five hundred years of progress, we've got Hip-Hop music and bungee jumping.

Voltaire (1694-1778)

"Now, now, my good man . . . this is no time for making enemies."

Voltaire was a writer, essayist, deist, and philosopher of the French Enlightenment period. On his deathbed, he was urged by a priest to renounce Satan.

George Washington (1732-1799)

"'Tis well."

George Washington was a hero of the American Revolution, the first President of the United States, and the Father of Our Country. Some have claimed that Washington requested a Bible with his dying breath, but neither his doctors nor his private secretary recorded any such request, and they were all with him until the moment he died. Washington did tell one of his physicians, "Doctor, I die hard, but I am not afraid to go. My breath cannot last long." A short time later, he expressed concern that he not be buried alive, "I am just going. Have me decently buried, and do not let my body be put into the vault in less than three days after I am dead. Do you understand?" "Yes, sir," the doctor replied. "'Tis well," answered Washington.

Daniel Webster (1782-1852)

"I still live."

Daniel Webster was a U.S. statesman and lawyer who became well known throughout the nation for his exceptional oratory and impassioned defense of the Constitution.

Herbert George "H. G." Wells (1866-1946)
"Go away. I'm all right."
H. G. Wells was an English writer and social theorist. One of his time's most influential writers, he, along with Jules Verne, is credited with inventing Science Fiction. His best-known novels, *The Invisible Man, The Time Machine*, and *The War of the Worlds* are still frequently read today, and his one-volume history of the world is recognized as the best ever compiled by a single author.

Oscar Wilde (1854-1900)
"Either the wallpaper goes, or I do."
Oscar Wilde was an Irish playwright, novelist, poet, author of short stories, and all-around degenerate. An outspoken socialist, anarchist, pacifist, and pedophile, Wilde was the defendant in a famous trial, where he defended his ongoing affair with a seventeen year-old boy named Robert Ross as "the love that dares not speak its name". How poetic. Wilde was convicted of "gross indecency" (less poetic perhaps, but much more accurate), and sentenced to two years of hard labor. After his release, and hardly rehabilitated, he dallied with "all the little boys on the Boulevard" and in his last letter to his boyfriend, Ross, Wilde laments, "Today I bade good-bye, with tears and one kiss, to the beautiful Greek boy . . . he is the nicest boy you ever introduced to me." Beautiful stuff, that. It was in the Left Bank hotel, while dying from syphilis, that he uttered his last words. Consider me a fan of the wallpaper.

Thomas Woodrow Wilson (1856-1924)
"I am ready."
Woodrow Wilson was a devout Presbyterian, intellectual, 28th President of the United States, and our Commander-In-Chief during World War I.

Henry Wirz, Captain, C.S.A. (1823-1865)
"This is too tight."
Captain Wirz was a Swiss-born Confederate officer who had the misfortune to be given command of the infamous Andersonville prison camp following his recovery from wounds received at the Battle of Seven Pines. Thousands of Union prisoners died from the poor conditions at Andersonville (as they did at nearly every other Civil War prison camp). Following the war, Wirz was tried for conspiring to "impair and injure the health and to destroy the lives of large numbers of Federal prisoners at Andersonville, and ordering or personally committing acts of assault or murder". Despite a complete lack of evidence Wirz was convicted and hung.

Hiram King "Hank" Williams (1923-1953)
"Nope."
Hank Williams is considered by all to be the Shakespeare of Country Music. His

lyrics were so haunting and filled with sad and beautiful imagery, that it is with great irony that, on Hank's last ride, when his driver stopped in Bristol, Virginia and asked him if he wanted anything to eat, Hank Williams, undeniably the greatest poet country music had ever known, said his last words on the planet, "Nope."

Malcolm X (1925-1965)
"Brothers! Brothers, please! Be cool, this is a house of peace!"
Malcolm X, born Malcolm Little, was an ex-convict, American Muslim minister, and a spokesman for the Nation Of Islam. On February 21, 1965, in Manhattan's Audubon Ballroom, Malcolm had just begun delivering a speech when a disturbance broke out in the crowd. Two men were staging a fight as a diversion, prior to shooting him. Malcolm was shot first in the chest with a sawed-off shotgun. Two other men charged the stage and fired handguns at Malcolm, who was shot sixteen times in all. All three men were captured, tried, and convicted. And all three killers were brothers of Malcolm's, members of the Nation Of Islam, the "religion of peace". Violent Muslims? Huge shock there.

Florenz Ziegfeld (1869-1932)
"Curtain! Fast music! Lights! Ready for the last finale! Great! The show looks good. The show looks good."
Florenz Ziegfeld was a famous Broadway producer whose musical reviews featured fantastic sets and beautiful women. He died hallucinating that he was directing one last show. In the 1936 Oscar winning movie, *The Great Ziegfeld*, William Powell plays Ziegfeld, and his last words are, *"I've got to have more steps! I need more steps! I've got to get higher! Higher!"*

EPITAPHS

Gracie Allen   George Burns
(1926-1964)   (1896-1996)

TOGETHER AGAIN

One of the most popular American comedy teams ever, George Burns and his wife, Gracie Allen, first performed together in vaudeville in 1922 and continued their act on radio and television until 1958, when illness forced Gracie's retirement. George's beloved Gracie died in 1964, but George continued to perform in movies and on television until his death at 100 in 1996.

Mel Blanc
(1908-1989)

THAT'S ALL, FOLKS!

Mel Blanc first achieved fame providing comical voices for radio programs to include The Jack Benny Program, Burns and Allen, and The Abbott and Costello Show. He found his true calling, though, as the voice of scores of cartoon characters during the golden years of American animation. Blanc's characters include Bugs Bunny, Daffy Duck, Porky Pig, Woody Woodpecker, Tweety Bird, Sylvester, Yosemite Sam, the Tasmanian Devil, Barney Rubble, Dino, Cosmo G. Spacely, Secret Squirrel, and many, many more. "That's all folks" is, of course, Porky Pig's sign-off for Warner Brothers cartoons.

George Washington Carver
(1864-1943)

HE COULD HAVE ADDED FORTUNE TO FAME,
BUT CARING FOR NEITHER,
HE FOUND HAPPINESS AND HONOR
IN BEING HELPFUL TO THE WORLD.

Botanical researcher and botanist, Carver worked at the Tuskegee Institute in Alabama, teaching former slaves farming techniques for self-sufficiency. He is most remembered for his research on, and promotion of, the peanut. He created about 100 existing industrial products from peanuts, including cosmetics, dyes, paints, plastics, gasoline, and nitroglycerin. Although his industrial products from peanuts excited the public imagination, none became a successful commercial product. There are many myths about Carver, especially the myth that his industrial products from peanuts played a major role in revolutionizing Southern agriculture.

Viscount Robert Stewart Castlereagh
(1769-1822)

POSTERITY WILL NE'ER SURVEY
A NOBLER GRAVE THAN THIS.
HERE LIES THE BONES OF CASTLEREAGH
STOP, TRAVELER, AND PISS.

Castlereagh was a productive and competent Anglo-Irish politician who represented the United Kingdom at Congress of Vienna and played an influential role in the passage of the Irish Act of Union. Despite his numerous successes and achievements, Castlereagh was despised by many. He began to exhibit signs of paranoia in 1821, and confided one of his long-standing, but unfounded worries to King George IV. He was afraid of being blackmailed for having homosexual contact with a soldier at a non-descript pub. King George advised him to consult with a physician for his paranoia. Instead, Castlereagh returned to his country estate and killed himself by cutting his own throat with a letter opener. Londoners jeered at his funeral procession, and cheered loudly when his casket was taken into Westminster Abbey for internment. Lord Byron, one of Castlereagh's many detractors, composed an epitaph that, mercifully, was not used.

Emily Dickinson
(1830-1886)

CALLED BACK

Although today Dickinson is one of the best-known American poets of the nineteenth century, she lived an isolated and secluded life and was practically unknown during her lifetime. Only seven of her 1800 poems were published while she lived, all anonymously.

Francis Scott Key "F. Scott" Fitzgerald
(1896-1940)

SO WE BEAT ON, BOATS, AGAINST THE CURRENT BORNE BACK CEASELESSLY INTO THE PAST

This is the last line in F. Scott Fitzgerald's classic novel, *The Great Gatsby*. Fitzgerald was an American writer, whose works are evocative of the Jazz Age, a term he coined himself. He is widely regarded as one of the twentieth century's great writers. Fitzgerald is considered a member of the Lost Generation, Americans born in the 1890s who came of age during World War I.

Benjamin Franklin
(1706-1790)

HERE LIES THE BODY OF
B. FRANKLIN, PRINTER
(LIKE THE COVER OF AN OLD BOOK
ITS CONTENTS TURN OUT AND
STRIPT OF ITS LETTERING & GILDING)
LIES HERE, FOOD FOR WORMS.
BUT THE WORK SHALL NOT BE LOST;
FOR IT WILL (AS HE BELIEV'D)
APPEAR ONCE MORE
IN A NEW AND MORE ELEGANT EDITION
REVISED AND CORRECTED
BY THE AUTHOR

Benjamin Franklin was one of the most important and influential Founding Fathers of the United States of America. Franklin was a leading author and printer, satirist, political theorist, politician, scientist, inventor, civic activist, statesman, diplomat, and revolutionary. As a scientist, he was a major figure in the Enlightenment and the history of physics for his discoveries and theories regarding electricity. He invented the lightning rod, bifocals, the Franklin stove, a carriage odometer, and a musical instrument Franklin called the "armonica" (the Italian word for harmony). He formed both the first public lending library in America and first fire department in Pennsylvania. He was an early proponent of colonial unity, and as a political writer and activist he, more than anyone, invented the idea of an American nation. As a diplomat during the American Revolution, he secured the French alliance that helped to make independence possible. When Ben Franklin was only 22 years old, he penned this epitaph. Sixty-four years later, he died peacefully in his sleep. His funeral in Philadelphia attracted over 20,000, which was at the time the largest gathering of mourners ever assembled in America. When Franklin's will was read, he left instructions not to use the epitaph, but to place a single line on his tombstone: "Benjamin and Deborah Franklin: 1790."

Robert Lee Frost
(1874-1963)

I HAD A LOVER'S QUARREL WITH THE WORLD

Robert Frost is a revered American poet. His work, frequently using themes from rural New England in the early 1900s, used the setting to examine complex social and philosophical themes. A popular and often-quoted poet, Frost was honored frequently during his lifetime, receiving four Pulitzer Prizes, and like many poets, Robert Frost wrote his own epitaph.

Herbert John "Jackie" Gleason
(1916-1987)

AND AWAY WE GO!

Jackie Gleason was an iconic American comedian, actor, and musician. One of the most popular stars of early television, Gleason was respected for both comedic and dramatic roles. However, his major legacy was his brash but lovable visual and verbal comedy styling, especially as delivered by the character Ralph Kramden on the pioneering sitcom, (and my own personal favorite), *The Honeymooners.* Jackie truly was what he always immodestly called himself, simply, "The Greatest." In the 1960s, he starred in *The Jackie Gleason Show*, filmed live from "the sun and fun capitol of the world, beautiful downtown Miami Beach", which became the second-highest rated television show in the country. Gleason would do an opening monologue, then, accompanied by "a little travelin' music" (*That's A-Plenty,* a Dixieland chestnut from 1914), he would shuffle toward the wing, clapping his hands and hollering, "And awa-a-aay we go!" The phrase became one of his trademarks and a national catchphrase.

Carl Jung
(1875-1961)

VOCATUS ATQUE NON VOCATUS DEUS ADERIT

(CALLED OR NOT CALLED GOD IS PRESENT)

Carl Jung was a Swiss psychiatrist, influential thinker, and founder of analytical psychology. His most notable ideas include the mystical concept of the Jungian archetype, the collective unconscious, and his theory of synchronicity. Jung emphasized the importance of balance and harmony. He cautioned that modern humans rely too heavily on science and logic and would benefit from integrating spirituality and appreciation of the unconscious realm.

Stan Laurel
(1980-1965)

IF ANYONE AT MY FUNERAL HAS A LONG FACE, I'LL NEVER SPEAK TO HIM AGAIN

In 1961, Laurel won a Lifetime Achievement Academy Award for his pioneering work in the field of comedy. He had achieved his lifelong dream as a comedian and had been involved in nearly 190 films. He spent his final years living in a small apartment in the Oceana Hotel in Santa Monica, California. Always gracious to fans, he spent much of this time meticulously answering fan mail. His phone number was listed in the Santa Monica telephone directory, and fans were amazed that they could simply dial the listed number and find themselves talking to Stan Laurel. Comic till the end, Laurel wrote his own epitaph.

Charles Augustus Lindbergh
(1902-1974)

IF I TAKE THE WINGS OF THE MORNING AND DWELL IN THE UTTERMOST PARTS OF THE SEA

The Lindbergh epitaph is taken from his favorite Psalm, Psalms 139:9, "If I take the wings of the morning and dwell in the uttermost parts of the sea, even there Your hand shall lead me and Your right hand shall hold me." Charles Lindbergh, known as "Lucky Lindy" and "The Lone Eagle", was an American hero, famous for the first solo, non-stop flight across the Atlantic Ocean. Lindbergh made history, flying from New York to Paris in 1927, in his equally famous plane, the *Spirit Of St. Louis*. In the ensuing deluge of fame, Lindbergh became the world's best-known aviator. James Stewart portrayed Lindbergh in the biographical motion picture, *The Spirit Of St. Louis* (1957), directed by Billy Wilder.

In an incident widely known as the "Lindbergh Kidnapping", the Lindbergh's first child, Charles III, was kidnapped at 20 months of age from their home in 1932. A $50,000 ransom was paid, but the infant was not returned. After a massive investigation, the baby's lifeless body was found, and two years later, a German convict and prison escapee, who had entered the United States illegally (sound familiar?) was arrested for kidnapping and murder. The trial, conviction, and execution of Bruno Hauptmann gained international infamy, and became known as "The Crime of the Century".

Lindbergh's speeches and writings later in life emphasized his love of both technology and nature, and a lifelong belief that "all the achievements of mankind have value only to the extent that they preserve and improve the quality of life." In honor of Charles and his wife Anne Morrow Lindbergh's vision of achieving balance between the technological advancements they helped pioneer, and the preservation of the human and natural environments, the Lindbergh Award was established in 1978. Each year since 1978, the Lindbergh Foundation has given the award to recipients whose work has made a significant contribution toward that concept of "balance".

Roger Eugene Maris
(1934-1985)
61/61
AGAINST ALL ODDS

Roger Maris grew up, a quiet kid, in Fargo, North Dakota. He was signed to the fabled New York Yankees in 1959, and in 1960, he led the league in slugging, RBIs, extra base hits, and total bases. He also won a Gold Glove and was named the American League's Most Valuable Player. In spite of all this success, the New York fans and press couldn't stand him. This was due to his introverted, "Aw shucks" Mid-Western background, and his lack of witticisms and one-liners to feed to the press. Maris just couldn't compete with Yogi Berra, Billy Martin, and Mickey Mantle when came to the media, and New York was a media machine. Unfortunately for Roger, he just played baseball. The following year, Maris and Mantle both attacked the revered Babe Ruth's long-standing and untouchable record of 60 home runs in a single season. The press and fans openly rooted against Maris and for Mantle.

On top of his lack of popular press coverage, Maris' chase for 61 hit another roadblock totally out of his control: along with adding two teams to the league, Major League Baseball had added 8 games to the schedule. In the middle of the season, baseball commissioner Ford Frick announced that unless Ruth's record was broken in the first 154 games of the season, the new record would be shown in the record books as having been set in 162 games while the previous record set in 154 games would also be shown. It is an urban legend, probably invented by New York sportswriter Dick Young, that an asterisk would be used to distinguish the new record. Commissioner Frick failed to consider that Ruth never had to play night games, or travel back and forth to the West Coast. According to *The Baseball Hall of Shame,* Frick made the ruling because, during his days as a newspaper reporter, he had been a close friend of Ruth's.

When Mantle went down with a leg injury late in the season, the New York fans and sportswriters continued to opine loudly that Maris would not eclipse their beloved Bambino's total. Maris became so affected by the pressure of the Babe's record, the constant hate mail and death threats, and his treatment by the local press, that even his hair started coming out in clumps. After being maligned so unfairly, for so long, Maris finally and flatly refused to talk to the press. That made matters worse. Throughout the spectacle that was the '61 season, and his chasing Ruth's record, Roger maintained his cool and his silence, which seemed to further infuriate his detractors. Maris failed to reach 61 in 154 games (he had only 59 after 154 games). He broke the record, hitting his 61st, on the last day of the season before only a few thousand fans in Yankee Stadium.

No asterisk was subsequently used in any record books – Major League baseball itself had no official record book, and Frick later acknowledged that there never was official qualification of Maris' accomplishment. However, Maris remained bitter about the experience. Speaking at the 1980 All-Star game, he said of that season, "They acted as though I was doing something wrong, poisoning the record books or something. Do you know what I have to show for 61 home runs? Nothing. Exactly nothing."

Roger Maris died in December 1985 of lymphoma, and is currently not in the Baseball Hall Of Fame, despite his two MVP awards and despite the fact that he held the major league home run record for three years longer than the Babe. The home run record, like all of baseball, is now a sham. The major league's hallowed home run record has been broken twice in the last ten years. Unfortunately, there are no asterisks used for players breaking records with steroids and human growth hormone.

Henry Louis "H. L." Mencken
(1880-1956)

IF AFTER I DEPART THIS VALE
YOU EVER REMEMBER ME
AND HAVE THOUGHT TO
PLEASE MY GHOST
FORGIVE SOME SINNER
AND WINK YOUR EYE
AT SOME HOMELY GIRL

H. L. Mencken was an American journalist, essayist, magazine editor, satirist, acerbic critic of American life and culture, and a student of American English. Mencken is perhaps best remembered today for *The American Language*, a multi-volume study of how the English language is spoken in the United States and his satirical reporting on Tennessee's Scopes Trial, which he named the "Monkey" trial. Mencken suggested this epitaph in *The Smart Set*. It is inscribed on a plaque in the lobby of The Baltimore Sun.

Leroy "Satchel" Paige
(1906-1982)

HOW TO STAY YOUNG

1. AVOID FRIED MEATS WHICH ANGRY UP THE BLOOD.
2. IF YOUR STOMACH DISPUTES YOU, LIE DOWN AND PACIFY IT WITH COOL THOUGHTS.
3. KEEP THE JUICES FLOWING BY JANGLING AROUND GENTLY AS YOU MOVE.
4. GO VERY LIGHT ON THE VICES, SUCH AS CARRYING ON IN SOCIETY. THE SOCIAL RAMBLE AIN'T RESTFUL.
5. AVOID RUNNING AT ALL TIMES.
6. DON'T LOOK BACK. SOMETHING MIGHT BE GAINING ON YOU.

Satchel Paige was one of the greatest baseball pitchers of all time. He played professional or semi-pro ball for over for over thirty-three years, his best seasons being with the Kansas City Monarchs of the old Negro League. Paige claimed to have mastered thirteen different, highly unusual pitches including the Hesitation Pitch (which was eventually ruled illegal), the Bat Dodger, the Four-Day Creeper, the Bee Ball, and the Two Hump Blooper. A baseball barnstormer and legend in his own lifetime, Paige pitched in the 1953 Major League All-Star Game at forty-seven years of age.

Buford H. Pusser
(1937-1974)

HE WALKED TALL

Buford Pusser was a legendary Tennessee sheriff who, despite repeated violent attacks, including one that killed his wife, used his wooden club to virtually single-handedly clean up the organized crime in McNairy County that had been long sanctioned by the local Democratic political machine. His story has directly inspired several books and movies, and at least one TV series. Joe Don Baker portrayed Pusser in 1973's *Walking Tall.*

Will Rogers
(1879-1935)

IF YOU LIVE LIFE RIGHT
DEATH IS A JOKE
AS FAR AS FEAR IS CONCERNED

Will Rogers was a Cherokee-American cowboy, comedian, humorist, social commentator, vaudeville performer and actor. When Will Rogers died in a plane crash with Wiley Post in 1935, he was the most read newspaper columnist in America, hosted the most listened to radio show in America, and was the number one male box office star in America.

George Herman "Babe" Ruth
(1895-1948)

MAY THAT DIVINE SPIRIT
THAT ANIMATED BABE RUTH
TO WIN THE CRUCIAL GAME OF LIFE
INSPIRE THE YOUTH OF AMERICA

Babe Ruth, also popularly known as "Babe", "The Bambino", and "The Sultan of Swat", was named the greatest baseball player in history in several surveys and rankings, his home run hitting prowess and charismatic personality made him a larger than life figure while a New York Yankee during the "Roaring Twenties".

He was the first player to hit 60 home runs in one season (1927), a record that stood for 34 years until broken by Roger Maris in 1961. Ruth's lifetime total of 714 home runs at his retirement in 1935 was a record for 39 years, until broken by Hank Aaron in 1974. The Babe died from cancer in 1948, shortly after he attended the premier showing of *The Babe Ruth Story*. John Cardinal Spellman wrote Ruth's epitaph.

William Shakespeare
(1564-1616)

GOOD FRIEND, FOR JESUS SAKE FORBEAR
TO DIG THE DUST ENCLOSED HERE
BLEST BE THE MAN
THAT SPARES THESE STONES
AND CURST BE HE
THAT MOVES MY BONES

William Shakespeare was an English poet and playwright, widely regarded as the greatest writer in the history of the English language, and the world's pre-eminent dramatist. Shakespeare is buried at the Holy Trinity Church in Stratford. It is said that he personally composed his epitaph.

Myra Maybelle Shirley "Belle" Starr
(1848-1889)

SHED NOT THE BITTER TEAR
NOR GIVE THE HEART TO VAIN REGRET
TIS BUT THE CASKET THAT LIES HERE
THE GEM THAT FILLED IT SPARKLES YET

According to legend, the Bandit Queen and outlaw, Belle Starr had been a spy, a Confederate General, the brains behind many outlaw gang, and the consort of nearly every western fugitive including all of the Younger Brothers. In 1889, she was killed by a shotgun blast while horseback riding. Although there were multiple suspects including both of her children, her killer was never identified.

Unknown U.S. Soldier
Arlington National Cemetery

HERE RESTS IN HONORED GLORY
AN AMERICAN SOLDIER
KNOWN BUT TO GOD

Unknown U.S. Soldier
Guadalcanal

WHEN YOU GO HOME
TELL THEM OF US AND SAY
FOR THEIR TOMORROW
WE GAVE OUR TODAY

Unknown U.S. Soldier
Guadalcanal

AND WHEN HE GETS TO HEAVEN
TO SAINT PETER HE WILL TELL:
ONE MORE MARINE REPORTING, SIR!
I'VE DONE MY TIME IN HELL.

A beautiful poem, written by W. H. Auden, *Epitaph For An Unknown Soldier*, goes like this:

To save your world, you asked this man to die.
Would this man, could he see you now, ask why?

Hiram King "Hank" Williams
(1923-1953)

THANK YOU FOR ALL THE
LOVE YOU GAVE ME
THERE COULD BE NO ONE STRONGER
THANK YOU FOR THE
MANY BEAUTIFUL SONGS
THEY WILL LIVE LONG AND LONGER

Hank Williams' cold cold heart finally stopped on a cold New Year's night somewhere between Knoxville, Tennessee and Canton, Ohio. Williams, scheduled to perform a show in Canton, and unable to fly due to bad weather, had been injected with B-12 and morphine by a quack doctor in Knoxville, and was carried into the back seat of his Cadillac for the trip. After a stop in Bristol, Virginia, where Hank uttered his last words, his chauffeur stopped again in Oak Hill, West Virginia. There he discovered Williams dead in the back seat, along with the lyrics to an unfinished song, "Then Came That Fateful Day."

MURDERER'S ROW

LAST WORDS OF CONDEMNED CRIMINALS AT THEIR EXECUTION

George Appel
"Well, gentlemen, you are about to see a baked apple."

Jeffrey Barney
"I'm tingling all over."

James French
"How about this for a headline? French fries."

Gary Gilmore
"Let's do it."

Thomas J. Grasso
"I did not get my Spaghetti-Os. I got spaghetti. I want the press to know this."

Edward E. Johnson
"I guess no one's going to call."

Richard A. Loeb
"I think I'm going to make it."

Dr. William Palmer
(as he stepped onto the trapdoor of the gallows)
"Is this safe?"

James Roges
(when asked if he had any last request before facing the firing squad)
"Why yes, a bullet proof vest."

John Spenkelink
"Capital punishment; them without the capital – get the punishment."

MARCH 2008

30

THE CURTAIN FALLS

On November 9, 1963, thirteen days before President Kennedy was killed, Bobby Darin gave his final, farewell nightclub performance at the Flamingo Hotel in Las Vegas. This song, *The Curtain Falls*, was his last number.

I wrote the first Lightnin' Lowdown in March 2005 (I posted it in April), three years ago, almost to the day, of this writing. During that time, a whole lot has happened to me, and for me, in my personal life, and in my professional life. The thing that has most impacted my life, both personally and professionally, was saying farewell to nightclub performances. The very first chapter of the Lightnin' Lowdown was written in response to my leaving the last of those old haunts behind. You see, for years I thought that since bars and nightclubs were where live music was being played (and where musicians were being hired), that bars and nightclubs were where I had to play my music to earn my living. But I was wrong. And when I stepped out of that world, in a leap of faith, my whole life opened up in new, exciting, and unbelievable ways for my music, my family, and me.

Now, three years later, I am playing more music, more often, for more money, and more happily, than I ever thought possible. The new and improved Lightnin' Charlie plays good music for good people. And all I had to do was let go and let God. He's put me here. He took me off the bottom. And He's not done with me yet.

Here we are at the beginning of a new chapter. It's been wonderful having a friend like you to tell all this to. Thanks for coming along. It's been great sharing the ride with you, but now, the curtain falls.

Off comes the makeup
Off comes the clown's disguise
The curtain's fallin'
The music softly dies.

*But I hope your smilin'
As you're filin' out the door
As they say in this biz
That's all there is...there isn't anymore.*

*We've shared a moment
And as the moment ends
I've got a funny feelin'
We're parting now as friends.*

*Your cheers and laughter will linger after
They've torn down these dusty walls
If I had this to do again
And the evening were new again
I would spend it with you again
But now the curtain falls.*

*Your cheers and laughter will linger after
They've torn down these dusty walls
People say I was made for this
Nothin' else would I trade for this
And to think I get paid for this...*

Goodnight Lightnin' Bugs.

God bless you,
Lightnin' Charlie

31

THE INDIAN ROPE TRICK
- OR -
AND LIKE A GOOD NEIGHBOR – SANSKRIT IS THERE
- OR -
HOW MUCH IS THAT DOGGIE IN THE RICKSHAW?

I try to be a good neighbor. In the nine years my wife and I have lived in our home, we have enjoyed our neighborhood, and have become fast and dear friends with our neighbors. Well...with two out of three.

We have wonderful neighbors to our north and south. But it's the luxurious rental house to our west – and its despicable, disgusting renters from the east – that is the problem, and is the subject of our saga.

An ancient Hindu proverb says, "These three take crooked ways: carts, boats, and musicians." But for the purposes of our story, and for the sake of the truth (and because the storyteller happens to be a musician!), let's change this thusly:

"These three take crooked ways: carts, boats, and physicians."

A wealthy Indian cardiologist named Raj and his wife Maarga, who immigrated here from that lovely land, the one nestled cozily between other dreamy vacation hotspots Iran, Pakistan, Viet Nam, and Bangladesh, have been a bigger nightmare to us (and to all our other neighbors) than if a colony of lepers had moved in. We need neighbors like these like Nancy Pelosi needs a Halloween mask.

In these trying times, that try men's souls, it is impossible to be critical of anyone who has an ethnicity other than White Anglo-Saxon Protestant (as I have lamented in this book, it's always open season on them, especially the male ones). Say anything against a person of color, or a person who has immigrated here – legally or illegally – from a foreign country, and you are automatically and instantly labeled a racist. As I have beat the drum loudly on this subject in the preceding pages, I see no need to go further into it here. But suffice it to say that, again, I am not a racist. This isn't about race. It's about Raj. Although I have never been a fan of curry, cobras, or Nehru jackets, I have never had anything against the people of India (with the possible exception that they helped to turn The Beatles from a guitar band that wore suits and played great rock 'n' roll into sitar-playing, consciousness-expanded, bearded and barefooted hallucinating gurus. But other than that...

Raj means "king" in Sanskrit (very apt), and his wife Maarga's name comes from "aghoramaarga" – a horrible sect of Indian Saivas (worshippers of Siva), who, according to Wikipedia, "eat loathsome food and are addicted to disgusting practices" (enormously apt as well). After doing a bit of online research on the Saivas and the ghastly Aghoris sect (after which Maarga's names comes from), I will only say that the Wikipedia definition above is the understatement of the century and say no more. Please trust me on this...you don't want to know anymore about it.

Dr. Raj and Maarga have two grown sons (both in medical school) and one dreadfully out of control and overgrown baby – a 100 pound Golden Retriever named Asim, (pronounced Ah-seem') which means "boundless, limitless" in Sanskrit (this is so apt it defies the imagination). Asim has become a neighborhood nuisance of the highest order, but Asim is not to blame. Setting, and enforcing, boundaries and limits with regard to one's animals is the responsibility of the owner and an absolute necessity, but that is completely lost on Raj and Maarga. They are the animals of this story in the true sense of the word (my apologies to animals). As you shall soon see, the personal depravity of Raj and Maarga is limitless and boundless as well.

I first met our new neighbors in my front yard as they were walking their baby (without a leash). I had just walked my Mother (also without a leash) to her car, helping her to back out of my driveway into the maniacal street below. As Mom was leaving, she had given me a decorative, stand-up bible that was open to the 23rd Psalm. So I was holding this bible in my hand, as I politely introduced myself to the couple I recognized as the ones who had just moved into the house behind me. The first thing I noticed about them was the thick black and grey fur protruding a good inch and a half from inside both ears of the gentleman (this will be the last time I refer to him in this manner), and the large ornamental blood-red dot between the eyes of an extremely misshapen and unattractive woman, who was nonetheless festooned from head to toe with very large and ornate jewelry.

A pretty good likeness of Raj,
except that this fellow's personal hygiene
habits have Dr. Charmin beat (notice no ear fur).

In spite of their appearance, I welcomed them to the neighborhood, and told them if there was ever anything they needed, to give us a call. I gave him a business card with my cellphone number on it. These were my first and second mistakes (big ones). Raj pocketed my card, and then introduced himself thusly: "I am Raj Charmin, a physician." (hmmm....did I look sick?) Then Dr. Charmin (just like the toilet tissue...again amazingly apt) introduced his wife Maarga, who was dressed in the traditional colorful Hindu garb (multi-colored garments really hide the dirt) and who made no effort to even make eye contact. That was fine with me...direct eye contact from Maarga probably turns one to stone. And then, last but not least, Raj Charmin (the physician) proudly presented their "beautiful baby boy...Asim". This whole exchange (along with the ear fur) should've rang some kind of a bell with me that I was talking to some kind of a nut, but alas, it's hindsight that's 20-20. Raj then asked me which roads were safe for them to walk Asim (without a leash) in the neighborhood. My third mistake (which I would also later live to regret) was telling them to avoid the dangerous street running up from the corner at my house – the same street I made famous in Chapter 26. Satisfied that they had met the neighborhood sucker (a guy in a cowboy hat holding a ceramic bible), they hurried off, chasing Asim, and the next time I saw Raj the physician, it was Thanksgiving weekend; and there was Charmin, ringing my front door bell, and holding a cherry pie.

'Beware of Hindus bearing gifts' is now my mantra. But at the time, I was too naive (and too anxious to be a good neighbor) to know. It is not every day that I am awakened early in the morning to see an Indian at my door with pie. So seizing the opportunity (carpe diem!), I opened the door and invited him in. This was mistake number four, but I made so many mistakes in this fiasco that I will cease to count them any further. Raj handed me the Marie Callender cherry pie, saying what good pie Marie Callender makes. I agreed and offered to make us some coffee (I am a coffee addict and cannot form a single cogent thought before ingesting a cup or two). Raj declined and, sitting down on the sofa, began telling me about how he and Maarga ("and the baby") had moved here from Salt Lake City, Utah ("Did you know the Marie Callender company is based out of Salt Lake City?"), and how they didn't know anyone in East Tennessee. He talked about his two sons ("in medical school") named Pankaja and Pitambara (which means "born of mud" and "yellow garments" respectively). Sounds like names for the incontinent (extremely apt yet again – it's amazing how Hindus can know the soul and character of their children when they name them as babies. Perhaps it's karma, but these names are all so accurate and right on the money!). I happen to know these Sanskrit names very well because they came up on my cellphone many dozens of times over the next few days and regrettably, I've memorized them (I'm now considering hypnotism to get rid of them). Raj continued chatting, saying that one of his sons – I don't remember which one – probably Yellow Garments – had carried (and was then given) the Olympic torch in the Beijing

Olympics. But a burglar subsequently broke into their home and stole it. I thought this was a shame and said so. Who breaks into a home in Salt Lake City and steals an Olympic torch? A Mormon on Meth? And what did they do with it...pawn it? These, and the good doctor's other long-winded, various and sundry subjects of conversation, might have been more interesting to me, had it not been for the fact that I was still in my bathrobe and without even a sip of coffee. After fifteen minutes or so of listening to his small talk (and stealing glimpses of his ear fur), I got up and suggested moving into the kitchen, where I could get to the bean grinder.

So Raj Charmin M.D. and me (me being at a slight disadvantage in my bathrobe, fuzzy slippers and only a bachelor's degree) went into the kitchen where Raj spilled the beans (not literally...if he had spilled my coffee beans – or if he had caused me to spill them – before I could get them from the grinder to the pot – from the pot into my mug – and from my mug into my veins – I would've thrown him out of my house – neighbor or no neighbor – and you would not be enjoying this story right now). No, Raj figuratively spilled the beans by getting to the point of his friendly little visit (finally) with the tried and true old preface for suckers: "Oh by the way..." Dr. Raj began by saying, "My wife and I have serious problem." I thought, "Oh no!" He went on to explain that he and his wife were "going out of town and we don't know anyone else here...we had someone who was supposed to help but now they can't do it...we don't know what to do..." I had thought that this was some life or death struggle he was having and I was perplexed as to why he was opening up so to me. Raj nimbly continued his plea, "We have person for overnight, but the person we had for day, they're moving house and can't do it". Oh. Is that it? In spite of the fact that I was operating (pun intended) without even a sip of caffeine, and in no way in full control of my faculties, I could still foggily figure out where this was going now, and sensing the opportunity to be a good neighbor and show some real Christian loving-kindness to my fellow man, I interjected (to put him out of his misery), "Do you need someone to take care of Asim?" Raj nervously answered yes. According to the curry man, they had someone who would be at their house overnight while they were gone, but the person who was supposed to take the day watch had backed out. I later learned that there was never anyone else who had agreed to house or dog sit for them, day or night. These were just two of the Indian witch doctor's many outright lies to me. I was being Hoodoo'ed by the Hindu Man (apologies to Junior Wells).

I don't have time to take proper care of my own family but I figured...what the heck? I'll make time to help out a neighbor. I had taken care of another neighbor's dog for them when they went out of town for an overnighter. I assumed Raj and Maarga were probably going to Gatlinburg or Nashville for the weekend, and now in the 11th hour their dog-sitter has backed out. This poor Indian (I mean rich Indian) was all alone in East Tennessee and needed a friend. And I could help him out. I could just hop the fence in my backyard, let the doggie out their back door, let him pee and poop real quick, put him back in the house, throw some food and water in his bowl, and split. No big deal. I'd be back home in 3 or 4 minutes. Surely I could make that sacrifice for a fellow human being for a couple of days. Three days tops. "How long are you going to be gone?" I asked, anxiously watching the coffee pot slowly fill up, drip by drip. "Three weeks", said the Indian doctor. "Three *weeks?*" asked the Tennessee sucker. "Yes, my wife and I are going to New Delhi. We leave tomorrow. If you could come by tonight, I'll give you key and show you where baby's food is, and let Asim get used to you a little bit."

I couldn't believe this. Had this person that I had just met and had spoken to for maybe two minutes on the street just come to me (bearing pie) and asked me to take care of his dog for three weeks? I wouldn't ask my best friend to do that for me; or a member of my family. I remember stammering, "Raj, I'm glad to help you out, but I am so busy right now...I've got gigs every day...sometimes several per day...my Mom is coming up to stay with our baby (human girl)...I've got major construction going on downstairs..." No response from the doctor (did the ear fur affect his hearing?). "But I guess I could hop the fence and feed him..." I faltered, "If it's just once a day, on the way to my gigs..." "Oh that's great Charlie! We have someone staying in the night", lied the doctor through his coffee-brown teeth (everything was looking like coffee to me at this point), "so if you can let Asim out and feed him in the morning, that will be fine. Then Dr. Raji added, "We appreciate this so much." As Raj Charmin, physician, made his quick getaway, I realized he never mentioned paying me to do this (not that all the money begged in all the boroughs of Bombay would be enough to compensate me for what was to come). What kind of devious, manipulating, medical malfunction was this?

My coffee was finally ready, and as I slurped my first sips of sanity, I was left alone to contemplate – soberly at last – what I had just gotten myself into. What had I done? I was grief-stricken. I felt sick all over. Is there a doctor in the house? Had I hallucinated what just happened?

[sung to the tune of *Strawberry Fields Forever* by The Beatles]
Let me take you down 'cause I'm going to...
Cherry Pie Fields...nothing is real...

Let's take a short break here...a little intermezzo if you will. A pause for the cause. A little levity before the gravity of what Our Hero has just committed himself to sinks in. Because it gets worse. So here are a couple of quickies...

> A Jehovah's Witness knocks on my door early Saturday morning. I open the door, invite him in, lead him to the dining room table, and ask him to sit down. After pouring him a cup of coffee, I sit down across from him and say, "So what would you like to talk about?" "I have no idea," he says. "I've never gotten this far before!"

> I went to see my cardiologist the other day to have him to check my heart. After running a battery of tests, he comes into the examination room and says, "You don't have to worry about your heart Charlie – your heart is going to last you for the rest of your life!

Ah yes a breath of fresh air...and stale jokes. Anyway, back to our story...

This gauntlet was thrown down Friday, the day after Thankgiving of last year. To say that November and December of 2010 was a busy time for me would be an understatement on the level of saying that American politics can be a slightly dirty business. I was in the middle of a particularly hectic run of gigs, and was already anticipating what was to be an extremely grueling December leading up to Christmas. I felt like a dizzy, tired, old prize fighter, gearing up for a fight that I wasn't sure I would even survive, let alone win, and now I've volunteered for more duty? I was going to need a cardiologist by the time this one got back from New Delhi (and I wonder if he works for free like he expects his dog-sitters to do?). Allow me to illustrate just how busy I was when Raj entered my life and living room. I had just finished up a stretch in November, when I played 10 shows in 13 days, culminating with Thanksgiving (complete with all the trimmings – three dinners in three different states – and traveling with three kids). And in December, while performing my act of Christian charity for the Charmins, I had 21 shows scheduled in 23 days. By the way, my wife works full time and we don't have a nanny or a maid (probably never shall). The rest of my December itinerary looked like this:

- Our baby girl (a real human baby – not a canine) was turning one year old and we were planning her a big first birthday party
- Our son was turning ten years old and we were planning his big birthday party too (not to be outdone by a child of one)
- Christmas (a little Christian holiday replete with shopping, gifts, and more traveling – not celebrated by Hindus)

- Completing a home renovation to our finished basement that involved lots of sheetrock, new ceilings, paint, new carpeting, new doors, new moldings, new recessed lighting, a complete whole house electrical service change, whole house hard-wired smoke alarms, insulation, and wall-to-wall custom built-in shelving
- Throw in an early winter that was record-breaking for snow, ice, and cold temperatures, just to make otherwise simple things difficult to impossible.

If you, the reader, are a parent (and you're not really a parent if you only have one child, because with only one child, you're always going to know who did it), you will understand, appreciate, and feel my pain. If you are a parent, you will realize that, in addition to the above itinerary (which would cripple a man half my age), was also added the relentless sufferings and mind-numbing hardships of the ordinary day-to-day raising of our three children, ages nine, eight, and one. If you are not a parent, then you won't.

That evening, I walked over to the Charmin house. I was still under the (false) impression that there would be someone spending the nights there and that my services would only be required once a day. Once inside, I became aware (through sight and smell) that housekeeping was certainly not the Charmin's strong suit. Apparently Asim the Boundless had no boundaries inside or out. There were what appeared to be (and smelled like) dirty clothes, shoes, socks, and an assortment of food stuffs (in various stages of decomposition) all over the living room floor. I shuddered to think of this man opening someone's chest cavity and sticking his hands in. But I guess that's why malpractice insurance is so high (and the doctors simply pass that savings on to their customers). Their rambunctious quadruped "baby" (without limits) was jumping up on me and tearing through the house, completely feral as usual. As Asim, the wild animal, was running across the sofa, picking up cushions in his teeth, barking, slinging spit, and tearing through the house, Mother Maarga was taking charge of the situation. She responded with a blood-curdling half scream, half yodel in her savage third-world falsetto that my neighbors and I have since come to know way too well. Let me explain...Each time Asim is outside, running amok, me and every other living soul within a quarter mile of our house is treated to this Sikh ghetto wail. And believe me, it's like a thousand fingernails on a thousand blackboards and everybody in the neighborhood jumps to attention when she does it. Everybody except for Asim, of course, who keeps right on doing whatever he was doing without the slightest twitch of acknowledgement. Remember, Asim is Sanskrit for "limitless, boundless". He is a free spirit who will not allow himself to be reigned in. And Raj and Maarga (please don't squeeze the Charmins) are too inconsiderate and too insane to bother. Obviously putting this carnal howl into print is phonetically impossible and is way beyond my talents as a writer to reproduce or transliterate it, but it goes very fast and very long and sounds something like this...

"AH-LEEEEEE-LEE-LEE-LEE-LEE-LEE-LEE-LEE-LEE-LEE-LEE-LEE!!!"

The only other time in my life I ever heard a yowl like this was while watching the news after 9/11. They were broadcasting a video shot live on the streets of some Arab nation where the peace-loving Muslims had taken to the streets in a wild celebration of all the innocent American civilians murdered in the Twin Towers. I remember a close-up of an Arab woman in burqa, who was squealing this same squall, only with unbridled ecstasy, teeming with joy at what her heroes had accomplished. Maybe that's why every time I hear it, I feel the urge to decapitate the source of it. But since I am a Christian (and not a Muslim), I am able to restrain myself from actually doing it. But my willpower cannot last forever.

Dr. Raj and Maarga the Dog-Mother began my tour of duty by showing me Asim's upholstered day-bed, which was situated in the middle of the living room, right in front of two large bay windows (the ones looking out at the stunning mountain view – the place where most people – sane people, that is – would put a sofa or chairs for *humans* to take in the lovely view). Maarga orders me to open the drapes for Asim in the morning, and then close them at dusk. This wasn't on my job description. Then on our way to the kitchen, I'm taken past a gigantic wall portrait of the four-armed Vishnu, who will without a doubt be watching over me and making sure I don't dodge any dog-duties (another nice one!). It strikes me that both of the Charmin's objects of worship, Vishnu the god and Asim the dog, have something striking in common – Vishnu's four arms, and Asim's four legs. And if you happen to be dyslexic, you can't tell any difference! Hey-Hey! Bucket-o-fish! God... Dog...Dyslexic? Thank you Ladies and Germs...I'm here all week.

[Editor's note: For those of you who didn't get the previous joke, maybe tonight, when you lie down in bed, you'll think about it, and get it. And if you go to bed and think of me, you shouldn't even be allowed to go to bed!]

Vishnu

Anyway...on to the kitchen. Achtung! Maarga shows me the jugs of distilled, filtered water that I am to provide for their baby. You see, Asim doesn't drink regular tap water (or filtered tap water) like us white trash. Asim gets only distilled, filtered water, purchased in gallon jugs (mommy and daddy can afford it). Then Mrs. Charmin points out the dry dog food. Misshapen Maarga then shows me several large Ziploc freezer bags filled with boiled baby carrots (for baby) in the refrigerator. *What?* She is barking (no pun intended) these orders at me in very broken English and madly pointing her fingers (which, like her wrists and neck, are covered with 24-karat gold and jewels) and jangling loudly like the bells of a gypsy tambourine. I am repeating my orders back to her, military-style, trying to make sure I understand her...

Maarga: "You put dry dog food in bowl. Two scoops. Then boiled carrots."

Me: "I put the boiled carrots in the bowl on top of the dry food?"

Maarga: "No! No! No! After he *finish* dry food. *Then* you give carrots."

Ya vol mein Fuehrer! I've got my mind right boss! Asim gets boiled carrots, al dente, ala carte, and on the side, and only at the *conclusion* of his first course. I am beginning to stare at the red dot on Maarga's forehead and see a target.

> Maarga: "Here is doggie biscuits. Give *one half* when you come in.
> And *one half* when you leave. So he know you are leaving."
>
> Me [muttering now]: "One half bye-bye biscuit when I leave..."

Keep in mind that this is how they are treating someone they just met, while receiving the largest favor done to strangers since Calvary. Now Maarga is upping the ante some more, sensing wounded prey, or complete gullibility, or both, telling me it's also my responsibility to get their mail, water the house plants, make sure to turn the porch lights on and off (what happened to the person spending the nights there?), take the trash can out to the street on Thursday night, all the while pointing and jangling, yowling and howling, and I must be in some state of shock (because I *know* I am not in the state of Tennessee anymore Dorothy). All the while, Raj is jabbering away to her in that beautiful, lilting Sanskrit language of theirs – obviously delegating – and Maarga then reluctantly turns over the reigns of this insane invective to her more polished, but equally dastardly husband (that's *dastardly*...I'm trying to watch my language here).

The only known photograph of Maarga smiling

Now it's Raj's turn at bat. Doctor Ear Fur begins by showing me the leash (unused) and giving me the rundown of the dog's daily medications. Yes, that's right. Daily prescription medications. On the countertop, Doctor Butt-Paper...I mean Charmin (they're synonymous right?) had lined up four or five prescription bottles of pills. Doctor's orders were stern and terse and went like this...

"This *arthritis* medicine. You give *one* tablet, *three* times a day."

"This *bowel* medicine. One *half* tablet, *twice* a day."

"This *worm* medicine. *Two* pills, *four* times a day, for *one* week."

"This *multi-vitamin*. *One* pill, *once* a day."

My head was positively swooning at this point and I know the question you are asking yourselves. Why didn't I just say no? Why didn't I politely (or otherwise) excuse myself and say, "Look, Raj. I cannot commit to all this. I am much too busy and this is way too much responsibility, and you are just going to have to find someone else."

I don't have a decent explanation as to why an otherwise clear-headed and un-shy guy like me would allow himself to be cornered and taken advantage of to this extent. I can only say that I was blitzkrieged by the magnitude of their chutzpah. This was gall to an exponential level. The unprecedented (in my experience) sum total of their nerve and the degree of their imposition, coupled with the lack of any consideration (or compensation) for someone they had just met basically numbed me into dumb acquiescence. It was kissin' cousins to Hitler's 'Big Lie Theory' (the more colossal the lie – the more likely people will accept it). So Raj and Maarga just kept piling it on. I bet that lots of otherwise rational German people, post World War Two, were probably scratching their heads in much the same manner as I am now, wondering how they could've been taken in by such an obvious lunatic. But also in my defense, is my suspicion that Raj came by his spellbinding aura honestly – he had undoubtedly been raised by street snake-charmers who trained him as a child to follow in their foul footsteps. But when student loans to American medical schools became so readily available to foreigners, and due to criminal Affirmative Action quotas, Raj the road beggar slithered down his rope, and opted for a more lucrative career in cardiology. The Slumdog Millionaire had me under his spell like a Calcutta cobra coming out of a dirty basket. And he didn't even play a flute.

Boy Raji and two assistants in training
(obviously upper class kids judging by their attire)

I got the house key and left to lick my wounds (after washing my hands). Needless to say, my wife was not at all happy about all these doings either. I hardly have time to be a husband and father – let alone a servant to the Charmins. And Beth (my Mrs.) was beside me the following day when my cellphone rang. We were in line at the checkout after an invigorating shopping trip through Wal-Mart. And behold! My heart has wings…it was Raj.

Me: "Hello?"
Raj: "Hello Charlie?"
Me: "Yes…"
Raj: "We are at airport and have just heard of a slight change of plans."
Me: "Oh…"
Raj: "The person who was going to stay overnight cannot do it. So we called Sandra next door to us, and she agreed to take Asim to her house overnight. We know how busy you are. You can pick him up there at 7AM and take him back to our house."
Me: "What? Listen Raj…this is getting to be just a bit more than I…"
Raj: "Charlie, our flight is boarding and I've got to go. But I gave my sons your cellphone number so they will be calling to check in with you. Bye."

The newest victim in our saga, Sandra, is Raj and Maarga's neighbor on the other side of their house. She is probably in her sixties and, with the exception of having a little dog of her own, lives alone. Sandra is homebound and had just undergone hip replacement surgery on one hip, was scheduled to have surgery on her other hip, and was having home health rehabilitation visits from a physical therapist. Now these lying pariahs have suckered Sandra into this nightmare too.

pa·ri·ah - (noun)

   1. an outcast.

   2. any person or animal that is generally despised or avoided.

   3. a member of a low caste in southern India and Burma.

Amen, double-amen, and triple-amen.

Sandra was no more able to take on this kind of responsibility than I was. And Raj and Maarga didn't know her any better than they knew me. They knew she was on crutches and homebound, but that didn't stop them from imposing their will (see definitions 2 and 3 above) upon her also.

That night, I reluctantly walked over to Raj's house to begin my beastly burden. Whilst he and Maarga were probably sipping bloody marys and chewing cocktail nuts in first class, I was trudging over to Filth City.

Determined to get in and out as fast as I could, I brought their mail in with me and set it on the dining room table (right next to the doggie brush and a big, half-chewed rawhide toy...*yecchhhhh...do these people eat dinner on this?*). I hurriedly closed the drapes to the doggie bed (even though it wasn't even dark yet), poured two scoops of dry food into the doggie dish, dispensed the proper amounts of medicine on top, filled the water bowl with filtered water, and while Asim began gobbling, I went to get the leash, water the plants, and turn on the porch lights.

I returned to the kitchen in what I thought was a quite respectable time indeed. Now for the boiled carrots al dente. I opened the refrigerator door and what do you think I saw? On the top shelf, stage center, was a large dinner plate, heaped to overflowing with brown beans and rice, not even covered with Saran wrap or aluminum foil (to keep the mold in), and left to decay for three weeks while they left the country. It hadn't been there the night before when they showed me the inside of the fridge where the carrots were. Apparently they just cooked it before they left and, instead of throwing the leftovers out like any self-respecting animal would've, the doctor and/or the doctor's wife piled it onto a plate and set it in the refrigerator. To turn into a science project. Then I noticed the stovetop had a large, dirty skillet on it with the same rice and beans scattered inside and all around the top of the greasy, grimy stove. They had left the country *(for three weeks)* and didn't even wash out the skillet they cooked in or cleaned the stove. Words fail me. To call them vermin wouldn't be fair to the vermin.

I was awakened from my trance-like stupor by Asim jumping up on my chest and barking. I put the leash on him and took him out in the backyard, him pulling me like a sled dog, and after finishing his business, I locked him up in the house and left, a much more worldly man than I had been when I arrived.

The next morning at 6:30AM, before going to my three shows, before having a cup of coffee, before *everything*, I staggered to Sandra's house to go fetch (the doggie). She answered the door looking haggard and upset. I asked if everything was okay and she said that the dog had kept her up all night, chasing her little dog and barking. And worst of all, when she put him on a leash to walk him, he had almost pulled her down the front steps to her house. She said she hoped that Asim would get more settled down with her and that tonight would be better. Obviously Sandra didn't know what "Asim" means in Sanskrit. After telling Sandra about how I was suckered into this situation too, and that I was so busy that I couldn't see straight, she felt sorry for me and offered to take more of the load. She said that since she was feeding her dog twice a day anyway, that I should just bring Asim's food and bowls (dry food, distilled water, boiled carrots, medications, etc.) over to her house (I didn't mention the bye-bye biscuits), and that she would be glad to take care of that too – to give me a break. This coming from a woman on crutches. She then suggested that she could put him out in her fenced-in yard in the mornings, and that I wouldn't have to be there at 7AM as prescribed (by the doctor). I could pick him up and deliver him to the House of Charmin, the Raj Mahal with roaches, whenever I got up and was leaving for the day. After making sure she was willing and able to do all that, and after almost starting to cry, I took all the aforementioned items over to Sandra's house, along with his brush and some of his toys, hoping it might make him more amenable (but I had already seen Asim at home, so I wasn't too optimistic).

That day, Sandra and I repeated our dog-duties (a pun so nice, I gotta use it twice!), and bright and early the following morning (really it was freezing rain and early the following morning) when I arrived at her house to get Asim, Sandra met me at the door looking worse than before. "What happened?" I asked. "I just can't do this anymore," she said. "The dog was running wild inside the house and he almost knocked me down a flight of steps last night. He barks constantly and I haven't slept in two nights now. I just can't do this for three more weeks." "What are we going to do?" I managed to mumble. "Well, my son called this morning, and when I told him what was going on with the neighbors' dog, he was very upset and said he was coming up here today to take it to a kennel and board it." Her son lives a hundred miles away in Knoxville, and when I spoke to Sandra that morning, he was already on his way. As I drove to my gigs that morning, I felt a lightness of heart and a festive freedom of spirit that I hadn't felt since the days of B.C. (Before Charmin). But glory be to God, the cavalry was coming and everything was going to be all right. I was on my way to play some out-of-town gigs, and wasn't going to be back home until that evening, and by then, things might be very different. And in the Zen, Buddhist, and Hindu tradition, all I had to do was nothing at all – and that included (especially) answering my cellphone.

Over the past couple of days, the Sons of Charmin, Mud Bottom and Yellow Pants (Indian braves), had called me constantly, to the tune of fifteen or twenty times a day. Most of these I let go to my voicemail so I could deal with their dozen calls with one callback. But since I was using a brand new smart phone, sometimes I wasn't smart enough to hit the right button. Or their incoming calls were coming in so fast and furious, that I was answering them inadvertently (while doing other phone business). Mud Botttom was in med school in Philadelphia and Yellow Pants was in residence at a hospital emergency room in Louisville, Kentucky. Since their parents in New Delhi were supposedly without a signal, the Olympic torch of ruining my life was passed to the sons (one of whom had experience in carrying it). And they called (clearly at the behest of Maarga the Dog-Mother) relentlessly. I didn't have time to take these calls. I didn't have time for any of this. Do you find it ironic that Our Hero, the soul singer and guitar slinger is too busy to take the *doctors' calls?* I found more than a bit of satisfaction in letting my receptionist (Ms. Verizon Voicemail) handle their bothersome and incessant inquiries. The only thing they wanted to know was if everything with Asim was okay. When I assured them that it was (Asim was fine...but of course, Sandra and I were quite the contrary), they would tell me, at length, how much they appreciated all that we were doing. Yeah right. Three doctors and one psycho-mama have the whole neighborhood jumping through filthy hoops for them without the offer of one nickel, and now I have to listen to this? It was adding insult to injury to keep saying, over and over, how they knew how busy I was, and how much they appreciated it, and it only served to make me madder. In the words of Judge Judy, don't pee on my leg and tell me it's raining. Thank you very much.

Teen Raj, Pre-Med
(standing behind in striped shirt)
taking notes and ready to follow in his father's sandalsteps

I had spoken to one of them – I think it was Mud Bottom – that morning and told him I had three shows, was going to be out-of-town all day, and wouldn't be back until evening. Perfect. So all I had to do until then was let my receptionist handle it (just like when a patient, or a patient's family, is frantically calling their doctor with a life or death situation, and the doc is busy on the golf course and can't be bothered). They had been calling Sandra ceaselessly too, and when they talked to her that morning, and found out that her son was coming to save the day (for us), they went ballistic. They didn't get angry over the phone to either one of us, they just went into hardcore-hyper-hindu mode and man, my phone started ringing like a slot machine gone haywire. Of course, I was not available to take their calls. My stoic and unflappable receptionist took a message and promised to have me call them back. Just as soon as possible. Sweet! They begged and pleaded for me to phone them back immediately and to stop this from happening (they were surely facing the wrath of Maarga if it did). They said in one message that the reason their parents wouldn't consider boarding Asim in a kennel was that they had a friend in Salt Lake City who had boarded their dog while away and that a terrible thing had happened. Yeah, they got a bill.

For someone who shared their name with a top-shelf toilet paper, these were the cheapest people in the world. I have since found out, from talking to their landlord (the owner of the house they're renting), that the Charmins haven't ever gotten the water and sewage utility put into their name. So their landlord has been stuck with paying their bill for the entire time they've lived there. Same story with the upkeep to their yard. They have never mowed their yard and the only time it's been mowed, the landlord has sent a crew over to do it (and paid for it). According to the landlord, Raj claims that they "had an agreement" that they wouldn't be responsible for water, sewage, garbage pickup (all on the same utility bill) or lawn maintenance. Funny...every other renter there has mowed their own lawn (or paid to have it mowed) and didn't have this special "gentlemen's agreement." But as we've seen, Raj and Maarga are special people. They don't have to play by the same rules the rest of us do. They play above the rim. And ever since moving in here, others have paid the freight for hauling all of their waste away. Be it their rubbish or their sewage, the Charmins don't wipe their own behinds.

While I was enjoying listening to another one of the impassioned pleas from one of the Sons of Charmin on my phone (what could I do anyway – I was working and was eighty miles from home), I tried to hit the "End Call" button for my voicemail, but as my finger was descending to the touch screen, it rang again (Yellow Pants this time), and an instant before my fingertip reached the touch screen, the screen had changed to an incoming call, and the button my finger hit was now "Answer Call". Grrrrrrr. "Hello...Charlie?" came the tremulous voice of Yellow Pants, Junior M.D. Gritting my teeth at the sheer number of calls coming in from these nuts, that I couldn't even touch my screen without answering one of them (I bet that never happens to a doctor on the golf course), I answered "Yes. Pitambara?" (I couldn't call him Yellow Pants, because at the time, I wasn't aware of the Karmic Sanskrit meanings of their names until doing the research for this story). "Charlie, we appreciate everything you are doing for my parents and Asim." Uh-huh. "But I spoke to Sandra and she said she is putting Asim in a kennel this afternoon." "Oh really?" came my disingenuous reply. "Yes Charlie. This is terrible." began Yellow Pants' even more disingenuous reply, "We know how busy you are but if you could please go there to Sandra's house and pick Asim up before her son gets there, we would appreciate it so much." I put on my best condescending, patronizing, and superior tone (the same one doctors learn in med school), "Listen Pitambara, I am in Morristown working. I am eighty miles from home. There's nothing I can do." I barely was able to contain myself from suggesting he take two aspirins and call me in the morning.

By the time I returned home that evening, Sandra's son had come and taken care of business. He got the name of Asim's vet (from the prescription bottles) and after phoning him and finding out that he had a huge, on-site, boarding service, took Asim and his belongings there, where he belonged in the first place. To be relieved of such a burden was so liberating that when I got home and found out from Sandra that Asim was no longer our responsibility, I danced naked before the Lord like David (not really, but that's how great I felt). My ensuing celebration of unbridled ecstasy, teeming with joy, rivaled that of my aforementioned enemy in burqa after 9/11. Super Duper...like Gary Cooper! Pankaja and Pitambara didn't seem to share my enthusiasm though, as my cellphone ringing off the hook proved. Once I had composed myself enough to speak, I answered the phone. It was Mud Bottom (and Yellow Pants was beeping in), "Charlie. What's going on? My brother said Asim has been taken to kennel." "Yes Pankaja." I struggled to suppress my elation, "I just got home and spoke to Sandra and she said that Asim is at Dr. Robinson's." (Danger! Will Robinson!) "But you know what Pankaja?" I continued, again mustering up my superior medical tone, "That's really better for everyone - including Asim. He's got round the clock care and attention, instead of being attended to for only a few minutes per day. He's at his veterinarian's office - in case he has some medical issue - he's where he can receive medical attention. (I'm really preaching to the choir here and putting on my most patronizing patois!) It's truly the best thing for all concerned - *especially* Asim." "Well Charlie, believe me, we know how busy you are, and we appreciate all you are doing for us" the boy born of mud beat on, "but my parents are going to be very upset to hear this news - my mother especially." Well *that* I believe. Mud Bottom plowed onward, "And I realize that so much of my Mother's demands are unreasonable." Preach on Brother! Preach on! Her own son admits she's crazy. The one born of mud is calling the kettle black! "But she is not going to allow Asim to stay at kennel." he opined. I interjected, "If they love their dog, why don't they want him to be well taken care of?" Ignoring this logic, and continuing to push further (family trait), Mud Bottom continued, "So Charlie, realizing that you are *so* busy (ad infinitum and ad nauseam), you tell me what *you* can do, within *your* busy schedule, that *you* would be comfortable with, to continue to care for Asim at home." "Paprika," I began, "I mean Pankaja", and these words were sweeter than honey upon my lips, "how can I say this as politely as possible? You ask what I can do, within my busy schedule that I would be comfortable with, and the answer to that, is *nothing.*" Without pausing for interruption, I carried on, sure of purpose and unstoppable, like Jim Brown with a football, or James Brown with some funk, I was not going to be denied, "And I don't feel that I am reneging on my original promise to your father either. When I offered to help with Asim, I had no idea -

because your father didn't offer that information – that I was being indentured for three weeks. And then, after this absurd length of time was revealed to me, my obligation was still only once a day. No medications were mentioned, no houseplants, no three-course meals, and no turn-down bed service. This has gotten so out of hand…" the church rolled on, "that I need to wash my hands (another pun!) completely of this – and let the professionals at the kennel handle it from here on out." Pankaja (and you've got to admire his ardor and perseverance – even in a losing cause) then countered with, "Well, Charlie I understand. And knowing how busy you are (broken record), how about this? If things don't work out at the kennel, and Asim is taken back home, how about you come to the house, once a day, and just *feed* Asim. You don't have to *walk* him – just *feed* him. Once a day." What? Was Pankaja, the Charmin Son, born of mud, actually telling me that it would be acceptable (to them) to leave a one-hundred pound animal inside the house, this rat and roach (and God only knows what else) infested Raj Mahal, for three weeks without going outside to do his business? And to be left alone for twenty-three hours and fifty-five minutes a day? Their beloved baby boy? Here I was, once again, after thinking that nothing they did or said could shock me anymore, being truly taken aback and caught completely off guard by the unparalleled perversity of these people. So after taking a moment to collect myself, I posed this question to Pankaja Charmin, Junior M.D., "Are you suggesting leaving the dog inside the house for three weeks?" "If that is the only way for him to be at home", he said "and make my mother happy, then yes." Make mother happy? I put an end to this indecent proposal with a curt response. Short, sweet, and to the point, a one-syllable answer that could not be misunderstood. One that rang with force and finality. One word that I should've used in the beginning, and a word not often heard by the Charmins and their sort (of which there are none). That word, my monosyllabic response, beautiful in its simplicity, and long overdue, was "No."

To his credit (and probably your disbelief), like a cockroach, Mud Bottom kept coming. This true mud slinger, born of mud, still pressed on, "Let me ask you this Charlie. Would you, and I know you're busy (*STOP IT!*), consider going to the kennel, and taking Asim some toys from the house, and take a look around at the facility, to see if it is a clean place? (*A WHAT?*) If you could do this, we would appreciate it so very much, and if you would let me know what you find, so I can put my mother's mind at ease…" His mother's mind? The terms these people toss around. I know I didn't have to, and I was finally out from under, but I gave in anyway (that old Christianity popping up again), and said, "OK Pankaja. I don't have time, but I'll do it. Me or my wife will go out there to Dr. Robinson's tomorrow. We'll take a bag of toys, although Sandra said she sent everything of Asim's that she had, down there with him. We will even take some cellphone pictures of Asim and the facility, and email them to you, so you can see for yourself if he appears to be doing all right."

Pankaja thanked me again, saying how much they appreciated it (*WHEW!*) and the following day, as promised, my wife Beth spent her lunch break going to the vet's with a bag of Asim's toys to get (and pass on) a report of how things were. No charge. What are friends for? Upon entering the office, Beth said everything was clean and nice. She was greeted by a friendly male receptionist who knew Asim by name, and immediately agreed to take Beth to him. The receptionist said Asim was doing fine – he barked a lot, but that he seemed to be settling down today, and that they had brushed him, walked him, and played with him. Beth was led into a large area with several kennels in it. Large kennels that, according to Beth, were the size of our kitchen and dining room combined. Spacious enough for Asim to even run around in. When Beth saw Asim, she said he was actually smiling (happy, no doubt, to be out of that stinky House of Vishnu and into a relatively speaking, immaculate bunch of dog cages). Beth handed the receptionist the bag of toys, saying she had brought them for Asim, to make him feel better and more at home. As he took them, he said, "Well, I'd be happy to hold onto them for him, but..." But what? "Someone phoned this morning from out of town and they are coming to pick Asim up this afternoon." That's de-lovely. That's de-lightful. That's de-licious. Perhaps that whole soiled pack of Charmins had lost my phone number overnight and that's why they didn't call me and tell me not to bother driving across town to take toys to, check up on, photograph, and send a report on *SOMEONE ELSE'S DOG!*

[Pardon me for yelling, but this abuse, all on my dime,
is beginning to make me furious all over again just retelling it to you]

Beth then relayed a small portion of this story to the receptionist, who listened with disbelief (especially at the fact that we barely even *knew* these people), and then asked, "How much are they paying you to do all this?" Beth replied, "Nothing." "Well" he said, "I'll house-sit with someone's dog, but not for free." And that was precisely why the Charmin baby wasn't getting the care he (or any other animal) deserved. It wasn't free.

So like the Quad-Armed Vishnu, Beth came home that day armed with:

1) this shocking news (how can anything shock me at this point?)
2) photos of Asim (smiling)
3) photos of Asim's big roomy kennel
4) photos of the squeaky-clean facility

For these New Delhi degenerates to worship a god with four hands I find fitting. For I suppose they aspire to having twice as many arms as they were born with so they could take twice as much from other people. By the way, Beth (sporting only two arms) also came home minus two things: an hour of her life she'll never get back, and a couple of gallons of gasoline in her van, both spent for nothing. Spent *on* nothings is more precise.

Playing dumb, I wrote my email and sent it to Mud Bottom's phone as promised. I copied it to Yellow Pants (if there's a Sanskrit word that means 'Rusty Zipper', then that must be his middle name), and also copied it to our eminent cardiologist, the scumdog millionaire, Dr. Raj Butt-Wipe. I attached the photos Beth took and sent it without mentioning the fact that we knew someone was coming to spring Asim. Because it didn't matter. It is finished. I was done.

Here's two pieces of good news:
1) I have unlimited minutes on my cellphone

2) I never heard from Punkaja (not a typo) or his brother with the yellow britches Pitambara, ever again

Strange, that after a hundred calls from these phonies (another good one!) in three days, that after receiving my detailed report as promised, no call came to say, "Oh Charlie, we know how busy you and your wife are, and we appreciate you so much driving to the vet to check on Asim and bringing him toys ..." Not a peep. At least I wasn't having manure spread on me like butter on bread anymore. I am sure that they think me an awful villain, refusing to rescue their poor sweet doggie from the dreadful place where he would receive food, grooming, walks, playtime, and medical attention if he needed it - and not returning their beloved baby boy to the home place where he would get food and water once a day, and lie in his own filth for three weeks. Shame on me. But of course, the poor doggie's rich parents would've been billed for all the care he would've gotten at the vet's, so that was out of the question.

Some people get wealthy squeezing pennies their whole life. And that must be a mighty miserable life. An old Yiddish proverb says, "A rich man who is stingy is the worst pauper." Some people become cardiologists and earn many hundreds of thousands of dollars per year, yet still steal the water it takes to fill up their bathtub. I guess it's lucky for Raj and Maarga's landlord that, from what I've seen (and smelled), they don't use very much water taking baths over there at the Charmin house.

Exactly three days less than three weeks later, the scourge returned to my neighborhood. I was downstairs painting some trim when my cellphone rang. It was 11:00 at night. And it was Raj. He was calling from the local airport, and said he didn't have a house key and needed to stop by my house and pick up the one he had given me. Not wanting him any closer to my house and family than my backyard fence would allow, I said I would put his key under his front door mat, and he could pick it up there. And oh by the way (to quote Raj), who leaves the country and has to depend upon a neighbor (the one they just met) to get back into their house when they return? I think by now we know the single correct answer to that question. Naturally Raj wasn't concerned about stopping by my house at midnight either. What's mine is theirs, and what's theirs is theirs. Dr. Charmin didn't seem happy about me leaving his key under their mat, but Bombay beggars can't be choosers. What was Raji the Haji afraid of? What did he think could happen...was some burglar going to use the key to enter the house and steal dog feces and bean mold? I didn't think so, but at any rate, I was willing to risk it. He asked me where his other key was (he said he had given me two keys). I said he had only given me one key, but that he or his wife had given

Sandra another key. That key, I told him, was on their dining room table, right next to the stack of mail that I continued to collect for them while they were gone. He didn't thank me, and I was glad of it. So I walked through the snow, and over to the House of Charmin for the final time, put the key under the mat, came home, and washed my hands. And I didn't hear from Raj again for three months.

I saw the dysfunctional duo from New Delhi only occasionally, walking Asim up the street, or in the backyard, but was spared any interaction with them (in the backyard, for example) due to it being the dead of winter, and not spending much time outdoors. I considered this God's Christmas gift to me.

God bless America, land that I love...

But one warm evening in March, as winter gave way to spring, I was cleaning out my limo, and saw our next door neighbor to the south, our lovable, sweet, and dear friend Betsy, walking over to our house, and she was ranting and raving and waving her arms, madder than a wet hornet, and certainly madder than I had ever seen her before.

When I asked Betsy what was wrong, she said through clenched teeth, "You're not gonna believe this..." We went into my living room and she started telling Beth and I about the visit our old pal Raj had just paid her. Still glowing with rage, Betsy told us how Raj had just knocked on her kitchen door and told her that she needed to stop putting food out on her compost and wood pile in her backyard. That's *her* backyard. Betsy and her husband Gary sometimes put out scraps on their woodpile to feed the squirrels and birds. Of course, on their way to their woodpile, Gary and Betsy have to watch where they're stepping, due to the Charmins' Golden Boy, who runs wild and free again, now that it's springtime, and spreads his waste all over our yards. I remember laughing one day, seeing Betsy cleaning the Charmin slumdog's poop off the wheels of her garbage can. I was not laughing *at* Betsy – I was laughing *with* her. Because we have the same problem.

We have run Asim off our lot and out of our flower beds many times. The Charmins are fortunate that wintertime has kept me and my family from enjoying our beautiful backyard, and also from stepping in any mementos their heir-apparent has left behind. Because it'll be on like Donkey Kong when that happens. When I see Asim in our yard, the scene usually plays like this: I jerk open the French doors to our deck and yell *"SKIT"* (or something to that effect). Then the be-jeweled, coffee-colored, Dog-Mother will come out onto her deck and bleat like the proverbial stuck hog *("AH-LEEEE-LEE-LEE-LEE-LEE-LEE-LEE")*, and then retreat into her house, regardless of what Asim does, or continues to do, or where he runs off to next. Asim has smartly overcome the definite language barrier between us, and does show good sense by bolting the instant he sees me. His daddy Raj and birth-mother Maarga should take a lesson from him on this. If they happen to be out on their deck or in their yard, and I, Beth, or the kids come out into our yard, they'll just turn and go back into their house. So they basically do the same thing their dog does when they see me, only not fast enough to suit me. They need to speed it up some. I want to hear the sound of Maarga's limbs jangling as she withdraws.

One of the places that I've caught Asim, rooting like a pig (major family resemblance) is in the flower bed in our backyard where our sweetheart cat Lucy is laid to rest. Now there are some things that I suppose are best just let go, and then there are others I will deal with violently if they happen again. This is the latter. But preferring to avoid any further contact with these Hindu heathens, for better or worse, we have just allowed Asim's running amok to go on unchecked. I'd really rather pick up Asim's feces with a plastic bag than shake hands with either of his owners without one. Sincerely. Knowing that personal responsibility is so far down their list (maybe tied for last with personal hygiene), it's pointless to confront them with it anyway. Any personal confrontation between Raj and I (the "king" and I) will not end well. We have complained about this to their landlord to no avail (she can't get them to mow their own lawn, pay for their own trash and water, etc., so how is she going to get them to obey the leash laws?). We've also called Animal Control a couple times, but by the time their paddy wagon gets out here, Asim is safely back inside the brown Butt-Paper estate. So at the suggestion of Animal Control, I have shot some cellphone pics of Asim in our yard unattended, and supposedly, with those photos as proof, they can write the Charmins a ticket for failure to control their animal. But the next time I catch him in my Lucy's flower bed, I'm going to do some shooting of another kind. Doggone. But hopefully that won't happen. And since the landlord told us that their lease is up in June (HALLELUJAH!), and they will not be given the option to renew, we have the blessed assurance that they'll soon be gone, dog and all (gone to victimize a new neighborhood), and we've been able to keep turning the other cheek. Because at least there's an end in sight. To paraphrase Billy Wilder, "I'd worship the ground you walked on, if you'd walk in another neighborhood." And since Raji's run-in with Betsy, Asim has not been seen outside nearly as much anymore (gee, I wonder where he's doing his dirty business?).

I do know of two places that Asim's doo-doo has ended up: in the trash can of another neighbor of mine, and in the bare hands of Maarga (of the aforementioned "addicted to disgusting practices" fame). My friend John, who lives around the corner from me, and is one of the general contractors who has done so much work on our house, told me that on more than one occasion, when he pulled his empty trash can from the street after the garbage men had run, that there was a gift from the magi in there. John's house is on a circle, and is part of the route that I originally suggested to the Charmins as a safe road to walk their beast. So I am to blame for John's present misfortune. John said that he often sees Raj and Maarga – they're impossible to miss – walking (chasing) Asim up his street, and that he knows they are the ones who are making the dirty deposit in his can. Why would they pick poop up off the ground and put it in someone's trash can? I'll tell you why. My next-door neighbor Gary has told me that he has seen (with his own eyes) Maarga picking up Asim's droppings in their yard with her *bare hands*. I don't see the need to expound on this detail any further, as I am growing sick of contemplating these people, and unfortunately, I am slowly but surely, in the writing of this diatribe, in danger of becoming the racist that I claimed not to be when I began. But I know in my heart of hearts (where no cardiologist can go) that the Charmins, and the snake charmers, and all the grisly religious sects of India are not indicative of a whole race – no more than Paris Hilton and Charlie Sheen represent me or my family as Americans. It doesn't take Sherlock Holmes and Watson to come to the conclusion that while walking their "baby" through my otherwise lovely neighborhood, Maarga occasionally picks up Asim's feces (with her bare hands) and drops it into my neighbor John's empty trash can. Why she does this, and which other neighbors they defile in this manner, I do not pretend to know. Likewise, what else Maarga does with dog poop gratefully escapes me as well (although after my much-regretted online research on the "aghoramaargas" and "saivas", I shudder to think what they're capable of).

Love thy neighbor as thyself, but choose your neighborhood carefully

But back to Betsy. Gary and Betsy, originally from Tupelo, Mississippi (Elvis' birthplace), have lived in their big, beautiful house on the corner (with their gorgeous, landscaped yard) for twenty-five years or more, and have never had a single problem with any other renter who has lived beside them, until now. They have become dear friends of ours and were therefore privy to the entire gory story of the Charmins trip to New Delhi and all it entailed for us. So, with regard to Raj and Maarga, they're forewarned, and forearmed (although not four armed like Vishnu next door). When Betsy asked Raj why she should stop putting food out for the squirrels and birds, our foul doctor began his lecture. He told Betsy that Asim is coming over there and eating the scraps, that it is unhealthy, and that it must stop. Betsy said what she does on her property is her business, and if he doesn't want Asim rooting like a pig (same family tradition) in her yard, then he should keep Asim on a leash and out of it. Raj, who lies just as well as he walks, said, "Asim is never out of our yard. He is always on a leash. The only time he comes over here to your yard is to get at this food." To which Betsy, who doesn't suffer liars gladly, replied, "You've got to be crazy. We've been stepping in your dog's poop ever since you moved in here." Dr. Raji held firm, "You must stop this. My wife and I are not used to living like this. As a physician, I must tell you that this is quite unsanitary." Well hot dog! Listen to Dr. Unclean's lecture on sanitary. Wow! Does his hypocrisy and gall know no bounds? (it's boundless – "asim" in Sanskrit) To this, Betsy said, in her finest, no-nonsense, Mississippi manner, "Well, we've all heard about how sanitary you and your wife are." The Slumdog Millionaire was momentarily rendered speechless, so the Tupelo Tornado pressed the attack, "So what you need to do right now is to get off my property, stay off my property, and keep your defecating dog (not the exact verbiage Betsy used) off my property. And when my husband gets home, I'm sure he'll be anxious to talk to you further about it.", and slammed the door.

When Gary got home a few minutes later, he went over to the Raj Mahal and had a little heart to heart with the heart doctor. Gary told him, in no uncertain terms, and with a deeper tone, basically the same thing Betsy had, but with a flourish at the end. He told Raj not to ever speak to his wife again, and if he did, that he would have him to deal with.

As Betsy is telling us this story, angry as a cow on astro-turf, Beth and I are once again put into a state of shock. Our mouths are hanging open as we're listening to this tale, and we're yet again staggered by the nerve of these noxious, no-good, neighbors. There's just no precedent for this kind of conduct, and even with our previous experience with Charmin atrocities, we were still horrified. So it really shouldn't have come as any surprise when, just as we're commiserating with our friend Betsy, that my cellphone rang. It was Raj.

I couldn't believe it. These parasites will make you distrust your own senses. Miscreants of their scale make you disbelieve your own eyes and ears (and nose). You tell yourself, "This just cannot *be*." I was staring at my cellphone like a farmer would stare at a flying saucer. These people could knock Howard Stern off the radio. So it was with (yet again) shock and disbelief that I let his call go to voicemail, and waited for him to hang up. Remember, I had not heard from him or his grubby wife, since the mayhem had ended the night they returned from New Delhi three months ago.

I put my phone on speaker and cautiously played my message.

"Hello Charlie? This is Raj Charmin, your neighbor. Um...I was wanting to get back to you and thank you for everything you did...um...taking care of Asim while we were gone...to India? We um...wanted to call to thank you earlier, but um... we've been sick since we got back, and um...but we are both fine now, so give us a call when you get a chance. I would like to talk to you. And um... thank you again. We appreciate it so much. Um...bye."

Now I know we Tennessee hillbillies are stupid and inferior (especially to Indian doctors) and we can hardly figure out how to get out of the rain, but just *how stupid does Raj think we are?* He doesn't call to say thanks for three months, and then, minutes after entering into heated hostilities with our neighbors Gary and Betsy, suddenly he and his wife feel well enough to call. To dub Raj and his motives 'transparent' here would be an understatement on the level of calling Bill Gates 'well off'.

My wife was licking her lips, waiting for me to call him back and let him have it, but I put the phone back into my pocket. "Aren't you going to call him back?" she asked. "No way", I said "I'm not calling him back for several reasons...

One, I don't jump the minute that scumbag cracks his whip, or ascend like a snake out of a basket when Raji, sitting cross-legged in a diaper, plays his flute (anymore).

Two, in the words of George Hammonds (my dear old bassist and brother), "Nothing says 'screw you' louder than an unreturned phone call."

And three, if I refuse to open this up for discussion, I will never have to speak to them, or have any contact with them again, ever."

And that has, until the time of this writing, remained true.

Before Betsy left that night, I said I wanted to tell her a funny story about the Marie Callender Cherry Pie that our neighbor had so generously bestowed upon us, that fateful morning last November. But Betsy said she had a funny story of her own. She said that Raj had brought her a pie too. He had showed up at their door, on Thanksgiving Day, the day *before* he came to mine, along with Maarga and the dog (now that's redundant), and a frozen pie. Nothing is sacred to these pigs – certainly not our Christian Holidays. Even though Betsy was in the middle of cooking Thanksgiving dinner, she told them they could come in, but the dog couldn't. Betsy said that remark made Maarga openly sneer at her. How dare her not invite the dog in for Thanksgiving dinner? It's no wonder the whole world hates Americans. Raj handed her the pie, saying they needed someone to watch Asim while they went out of town. Betsy said she was sorry, but "we don't do dogs". "Well", Raj hissed, "if we gave you a key, could you possibly just come over and water our plants while we're away?" "No", Betsy replied (she smartly doesn't want to be in someone else's house that they don't know well, and then be responsible – and liable – for anything that's wrong, imagined or otherwise, when they return), "but if you want to bring all your houseplants over here, we'll be happy to keep them watered." Betsy then continued to offer, "And if you need someone to get your mail, or newspapers, we'd be glad to do that for y'all." To which Dr. Raj and his two dogs (neither one on a leash) abruptly turned around, without a word, and left.

This proves a couple of things. First, it proves the veracity of my mantra 'Beware of Hindus bearing gifts', and second, it proves that Dr. Raji the Haji and Dog-Mommy the Swami are loathsome liars.

Raj never had anyone scheduled to house-sit overnight. And I don't believe he ever had anyone who had agreed to house-sit during the day either. If they did have someone spending the nights there, as the bogus Dr. Krishna had pretended to me they did, they wouldn't have had to ask Betsy and Gary to go into their house and water their plants. The day before he slithered into my living room, he tried the same trick with Betsy. Raj supposedly didn't know of the "change of plans" regarding his overnight house-sitter until the next day as he was leaving (when he phoned me from the airport hurriedly and couldn't discuss it). Wouldn't the person spending nights at the house for three weeks be the one to water the plants, get the mail, etc.? The Charmins - predators and liars of the first order - were simply fishing for a sucker. Someone to take a key and take the responsibility that went along with it - either in part or in full - who would be given as much extra responsibilities as he or she would bear, all based on deception, and who would then get a counterfeit call from the airport, when a frantic snake charmer would say that you're now on your own, and you'd be treated to hear, ad nauseam, just how much the despicable doctor and his lurid wife appreciated everything, and so on, and so on, and so on.

The funny part of my pie story was that weeks after all the pandemonium, that Marie Callender cherry pie was still in our freezer. One night, after dinner, we thought we would go ahead and bake it. Hopefully the statute of limitations (for disease) had run out, and between freezing and baking, that it would be safe to eat. And Lord knows, we had earned our piece of pie. But inside the box, was still another surprise. Inside, we realized that the good doctor had evidently saved a few shekels by purchasing a pie that was either in the garbage, on clearance, or up for recall. Cementing his title as the world's cheapest physician and most wretched neighbor, Dr. Raji's pathetic bribe at my front door, his generous gift of pie, his carrot-on-a-stick, turned out to be this distorted, aborted mess that will end our saga.

The Marie Callender Cherry Pie had apparently been completely thawed, and then refrozen (God knows what else). And when it was refrozen, it apparently had been stored on its side or upside-down, because the pie had taken on the shape of a gourd. Had it karmically morphed and taken on the misshapen physical form of its original owner, Maarga Charmin? The apple don't fall far from the tree, and I guess it's the same with cherries. Not knowing which of these two bargain hunters had purchased it, but knowing that both of them are equally perverted and ugly on a soul level, it really makes no difference. The funny thing is that karma is alive and well, and that even frozen desserts touched by these New Delhi deformities become warped and bent and our cherry pie had the scars to prove it.

What is this mess...an aerial map of India?

So let me bid you all adieu, and I hope you have enjoyed traveling this long and winding road with me. I would like to thank my soon to be ex-neighbors, those contemptible cretins of Krishna, those vile vermin of Vishnu, those indecent Indian ingrates, this pair of sick and sleazy scoundrels from Salt Lake City, those absolutely detestable, deceitful, and downright degenerate dirt-bags of New Delhi, for making this story possible. If it weren't for you, and your twisted Indian rope trick, which roped me, my family, and my entire neighborhood into your sick schemes, I would be minus the lessons learned from my association with you in this debacle, and we would all be without this extraordinary story. Film at eleven.

I leave you now with the Sanskrit word for goodbye, which is "vigama". I had wanted to make a final comic and Karmic connection to Raj and Maarga Charmin's astoundingly appropriate last name (as these Sanskrit names and their meanings have been so funny and apt throughout). I searched thoroughly the online dictionaries to find the Sanskrit word for "toilet paper", but not surprisingly, there isn't one.

The End ("anta" in Sanskrit)

LC

"Honesty is the best policy, but insanity is a better defense."
Steve Landesberg

"One disadvantage of being a hog is that at any moment
some blundering fool may try to make a silk purse out of your wife's ear."
J.B. Morton

"A good neighbor is a fellow who smiles at you over the back fence, but doesn't climb over it."
Arthur Baer

P.S. I couldn't say goodbye without a song, so here's one for the road...
[sung to the tune of *My Blue Heaven*]

When Whippoorwills call, and evening is nigh
I hurry to my Hindu heaven

Dog poop marks the spot, my Maarga's little red dot
Will lead you to my Hindu heaven

You'll see Asim's rear end, a Vishnu den, a smelly room
A rental rat's nest that's nestled where roaches bloom

Just Maarga and me, and baby makes three
We're filthy in my Hindu heaven
We're filthy in my Hindu heaven

MAY 2011

32

THE WORLD'S FAIR

If this world was fair, Elvis would be alive, and all the Elvis impersonators would be dead.

As we move forward, please keep referring to this mission statement. Not I, but the facts of this case, will prove it beyond any shadow of a doubt.

This story has to do with one Elvis impersonator in particular, whom I carried and coddled, whom I gave a vehicle to, and whom I gave other large gifts to. I was the one (nice allusion to an Elvis song title there!) who was truly impersonating Elvis – the real Elvis – who was famous for giving away cars and jewelry and houses to friends and strangers alike. But Elvis impersonators don't seem to have any more of a clue on how to impersonate Elvis the man than they do with his music. And you could take all of this Elvis impersonator's talent and fit it on the head of a pin, and have enough room left over for the Library of Congress.

In previous chapters, you have heard lots of my ranting and raving. And since the first edition printing of this book, my rants have been very well received, critically-speaking. One could say that my rants have received raves! And when I am ranting about a particular person's shortcomings, I often have to point out their physical or ethnic characteristics for descriptive purposes and for the sake of the story. But I am careful to always point out that one person's bad behavior and/or lack of character should not reflect upon their group as a whole. One bad apple don't spoil the whole bunch girl. There's some good in every group. That's the rule. But the exceptions to that rule must be mosquitoes and Elvis impersonators. There is not, and could not, be such a thing as a "good mosquito" or a "good Elvis impersonator". It would be a contradiction of terms to say there is. The terms are oxymorons. Some examples of oxymorons are: "civil war", "act naturally", and "a fine mess". An example of a moron: Elvis impersonator. I can say, unequivocally and without fear of reprisal, that *all* Elvis impersonators are bad. If you are reading this, and you are an Elvis impersonator, you too, are bad. You may *think* you are good, but you are mistaken. If you are reading this, and you have seen an Elvis impersonator that you think is good, he is not. You may think he is, but you're wrong.

You may think there is no such thing as a good debt, but I'm here to tell you there is. If you lend a scoundrel twenty dollars, and they spend the rest of their life avoiding you like the plague, then that's money well spent. You are out twenty bucks, granted; but you are rid of the scoundrel forever. Try getting an exterminator for twenty bucks.

"Running into debt isn't so bad. It's running into creditors that hurts."
– Unknown

"Some people use one half their ingenuity to get into debt, and the other half to avoid paying it."
– George D. Prentice

"Tis against some men's principle to pay interest, and seems against others' interest to pay the principle."
– Benjamin Franklin

It's been said by many, but I think it's said best by this ancient Hebrew proverb, which says, "Eat vegetables and fear no creditors, rather than eat duck and hide."

So this is the story of a lousy Elvis impersonator (redundant), and how he ripped me off (and how!), and how I don't have to be subjected to his company ever again. So our story does, at least, have a happy ending.

How The Web Was Woven

The Elvis impersonator, who is the subject of our story, shares his first name with the first book of the New Testament, the first synoptic Gospel (but shares nothing of the content). Our poor, short Matthew the Elvis impersonator (short in stature, short in character) goes by the shortened first name "Matt". Matt (his real name) shares his uncommon last name with a common unit of American currency. But due to inflation, I am going to change his last name a little. So without any further ado... Ladies and Gentlemen...Let me introduce...(and please do not even hum the theme from "2001: A Space Odyssey" and "See See Rider" here)...

Matt Penny
(not his real last name, but closer to his real worth).

I don't like to use the real names of the villains in my stories, not because I am afraid of retribution (legal or otherwise), but because I do not wish to give them any additional notoriety or glory, even ignominiously. They've already profited enough off my name and on my back, and Matt Penny is no exception. So I will change his last name. And I deserve to get some change back.

Rubberneckin'

I first became aware of Matt Penny from seeing him hanging around local music stores, beating up beautiful guitars. I would be in the store to buy supplies – picks, strings, or whatever – and I would see him, sitting and strumming some real nice acoustic guitar. I would usually notice him – not because he stood out in a crowd or was a good guitarist – quite the contrary, but I would involuntarily rubberneck because of the *kind* of guitar he would be playing. Matt Penny would always be banging away on a super cool Elvis guitar.

Guitar Man

Elvis owned and operated a big variety of acoustic and electric guitars, but certain axes are associated with him particularly – the Gibson J-200 and the Martin D-28, for example. Certainly these guitars were used and popularized by tons of other artists, but these two were used by Elvis, in the studio and onstage, throughout his career. There are certain ones that have been replicated as Elvis signature models, that hang in music stores (with big price tags hanging from them) like the D-28 that has a leather guitar cover on it with "Elvis Presley" emblazoned on the front (Elvis used a 1955 Martin D-28 through most of the Sun years and on the early RCA sides that sported this leather cover). Then there's the famous blonde 1956 J-200 that Elvis used through the '50s and is shown in lots of movies, and was a favorite of Elvis', even into the late '60s and early '70s, when it was customized with a mod starburst pickguard. Elvis also had another, almost identical, Gibson Jumbo, a 1960 J-200 that was immortalized by Elvis and Scotty Moore in the '68 Comeback Special. Elvis played an ebony black 1968 Gibson J-200 and an ebony black Gibson Dove Custom in concert throughout the 1970s (with the Kenpo Karate decal added). But Elvis poetically returned to a Martin D-28 for the final shows of his life, the same kind of guitar he began his career with. Although Elvis is much underestimated as a guitarist, he was a very good guitar player. Johnny Cash called him a "fabulous rhythm player."

Elvis in the beginning with his Martin D-28, before and after the leather cover

Elvis and his 1956 Gibson J200, before and after the modifications

Elvis and his ebony black Gibson J-200, with and without the Kenpo decal

Elvis with a Martin D-28 again, on June 26, 1977, the last concert of his life

Being a fan of Elvis, and a fan of great guitars, I would naturally do a double-take if I happened to see one, even out of the corner of my eye. I'm a well-trained Elvis Man. So it was that from time to time, I would see this squirrelly-looking little guy, with bad teeth, and dyed black hair, sitting in a music store, and playing one of these expensive Elvis guitars. It is unfortunate that in music stores, guitars are often scratched and dented from being abused by amateurs. And it should be noted, with no small amount of irony, that when I first met Matt Penny, he was devaluing some very fine instruments through their association with him. I was soon to be devalued through my association with him as well.

That's When Your Heartaches Begin

On one of these occasions, I remarked while passing, something like, "Man, that's a nice Gibson Jumbo." "Yeah it is. You're Lightnin' Charlie, right?" he asked, missing another chord change. "Yes." I said, "Have we met?" "No, but I've seen you lots of times. I'm Matt Penny", he said, "I impersonate Elvis...professionally." (Well...is there any other way?) Matt Penny had to immediately distinguish himself from the no-talent hacks, who share not a strand of Elvis' DNA, who warble and wiggle with their karaoke machines, horribly desecrating the music and image of America's greatest rock 'n' roller. Oh...wait a minute...that's exactly what Matt Penny does! "Yeah. That's cool." I lied, "That was "Polk Salad Annie" you were playing a minute ago, wasn't it?" (I knew he was *trying* to play "Polk Salad Annie", but it was closer to "Tuna Salad Ernie".) Hearing this, and mistaking it for a request, Matt fingered an E-chord (one finger at-a-time), and launched back into "Tuna Salad", sounding more like the Wreck of The Old 97 (not the song, but the actual train wreck), and before I could excuse myself to leave, it happened. He started singing.

Compared to his singing, Matt was Merle Travis on guitar. It never ceases to amaze me how bad someone can be, and not be aware of it. But I have seen enough "American Idol" episodes to know it is rampant. I suffered through a verse (by this "professional"), then quickly excused myself.

I left, shaking my head (trying to get the sounds of Matt Penny out), and pondering the many injustices of the universe, not the least of which is why the world's most untalented feel compelled to impersonate one of the world's most talented.

T-R-O-U-B-L-E

The next time I saw Matt Penny, was (you guessed it) in the music store, strumming a Martin D-28 with the Elvis cover (list price $8,500), and was butchering it and "Suspicious Minds" simultaneously. He mercifully stopped playing and said, "Hey man, I'm glad I ran into you. I've got something for you." Uh-oh.

'Beware of Elvis impersonators bearing gifts' has since become my mantra [see Chapter 30 for more personal mantras]. But at the time, I was suckered in by the promise of a cool Elvis item. P. T. Barnum, the original carny, once said, "You can't cheat an honest man", meaning that someone has to be looking to get ahead to get swindled. "I have a pair of Elvis replica sunglasses", Matt began, "not the typical ones you see all the time, but the pair he wore in 'Elvis On Tour' the movie. I had them custom-made and nobody has these. They've got tinted, gradient lenses and the TCB logo on the sides." Well, I was hooked like a big fat catfish, and proved it by responding, "Really?" "Yeah", said P. T. Penny, "I want you to have them." He didn't have the glasses on him that day, nor did he have the $8,500 for the Martin he was destroying, but suggested he bring them by my house sometime. "Oh that would be great", was my fish-hooked reply. I knew the glasses he was talking about and I had never seen a replica of them – these are the glasses Elvis is wearing while singing "Lead Me Guide Me" and "Bosom Of Abraham" with JD Sumner and the Stamps in *Elvis On Tour*. So that was how Matt Penny managed to get my home phone number, along with an invitation to my home. I had sold out my privacy (and that of my family) for the promise of a pair of Elvis sunglasses. But at the time, that sounded like a fair deal to me.

He Knows Just What I Need

Matt called me a few days later and said he was coming to Johnson City (he lived about 30 miles away in Bristol) and asked if it would be okay for him to stop by. I said yes, and gave him directions to the house, and he arrived safe and sound, shortly thereafter. Two surprises greeted me at the door. The first surprise was just how bad his teeth were in the bright sunlight (for the record, dyed blue-black hair and rotten yellow-brown teeth are not a good combination). The second surprise was that Matt had someone with him, a pimply guy dressed like one of JFK's secret service men, in a cheap, high-water, Salvation Army black suit, white shirt and tie. He was wearing dark sunglasses and Matt introduced him to me as, "Junior – my bodyguard."

One Broken Heart For Sale

I suppressed laughter and invited them in, introduced Matt and Junior to my wife, and was anxious to get down to business (my Elvis glasses). But as I was graciously giving them the ten dollar tour of the house, and showing them my man-cave basement and a few of my Elvis items, I realized that bad teeth and complete lack of any musical talent were not the only things holding Matt Penny back. I realized that Matt Penny was cross-eyed. Not completely cross-eyed, but more than halfway there (like Reba!). I was taken aback by this disquieting development, and when Matt finally handed over the Elvis glasses, I felt like I was taking a wheelchair from a cripple. "I had these custom-made by a guy in Nashville", was Matt's opening line, "and nobody has a pair of these. I want you to have them." Matt handed me these plastic sunglasses, that had purple gradient lenses, and really cool TCB lightning bolt logos on the sides, but were broken and taped at the ends. One of the black plastic pieces that rests on top of the ear was broken completely off, and the other one had scotch tape wrapped around it. I politely (and disingenuously) said, "Wow, man. Thanks. These are... something. They're just like the ones he wore in *Elvis On Tour*" (except that Elvis' were 24-karat white gold and in one piece – not broken pot-metal and plastic, held together with scotch tape). I tried them on and started singing "Lead me...guide me...along the way..." They of course tilted sideways across the front of my face due to the fact that they only had one side going across my ear. "You can fix that with a little piece of plastic and some scotch tape." was Matt's offering. "Junior!" Matt barked, both eyes looking at the end of his nose, "Go out to the car and grab that pair of sunglasses off the floorboard in the back. We can break off one of the ear things and tape it on here." Well that's one good thing about having a bodyguard on call. "That's okay man", was my rebuttal, "I can do something with them. You don't have to bother now." "No way man." retorted Matt Penny, Professional Elvis impersonator, "Go grab those shades Junior!" While Junior scurried out to Matt's car (which, by the way, was a primered, Bondo-mobile) to fetch another pair of broken shades, Matt sat down and, while talking to Beth and I, casually mentioned that he "hadn't had a home-cooked meal in a long time." "Well, you should stay and eat with us." was Beth's innocent reply. "Well that would be great ma'am." Matt drawled, "Is it alright for Junior to eat with us too? Or he can wait in the car." "Of course not!" replied Beth, "We've got plenty." We were *getting* plenty was more like it. It's a shame that we weren't having catfish for supper, served with the hook still in. Or better yet, fried sucker fish.

 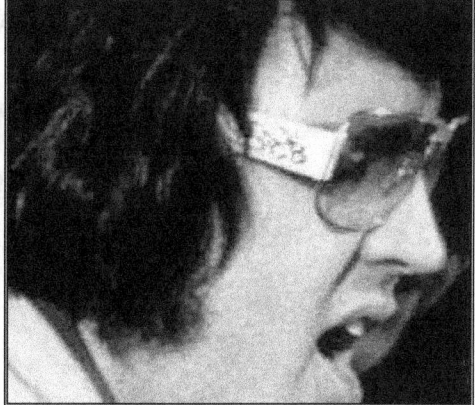

Elvis singing "Lead Me Guide Me" with the TCB glasses

I found a guy online who sells Elvis replica items, and what do you know... there's the gospel glasses, with 14-karat gold TCBs.
Price: $500 (scotch tape sold separately)

Ito Eats

So we sat down to dinner. It was Beth and I, our two sons Sidney and Sam (who were eighteen months and newborn, respectively), Matt Penny and Junior. And the aroma was sickening. Not Beth's cooking, or Sam's diaper, but Matt and Junior's body odor. Are you beginning to see that there's just no end to what separates this Elvis impersonator from Elvis the person? And for whatever reason, after dropping the not-so-subtle hint to insure his dinner invitation, Matt (and Junior – following his master's lead) just picked at their dinner and hardly ate – once again the polar opposite to the real Elvis. But I didn't eat much either, due to the smell.

He Touched Me

After dinner, Matt regaled me with stories about how he hand-makes his own Elvis jumpsuits, and how he had sold some of them for thousands of dollars to other impersonators. He could do "anything with a sewing machine." Matt loved talking about himself, and was extremely self-centered in his manner and conversation, but then he would throw you a curve by making these seemingly selfless and generous offers. This certainly wasn't his first rodeo. He set the hook thusly, "Man, you need to let me make you some custom stage clothes. Not jumpsuits, but something that would reflect your style. I'm thinking high-collared shirts, tailored jackets..." What I heard in my head was "Watch yourself...this guy's a psycho. You don't want to hitch your wagon to this.", but what I heard coming out of my mouth was, "Really? Man...that would be awesome!"

A Little Less Conversation (A Little More Action)

'Pride goeth before a fall' is now my mantra. But I went for this bait like a bat out of... well...I immediately started reeling off examples of all the jackets and stage clothing that I had always dreamed of owning. These things may sound hideous to you, the reader, but they sounded like a fairytale Christmas to me. Now, for the first time in my life, I was being offered the chance at a zebra-skin tuxedo jacket ala bluesman J. B. Lenoir. And what about a black sport coat with leopard-skin lapels and trim ala Jerry Lee Lewis? Don't forget the custom-tailored, high-collared dress shirts and dinner jackets ala the offstage Elvis. Suddenly I was the proverbial kid in the candy store. Finally, every piece of fantasy stage clothing I had ever dreamed of, Matt Penny said he could do it for me, no problem. It was raining...pennies from heaven. Or so I thought, but boy was my map wrong!

Follow That Dream

I learned very early in my career the importance of how one looks on stage. I believe that how one looks is ultimately more important than how one sounds, and I have always taken my appearance on stage very seriously. People basically "hear" with their eyes, and their musical judgments and opinions, at least in a concert setting, are based more on what they see than what they hear. I have been called lots of names at gigs in the span of my twenty-eight years in show business, but because of the way I am always dressed for the show, "busboy" and "dishwasher" have never been among my many soubriquets.

So painstaking was my obsession with my work (and my work clothes) that I gave my wife, as a graduation present (when she graduated from college with a degree in physical therapy), a Singer sewing machine. She thought (but didn't say) that it was the worst gift she had ever gotten. A sewing machine? But I was convinced that soon she would be making me some of these funky stage clothes I had always wanted. Not the ridiculous kind of pseudo-Elvis handmade jumpsuits with bedazzlers and dimestore sequins all over it, but classy garb, like zebra-striped tuxedo jackets with tails!

Matt told me if I would buy the material, that he would be glad to do it for me, "as a friend." Of course I told him that I wouldn't consider him doing the work without getting paid for his time. So we reached an agreement that I would buy all the materials, and he would make the clothes to my exact size and specifications for a nominal fee ("as a friend"). Matt also told me that, "If you need t-shirts, I have a silk-screen machine at home and can do that for you dirt cheap." Well had I struck gold here or what? (There's gold in them there brown teeth!) I always needed product to sell. I could get Lightnin' Charlie t-shirts printed ("dirt cheap") and sell them for a profit, and take the profits, and pay Matt to custom-tailor me the stage wardrobe of my wildest dreams. Sound too good to be true? Well, of course it was, and this was only the beginning.

Fools Rush In (Where Angels Fear To Tread)

Matt and I next visited the local fabric store, and picked out lots of exotic materials for my jackets. I wanted to start out with the "big three" – the J. B. Lenoir zebra-skin tuxedo jacket with tails, the Jerry Lee black sport coat with leopard-skin trim, and an Elvis-inspired black paisley dinner jacket with high collar. But we found some wicked-cool tiger fur material and I placed my order with Matt for a Tiger Man sport coat with black satin lapels and cuffs. We picked out all the materials for the four jackets, buttons and trim, and I was feeling groovy. Matt, armed with my measurements, then took off for Bristol to get started, along with a little bit of "up-front cash" that I insisted he take.

In the weeks that followed, while Matt was supposedly working on my jackets, he called me and said he had lucked into a big warehouse full of plain white short-sleeve t-shirts. Not just any flimsy, flea market tees, but Hane's Beefy-T shirts (the best). According to Matt Penny, Elvis impersonator, the owner of this warehouse had recently gone out of business, and all of his stock was being liquidated. Would I be interested in buying up some of these primo t-shirts for next to nothing? Does the Pope wear a funny hat? Why sure! I could buy several cases of plain white tees, in assorted sizes, and have them on hand forever, for my screen printer and custom clothier, Matt Penny (my new best friend!) to print new shirts, and new designs, as needed, from now until the end of time (or until I ran out of shirts, which, by the time that happened, I'd be rich enough to retire). I found out (from Matt) how much twelve dozen (a gross) of shirts would cost me, and then the sucker fish (me) wrote him a check for several grosses of mediums, larges, extra-larges, and double extra-larges. Since plain white t-shirts don't go out of style, and Hane's Beefy T's were the best quality t-shirt you could buy, I figured, "Why not get set for life?" (with t-shirts), and like my Daddy always said, "Get while the gettin's good." Oh, I was getting it all right.

(Now And Then There's) A Fool Such As I

I gave Matt a digital image of what I wanted on the shirt fronts (after giving him a check), and suggested we start slowly with a couple dozen in each size. I need to say that which I alluded to already, that Matt Penny had no regular job and he told me he would be working on these things for me full-time. I had no reason to disbelieve him, but I had no reason to believe him either. I hadn't gotten anything from him at this point, but a pair of broken pot-metal sunglasses. So needless to say, to you my ultra-wise and street-smart reader, that I never got a single shirt. So much for early retirement!

Tiger Man

I did get a call from him regarding the Tiger Man sport coat. He was working on this one first, and it was finished, but he said he wasn't happy with the way the shoulders and lining had turned out. He asked if I could come to his apartment in Bristol and try it on and see what I thought. I did, and what I thought was, and is, unprintable. The jacket was at least two sizes too small, but Matt said he could fix this, no problem. He needed me to bring him a jacket of mine that fit me perfectly, and he would take the measurements off of it. This I did and the second trip to his apartment yielded me another benefit. It was the first and last time I ever saw the cases of Beefy T's I bought. So at least I know that they existed. It's just a shame that instead of having my clean likeness and logo on their fronts, they were undoubtedly silk-screened with a full color image of Matt Penny, Elvis impersonator, yellow teeth and all.

Up to this point, as far as my dealings with Matt were concerned, I was still being penny wise and pound foolish (pun intended). But that too was about to change, and not for the better. Up to this point, I had put up small amounts of money for material and buttons, some up-front money for Matt's time sewing, and the money to purchase the plain white t-shirts. So I was, by no means, penny wise (wise to Penny), but I was about to become a lot more foolish by the pound.

When It Rains, It Really Pours

A bad penny always comes back, and a few days after my first fitting with the sport coat, Matt phoned me, frantic. He was in Nashville and had played a show the night before (nice Beatles song there!). It should come as no surprise to us by now that, instead of getting (and paying for) a hotel room for the night, Matt (and his bodyguard Junior) had stayed the night at a friend's apartment (no charge). But what seemed like a good way to save some money had backfired badly. Because when he went out to his car the next day, he found his car windows smashed out, his small PA system stolen, and his gold lame Elvis suit gone.

Matt sobbed about how sick he was about this, that he started to take his gold lame suit into the apartment, but didn't. "Thank God I didn't leave my guitar out there," he bawled, "but what am I gonna do? I've got all these shows coming up..." He said this happened in a gated complex, and doesn't know how someone could have gotten in. In the months that followed, I wondered if one of Matt Penny's old sucker fish had come back home to roost.

Matt said he wanted to talk about buying some PA equipment from me. Tearfully, he explained that if he didn't have a PA, he couldn't play his gigs. And if he couldn't play his gigs, he couldn't pay his rent. And if he couldn't pay his rent, who knows what would happen (to my custom clothier and silk-screener). At this time, I had yet to completely retire from playing the nightclubs, but had retired from playing the ones that I had to haul a sound system into. Not only was the burden of hauling, loading-in, setting up, sound checking, then tearing down, loading out, and hauling out a huge PA system a back-breaking chore, but it was counter-productive. I finally came to realize this truth: that a club that didn't have a PA of its own was just not a club worth playing – not just because (another Elvis song!) of the overwhelming amount of extra work for me, hauling and setting it up, but because a club without a sound system wasn't a music club. Music and musicians were so far down their list of priorities that I didn't want anything to do with them or their clientele (and they felt likewise). If a night club was interested in presenting good music, they would, by definition, have a house sound system. But if I had to wait for the salad bar to be moved, or the game to be over, before I could set up the bandstand, then I was in the wrong place and didn't belong there. It took me more than twenty years to figure this out, but that probably comes as no surprise to you, the reader, since we are this deep into the story, and I still haven't figured Matt Penny out.

You're A Heartbreaker

So I had a lot of PA equipment that I wasn't using and needed to sell. Matt "the bad" Penny turned up at my house one night (Hey! Elvis song!), and I showed him what I had. I thought it would be equitable for Matt and for me, to trade some of this equipment towards the tailoring and t-shirt work that he was (supposedly) doing for me. But PA equipment is very expensive, and when Matt had picked out the speakers and PA head that he wanted, along with cables and stands, and some lighting equipment (also very expensive), and even a light truss, he was way over budget as far as an even trade for silk-screening t-shirts and sewing some jackets. So we figured out a fair price for the work he was doing and subtracted that from the price of the gear he wanted. Naturally, for my good friend Matt Penny, I discounted the price way down (Elvis song!). All this was put into writing, and signed. So we had a deal, except for the fact that Matt had no money. Matt didn't have a penny. He couldn't pay me anything on it. But if he had the equipment, of course he could play all these gigs he had booked, and he could pay me a little at a time. So being that it was for my newest, bestest friend Matt Penny, I agreed. And this was no small amount of money. I don't remember the exact amount, but it was around two thousand dollars.

Doncha Think It's Time

Matt Penny finally had my Tiger Man sport coat finished (again), and boy was I ready. It seemed that in our relationship, everything was going out, and nothing was coming in, but that was about to change. Now I was going to have a stage jacket that would make me look like the wild, rock 'n' roll animal I pretended to be onstage. But when I put that jacket on, instead of being transformed into a loose and hungry jungle cat, I felt like I was toothpaste being squeezed into the tube. It was a strait-jacket with stripes. The thing was even smaller than before! Matt instantly apologized, saying his girlfriend had been doing some of the sewing for him, and must not have followed the measurements and his instructions very well. "But don't worry", he said, "I can fix this up. No problem." And then Matt Penny, being the seasoned sucker fisherman he was, sensed my distress, and feeling the line start to tighten and maybe break, quickly offered this bone, "Charlie, I have something really cool for you. You've been so good to me man. I made something for you and I can't wait for you to see it."

Puppet On A String

Matt returned with a high-collared Elvis shirt, with a black and white mosaic pattern, frilled cuffs and a V-neck. V for very cool. Rendered momentarily speechless, I took the shirt, tried it on, and it fit perfectly. "I made this one out of some extra material I had." began Penny's penance, "I guessed at the measurements. It looks like it fits great. How does it feel?" "It fits perfectly." I stammered. Matt continued his play, seeing me go for the bait, "I could make you as many of these as you want, quickly too. They don't take no time to make." (I realize that's a double-negative, but I'm quoting Matt Penny.) He set the hook, "I could make you two or three in a day - silk or satin - solid colors or patterns - black, white, candy apple red, royal blue, whatever you want."

Penny was playing me like a fish all right. And this play earned him another shot at me. Maybe he sensed he only had one more shot, so he made it a good one.

I Got A Feelin' In My Body

I am usually generous to a fault, especially with my friends, but this was at a breaking point. Being fairly free with my money, and not being a penny pincher (Hey!), I was letting this dough ride, with the hope that he could eventually come through with everything he had promised. Although my doubts were certainly raised, I was too deep in to fold now. This was no penny ante game either (nyuk-nyuk!) Like Kenny Rogers said, "You got to know when to hold 'em, know when to fold 'em. Know when to walk away, and know when to run." But I didn't listen to Kenny Rogers, and tragically, I didn't listen to that voice of reason inside my head – the one that told me from the get-go not to get into a game with this weirdo. But here I was. And Lord help me, I was all in...almost.

Too Much Monkey Business

Let me present this, in self-defense...all this monkey business was going on at the time when Beth and I had just purchased our first home. We had moved in just three weeks prior to her scheduled C-section delivery of our second child. I was gigging five nights a week, traveling to my house gig at the hotel and convention center I made famous in Chapter 1. I was producing and recording a very long and difficult CD (see also Chapter 1), and was writing the blogs that eventually became this book. All this work-related pressure, plus a new house and (another) new baby, surely contributed to my mental lapses of judgment. At least that's my story, and I'm sticking to it. I hate to admit here that I could be that stupid. But like I've said before in this book, quoting Forrest Gump, "Stupid is as stupid does." And like Matt Penny, who thought he was a great singer, but was mistaken (or deluded), I must not be as smart as I think I'm is.

Bitter They Are, Harder They Fall

Just before we moved into our new house, I had bought a new car, and was selling my GMC diesel van and twelve-foot trailer that had lugged the Upsetters and me all over the country. Since I was in the middle of this regular hotel gig, playing five nights a week for three years, I didn't need a big diesel van and a trailer anymore. At the time, when I had a show booked with the band somewhere (which was not very often), the hotel would let me off to go play it, and I would meet my band (who all lived in North Carolina) at the gig. And since I refused to play clubs that didn't have a sound system, I didn't have to carry anything with me except my gear. Therefore, my van and trailer were of no use to me anymore and were both up for sale, and by a highly-motivated seller (I had learned that term while house-hunting!). My van and trailer was close to forty feet of rig, and due to the fact that it was very much in the way, and an eyesore, sitting in the yard, alongside one of our two driveways, we were very anxious to get rid of them. My new car, my two Cadillacs, and Beth's car took up the rest of the real estate. I had just sold the trailer a day or two before, to a neighbor, when Matt the bad penny turned up again and asked to buy my van.

How Can You Lose What You Never Had

I had invested so much into this "friendship" that basically anything I did to end that so-called friendship, by calling him at his game, would surely get me nothing. I might stay in the game and get nothing, but I might get at least a portion of the things I was due, and you gotta be in it to win it. In for a penny, in for a pound, right? I could threaten to kill and even make good on the threat to kill Matt Penny, but that wouldn't get me a nickel back either. I know you, the reader, must be yelling out loud for me to wake up and not get in even further with this liar, but I was just not making good, sound, business decisions at this point in my life. I was so exhausted and busier than a monkey without a tail [see Chapter 1], that I was doing well just to find my way home at night. Not all of my decisions were bad ones though: I had just purchased the house of our dreams, and we were joyously making it into a home, furnishing and decorating it around our newborn, beautiful baby boy. But I was worn out, mentally, physically, and emotionally, and there were nights that I remember driving home from my hardcore hotel gig [see Chapter 1 again] with the migraine that killed Bruce Lee. I used to get these stress-induced migraines [see Chapters 4 and 17], when I was surrounded by madness. When Matt Penny, Elvis impersonator was in my life (and while I was playing the hotel and correctional center in Bristol) they were coming fairly often and were crippling in their ferocity. I remember driving home from Bristol one night, in the rain, blinded by pain, and literally having to crawl out of my car, and into my house, on all fours, after another typical night at the office. Ah yes, those were the days...

Double Trouble

By now, as you all know I am a huge Elvis fan, and really feel like he is a member of my family [see Chapter 21]. In spite of that fact – or more correctly *because of it* – I don't have a good track record with impersonators. I think it bears mentioning that Matt Penny was not the first one that gave me trouble (great Elvis song). Read on...

Memphis, Tennessee

In August of 1997, the band was booked to play in Memphis during 'Elvis

Week', which annually commemorates the anniversary of his death. This is an insane week to be in Memphis, as fans and freaks (these are not synonymous) from all over the world gather to mark the anniversary of his death on August 16, 1977. This was an even crazier 'Elvis Week' than usual, as it was the twentieth anniversary, and the nutjobs were everywhere. It was like the world had gotten shaved by a drunken barber.

When we arrived at our hotel in West Memphis, Arkansas (you couldn't get a hotel reservation in Memphis, Tennessee for months in advance), and waiting in line to check in, someone tapped me on my shoulder. I turned and saw something that my senses just couldn't make sense of. I thought I was having a mini-stroke or something. I had driven five hundred miles through the night after playing another show and was a bit toasted (no...a lot toasted). At ten o'clock in the morning, in a hotel lobby in West Memphis, Arkansas, an Elvis impersonator, dressed in the beaded, fringe jumpsuit El wore in *That's The Way It Is*, with sunglasses (of course) says to me, "Hey man, which way to the men's room?" I pointed in the general direction that the restrooms reside in every other hotel lobby in America, and he struck a karate pose and said (you guessed it), "Thank you very much!" The phrase 'nuttier than squirrel poop' seems to apply here.

We were playing a neat little downtown blues club, just off Beale Street, and Ray, the club owner, and I got along well. Ray had booked me through the years, and called me prior to this gig to ask a favor. He said that since his place (which is usually frequented by locals – not tourists) would be so jam-packed for 'Elvis Week' with out-of-towners expecting an "Elvis" fix (especially on the weekend when we were there), that he had booked an impersonator to do just one song during our show – and that the impersonator wanted to do the rock 'n' roll medley from Elvis' 1974 Recorded Live In Memphis record. I'll call the impersonator "Joe Bent" (real close to his real name). Ray wanted to check with me and see if that would be all right. Ray was hoping we could play the medley, so it would come off a lot better than the guy singing to a pre-recorded track. I said that would be fine – fun even – that I knew the medley, would teach it to the band, and we'd be ready. The medley Joe Bent wanted to do is from Elvis' Recorded Live In Memphis album, recorded just a few miles from Graceland at the Mid-South Coliseum. This medley consisted of six songs: "Long Tall Sally", "Whole Lotta Shakin' Goin' On", "Flip Flop And Fly", "Your Mama Can't Dance (And Your Daddy Don't Rock 'n' Roll)", "Jailhouse Rock", and "Hound Dog". I knew this medley – and this album – well, due to it being recorded on my twelfth birthday, and also for having a spectacular version of "How Great Thou Art". So we were all set to do this medley, with an Elvis impersonator in

Memphis during Elvis Week. Awesome possum...I was looking forward to it (because of being afflicted with naïve optimism in my younger days).

In 1997, besides being newly married, Lightnin' Charlie was touring with a brand new CD *(Don't Touch That Dial!)*, which like all of my CDs, before and since, includes an Elvis song. Our live show, at that time, also included Elvis songs in our three-set show. We had recorded "Burning Love" on this record and it was included in our live sets, along with Elvis' great inspirational ballad, "If I Can Dream", which was in our show at this time too. We had been on the road for a while, and had our setlist down pat with songs from the new CD, old songs of ours, covers, etc. But it wouldn't be a problem to plug this Elvis impersonator and the one medley into our show that night.

Stranger In My Own Hometown

When we got to the club that afternoon to set up, I realized that things in Memphis weren't quite the way Elvis had left them. I saw a show poster hanging in the window for a band that had played there earlier in the week, a lesbian Elvis impersonator called Elvis Herselvis and Her Straight White Males. Ugh. I also saw the only Mexican Elvis impersonator in the world (thank God) walking up the center of Beale Street striking more karate poses and getting lots of laughs and jeers from local soul brothers. His name is (are you ready for this?) Elvez. What a world. Matt Penny looks like Cary Grant next to these superfreaks. A penny for my thoughts? I refer you back to the first sentence of this chapter.

The place was packed that night, and we were about to finish our first set, when a guy came up to the edge of the stage and handed one of my bandmates a note. He passed it to me between songs, thinking it was a request. I opened it and it read, "Take a break. Joe Bent wants to talk to you." Excuse me? I walked over to the edge of the stage where this tick was waiting (Joe Bent's version of "Junior") and put it in plain English for him, "Let me explain something. Our break will begin when I say it begins. Not when Joe Bent says, and not when his lackey says. Okay?"

So after stretching our set a little, we took our break, and Joe Bent's pet schmuck was waiting to take me into the kitchen to discuss our song with Joe Bent. Why do these wack-jobs always have bodyguards and an entourage? How pathetic can you get? The flunky and I walked into the kitchen where Joe Bent was waiting. He was obviously annoyed at being kept waiting, but he had apparently passed the time by snorting gigantic lines of cocaine off the stainless steel dishwasher. He continued to do this while we were talking and our conversation went like this…

Joe Bent: "OK. You guys got the Mid-South Coliseum medley, right?"

Me: "Yep. Key of C. We've got it.

Joe Bent: "What about 'See See Rider'?"

Me: "Well, the boss said we were only supposed to do the one tune."

Joe Bent: "C'mon, let's do 'See See Rider' in G."

Me: "Well, alright." (great Buddy Holly tune – not included in the medley)

Joe Bent [bending over the dishwasher and snorting more dust]: Then we'll do 'I Got A Woman'. Key of E."

Me: "What?"

Joe Bent: "C'mon man. This is Memphis. It's Elvis Week. And I'm Joe Bent. Do you realize how big a star I am? I'm in 'Honeymoon In Vegas', I'm in 'The Client', I've been on Jay Leno!"

Me [realizing that he was a big one, alright]: "Are you kidding?"

Joe Bent [thinking me star-struck]: "No I'm not kidding. C'mon man. Let's go. There's a lot of people out there waiting to see Elvis."

Part of me wanted to punch this idiot in the nose and watch him bleed to death. But I meekly agreed to let him do all these songs, partly because my wife was videotaping from the audience, and I thought it might be something special to have filmed – us backing up an obnoxious, coke-head, Elvis impersonator in Memphis (sadly on the twentieth anniversary of the real Elvis' death). And to his credit, Joe Bent was rightfully excited by the prospect of fronting a real band for the first time in his life. Ray the club owner (who was naturally not present the night of our performance) had sent me Joe Bent's terrible cassette tape for me to hear his version of the Mid-South medley (which ran about eight minutes). It was horrible. An amateur recording sung to bad tracks, and some tracks recorded with an equally horrible studio band, it gave insight into the fact that Joe Bent, like many other 'movie stars', was understandably chomping at the bit to get to perform with a real live rock 'n' roll band – one that could take care of business in a flash.

We went out and started our set, and then brought up the fake Elvis. But naturally before the fake Elvis could take the stage, his fake Memphis Mafia man (the pet schmuck and the junky's flunky) introduced him with much fake fanfare. Then the band ripped through "See See Rider", then "I Got A Woman", then "Washed My Hands In Muddy Water" and "Johnny B. Goode", then the six-song medley, then "Polk Salad Annie", and in between, Joe Bent called off a couple more as well. The band was so good on this stuff, hitting every stab and break, that Joe Bent even remarked to the audience between songs (and kicks and punches), "How 'bout it for these guys, huh?" It wasn't that he didn't know our name, because he would be using it in a few minutes (with curse words attached). I remember doing "Love Me Tender" while the fake Elvis walked into the audience to give out fake scarves, and fake kisses – laced with real cocaine (the faces of the women he kissed had to go numb immediately, like they'd been to the dentist!). So all told, we let this fool do almost a whole set. We stopped our show to let him do his thing. Let him do ten songs instead of one. Was this because I'm a nice guy? No, it's because I'm a moron (see almost any chapter in this book). If I were twice as smart, I'd be an idiot. And here's how this freak of nature thanked me...

One-Sided Love Affair

After the freak's finale ("Can't Help Falling In Love", his eleventh song?), we finished up with a couple songs to end the set. I thought it only fitting to end the set with our two Elvis offerings. It was during the first of our two songs, "If I Can Dream" that the trouble started. Apparently Joe Bent got angry that we had the gall to do an Elvis song while he was in the building. Very angry. We followed "If I Can Dream" with our set-closer, our rocked-up version of "Burning Love", and went to break. As I said before, "Burning Love" was one of our set pieces in our show, and was on the CD we were supporting on that tour, and it's customary to do songs from the album you're trying to sell. But Joe Bent (movie star, Elvis impersonator, and guest on our stage), didn't see it that way, because while we were playing these last two songs, Joe Bent was going berserk. However all the carrying on he was doing from the audience was on the opposite side of the stage from me, and lucky for him, I couldn't see or hear him. But my rhythm guitarist, "BB" could. And when we finished, as I was putting my guitar on the stand to take our break, BB came over to me and told me what this imbecile had been doing (and saying) from the audience. Folks, I apologize for the language here, and for my alluding to it, but there's just no other way to tell this tale without quoting him. The four-letter word I'm omitting in these phrases is the big one. The big bad F-Bomb. BB told me that while we were doing "Burning Love" and

"If I Can Dream", the coke-headed movie star (redundant) was jumping up and down and screaming,

*"[F***] Lightnin' Charlie! [F***] him!
Those songs are a central part of my act!!!"*

What? Well, excu-u-u-se me! I didn't realize Joe Bent had the rights to every song Elvis ever recorded. And pardon moi for having the nerve to play an Elvis song in the presence of an "Elvis". You, my dear reader, will understand the world of difference a couple of quotation marks make here, distinguishing between Elvis and "Elvis". This coked creep, that we had just allowed up on our stage, during our show, at our gig, gets bent out of shape (perfect pun!) because we have the nerve to play a couple Elvis songs – one of which is on our album? I'll bet I would've been afforded that luxury if I were a lesbian.

Rip It Up

Now I was enraged. I leaped off the stage like a late freight looking for him. But like his brethren, the cockroach and the fly, Joe Bent had managed to vanish the moment he was about to get smushed and sent into the next world. Maybe he saw BB telling me what was up, and he (and his handler) high-tailed it out of there, or maybe he just got very lucky, but I couldn't find him anywhere. I looked all through the audience (he should've been easy to spot, in his Aloha From Hawaii jumpsuit), and I looked in the kitchen (at the dishwasher where he was doing his drugs), but no Joe. I furiously went outside the club, and ran completely around the block, desperate to find him. And if I had found him, I had only one thing on my mind, and that was dropping him like a wet egg out of a loose goose, and then ripping out, by the root, handfuls of the black sideburns from both sides of his face that gave him his identity. Oh Lord, if I could – I surely would. If only I could find this jerk, he would be impersonating Elvis with two swollen-shut eyes, glue-on sideburns, and minus a few teeth. Good luck with that Joe Bent. Take that to the makeup department of the next big Hollywood movie you do. But as fate would have it, Joe Bent was nowhere to be found. "Elvis" had left the building, and not a second too soon. So I returned to the club to finish our show, feeling very much used and abused, and still very hot.

Stay Away Joe

 The club happened to have little CB-style hand microphones hanging from the walls at various places in the room. It was primarily a restaurant, and when waitresses were taking orders, I suppose they would call out the orders on these to the kitchen, for kitschy effect. But the mics were live and very loud in the room also. We had fooled around with them a little while we were setting up that day. They were real distorted, and "dirty-sounding", like the bullhorns police use. And there just happened to be one at the back of the stage. When I went back up on stage to begin our third and final set, I was still fuming with fury and fit to be tied. I began by saying quietly (on my vocal mic), "The Elvis impersonator that I allowed on stage tonight seems to have taken offence that we had the nerve to play a couple of Elvis songs in his presence. Some of you in the audience might have heard the way he thanked me for the privilege. But I would like say something to Joe Bent. And that is, if Joe Bent doesn't like it, Joe Bent should..." And I grabbed that dirty-sounding CB mic off the wall and yelled, *"...KISS MY [expletive deleted]!!!"* I threw down the bullhorn mic and tore into our first song, seeing the black rib cooks at the rear of the restaurant going crazy with laughter, and slapping each other fives in absolute appreciation of my glorious speech. Justice was served, although not as viciously and as personally as I had wanted. The rib cooks' reaction to my inspired speech was an indication of how bent (pun intended...a good pun is its own reword!) the celebration of America's greatest star had become. And how perverse the handling of his legacy. Lesbians, coke-heads, and Elvez? If "Elvis Week" and the freaks and geeks that abounded in it were offensive to me, a musician and Elvis fan in Memphis for a weekend, I can only imagine what a joke it is to Memphian rib cooks.

How's The World Treating You

 I am reluctantly including a couple photos of these freaks, thereby saving (another) couple thousand words. The first photo is "Elvis Herselvis" and "friend", proving mightily that you can take the girl out of the trailer park, but you can't take the trailer park out of the girl. The second freak in this pictorial freak show is "Elvez", shown here in his "movie soundtrack" album cover from G.I. (Ay, Ay!) Blues. No comment necessary here (other than eloquently illustrating the need for immigration reform). I sadly placed Elvis next to these deviants for contrast, and to further demonstrate the accuracy of the first sentence of this chapter ("If this world was fair...").

Don't Be Cruel (To A Heart That's True)

Matt Penny needs his butt kicked. Since my brief association with him, I have heard from countless other people who share the same experience and the same fate as I, in regard to Matt Penny. He is infamous. He has ripped off so many people, and I know not how he has continued to get away with it. I live in a part of the country where one might meet with a swift justice when caught stealing. I only wish thieves had to register like sex offenders, so others might have some knowledge of who they're dealing with. And the fate of Matt Penny and other liars is expressed here eloquently by George Bernard Shaw:

> "The liar's punishment is not in the least that he is not believed, but that he cannot believe anyone else."

So even though this escapade cost me a pretty penny (!!!), I am resigned to the fact that while I was trying to help myself, my family, and my career (and my fellow man), I got burnt. No good deed goes unpunished. But I have learned my lesson when it comes to Elvis impersonators. They're all bad, every one. As it is written: "None is righteous, no, not one." I will never trust another one of them, never help another one of them, and never bail another one of them out of trouble. I've learned my lesson. And one doesn't learn anything the third time the mule kicks you.

I Got Stung

I saw much less of Matt Penny after he had made his final big "sting" for my van. I finally realized that I could toss a penny into a wishing well and expect more in return than I was ever going to get from Matt. Like Bing Crosby before me, I too had lost hope. Although he had signed a written contract for the van, and the sound and lighting equipment, with how much he would pay per month, it never amounted to anything. Matt Penny's autograph isn't worth the paper it's written on. He never made one single payment to me on the van and all the gear. I never got a single t-shirt. I never got a high-collared Elvis shirt in royal blue, or the zebra-skin tuxedo jacket. I did get the Tiger Man sport coat with the black satin trim, but it is so small, it's unwearable. One thing about having an orange-and-black, tiger-fur sport coat is it must fit well. Nothing says tacky quite like a fur dinner jacket that's three sizes too small! I do have the Elvis glasses with the scotch taped arms, and the black and white mosaic Elvis shirt. I also have a guitar that Matt Penny gave to me one Halloween night when he showed up at my gig in full Elvis jumpsuit with a girlfriend who had bad teeth and a black, bee-hive hairdo (perfect match, that). When I saw him from the stage, I made a mad dash to catch him before he disappeared (as Elvis impersonators are known to do), and before I could start choking him, he held out this cheap (but new – with tags) electric guitar and said he wanted me to have it, "You've been so good to me man, and I know I haven't been able to pay you much." "Much?" I said, "Nothing's more like it." He told me how sorry he was, and how things were going to be different, and he was going to start paying me regular payments, and all the gigs he's got, and blah-blah-blah. I eventually sold the guitar to a local music store for $100, and when I told them I had gotten it from Matt Penny, they said, "How much does he owe you?"

Trying To Get To You

I finally tired from the chase, and gave up. I got tired of calling him, leaving messages, finding his number had been changed, getting his new number, and beginning again. In the words of Lily Von Schtupp, I just got tired of playing the game. Tired of trying to find out where he was living (since he had been evicted from his old apartment), tired of saving and re-saving his one voicemail message where he admitted his huge debt to me. Just ran ragged and hopeless, I finally had to surrender (great Elvis song). So like a hound dog (uh-huh) on a fox hunt, I eventually gave up, and I never saw or heard from Matt Penny again. I did hear of him driving around Bristol though, in a fully restored pink 1955 Cadillac. How he came by that, I'll never know (beautiful and obscure Elvis song). But he's lucky I never saw him in it. If you pick up a starving dog and make him prosperous, he will not bite you. This is the principal difference between a dog and Matt Penny.

Something Blue

I was at an auto salvage yard in Bristol a couple weeks ago, buying a timing cover for my '66 Coupe de Ville, and the man at the yard said to me, "You play music, right? Do you know an Elvis impersonator named..." (Oh no!!!) "...Matt Penny?" "Know him?" I laughed, "He stole thousands from me." "Me too!" came his reply, "He took a car from my lot, and left his van as collateral until he could pay me on it. Then he came back with his key and drove his van off and had my car crushed." "Was it a blue GMC diesel van?" I asked. "No", he said, somehow putting my mind at ease, "it was a gasoline van." So I told him a bit of my saga, and we shook hands laughing, happy to have the company of another's misery.

"A small debt produces a debtor; a large one, an enemy."
– Publilius Syrus

Preach on Publilius! Preach on!

You're The Devil In Disguise

I just googled Matt's real name and saw some interesting items. I saw a youtube post of Matt onstage horribly butchering "Burning Love", but it was the comments that struck me. There were literally dozens of angry comments from people he had ripped off. From all over the world. There was one from somebody in the UK, warning people from buying "authentic Elvis scarves" from Matt Penny for $200 on ebay (they're fake). Many of the comments had been removed (by Matt) but I guess they're coming in faster than he can delete them. There are dozens. Matt misspelled some lame responses to a few, and in one response, even claimed to be a friend writing *for* Matt Penny, who "had passed away nine months ago." Many were from ETAs who Matt Penny had ripped off for expensive jumpsuits and accessories (ETA is an acronym for Elvis Tribute Artist – I guess it's politically incorrect to call them impersonators anymore, but ask me if I care). Then there is the youtube video of Matt Penny selling (and modeling) a complete custom-made Bigfoot costume for $800. Yes, Bigfoot costume...a sasquatch. I am not – and could not – make this up. I think I recognized some of my faux fur on its backside. I did see one thing I surely recognized though – my light truss, which was onstage with snaggle-tooth somewhere in an empty room in Las Vegas...way *way* off the strip (it looked like a Shoney's.) Just to make this story more unbelievable, there is a home-made video on Matt Penny's youtube channel of "Bigfoot" trampling through the woods, peering around trees, and even "attacking" the camera (but the video and the videographer somehow survived). Behind all this is a soundtrack of scary noises and rushing wind, and the words "Directed by: Matt Penny" scrolling over and over, along with the claim that this film is "undisputable evidence of the existence of Sasquatch". A portion of the film, which the director said was shot on location in Tennessee showed "Bigfoot" walking in the woods through bunches of palm trees. This must've been shot on the Tennessee coast.

Don't

Then I read a couple hilarious interviews where Matt tells of his thirty-five year career as a "Tribute Artist", and how he incorporates gospel music into his act...what? Gospel music? I remember when I first met this cock-eyed heretic, I mentioned something about the great gospel singer, Jake Hess, saying how Elvis in some particular gospel song was obviously emulating the voice of Jake (Elvis' favorite gospel singer). Matt Penny not only had never heard of Jake Hess, he had never heard the Elvis gospel song. Now that doesn't make someone a bad person, not anymore than crossed eyes and rotten teeth makes a bad person, but it makes an Elvis impersonator a bad person. Can you imagine a Beatles tribute band that had never heard Sgt. Pepper? To not know Elvis' gospel material is to not know Elvis.

Almost Always True

I also saw an ad Matt posted selling his (somebody's) '55 Cadillac, but I didn't see anything about it having a clear title. Also saw a Matt "Elvis" Penny fanpage (which boasted zero members). Then I went on Matt Penny's official website, on which only the home page was still active, and none of the links worked (due to non-payment of fees, no doubt). The bio on his home page is obviously written by Matt himself, judging by the amazing number of misspellings and grammatical faux pas that are on the level of a second-grade crack baby (if you gave Matt a penny for his thoughts, you'd get change back!). I laughed out loud at this one – that Matt Penny's music was "unique In Its own Way!" (I am leaving the capitalizations as they were for your complete mental picture). And how exactly can an Elvis impersonator be unique, when he's copying every single thing he's doing from someone else? (and stealing every single thing he's using from someone else too). The main thing the website was touting was the claim that Matt has legally changed his name to "Elvis" (his site claims he is the only Elvis Tribute Artist to have legally earned the right to the name "Elvis"). Hey, you know what? Instead of me continuing to try and paraphrase this chaos for you, here is the actual text from his website homepage and I swear I haven't touched it:

> The only man in todays music that bares the legal name "ELVIS" named after the great legendary KING OF ROCK-N-ROLL, Matt makes his own statements in music and style.
>
> He has been a Full time "working" Elvis Impersonator for 24 years. since the
> age of only 8 years old! and today still performes as THE KING throughout the eastern United States. His act has taken him all over the country, even to
> Canada and Japan.
>
> Matt has been on several documented TV Programs where he has portrayed
> the legendary ELVIS A. PRESLEY on numerous occassions. along with several Radio ads and comercials. He even played ELVIS in the documentary
> Film in 1999 called "Crawdaddy" which was shown in Bristol, England.
>
> So after hundreds of stage performances and Tribute shows, Matt is ready to
> make his own statements in MUSIC! order his newest CD today for only $10.00 + Shipping to hear why he has earned the name "ELVIS!"

Too bad you aren't seeing all the pretty, green and red squiggly lines Microsoft Word has provided for me here. This page of text looks like Christmas wrapping paper! Hey, want to have some fun? Share this with your friends and see who can come up with the most mistakes! And take it from me...he smells worse than he spells.

Who Am I?

So this thief and chief scumbag's official (and legal) name on all these sites and online wanted posters is 'Matt "Elvis" Penny'. What an absolute disgrace to whom Elvis Presley was and what kind of man he was, and everything he stood for. Could cock-eyed Mister Penny have changed his name to anything more polar opposite in nature than this? What if the fuehrer changed his name to 'Adolph "Jesus" Hitler' and started incorporating gospel music into his speeches? Oh, I want to buy a button! It's so disgusting on so many levels.

Take Me To The Fair

Also of note is that I couldn't find a single photo of Penny Dreadful smiling, but that's because he's the one who is taking all the pictures and posting them on the web, and the snaggle-toothed swine won't dare bare his broken brown fangs (see "bares the legal name" above!). Who else is interested in taking his photograph, except maybe the bunko squad? There are several of him looking directly into the camera (in two different directions) with "Copyright by Matt Penny" written underneath each photo. He wouldn't want anybody to steal one. A thief always locks his doors. Meanwhile this crook has posted photos of another one of his home-made CDs that is supposedly on "Sun Records" and even has the (stolen) Sun Records logo on the CD cover (I spotted this as a fake because the CD cover has "Label" spelled "L-A-B-L-E"). He has lots of assorted Matt "Elvis" Penny crap for sale – buttons, t-shirts (high-quality Hane's Beefy-Ts no doubt), coffee mugs, along with more big news – that Matt "Elvis" Penny has released a brand new Johnny Cash Tribute CD (on Penny Records), so Cash's music and memory is now fair game too, and being drug through the mud by this sorry scoundrel. Sadly, everything about Matt "Elvis" Penny has been stolen – his music, his look, his clothes, his mannerisms, his stage equipment, his name, and even the vehicle he rode in on. I hate a thief. A word to the wise...if Matt "the Counterfeit" Penny kisses you, you'd better count your teeth.

Are You Sincere

I am grateful for you lending me your ear. But don't make a habit of it. There are some people (in jumpsuits) who would take it and not give it back. Then you'd only have one ear, and couldn't wear sunglasses. Except for the special, custom pair I have, made especially for one-eared Elvis fans, that I could make you a real deal on... And if you know a thin ten to thirteen year old boy that is looking for a tiger-striped dinner jacket, send them my way (my way...Sinatra and Elvis).

Good Time Charlie's Got The Blues

I turned this in on my federal tax return a few years ago as a bad debt, trying to alleviate some of my tax burden (see lucky Chapter 13), and got a few pennies back (no pun intended). So for all intents and purposes, and as far as the IRS is concerned, it's a done deal. Case closed, unless of course, Matt Penny was to return to me (Dean Martin song!) even a small portion of the money he owes. Then I would naturally have to report that as income, and pay a hefty income tax on it. Nice system. Hey IRS agents, if you're reading this, you might want to consider Matt "Elvis" Penny for an audit. I think you'll find it worth your while.

My Happiness

Although I have the misfortune of being subjected to a criminal tax code and answering to the Immoral Revenue Service (to whom I cannot ever mention this debt again), I have the great good fortune of being a celebrated author with legions of fans and readers (to whom I can whine away at incessantly). Thank you Lightnin' Bugs, for enjoying my calamities so! I am laughing out loud as I write this. That's good for the soul. Proverbs 15:13 says,

"A merry heart doeth good like a medicine."

Choo Choo Charlie says, "Love my good and plenty!" The bible says it's good and healthy to laugh. And I say it's good and plenty healthy to laugh at oneself (and one's stupid mistakes...of which I have plenty...and enough funny material for several more books). It's also the only true revenge. As Shakespeare said,

"The robbed that smiles, steals something from the thief."

Amen Brother Bill! That's telling it like it is! Take *that* Matt Penny! I'm smiling (and I hope you, the reader, are too). What soap is to the body, laughter is to the soul. Here's some more Shakespeare, but I can't dispense many more of these pearls of wisdom...I gotta go...I'm supposed to get a tattoo in ten minutes...

"Parting is such sweet sorrow."

That's sweet, Sir William. Big Bad Bill is Sweet William now! Yes indeed. Well, I'm out-a-here. Time flies like a bullet...fruit flies like a banana. I love you Lightnin' Bugs! Farewell! God knows when we shall meet again (more Shakespeare).

So as we close, I say farewell to you, goodbye for now and thank you for being my friend. And remember, goodbyes are not forever, goodbyes are not the end. They simply mean I'll miss you, until we meet again!

May God bless and keep you,
Lightnin' Charlie

"Debts and lies are generally mixed together"
- Francois Rabelais

"Forgetfulness - *noun*
A gift of God bestowed upon debtors
in compensation for their destitution of conscience."
- Ambrose Bierce

"Sin has many tools, but a lie is the handle that fits them all."
- Oliver Wendell Holmes, Sr.

33

PROVERBS

proverb *n.*

1. A short pithy saying in frequent and widespread use that expresses a basic truth or practical precept.

pithy *adj.*

1. (of language or style) Concise and forcefully expressive.
2. (of a fruit or plant) Containing much pith.

Here, offered for your approval, is a list of some pithy proverbs. I hope you will agree with me that these are they that contain much pith. I have laughed much while compiling them, and have intentionally included the ancient alongside the new. Truth is timeless, and the thing that makes these proverbs funny is the amount of truth in them, no matter how old they are. I've heard it said that a proverb is a short sentence based on long experience.

You will find that I have included a large number of Yiddish proverbs, because they are the ones that are loaded with truth, humor, and experience (and contain the most "pith"!).

There are some true gems that aren't Yiddish, like the Amish proverb that boldly states,

> "The man who claims to be the boss in his own home
> will lie about other things as well."

Then there's the timeless Texas proverb,

> "When you throw dirt, you lose ground."

But for my money, the Yiddish ones are tops. And here they are…

"A chip on the shoulder indicates wood higher up."

"The girl who can't dance says the band can't play."

"After nine months the secret comes out."

"Cancer, schmancer! -- as long as you're healthy."

"Dear God: You do such wonderful things for complete strangers; why not for me?"

"If you want your dreams to come true, don't sleep."

"Man plans and God laughs."

"If you ever need a helping hand you'll find one at the end of your arm."

"The soldiers fight, and the kings are heroes."

"Everyone is kneaded out of the same dough but not baked in the same oven."

"God made man because He loves stories."

"If God wants people to suffer, he sends them too much understanding."

"An advantage of poverty: your relatives gain nothing by your death."

"Bygone troubles are a pleasure to talk about."

"If rich people could hire other people to die for them, the poor could make a wonderful living."

"Flattery makes friends and truth makes enemies."

"All is not butter that comes from a cow."

"One must not wish a doctor a good year."

"They are both in love: he with himself, and she with herself."

Since we are living in a world driven by the internet (and its fans), I am including a bunch of proverbs, axioms, and puns that I have culled from the World Wide Web. I have alphabetized them for no practical reason. Apply amens where appropriate…

"A clear conscience is usually the sign of a bad memory."

"A conclusion is simply the place where you got tired of thinking."

"A little inaccuracy sometimes saves a ton of explanation."

"A smoking section in a restaurant is like a peeing section in a pool."

"After all is said and done, more is said than done."

"All work and no play, will make you a manager."

"Always keep your words soft and sweet, just in case you have to eat them."

"An apple every eight hours will keep three doctors away."

"An atheist is a man who has no invisible means of support."

"Any clod can have the facts, but having an opinion is an art."

"Any time things appear to be going better, you have overlooked something."

"As long as there are tests, there will be prayer in public schools."

"Attitude determines your altitude."

"Biology grows on you."

"Bravery is being the only one who knows you're afraid."

"Change is inevitable, except from vending machines."

"Clones are people two."

"Don't be sexist. Broads hate that."

"God is a comedian playing to an audience too afraid to laugh."

"Hospitality: making your guests feel like they're at home, even if you wish they were."

"I couldn't repair your brakes, so I made your horn louder."

"If you pay peanuts, you get monkeys."

"Men marry women with the hope they will never change. Women marry men with the hope they will change. Invariably they are both disappointed."

"Never get into fights with ugly people, they have nothing to lose."

"The main reason Santa is so jolly is because he knows where all the bad girls live."

"There are no short cuts to any place worth going."

"There is no such thing as an atheist in a foxhole."

"There will come a time when you believe everything is finished. That will be the beginning."

"The trouble with being punctual is that nobody's there to appreciate it."

"What happens if you get scared half to death twice?"

"Why is the alphabet in that order? Is it because of that song?"

"Worrying works! 90% of the things I worry about never happen."

"Worry is like a rocking chair; it keeps you busy, but gets you nowhere."

"You cannot get to the top by sitting on your bottom."

So there you are. Amen? Amen! Just because (as you must know by now) I adore quotations, here are a few for the road, just for the fun of it...

"A man in love is incomplete until he has married. Then he's finished."
- Zsa Zsa Gabor

"When I die, I want to go peacefully like my Grandfather did, in his sleep... not screaming, like the passengers in his car."
- Unknown

"When I was born the doctor took one look at my face... turned me over and said, 'Look... twins!'"
- Rodney Dangerfield

You know you've read a good book when you turn the last page and feel as if you've lost a good friend. Well friend, feel free to read this one over and over again, and maybe it will even improve over time. Hopefully you are not of the opinion that the covers of this book are too far apart! Maybe you are even a little sad (as I am) that you have reached the end. But (to paraphrase Dr. Seuss) don't be sad because it's over – smile because it happened.

And here's another one from Dr. Seuss, a closing shot, dedicated to all those that I have perhaps offended with my opinions and my ruthless representation of the truth,

"Be who you are and say what you feel because those who mind don't matter and those who matter don't mind."

This is your spunky, singing, sideburned scribe saying so long. Adieu! How lucky I am to have known someone who was so hard to say goodbye to. But remember this... I love you and the Lord loves you. Now go and be well, do good work, keep your hands on the plow, and your eyes on the Prize. I have fought the good fight, I have finished the race, and I have kept the faith. Until we meet again, I wish you love.

LC

photo courtesy of Rita Eggers

JULY 2012

AFTERWORD

A lot has happened in Lightnin' Land since the first edition of *Off The Record* was published four years ago. I've built a professional digital recording studio in our home, and recorded and released a new gospel CD called *Trust In God – Family Album Volume One*, in which I play all the instruments and all the vocals are sung by my wife, our sons, and I (it's a family affair!). I have also just released a rockin' retrospective CD called *The Essential Upsetters,* which chronicles my 28 years as a bandleader. I continue to perform an amazing 250 to 300 shows per year, happily playing good music for good people. I have been blessed with the remarkable success of *Off The Record,* which is now in its second edition, and is already in over 18,000 bookstores worldwide. This second edition of *OTR* contains three brand new chapters, a new cover, and this new afterword. But you could read all that on a cold and impersonal press release. Since we have become family (on our journey through these pages together), I feel it is proper to give you a closer and more intimate glimpse of what's happening – not in my show business life – but in my real life. So here goes...

Our two sons are growing up so fast (they're ten and eleven now) and have both accomplished so much. We're very proud of the young men they are fast becoming. They were only three and four years old when I started writing the blogs that would become *Off The Record.* My boys and my book have grown up together. There are plenty of things that have happened to me (and for me) as a performer, recording artist, author, etc. in the four years since the first edition of this book was published. But the biggest thing to report, in this second edition, is actually a little thing. She's a little thing now, but she's growing. And that is our third edition, our sweet little baby girl, Lily.

Lily is our joy. My wife and I, and our two sons (our first and second editions), have never been in love with anything quite like this before. She is a doll. But "joy" and "love" weren't among the list of emotions I felt when my wife Beth first told me the news. I was shell-shocked. Dumbfounded. You could've knocked me over with a bendy straw. You see, we thought we were through with the baby-business (I *knew* I was through), but apparently the Lord had other plans. And I can describe the way I felt when I heard the news in three words...

SURPRISE!!!...SURPRISE!!!...SURPRISE!!!

After making fairly sure of our situation with three home pregnancy tests (well the first two could be wrong, couldn't they?), my wife went to her doctor to find out for sure. After telling him all our personal business, the birth control niceties, and other sordid and gory details, the doctor said, "You can't be pregnant." Beth replied, "That's exactly what my husband said!" But the examination proved otherwise. Me and Fertile Myrtle were gonna have another one, and forever be outnumbered.

Once we were sure of this impending life-changer...this ticking time-bomb...this most blessed event, there was one overwhelming sense that I felt, and could not get rid of. It fell on me like a ton of bricks. What I felt was old. I felt really, really old. Too old. Ancient even. I felt like Methuselah's great-grandfather (that's old!). I felt like I was the guy who had introduced young Abe Lincoln to Mary Todd. I felt like the guy who was so old, that when he was in school, there was no such thing as history class! Lord knows I was too old to start with another baby...doesn't He?

Due to our work schedules and the fact that we have never used day care, I was daytime Mister Mom to both of our boys. After the exhaustive job of raising two babies who are eighteen months apart, and daily hauling them, their snacks and drinks, and all the baby gear, to my 250 daytime shows per year, for five or six years (until they started school), I was simply not ready, willing, or able to start all over again. I had just been pardoned from that duty. Now that our sons were in school, I had the freedom to go to work by myself (which seemed like a Hawaiian vacation!), and they had reached an age where they were largely self-sufficient (they could get their own drinks and snacks, dress themselves, bathe themselves, etc.). I had just gotten some of my TV room back. And now Beth drops this bomb on me? Not only did I feel unwilling to embark on that rugged road with a newborn baby again, I felt completely unable to provide all that's required to raise another child from scratch. But thankfully, I know a Man who is. God is able. Always able and always faithful. And He's made a way for us.

But at the time, more than anything else, when Beth told me the news, I just felt plain old. I remember telling her,

"Honey, I'm going to be forty-eight years old. Do you realize that by the time we get this baby out of diapers...that I'll be in 'em??!!!"

Yeah, laugh it up Lightnin' Bugs. Everything's funny...as long as it's happening to somebody else. But regardless of whether I'm old or not, and regardless of how I feel, our God is good, all the time. He gave Beth and I just what we needed – a beautiful, bouncing, healthy baby girl – Daddy's little fattie! Beth had always dreamed of having a little girl, putting her in frilly dresses, and fixing her hair, ever since she herself was a little girl. And Lillian Jeanette is our dream-come-true.

Lily is named after Beth's Great-Aunt Lillian, who adopted a son, but never had children of her own; and my Aunt Jeanette, who never had children of her own, but was a second mother to me and my brother and sister (and who is celebrated in Chapter 21 of this book). We also have dear, dear friends named JC and Jeanette Price who have been like grandparents to our sons. So we've nailed three birds with one stone. One stone-cold, living doll named Lillian Jeanette. Our Lily is now two-and-a-half years old, and is the cute and cuddly center of our universe. And although it's been tough, I'll quote Vestal Goodman by saying, "I wouldn't take nothin' for my journey now." Our journey, as far as raising babies is concerned, should be finalized with Lily. This should be the last adorable addition to our family for me to report to you (for a while at least...until grandchildren!) because when the doctor took Lily out of my wife's oven, we had him blow out the pilot light!

And so, in this afterword, I'd like to announce that we are living the good life, loving God and loving each other. I'm still doing my best at being Dad to our two boys, a husband to my wife, and Daddy to our baby girl. I haven't forgotten how to change diapers, or how to sing without sleep. I remember all the songs and characters on Sesame Street and the Muppet Show, and we have all adjusted very nicely thank you very much.

We even have a storage building full of our boys' old toys, so Lily always has something new to play with. And that leaves me more money to spend on other things. Like shells (and I don't mean pasta!). I mean 12 gauge, pistol grip, sawed off, heat shield, pump action, by God and Greyhound, shotgun shells. Because there's a big difference between raising boys and raising girls. When you raise boys, you worry about your boys. But when you raise girls, you worry about everybody's boys.

When my Lily is sixteen, I'll be sixty-four. When I'm sixty-four, I want to be the scariest, rootin'-est, tootin'-est, crazy-eyed, shotgun-totin', old wise man that any of the local high school boys have ever seen or heard of. Put that in your Beatles song, Paul McCartney! My only hope is to be feared. And I expect the assistance of my two sons, Lily's big brothers, who will at that time, be twenty-six and twenty-seven (which is the perfect age for taking care of that kind of business).

My father-in-law Bob (Beth's Dad) had the right idea. Before allowing his daughter to go out on a date, Bob used to have her date come in the house and sit down at the table, old-school-style, and talk about what they were going to do, where they were going to do it, and who they were going to do it with. That's old-school. But while the boy was explaining the evening he had planned, Bob always added a personal touch which seemed to resonate with the teenage boys. Bob would be cleaning his guns while he listened. He would listen intently, and ask lots of questions, always looking the boy straight in the eye without blinking, and all the while cleaning his various and sundry rifles and shotguns, looking from the chamber to the boy and back again. According to Beth, this had a huge effect on the boys, and led to many an evening spent at her house watching television instead of going anywhere.

Thankfully, Beth had long moved out of her Dad's house before we started dating. Because if she hadn't, we probably wouldn't have had a second date (or a first, for that matter...I wouldn't have stuck around to even watch TV!). And I wouldn't be writing this now, with our beautiful daughter Lily pulling on my pant leg, eating Cocoa Puffs, and watching Elmo. Don't get me wrong...it's not that I don't want Lily to date boys; it's just that I don't want her to date boys until she's at least thirty years old. By then I'll be seventy-seven and probably too feeble to scare any of her suitors, or too senile to care.

But for now (and for the next thirty years at least), I'm a card-carrying member of D.A.D.D. (Dads Against Daughters Dating).

The morning after Lily was born, I woke up in the hospital room and randomly opened my bible to somewhere in the middle. I was reading a wonderful translation of the Old and New Testaments called the *Complete Jewish Bible* by David Stern. But we must keep in mind that "random" and "coincidence" are not kosher words! Everything happens for a reason. My bible fell open to the middle and I began reading from the 35th chapter of the book of Isaiah,

> *The desert and the dry land will be glad;*
> *the 'Aravah will rejoice and blossom like the lily.*
> *It will burst into flower,*
> *will rejoice with joy and singing,*
> *will be given the glory of the L'vanon,*
> *the splendor of Karmel and the Sharon.*

> *They will see the glory of* ADONAI,
> *the splendor of our God.*
>
> - *Isaiah 35:1-2 CJB*

Beth and I see the splendor of our God every day, as we rejoice with joy and singing, with our Lily.

Another instance of God speaking to us through a flower is the story of our son Samuel and our magnolia tree. We moved into our home on Memorial Day weekend of 2002. Sam was born in June of that year. The house was nicely landscaped and I was happy that a large magnolia tree, one of my favorite trees, was in our new backyard. I've always loved magnolia trees for their huge blooms. But the magnolia in our backyard has never bloomed. It is otherwise healthy, large and growing. We have tried fertilizers, compost, phosphorus, etc. and nothing has worked. It is a fully mature tree, probably twenty feet tall, but after seven summers, I had given up on the idea of ever seeing a beautiful, white, fragrant flower on our magnolia tree.

Then at the end of May, 2010, our Samuel came to Beth and I to say that he wanted to accept Jesus Christ as his Lord and Savior and that he wanted to be baptized. This was, of course, glorious news for his mother and me. We talked to our pastor and set it up for Sam to come forward during the altar call the following Sunday during worship service. Before Sam went forward that Sunday, I asked him if he wanted me or his mother to go with him to the altar. Sam whispered back, "No thanks Dad, I'll be fine." And he was, and is, thanks to Calvary. So that was how our beloved Samuel got saved. Our pastor was to baptize Sam the following Sunday evening. The evening Samuel was baptized was during Memorial Day weekend.

Memorial Day weekend of 2010 was the eighth anniversary of us moving into our first and only home we've ever had as a family. Samuel was turning eight years old. The number eight is very significant. The number eight in Scripture always pertains to resurrection and rebirth through salvation. Even the mathematical symbol for infinity is the number eight on its side. So it is without a small sense of irony that our son Samuel was being baptized and "reborn" on this eighth anniversary and just three weeks before his eighth birthday.

Taking all this into account, imagine my awe and wonder, when we returned from Sam's baptism, and saw a big, beautiful, white bloom on our magnolia tree! On the first day that our eight year old Samuel was officially washed white as snow from sin, here was this first snow-white bloom, on a previously barren tree. And all this occurred on exactly the eighth anniversary of God giving us our home – and our magnolia tree. This stands as proof to me that our God is still God and He alone controls the universe, and He is working mightily in our lives, every moment. This was no accident (not a kosher word!). To quote Albert Einstein (again), "God does not play dice with the universe." And to quote myself (again), "Coincidence is really God working anonymously." Amen.

Our eldest son Sidney has matured into an awesome kid. Sidney is fearless in all situations, makes friends instantly, and is (and always will be) our Number One Son. When we sing onstage as a family, Sidney isn't nearly as "into it" as his brother Sam. Sam has taken piano lessons since he was four years old (and has received many superior ribbons, trophies, and cups from his recitals). Sidney is more into sports and video games, and only sings with us because we want him to. If he ever says to us that he doesn't want to do it, we will not force him to. Right now, music is like brushing teeth to Sidney. It is just something that is expected of him, but not necessarily something he enjoys. Sidney is, and always has been, very athletic. Sidney's first word was not "da-da"…it was "up!" And his second word was "ball". Sid has played Little League baseball since he was five, and loves the outdoors. He loves shooting guns at Paw-Paw's house, fishing, etc. and we have had him in Boy Scouts and 4-H Camp since he was little. Sidney is also the family's historian and scholar on all things military. From B-24 Liberators to M14 rifles, Sidney can tell you more than you would ever need to know. I am very proud of him for learning more American History than any other kid his age I have ever seen. He has pursued this all on his own, and has had this zeal for American History ever since he could talk. This has been Sidney's passion since he was a baby. He is particularly interested in WW2, which makes him even more special. When Sidney was a baby, his word for airplane was "dee". Don't ask me where he got that, it just was. But when Sidney was about a year old, he could tell the difference between a passenger jet and a military jet. If we were outside, and a commercial, passenger jet flew overhead, Sidney would look up and say "dee!!!" But if a military fighter jet flew overhead, Sidney would look up and say, "dee-boom!!!" He was always consistent with this, and was always 100% correct in recognizing the difference between civilian and military planes. Don't ask me how.

In May of 2012, almost two years to the day from his brother Sam's baptism, I baptized Sidney in the name of the Father, and of the Son, and of the Holy Spirit, to walk in newness of life. That was the greatest day in both of our lives, and – not to be outdone by Sam's story – God intervened here also. On the Sunday morning when Sidney went forward in our home church to pray the sinner's prayer, his Mom and I were taken completely by surprise. Sidney had already accepted Jesus Christ as his Lord and personal Savior, but had been sheepish about going forward to publicly confess in a crowded church. After church that day, we went home and prayed together as a family. Later that afternoon, we all went out to a restaurant to celebrate a family birthday – Beth and Sidney in her van – and Sam, Lily, and I in my limo (we took two cars because I had to go straight from dinner to a gig). Since Mom and Dad were riding separately, Sidney got to ride shotgun, in the front seat of Beth's van. On the way to the restaurant, God sent a dove that flew directly at the passenger side of the windshield where Sid was sitting. Beth had to slow down to keep from hitting it. The dove hovered there – right in front of Sidney's face for a moment, as if delivering a message, and was gone. As with Jesus and John, God sent His Holy Spirit in the form of a dove. Beth and I wanted to find Sidney a special bible to present to him at his baptism the following week, and we found just the right thing – a military bible with a camouflage cover. To make it all the more special for him, we had the printer engrave a dove symbol on the front cover. Our sons are awesome sons, and our God is an awesome God!

Since the first edition of *Off The Record* was published, I have somehow become even more in love with my wife. She is my everything. My love for her has grown since my first sight of her (and I was in love with her even then). My Beth is the sweetest, kindest, most tender, caring and loving woman in the world. She's also the most beautiful. She completes me. I am so glad she is mine, and I am so lucky that she continues to put up with me and my many faults.

Our music has continued to grow also. We have developed such tight, pretty harmonies together, that it truly sounds like one voice coming from one flesh. Ours is One Love blessed by One God. Our sound comes from two souls, joined forever in love, knotted together as the two lovers immortalized in the ballad "Barbara Allen"...

> *They grew and grew to the steeple top*
> *Till they could grow no higher.*
> *And there they twined in a true love's knot*
> *Red rose around green briar.*

Beth, if you are reading this...I love you. And if not, I'll read it to you! A certain verse of Scripture always speaks to my heart of how I feel about you, and it's no accident that its chapter and verse is the same as our wedding date. It is Proverbs 3:15...

> *She is more precious than rubies:*
> *and all the things thou canst desire*
> *are not to be compared unto her.*

In closing, the thing that has made me the happiest about *Off The Record* over the past three years is simply that it has made others happy. I have received many glowing reviews from readers and critics all over the globe. But there is one review that stands out in my mind. It is from a lady who had purchased a copy of *Off The Record* from me at a local nursing home I play regularly. Her husband was a resident there, and he was dying. She was dealing with all of the grief and sorrow of watching the one she loved most in the whole world slowly pass away. She would spend fifteen or twenty hours a day at the nursing home, at her husband's bedside, in spite of the fact that he was slipping into a coma and unconscious most of the time. She told me that she would go home late at night to try and get a few hours of sleep before returning the next day, and that when she would lie down in her bed, consumed with grief, she would read some of my book, trying to unwind a little before dozing off. Despite the pain and sadness that was filling her heart, she would just crack up and laugh uncontrollably hard at some of my stories. This belly laughter occurred during the saddest time of her life. After her husband had passed away, she told me about this, about how my book helped to get her through a very dark and lonely time, and I'll never forget it. This still stands as the greatest compliment I have ever gotten as an author. Laughter truly is the best medicine. This, plus the fact that it is not enough to be good, but to be good for something, or someone, that is the real reason for this writing. Mother Teresa once said...

> *"I am a little pencil in the hand of a writing God*
> *who is sending a love letter to the world."*

We are all called to find a need, and fill it. Let us heed the words of Walt Whitman, the Good Grey Poet...

> *Love the earth and sun and animals,*
> *Despise riches, give alms to everyone that asks,*
> *Stand up for the stupid and crazy,*
> *Devote your income and labor to others...*
> *And your very flesh shall be a great poem.*

I hope you have enjoyed reading this book as much as I have enjoyed writing it. It's been a wonderful ride. I may not be where I want to be, but – praise God – I'm not where I used to be. *Off The Record* chronicles a very large portion of my life and career, but not all of it; and not the best of it.

The best is yet to come.

Lightnin' Charlie
Johnson City, Tennessee
July 28, 2012

ABOUT THE AUTHOR

Lightnin' Charlie was born in Miami Beach, Florida in 1962. He has been a relentless full-time musician for twenty-eight years. He has long been a favorite of music fans locally, nationally and internationally. Known for his charismatic personality and dynamic stage show, he is a natural entertainer and a virtual encyclopedia of classic American music styles. Whether fronting his band the Upsetters at a theater or music festival, or performing with his wife as a duo in a church concert or charity fundraiser, or as a solo acoustic act in a restaurant or nursing home, Lightnin' Charlie, voted "Favorite Musician/Group and Favorite Artist in The Mountain Empire 2005-2011", is a master showman and always leaves audiences smiling and begging for more.

*"Lightnin' Charlie DELIVERS! * * * * * (Five Stars).
If this don't get your party going, call it a wake!"*
– Amazon.com

"Charlie's charismatic stage persona and off-the-wall guitar antics grab an audience's attention like a snake-handling preacher."
– The Creative Loafer

"A unique combination of gutsy vocals, smokin' guitar, and high-energy showmanship, Lightnin' Charlie is simply amazing – not because he'd play his guitar behind his head and with his teeth, but because of the way he could make it SOUND! An exceptional guitarist."
– Carolina Bluesfest Newsletter

"While his shows run the gamut from a slow boil to torrential fury, Lightnin' Charlie keeps the temperature hot. A deft instrumentalist, Lightnin' Charlie performs astounding guitar histrionics that will amaze everyone from blues neophytes to the most studied guitar aficionados."
– John Sewell, TriCities.com

"Lightnin' Charlie Dolinger, looking disreputably cool, sang like Howlin' Wolf while the Upsetters smoked behind him. Displaying exquisite timing and dynamics, tonal variety, and electric communication, the small band put out big sound and feeling on blistering blues."
– Style Magazine

"Charlie is an exciting, accomplished guitarist, but there is no great shortage of wonderful guitarists. The thing that sets Lightnin' ahead of the others is that this boy can sing, too!"
– Ann Rabson, Saffire The Uppity Blues Women

"I've been to every one of these [National Blues Talent Contest, Memphis, TN], and Lightnin' Charlie might be the hottest guitarist they've ever had. He's got Stevie Ray Vaughan written all over him."
– ESP Entertainment Guide

Lightnin' Charlie's 2005 CD, *A New Leaf*, features Lightnin' Charlie and the Upsetters in both electric and acoustic ensembles, and rave reviews abound.

*"A stellar release. A New Leaf contains so many great cuts,
it's hard to single out simply one or two as standouts
Shines as bright and bold as autumn colors."*
– Joe Tennis, Bristol Herald-Courier

*"Rockin' swamp blues and rock 'n' roll just the way I like it. Lightnin'
Charlie's A New Leaf doesn't have a weak song on it.
Can't wait for his next CD."*
– Bernard Boyat, Le Cri Du Coyote (The Coyote Cry, France)

"A powerful, polished and fresh original release. Atomic-powered roots music, somewhere between classic rock 'n' roll and Chicago blues. Vibrant remakes and superb originals. In an age when the Americana genre has become increasingly commercialized and more bloated than ever, here is a release that is purely American."
– Aaron Crawford, Loafer Magazine

"An authentic American original, Lightnin' Charlie, with his Stetson hat and Fender Stratocaster, has hit the mark with a FANTASTIC new CD, A New Leaf on Blue Chip Records. GREAT ALBUM!"
– Rootstime (Belgium)

"Tennessee's Lightnin' Charlie proves a versatile guitarist and a smooth singer on A New Leaf (Blue Chip Records). Musicians will dig his range of punchy tones, and most listeners will enjoy the way he and his band (and engineer) blur distinctions between vintage and modern. Top-notch material. A-PLUS!"
– Blues Revue

"Lightnin' Charlie covers some all-time blues classics with sheer magnificence, and his five original songs are polished with creative soul, rock, and harmony. The boppin' tunes on A New Leaf could bring joy to watching paint dry."
– Josh Mancuso, News And Neighbor

"The best blues-based CD I have ever heard, including all the classic recordings. There is always some deficiency in all records, but not in this one. Listening to A New Leaf from beginning to end is truly a musical experience."
– Ron Baisden, Blue Rapture

Lightnin' Charlie is currently enjoying the successes of his book and his music, and capitalizing on his unique ability to appeal to a huge range of audiences with his extraordinary repertoire and brilliant showmanship. He performs an incredible 20 – 30 shows per month and the venues he plays are as diverse as his music. Lightnin' Charlie rocks churches, nursing homes, assisted living centers, concert halls, theaters, charity fundraisers, music and arts festivals, radio and television.

He is in regular rotation on radio stations worldwide, XM and Sirius satellite radio, and has been featured on national television.

In 2010, LC released *Trust In God – Family Album Volume One,* an acoustic gospel CD with his wife Beth. Reviews are glowing...

"I was simply amazed [listening to 'Trust In God']. Lightnin' Charlie just makes it go straight to my heart. This is Gospel the way it should be. A great CD."
– CheriasChatter.com

"Thirteen of the greatest hymns and inspirational American songs ever recorded, delivered in the way that only the great Lightnin' Charlie can deliver them. There are two kinds of people in the world: Those who love Lightnin' Charlie, and those who haven't had the good fortune to hear him yet. If you fall in the second group, you can take care of that right now by ordering 'Trust In God'".
– RickRouse.com

Lightnin' Charlie's legions of die-hard, dedicated fans, affectionately known as "Lightnin' Bugs", are anxiously awaiting the release of his upcoming CDs, these two presently in the works:

- *Lightnin' Charlie Family Album Volume Two – Songbook*
  popular favorites featuring the pure harmonies of LC and his wife Beth
- *Lightnin' Charlie – Good News*
  LC's highly touted, tour-de-force, "old school" gospel album, chock full of original music and cool covers – unplugged and with the Upsetters (plus some very special guests!)

Watch www.lightnincharlie.com for these and other new releases on Blue Chip Records.

"Lightnin' Charlie is a veritable icon here in the Mountain Empire. Everyone who has seen Lightnin' perform is astounded by his talent, range, and showmanship. This man knows how to entertain a crowd. And when Charlie and his wife, Beth raise their voices in harmony to praise the Lord in song, the sound they produce is nothing short of perfection. Charlie can pick and sing everything from country to rock 'n' roll to the blues, and he does it as well as anyone on the planet. Lightnin' Charlie is one of the most entertaining, yet down-to-earth guys around, and if you have never seen him in concert, you are missing out on something really special."
– PickinPorch.org

Lightnin' Charlie Dolinger, the hardest-working man in show business, lives happily in Johnson City, Tennessee with his wife Beth, their two sons, Sidney and Sam, and their baby daughter Lily. He divides his time between being singer and songwriter, recording artist and lawn mower, showman and storyteller, celebrated author and family dishwasher. But his full-time job is Christian, husband, and Dad.

Join the Lightnin' Charlie Fan Club and receive free monthly Lightnin' Bug Newsletter at www.LightninCharlie.com

Other works by Lightnin' Charlie:

CDs

*Lightnin' Charlie
and the Upsetters*
(1994)

*Don't Touch
That Dial!*
(1997)

A New Leaf
(2005)

*Trust In God
Family Album Volume One*
(2010)

The Essential Upsetters
(2012)

Watch for Lightnin' Charlie's upcoming CD releases on Blue Chip Records:

Songbook – Family Album Volume Two
Good News

DVDs

By Request
(2006)

Books

Off The Record
The Trials and Tribulations
of a Travelin' Troubadour
1st Edition (2008)
2nd Edition (2012)

About The Author photo credits (in order of appearance): Rita Eggers, Lightnin' Charlie, John Edwards, Bill W. Bryant, Rita Eggers, Rick Rouse, Beth Dolinger, Charlie Warden, Jerry Greene, Rita Eggers, Tom Netherland, Rita Eggers, Rita Eggers, Rita Eggers

This book is lovingly dedicated to my Mother and to my Brother,
William H. Livesay Jr. (1949 - 2007)

For I consider that the sufferings of this present time
are not worthy *to be compared* with the glory which shall be revealed in us.
- Romans 8:18 NKJV